INTELLECTUAL PROPERTY JURISDICTION STRATEGIES

ELGAR INTELLECTUAL PROPERTY LAW AND PRACTICE

Series Editors: Trevor Cook, *Partner, WilmerHale* and Johanna Gibson, *Herchel Smith Professor of Intellectual Property Law, Queen Mary University of London*

The Elgar Intellectual Property Law and Practice series is a library of works by leading practitioners and scholars covering discrete areas of law in the field of intellectual property. Each title will describe the law in detail, but will also be deeply analytical, highlighting and unpicking the legal issues that are most critical and relevant to practice. Designed to be detailed, focused reference works, the books in this series aim to offer an authoritative statement on the law and practice in key topics within the field, from *Trade Marks* to *Pharmaceuticals*, from *Patent Standards* to *Trade Secrecy* and from *IP Licensing* to *IP Valuation.*

Titles in this series include:

The Law and Regulation of Franchising in the EU
Mark Abell

The Protection of Geographical Indications
Law and Practice
Michael Blakeney

Patent Law in Greater China
Edited by Stefan Luginbuehl and Peter Ganea

Trade Secrecy and International Transactions
Law and Practice
Elizabeth A. Rowe and Sharon K. Sandeen

The Law and Practice of Trademark Transactions
A Global and Local Outlook
Edited by Irene Calboli and Jacques de Werra

Certification and Collective Marks
Law and Practice
Jeffrey Belson

Intellectual Property Jurisdiction Strategies
Where to Litigate Unitary Rights vs National Rights in the EU
Torsten Bjørn Larsen

INTELLECTUAL PROPERTY JURISDICTION STRATEGIES

Where to Litigate Unitary Rights vs National Rights in the EU

TORSTEN BJØRN LARSEN

Associate Professor, Aalborg University, Denmark

ELGAR INTELLECTUAL PROPERTY LAW AND PRACTICE

Edward Elgar
PUBLISHING

Cheltenham, UK • Northampton, MA, USA

Published by
Edward Elgar Publishing Limited
The Lypiatts
15 Lansdown Road
Cheltenham
Glos GL50 2JA
UK

Edward Elgar Publishing, Inc.
William Pratt House
9 Dewey Court
Northampton
Massachusetts 01060
USA

A catalogue record for this book
is available from the British Library

Library of Congress Control Number: 2017939829

This book is available electronically in the **Elgar**online
Law subject collection
DOI 10.4337/9781786437518

MIX
Paper from
responsible sources
FSC® C013604

ISBN 978 1 78643 750 1 (cased)
ISBN 978 1 78643 751 8 (eBook)

Typeset by Columns Design XML Ltd, Reading
Printed and bound by CPI Group (UK) Ltd, Croydon, CR0 4YY

DEDICATION

To my dear mother and father.

To whom I shall always be grateful.

CONTENTS

EXTENDED TABLE OF CONTENTS

FIGURES

TABLES

PREFACE

This study is the result of my employment at the Faculty of Law, University of Copenhagen. Since the first draft in 2014 both intellectual property law and private international law have been subject to changes. In intellectual property law the European Trademark Regulation has replaced the Community Trademark Regulation and in private international law the new Brussels I Regulation has replaced the old Brussels I Regulation. Also, new case law has brought about some changes. These developments have all been written into the study. Brexit is, however, not addressed.

I wish to thank my parents and my partner in life, Tina, for being supportive, encouraging and helpful. Even in the toughest of times you still believe in me. Also, thank you to my former colleagues at the University of Copenhagen and to my new colleagues at Aalborg University for an inspiring and cheerful environment. Thank you also to my colleagues in legal practice for your comments. Thank you in particular to Professor PhD Morten Rosenmeier for always being so fair, to Professor dr. jur. Thomas Riis for your time, your patience and your advice in the process and to Professor Dr. Annette Kur for being an inspiration. Also, a special thank you to Associate Professor Andreas Ehlers, attorney-at-law, partner Simon Krogh and Professor PhD Rasmus Kristian Feldthusen for the talks and laughs in the process. Especially the latter kept me going. Finally, thank you to Professor PhD Peter Arnt Nielsen for your comments in the final phase and to all of you at Edward Elgar Publishing for being so kind and professional.

Finally, the text may at times appear mechanical and staccato. The style is chosen in order to compress the text and to apply the same structure throughout the study. My apologies to the reader for the inconvenience. All errors are, of course, my responsibility. The law is stated as 1 January 2017.

'Ikkun fremad og fremad og aldrig forknyt
Har til målet man nået sætter straks man et nyt'

Torsten Bjørn Larsen
Copenhagen
February 2017

ABBREVIATIONS

ACTA	Anti-Counterfeiting Trade Agreement
AG	Advocate General
ALI	American Law Institute
AUPC	Agreement on a Unified Patent Court
BR	Brussels Regime
Brussels Convention	Convention on Jurisdiction and Enforcement of Judgments in Civil and Commercial Matters
Brussels I Regulation	Regulation on Jurisdiction and Recognition and Enforcement of Judgments in Civil and Commercial Matters
CD	Community Design
CDR	Community Design Regulation
Charter	Charter of Fundamental Rights of the European Union
CJEU	Court of Justice of the European Union
CLIP	Conflict of Laws in Intellectual Property
CMS	Contracting Member State
Commission	European Commission
Council	European Council
CPV	Community Plant Variety
CPVO	Community Plant Variety Office
CPVR	Community Plant Variety Regulation
CTM	Community Trademark
CTMR	Community Trademark Regulation
DD	Design Directive
ED	Enforcement Directive
ECHR	European Convention on the Protection of Human Rights and Fundamental Freedoms
ECtHR	European Court of Human Rights
EFTA	European Free Trade Association
EPC	European Patent Convention
EPLA	European Patent Litigation Agreement
EPO	European Patent Organisation
EU	European Union
EUIPO	European Union Intellectual Property Office
EUTM	European Union Trademark

EUTMR	European Union Trademark Regulation
ILA	International Law Association
IP	Intellectual Property
Lugano Convention	Convention on Jurisdiction and Recognition and Enforcement of Judgments in Civil and Commercial Matters
N/A	Non-applicable
PDO	Protected Designation of Origin right
PGI	Protected Geographical Indication right
RCD	Registered Community Design
Rome II	Regulation on the Law applicable to Non-Contractual Obligations
ROP	Rules of Procedure of the Unified Patent Court
SPG	Speciality Guaranteed right
TFEU	Treaty of the Functioning of the European Union
TMD	Trademark Directive
Transparency	Transparency Proposal on Jurisdiction, Choice of Law, Recognition and Enforcement of Foreign Judgments in Intellectual Property
TRIPS	Trade Related Aspects of Intellectual Property Rights
UCD	Unregistered Community Design
UP	Unitary Patent
UPC	Unified Patent Court
UPOV	Union for the Protection of New Varieties of Plants
UPR	Unitary Patent Regulation
VC	Vienna Convention on the Law of Treaties
Waseda	Principles of Private International Law on Intellectual Property Rights

TABLE OF CASES

EUROPEAN COURT OF JUSTICE

Advocate General opinions

NATIONAL COURTS

Austria

Oberster Gerichtshof

Belgium

Lower courts

Denmark

Maritime and Commercial Court

France

Cour de Cassation

Lower courts

Germany

Bundesgerichtshof

Bundesarbeitsgericht

Lower courts

Italy

Corte di Cassazione

Lower courts

Netherlands

Hoge Raad

Supreme Court

Lower courts

Norway

Høyesteretts kjæremålsutvalg

Scotland

Sweden

Högsta Domstolen

Switzerland

Bundesgericht

Handelsgericht Zürich

United Kingdom

House of Lords

Supreme Court

Lower courts

ADMINISTRATIVE DECISIONS FROM THE EUIPO

TABLE OF LEGISLATION

REGULATIONS

DIRECTIVES

TABLE OF TREATIES, CONVENTIONS AND OTHER INSTRUMENTS

TREATIES

CONVENTIONS

AGREEMENTS

DECISIONS

PREPARATORY WORKS

SCHOLARLY REPORTS

CJEU OPINION

EVALUATION REPORTS

GREEN PAPERS

RECOMMENDATIONS

Part I

INTRODUCTION

1

INTRODUCTION

A. INTRODUCTION

This volume deals with intellectual property (hereinafter IP) jurisdiction strategies. For the purpose of the study the term 'IP jurisdiction strategies' is defined as the advantages for the plaintiff to litigate based on a national IP right compared to litigating based on a corresponding European unitary IP right as further defined in section 4 below. **1.01**

1. Purpose

The purpose behind the study is twofold. One purpose is that the approach – whereas the international jurisdiction rules,[1] which apply to a national IP right are compared vis-à-vis the international jurisdiction rules, which apply to a corresponding European unitary IP right – has not yet been taken in legal literature and is therefore new[2] and that the study addresses, inter alia, new **1.02**

1 The terms 'jurisdiction rules' and 'forum rules' are used synonymously for the purpose of the study.

2 This is not to say that the jurisdiction rules have not been subject to an examination in the legal literature see, inter alia, Joseph Drexl and Annette Kur (eds), *Intellectual Property and Private International Law, Heading for the Future,* IIC Studies, vol. 24, Hart Publishing, 2005; James J. Fawcett and Paul Torremans, *Intellectual Property and Private International Law*, second edn, Oxford Private International Law Series, 2011; *Conflict of Laws in Intellectual Property, The CLIP Principles and Commentary*, European Max Planck Group on Conflicts of Laws in Intellectual Property, Oxford University Press, 2013; Stefan Leible and Ansgar Ohly (eds), *Intellectual Property and Private International Law*, Mohr Siebeck, 2009; Arnaud Nuyts (ed.), *International Litigation in Intellectual Property and Information Technology*, Kluwer Law International, 2008; Marta Pertegás Sender, *Cross-Border Enforcement of Patent Rights*, Oxford Private International Law Series, 2002; Eike Scharper, *Durchsetzung der Gemeinschaftsmarke*, Internationale Zuständigkeit, anwendbares Recht und Rechtsfolgen bei Verletzung, Carl Heymanns Verlag, 2006; Benedetta Ubertazzi, *Exclusive Jurisdiction*

forum rules[3] and new decisions.[4] Another purpose is that the study provides practitioners with a platform that enables them to decide whether to litigate based on a national IP right rather than on a corresponding European unitary IP right, which in turn is valuable knowledge in cross-border IP litigation cf. section 4.

1.03 For illustration purposes an example is given in section 2. In section 3 the scope of the study is addressed and in section 4 the term 'IP jurisdiction strategies' is defined. In section 5 the limits of the study are laid down and finally in section B the structure of the study is outlined.

2. Example

1.04 The example below may illustrate the subject of the present study. The example is referred to throughout the study. The example reads as follows:

> Frogs GmbH is a shoe manufacturer based in Munich, Germany. Frogs GmbH markets and sells a foam shoe throughout the EU under the name Frogs. Frogs GmbH owns a number of IP rights:
>
> *First*, the shoe name Frogs is trademark protected at national levels in the Member States and at EU level as a European union trademark right (EUTM).
>
> *Secondly*, the look of the shoe is design protected at national levels in the Member States and at EU level as a registered and unregistered Community design right (CD).
>
> *Thirdly*, the technical impact of the shoe sole is patent protected at national levels in the Member States and as a unitary patent right (UP).
>
> *Fourthly*, Frogs GmbH has established a research and development (R&D) department, which is being funded by the income of an attractive plant variety right owned by Frogs GmbH. The plant variety is protected on national levels in the Member States and on EU level as a Community plant variety right (CPV).
>
> A situation has now come up where a farmer from Sicily has copied Frogs GmbH's business model and has started a company under the name Frox SpA. The company

---

in Intellectual Property, Max Planck Institut für Ausländisches und Internationales Privatrecht, Mohr Siebeck, 2012 and Toshiyuki Kono, *Intellectual Property and Private International Law, Comparative Perspectives*, Hart Publishing, 2012.

3 Art. 33 AUPC.

4 Case C-523/10, *Wintersteiger AG v Products 4U Sondermaschinenbau GmbH*; Case C-133/11, *Folien Fischer AG, Fofitec AG v Ritrama SpA*; Case C-170/12, *Peter Pinckney v KDG Mediatech AG*; Case C-387/12, *Hi Hotel HCF SARL v Uwe Spoering*; Case C-360/12, *Coty Prestige Lancaster Group GmbH v First Note Perfumes NV*; Case C-441/13, *Pez Hejduk v EnergieAgentur NRW GmbH*; Case C-25/16, *Nintendo Co. Ltd. v BigBen Interactive GmbH, BigBen Interactive SA* (pending); Case C-230/15, *Brite Strike Technologies Inc. v Brite Strike Technologies SA*; Case C-433/16, *Bayerische Motoren Werke AG v Acacia S.r.l.* (pending); Case C-618/15, *Concurrence SARL v Samsung Electronics France SAS and Amazon Services Europe Sàrl*; and case C-617/15, *Hummel Holding A/S v Nike Inc. and Nike Retail BV* (pending).

has its statutory seat in Palermo, Italy whereas its management and control centre is located in Amsterdam, the Netherlands and its principal place of business is in Paris, France. Frox SpA also has an establishment in London, UK. Furthermore Frox SpA has an independent legal entity in Copenhagen, Denmark (Frox ApS) and another independent legal entity in Stockholm, Sweden (Frox AB).

Frox SpA is – in line with Frogs GmbH – funded by the income of a plant variety marketed and sold throughout the EU. The plant variety is similar to the one owned by Frogs GmbH. Frox SpA markets and sells thousands of 1:1 counterfeited foam shoes in Italy, Spain, France and Austria under the name Frox. The shoes are manufactured in Italy. The plant variety and the shoes are distributed from both Italy and the UK. The shoes are advertised for on frox.com.

Frogs GmbH has become aware of the infringements of their trademark, design, patent and plant variety rights and has sent Frox SpA a cease and desist (C&D) letter, however, with no effect. Frogs GmbH intends to enforce their IP rights but has two overall concerns:

The *first* concern relates to the advantages from a jurisdictional viewpoint for Frogs GmbH to litigate on the basis of their national IP rights compared to doing so on the basis of their corresponding European unitary IP right.[5]

The *second* concern relates to the advantages from a jurisdictional viewpoint for their counterpart, Frox SpA, to litigate on the basis of Frogs GmbH's national IP rights compared to doing so on the basis of Frogs GmbH's corresponding European unitary IP right.[6]

The strategic jurisdictional reflections raised in the above example have most **1.05**
likely also been done in the series of ongoing lawsuits between Samsung and Apple.[7] Here Samsung brought, inter alia, an action for a declaration of non-infringement[8] also known as a negative declaration[9] or just a declaratory

5 A non-exhaustive list of factors determining the jurisdictional advantages for the plaintiff is provided for in section 4.

6 Ibid.

7 *Infra* note 11.

8 The term 'action for declaration of non-infringement' is used, inter alia, in arts 96(b) EUTMR, 81(b) CDR and 32(1)(b) AUPC and by legal scholars, inter alia, Sender, *supra* note 2, 81.

9 The term 'negative declaration' is used by the CJEU in case C-133/11, *Folien Fischer AG*, n. 4, para. 56 and by legal scholars, inter alia, Fawcett and Torremans, *supra* note 2, 5.37; Ulrich Magnus and Peter Mankowski, *Brussels I Regulation* European Commentaries on Private International Law, 2nd revised edn, 2012, 229; Anna Gardella, 'Torpedoes and Actions for Negative Declarations in International IP Law Litigation' in Arnaud Nuyts (ed.), *International Litigation in Intellectual Property and Information Technology*, Kluwer Law International, 2008, p. 181; and Ulf Maunsbach, 'Jurisdiction in Relation to Online Cross-Border Infringements: The Code and the Law' in Dan Jerker B. Svantesson and Stanley Greenstein (eds), *Internationalisation of Law in the Digital Information Society*, 2013, p. 182.

action[10] against Apple in the UK[11] claiming that Samsung's Galaxy tablets did not infringe Apple's registered CD.[12] The reason for doing so could be that it would be advantageous to Samsung *since* the action could be brought at their own domicile in the UK[13] and *since* the UK courts would have unrestricted jurisdiction.[14] The strategy appeared successful since Samsung's Galaxy tablets were found not to infringe Apples registered CD.[15]

3. Scope

1.06 The scope of the study is defined by three factors. The first factor is the IP rights covered by the study (section a); the second factor is the litigations covered by the study (section b) and the third factor is the international jurisdiction rules covered by the study (section c).

(a) The IP rights

1.07 The IP rights covered by the study include trademark, design, plant variety and patent rights. The choice of those four kinds of IP rights has been predefined given that European unitary IP rights only exist within these areas.[16]

1.08 Thus, the position for a national trademark right is compared with the position for the corresponding EUTM having a unitary character;[17] the position for a national design right is compared with the position for the corresponding CD having a unitary character;[18] the position for a national plant variety right is compared with the position for the CPV having a unitary

---

10 The term 'declaratory action' is used, inter alia, in the *CLIP Principles and Commentary*, *supra* note 2, 173 (2:602.C01).

11 High Court of Justice, Chancery Division Patents Court, *Samsung Electronic (UK) Ltd. v Apple Inc.*, case no HC 11 C 03050, 9 July 2012.

12 Community Design No. 000181607–0001 of 24 May 2004. For the purposes of the present study it is explicitly noted that Apple Inc. did not have any corresponding national design right in, inter alia, the UK.

13 The question of jurisdiction is not mentioned in the judgment. Given, however, that non-infringement actions cannot be brought at *forum delicti* making art. 82(5) CDR inapplicable the action must have been brought either at Apple Inc's establishment in the UK following art. 82(1) CDR or at Samsung Electronics (UK) Ltd's domicile in the UK following art. 82(2) CDR. Either one equals Samsung Electronics (UK) Limited's home domicile.

14 Art. 83(1) CDR. The distinction between unrestricted and restricted jurisdiction is addressed in section 4 (factor 4).

15 *Samsung Electronic (UK) Ltd. v Apple Inc.*, n. 11, para. 191.

16 Two modifications apply i.e. *that* a UP is not yet obtainable cf. art. 18(2) UPR and *that* a protected designation of origin right (PDO), a protected geographical indication right (PGI) and a speciality guaranteed right (SPG) are also found in European unitary versions but are excluded from the scope of the study since they are all subject to the same jurisdiction rules, which apply to national IP rights cf. s. 5(a).

17 Art. 1(2) EUTMR.

18 Art. 1(3) CDR.

character[19] and the position for a national patent right is compared with the position for the UP having a unitary character,[20] which contrary to the above does not set in automatically but is granted upon request by the applicant.[21]

For the purpose of the present study it is clarified *that* CPV protection cannot be combined with national plant variety protection,[22] which is available in almost every EU Member State[23] and that therefore the jurisdictional advantages of litigating based on a national plant variety right rather than litigating based on the CPV must be determined at registration level and not, as the remaining IP rights covered by the study, on infringement level; *that* the IP rights covered count also unregistered versions on both national[24] and EU levels;[25] *that* a national IP right is covered regardless of whether it has been applied for centrally[26] or on a Member State-by-Member State basis and *that* a European unitary IP right is covered regardless of whether it extends to every 28 EU Member States (such as the EUTM, CD and CPV)[27] or only to 26 EU Member States (such as the UP).[28] **1.09**

(b) The litigations

The litigations covered by the study count infringement actions where invalidity is not raised, non-infringement actions[29] where invalidity is not raised and finally infringement and non-infringement actions where invalidity is raised. **1.10**

19 Art. 2 CPVR.

20 Arts 2(c) cf. 3(2) UPR and art. 2(f) AUPC.

21 Art. 9 cf. recital 5 UPR.

22 Art. 3 cf. 92(1) CPVR.

23 Members of the International Union for the Protection of New Varieties of Plant of 1961 as revised in Geneva in 1972, 1978 and 1991 number every Member State except Cyprus, Greece, Luxembourg and Malta cf. upov.int/members.

24 An example of an unregistered IP right at national level could be a Danish trademark acquired through use cf. § 3(1)(2) Danish Trademarks Act.

25 An example of an unregistered IP right at EU level could be the unregistered CD cf. art. 11 CDR.

26 A central application procedure is available for *trademarks* cf. Madrid System for the International Registration of Marks and the Protocol Relating to the Madrid Agreement Concerning the International Registration of Marks, adopted at Madrid on June 27, 1989; for *patents* cf. Convention on the Grant of European Patents of 5 October 1973 as revised by the Act revising art. 63 EPC of 17 December 1991 and the Act revising the EPC of 29 November 2000 and Patent Corporation Treaty done at Washington on June 19, 1970 as amended on September 28, 1979 as modified on February 3, 1984 and on October 3, 2001 and for *designs* cf. Hague Agreement concerning the International Registration of Industrial Designs.

27 The EUTM, CD and CPV extend also to Croatia being a new Member State as from 1 July 2013 cf. Treaty concerning the Accession of the Republic of Croatia, Council of the European Union, Brussels of 7 November 2011 14409/11 cf. Communication no. 4/12 of the President of OHIM of 12 December 2012 concerning the Enlargement of the European Union to Croatia and Press Release of 1 July 2013 of CPVO concerning the Enlargement of the European Union to Croatia.

28 The UP extends only to 26 Member States since Croatia and Spain are not parties to the UPR.

29 The term 'non-infringement action' is synonymous to the terms 'action for declaration of non-infringement', 'negative declaration' and 'declaratory action'.

1.11 The choice of those three kinds of actions has also been predefined given that they express the claims, namely infringement, non-infringement and invalidity, which may be raised between the rightholder (being the party claiming IP protection) and the infringer (being the party allegedly infringing the IP right). For the purpose of the present study, therefore, the actions relate to IP rights, which have allegedly been infringed. For reasons of clarity the actions are dealt with separately below.[30]

1.12 Infringement actions are the first kind. In these actions, which also include threatened infringements, the rightholder claims infringement of his/her trademark, design, plant variety or patent right. As a defence the infringer claims non-infringement of the IP right e.g. *since* the use of the mark/sign creates no risk of confusion,[31] *since* the use of the design produces a different overall impression on the informed user,[32] *since* the use of the plant variety is subject to the farmers privilege[33] or *since* the use of the technique is outside the scope of the patent claims.[34] In infringement actions the initiative lies with the rightholder being the one choosing the forum.

Applying the example in section 2 Frogs GmbH may bring an infringement action against Frox SpA. During the action Frogs GmbH claims infringement of their IP rights and as a defence Frox SpA claims non-infringement e.g. *since* the sign Frox is not confusingly similar to the trademark Frogs; *since* their design imposes an overall different impression on the informed user compared to Frogs' design and/or *since* their shoe sole is based on a different technique outside the scope of Frogs' patent claim.

1.13 Non-infringement actions are the second kind. In these actions the infringer acts as the plaintiff and the rightholder acts as the defendant and so the parties trade places. The idea of bringing any such action is not to impose any liability on the rightholder. Rather the idea is to rule out the infringer's own liability by seeking a finding that his/her conduct does not infringe the rightholder's trademark, design, plant variety or patent right.[35] As a defence the rightholder claims infringement of his/her IP right. In non-infringement actions the initiative lies with the infringer being the one choosing the forum.

---

30 The claims raised in the below actions can be (and are often) combined in various ways e.g. may the infringer claim invalidity and in the alternative non-infringement.

31 Art. 5(1)(b) TMD and art. 9(1)(b) EUTMR.

32 Art. 9(1) DD and art. 10(1) CDR.

33 For national plant variety rights the substantial law has not been harmonized at EU-level cf. therefore the Member States own plant variety acts. For the CPV cf. art. 14 CPVR.

34 For national patent rights the substantial law has not been harmonized at EU-level cf. therefore the Member States own patent acts. For the UP cf. arts 7 UPR cf. 24(c) AUPC cf. 69 EPC.

35 Opinion of Advocate General Jääskinen in case C-133/11, *Folien Fischer AG*, n. 4, para. 47 and judgment of the CJEU, para. 42.

Applying the example in section 2 Frox SpA may bring a non-infringement action against Frogs GmbH seeking a finding, inter alia, that the marketing and selling of their shoes under the name Frox in Italy, Spain, France and Austria does not infringe Frogs GmbH's trademark, design and patent rights e.g. *since* the sign Frox is not confusingly similar to the trademark Frogs; *since* their design imposes an overall different impression on the informed user compared to Frogs' design and/or *since* their shoe sole is based on a different technique outside the scope of Frogs' patent claim. As a defence Frogs GmbH claims infringement.

Invalidity actions are the third kind. Invalidity may be raised in various ways i.e. *as* a claim in infringement actions; *as* a counterclaim/(defence) in infringement actions; *as* a claim in non-infringement actions and *as* a counterclaim/(defence) in non-infringement actions.[36] In trademark cases invalidity can be raised e.g. *if* the trademark lacks distinctiveness;[37] *if* the trademark has not been used for five years[38] or *if* the trademark has become the common name of the product or service in respect of which it is registered.[39] In design cases invalidity can be raised e.g. *if* the design lacks novelty or individual character.[40] In plant variety cases invalidity can be raised e.g. *if* the variety lacks novelty.[41] Finally, in patent cases invalidity can be raised e.g. *if* the invention lacks novelty or inventive step.[42] In invalidity actions the initiative is either split between the parties (e.g. where the rightholder chooses the forum and the infringer claims invalidity) or lies fully with one of the parties (e.g. where the infringer chooses the forum and claims invalidity). **1.14**

Applying the example in section 2 Frogs GmbH may bring an infringement action against Frox SpA. During the action Frogs GmbH claims infringement of their IP rights and as a defence Frox SpA claims invalidity by way of a counterclaim/(defence) *since* the CD has not been subject to any substantial law examination and if it had the design would show the lack of novelty and individual character because the design is known from wooden clogs and/or *since* the technique of the shoe sole lacks inventive step since it is obvious to a person skilled in the art. Alternatively, Frox SpA may bring a non-infringement action against Frogs GmbH claiming invalidity of Frogs GmbH's IP rights by way of a claim and as a defence Frogs GmbH claims infringement *since* the sign Frox is confusingly similar to the trademark Frogs; *since* the shoes imposes an overall similar impression on the informed user compared to Frogs' design and/or *since* the shoe sole is based on the same technique within the scope of Frogs' patent claim.

---

36 See below for examples.

37 Arts 3(1)(a) TMD and 7(1)(b) EUTMR.

38 Arts 16(1) TMD and 51(1)(a) EUTMR.

39 Arts 20(1)(a) TMD and 51(1)(b) EUTMR.

40 Arts 11(1)(b) cf. 4–5 DD and arts 25(1)(b) cf. 5–6 CDR.

41 For national plant variety rights the substantial law has not been harmonized at EU-level cf. therefore the Member States own plant variety acts. For the CPVR cf. art. 20(1)(a) cf. 10 CPVR.

42 For national patent rights the substantial law has not been harmonized at EU-level cf. therefore the Member States own patent acts. For the UP cf. arts 7 UPR cf. 24(c) AUPC cf. 54 and 56 EPC.

(c) The international jurisdiction rules

1.15 The international jurisdiction rules covered by the study count the defendant's domicile,[43] establishment,[44] multiple defendants'[45] *forum delicti*[46] and exclusive jurisdiction[47] rules which, with variations, all apply to both a national IP right and to every European unitary IP right; the plaintiff's domicile rule, which applies to the EUTM, CD and CPV[48] and likely in a camouflaged version to the UP[49] and finally the central division rule, which applies to the UP.[50] In addition to the above 'fall back' rules may apply under the EUTM, CD and CPV cf. Chapter 2. For the purpose of the study focus lies with the following two areas:

1.16 The *first* focus area is the number of international jurisdiction rules available to the plaintiff. The reason that the number of international jurisdiction rules is a focus area is that the jurisdiction framework is very complex given that a variety of factors decide what rules apply, inter alia, the territorial extent of the IP right (whether national or European unitary); the character of the national IP right (whether registered or unregistered); the character of the European unitary IP right (whether a trademark, design, plant variety or patent right with different rules remaining applicable in the background); the action (whether infringement, non-infringement or invalidity) and on the domicile of the defendant (whether in the EU, in the EFTA or outside the EU/EFTA). The number of international jurisdiction rules available to the plaintiff is addressed in Chapters 2–3.

1.17 The *second* focus area is the nature of the international jurisdiction rules available to the plaintiff. Any such count in the ones mentioned above. Not every international jurisdiction rule is in focus e.g. is the exclusive jurisdiction rule[51] not in focus given that it has recently been subject to a thorough study[52] and the same goes for the central division rule[53] given its limited application. Rather focus lies with, but is not limited to, *forum delicti*. The reason is that in IP litigation *forum delicti* is the real alternative to the defendant's domicile in

43 Arts 4 BR, 97(1) EUTMR, 82(1) CDR, 101(2)(a) CPVR and 33(1)(b) AUPC cf. Chapter 5.
44 Arts 7(5) BR, 97(1) EUTMR, 82(1) CDR, 101(2)(a) CPVR and 33(1)(b) AUPC cf. Chapter 6.
45 Arts 8(1) BR, 94(2)(a) EUTMR, 79(3)(a) CDR, 101(1) CPVR and 33(1)(b) AUPC cf. Chapter 8.
46 Arts 7(2) BR, 97(5) EUTMR, 82(5) CDR, 101(3) CPVR and 33(1)(a) AUPC cf. Chapter 9.
47 Arts 24(4) BR, 96(d) and 99(2) cf. 56 EUTMR, 81(d) and 84(4) cf. 52 CDR, 20 CPVR and 33(3) and (4) AUPC cf. Chapter 11.
48 Arts 97(2) EUTMR, 82(2) CDR and 101(2)(b) CPVR cf. Chapter 7.
49 Arts 33(1)(a) cf. 34 AUPC cf. Chapter 7.
50 Art. 33(1), (2), (3) and (4) AUPC cf. Chapter 10.
51 Chapter 11.
52 Ubertazzi, *supra* note 2.
53 Chapter 10.

situations where there is only one defendant[54] and that the CJEU has recently handed down a number of decisions, which to some extent clarify the scope and impact of *forum delicti* to both national IP rights[55] and to European unitary IP rights.[56] The *forum delicti* rule is addressed in Chapter 9.

In sum, the IP rights, the litigations and the international jurisdiction rules covered by the study can be illustrated as in Table 1.1 below. **1.18**

Table 1.1 Scope of the study

	SITUATION 1 (National IP rights)	**SITUATION 2 (European unitary IP rights)**
IP rights	• National trademark rights • National design rights • National plant variety rights • National patent rights	• European union trademark (EUTM) • Community design (CD) • Community plant variety (CPV) • Unitary patent (UP)
Litigations	• Infringement actions • Non-infringement actions • Invalidity actions	• Infringement actions • Non-infringement actions • Invalidity actions
International jurisdiction rules	• The defendant's domicile rule • The establishment rule • The multiple defendants' rule • The *forum deliciti* rule • The exclusive jurisdiction rule	• The defendant's domicile rule • The establishment rule • The multiple defendants' rule • The *forum delicti* rule • The exclusive jurisdiction rule • The plaintiff's domicile rule (EUTM, CD, CPV, (UP)) • The central division rule (UP)

4. IP jurisdiction strategies

In IP litigation a number of strategic decisions must be made by the plaintiff – whether acting as the rightholder or as the infringer[57] – prior to bringing the action against the defendant in a given Member State. Such decisions have one thing in common: to bring the action where it is most advantageous for the plaintiff. To determine what is most advantageous for the plaintiff, a large number of issues must be addressed. Some have a procedural law nature,[58] **1.19**

54 Christian Heinze, Jurisdiction under the CLIP Principles available at http://www.tomeika.jur.kyushu-u.ac.jp/chizai/symposium/paper/004_08May09_Heinze.pdf p. 8.

55 Case C-523/10, *Wintersteiger*, n. 4; case C-133/11, *Folien Fischer*; case C-170/12, *Peter Pinckney*; case C-387/12, *Hi Hotel*; case C-441/13, *Pez Hejduk*; case C-230/15, *Brite Strike* and case C-618/15, *Concurrence SARL*.

56 Case C-360/12, *Coty Prestige*, n. 4; case C-25/16, *Nintendo Co. Ltd.*, n. 4; case C-433/16, *Bayerische Motoren Werke AG*and case C-617/15, *Hummel Holding A/S v Nike Inc. and Nike Retail BV* (pending).

57 Section 3(b).

58 The procedural law issues include, inter alia, the rules on examination of witnesses; the rules on expert evidence; the rules on disclosure of documents; the rules on obtaining and preservation of evidence; the rules on search and seizure; the rules on possible suspensive effect of decisions and the rules on legal costs. Any such rules are subject to the laws of the Member State where the case is being litigated, the so-called *lex fori*, regardless of whether the IP right in question is a national IP right or a European unitary IP right cf. arts

some have a substantial IP law nature,[59] some have a penal law nature,[60] some have a non-law nature[61] and some have a private international law nature. The study does not deal with the former four i.e. the procedural law, substantive IP law, penal law and non-law issues. Rather the study deals with the latter i.e. the private international law issues.

1.20 For the purpose of the study such issues are defined as the jurisdictional advantages for the plaintiff to litigate based on a national IP right compared to litigating based on a corresponding European unitary IP right.[62]

1.21 Crucial, therefore, is what can be considered a jurisdictional advantage for the plaintiff in IP litigation. For that purpose, a non-exhaustive list of factors can be identified. The factors – where some are general because they apply irrespectively of whether the plaintiff acts as the rightholder or as the infringer[63] and others are specific because they depend on whether the plaintiff acts as the rightholder or as the infringer[64] – can be divided into overall two groups (A and B).[65]

1.22 Group A, which is also factor 1, relates to the number of international jurisdiction rules available to the plaintiff (Chapters 2–3). More jurisdiction rules is an advantage for the plaintiff since they leave him/her a discretion on where to sue, which in turn may limit his/her risks. The concept is known as forum shopping (Chapter 4 section C.3).

101(3) EUTMR, 88(3) CDR and 103 CPVR with the sole exception of the UP, which has its own procedural laws cf. Rules of Procedure of the Unified Patent Court of 19 October 2015. The above elements are included in the critique of *Wintersteiger* cf. Chapter 9 section B.1(a)(ii), Principle 3: Avoiding forum shopping.

59 The substantial IP law issues include, inter alia, the scope of protection for national patent or plant variety rights where the rules have not been harmonized at EU level.

60 The penal law issues include, inter alia, the damages awarded by the courts. Any such damages vary widely among the Member States.

61 The non-law issues include, inter alia, considerations in terms of not harming the brand of the plaintiff and/or harming the brand of the defendant.

62 Section 1.

63 Factors 1–4.

64 Factors 5–9.

65 Factors 1–9 are defined in terms of what is usually considered an advantage for the plaintiff. The risk of doing so is that the details fade. For example where in factor 6 joint adjudication is listed as an advantage for the plaintiff acting as the rightholder this does not preclude that split adjudication may sometimes be an advantage for him/her. This would typically be the case where the rightholder has a weak IP right. In that case he/she may take an interest in having the validity of the IP right tried in a number of Member States in the hope that one of these Member States will declare the IP right valid which, in turn, can be used by the rightholder to have the infringer stop marketing a product in the EU cf. Fawcett and Torremans, *supra* note 2, 7.32 with references.

Group B relates to the nature of the international jurisdiction rules available to the plaintiff (Chapters 4–11) and covers the following factors, which are counted consecutively from the one above. 1.23

Factor 2, therefore, is whether a jurisdiction rule allows for more available fora (Chapters 5, 6 and 9). The factor differs from the one above since it addresses available fora within one same jurisdiction rule. The advantages above apply *mutatis mutandis* unless only one party benefits in which event it may only be an advantage for the plaintiff acting as the rightholder or as the infringer. 1.24

Factor 3 is whether the action can be brought in the plaintiff's home Member State. This is possible, inter alia, if a plaintiff's domicile rule is available (Chapter 7) or if the infringement occurred there (Chapter 9 section C.4). The advantage of bringing the action in the plaintiff's home Member State are, inter alia, that the plaintiff saves time and costs for travelling and for foreign external counsels provided that any such are hired along with national external counsels;[66] that the plaintiff saves time and costs for translation of written submissions and translation of the oral procedure given that the proceedings are conducted in the plaintiff's own mother tongue[67] and that the plaintiff may feel more confident given that the case is conducted on the basis of his/her own procedural laws. 1.25

Factor 4 is the extent of jurisdiction. The extent of jurisdiction can either be unrestricted or restricted. Unrestricted jurisdiction also known as, inter alia, extraterritorial jurisdiction,[68] cross-border jurisdiction,[69] global jurisdiction,[70] general jurisdiction[71] or central jurisdiction[72] allows a competent court to hear 1.26

---

66 If, applying the example in section 2, Frox SpA brings a non-infringement action against Frogs GmbH in Italy following art. 7(2) Brussels I Regulation as interpreted in *Folien Fischer* cf. Chapter 9 Frox SpA will most likely hire their local Italian legal counsels contrary to the situation where any such action is brought in Germany following art. 4 Brussels I Regulation where Frox SpA will most likely hire both foreign German legal counsels along with their own Italian legal counsels.

67 If, applying the example in section 2, Frox SpA brings a non-infringement action against Frogs GmbH in Italy following art. 7(2) Brussels I Regulation as interpreted in *Folien Fischer* cf. Chapter 9 the action will be conducted in Italian on the basis of Italian procedural laws being *lex fori* and Frox SpA will save time and costs for translation of the written submissions and the oral proceedings into German.

68 Alexander Peukert, 'Territoriality and Extraterritoriality in Intellectual Property Law', in Gunther Handl and Joachim Zekoll (eds), *Beyond Territoriality: Transnational Legal Authority in an Age of Globalization*, Queen Mary Studies in International Law, Brill Academic Publishing, Leiden/Boston, 2011; and Graeme Dinwoodie, 'Developing a Private International Intellectual Property Law: The Demise of Territoriality' (2009) 51 *William and Mary Law Review* 711.

69 Sender, *supra* note 2, 3.115 *et seq.*

70 Magnus and Mankowski, *supra* note 9, 246.

71 *Conflict of Laws in Intellectual Property, The CLIP Principles and Commentary*, *supra* note 2, 56 (2:101.C01) and 85 (2:203.C03) and Kono, *supra* note 2, 23.

72 Annette Kur, 'Case C-235/09, DHL Express v. Chronopost, Judgment of the Court of Justice (Grand Chamber) of 12 April 2011' (2012) 49(2) *Common Market Law Review* 753–66, 753 note 2.

a claim for infringement irrespectively of where the infringement occurred[73] (hereinafter unlimited full jurisdiction)[74] whereas restricted jurisdiction also known as territorial jurisdiction[75] or country-by-country jurisdiction only allows a competent court to hear a claim for infringement, which occurred in the Member State where the court is located[76] (hereinafter limited forum jurisdiction).[77] The advantages of bringing the action in a forum having unlimited full jurisdiction is that it allows the case to be addressed in one operation, which in turn saves the plaintiff time and costs for later court cases (winner takes it all) whereas the advantages of bringing the action in a forum having limited forum jurisdiction is that it allows the plaintiff to bring a test case, which can later be used as a reference or as a means of pressure to have the defendant enter into a settlement. For the purpose of the present study discretion between unlimited full and limited forum jurisdiction is an advantage for the plaintiff. The extent of jurisdiction is addressed for every forum rule subject to the present study cf. Chapters 5–11.

1.27 Factor 5 is whether change of forum principles and rules apply. Any such principles and rules include, inter alia, whether a court may decline jurisdiction of its own discretion because it finds that another court is better suited to address the case (*forum non-conveniens*)[78] or whether a defendant by so requesting may force a court (regional division) to refer the case to another court (central division).[79] Any such change of forum principles and rules are an advantage for the plaintiff acting as the infringer since they allow the action to be prolonged.

---

73 See e.g. within the meaning of art. 7(2) Brussels I Regulation for infringement of personality rights case C-68/93, *Fiona Shevill, Ixora Trading Inc., Chequepoint SARL and Chequepoint International Ltd. v Presse Alliance SA*, para. 25.

74 Applying the example in section 2 Frogs GmbH may bring an infringement action against Frox SpA in Italy being the defendant's domicile cf. art. 4 Brussels I Regulation. The courts at any such place have unlimited full jurisdiction cf. Chapter 5 and are therefore competent, if Frogs GmbH so claims, to order Frox SpA to stop manufacturing the foam shoes in Italy, to stop distributing them through the branch office in London and to stop marketing and selling them in Italy, Spain, France and Austria, see also *Conflict of Laws in Intellectual Property, The CLIP Principles and Commentary*, *supra* note 2, 85 (2:203C03) and Fawcett and Torremans, *supra* note 2, 5.08.

75 *Conflict of Laws in Intellectual Property, The CLIP Principles and Commentary*, ibid.

76 See e.g. within the meaning of art. 7(2) Brussels I Regulation for infringement of personality rights case C-68/93, *Fiona Shevill*, para. 30.

77 Applying the example in section 2 Frogs may bring an infringement action against Frox SpA in Spain being a place where the IP right is registered cf. art. 7(2) Brussels I Regulation. The courts at any such place have limited forum jurisdiction cf. Chapter 9 and are therefore only competent, if Frogs GmbH so claims, to order Frox SpA to stop marketing and selling the foam shoes in Spain. The Spanish courts cannot order Frox SpA to stop manufacturing the foam shoes in Italy or order them to stop distributing them to, inter alia, France or Austria through the branch office in London, see also *Conflict of Laws in Intellectual Property, The CLIP Principles and Commentary*, *supra* note 2. 85 (2:203C03) and Fawcett and Torremans, *supra* note 2, 5.08.

78 Annette Kur and Thomas Dreier, *European Intellectual Property Law, Text, Cases and Materials*, Edward Elgar Publishing, 2013, p. 489.

79 Art. 33(2)(second sentence) AUPC.

1.28 Factor 6 is the interrelation between infringement and invalidity. The interrelation may take different forms, inter alia, that the same court of the same Member State is competent to address both infringement and invalidity;[80] that different courts of the same Member State are competent to address infringement and invalidity;[81] that the courts of a Member State are competent to address infringement whereas a public authority in the same Member State is exclusively competent to address invalidity;[82] that the courts of different Member States are competent to address infringement and invalidity[83] or finally that the courts of a Member State are competent to address infringement whereas a public authority of another Member State is exclusively competent to address invalidity.[84] For the purpose of the present study the former three (where infringement and invalidity are decided in the same Member State) are referred to as joint adjudication whereas the latter two (where infringement and invalidity are decided in different Member States) are referred to as split adjudication. If the plaintiff acts as the rightholder joint adjudication is (usually) an advantage since it speeds up the process, which in turn saves him/her time and costs[85] whereas split adjudication is (usually) an advantage if the plaintiff acts as the infringer since the action will be prolonged. The interrelation between infringement and invalidity is addressed for every forum rule subject to the present study cf. Chapters 5–11.

1.29 Factor 7 is the interrelation between non-infringement and invalidity. The interrelation may take different forms namely that invalidity may be raised in

80 An example would be, inter alia, arts 96(a) and (d) EUTMR and 81(a) and (d) CDR cf. Fawcett and Torremans, *supra* note 2, 8.48 and 8.117.

81 An example would be, inter alia, where a local or regional division is located within the same Contracting Member State as the central division within the meaning of art. 33(3)(b) AUPC.

82 An example would be, inter alia, where the courts of France are competent to address infringement of a CPV cf. art. 101(2)(c) CPVR whereas the CPVO located in France are exclusively competent to address invalidity cf. art. 20 CPVR.

83 An example would be, inter alia, where the defendant's domicile in art. 4 BR does not coincide with the place(s) of registration in art. 24(4) BR cf. case C-4/03, *Gesellschaft für Antriebstechnik mbH & Co. KG v Lamellen und Kupplungsbau Beteiligungs KG*, para. 32.

84 An example would be, inter alia, where the defendant's domicile in art. 101(2)(a) CPVR does not coincide with the location of the CPVO.

85 Joint adjudication may, however, not always be an advantage for the plaintiff acting as the rightholder even though infringement and invalidity are addressed within the same Member State. The reason is that the infringement action risks being stayed pending the result of the invalidity action cf. art. 106(2) CPVR. The stay of procedure rules are, however, not addressed for the purpose of the present study cf. section 5(a) (limit 7).

non-infringement actions,[86] which may lead to either split[87] or joint[88] adjudication or *that* invalidity may not be raised in any such actions,[89] which usually leads to split adjudication.[90] The above advantages apply *mutatis mutandis* even though split adjudication is sometimes not up to the free will of the plaintiff acting as the infringer but is decided for him/her.

1.30 Factor 8 is whether threatened infringement actions are allowed. Allowing such actions is an advantage for the plaintiff acting as the rightholder *since* he/she by being the first mover may choose the forum, which, in turn limits his/her risks and *since* he/she may save time and costs given that a possible infringement is addressed even before it starts.[91]

1.31 Factor 9 is whether non-infringement actions are allowed. Allowing non-infringement actions is an advantage for the plaintiff acting as the infringer *since* he/she by being the first mover may choose the forum, which, in turn, limits his/her risks.

1.32 In sum, the advantages for the plaintiff can be illustrated as in Table 1.2 below:

Table 1.2 Jurisdictional advantages

Factor	Nature	Impact	Advantages for the plaintiff
1	General	Whether more forum rules are available	• More forum rules is an advantage for the plaintiff *since* they provide for a discretion where to sue
2	General/ Specific	Whether one forum rule allows for more available fora	• More available fora is an advantage for the plaintiff *since* they provide for a discretion where to sue unless only one party benefits in which event it may only be an advantage for the plaintiff acting as the rightholder or as the infringer
3	General	Whether a plaintiff's own domicile is available	• A plaintiff's own domicile is an advantage for the plaintiff *since* it saves him/her time and costs for travelling, external counsels and translation and *since* it makes him/her feel more confident given that the case is conducted on the basis of home procedural laws
4	General	Whether the extent of jurisdiction is unlimited or limited	• A discretion between unlimited full and limited forum jurisdiction is an advantage for the plaintiff

86 Arts 4, 7(2) and 7(5) Brussels I Regulation and art. 63(e) ROP.
87 Art. 24(4) BR.
88 Art. 33(4) AUPC.
89 Arts 99(2) EUTMR and 84(4) CDR.
90 Arts 56 EUTMR and 52 CDR concerning the registered CD.
91 Report on the Convention on the Association of the Kingdom of Denmark, Ireland and the United Kingdom of Great Britain and Northern Ireland to the Convention on Jurisdiction and the Enforcement of Judgments in Civil and Commercial matters and the Protocol on its Interpretation by the Court of Justice by Professor Dr. Peter Schlosser (Sclosser report) at 134.

Factor	Nature	Impact	Advantages for the plaintiff
5	Specific	Whether change of forum principles and rules apply	• Change of forum principles and rules are an advantage for the plaintiff acting as the infringer since they allow the action to be prolonged
6	Specific	Whether invalidity in infringement actions leads to joint or split adjudication	• Joint adjudication is an advantage for the plaintiff acting as the rightholder *since* the action is speeded up • Split adjudication is an advantage for the plaintiff acting as the infringer *since* the action is prolonged
7	Specific	Whether invalidity in non-infringement actions leads to joint or split adjudication	• Joint adjudication is an advantage for the plaintiff acting as the rightholder *since* the action is speeded up • Split adjudication is an advantage for the plaintiff acting as the infringer *since* the action is prolonged
8	Specific	Whether threatened infringement actions are permitted	• Threatened infringement actions is an advantage for the plaintiff acting as the rightholder *since* he/she is the first mover and *since* an infringement can be addressed before it starts
9	Specific	Whether non-infringement actions are permitted	• Non-infringement actions is an advantage for the plaintiff acting as the infringer *since* he/she is the first mover

5. Limits

The limits of the study can be divided into overall four groups i.e. the jurisdiction limits (section a), the applicable law limits (section b), the substantive IP law limits (section c) and the recognition and enforcement limits (section d). 1.33

(a) Jurisdiction limits

The jurisdiction limits, which relate to the first stage of the infringement procedures, count seven sublimits. 1.34

Limit 1 relates to the IP rights. Following this limit, IP rights other than the ones mentioned in section 3(a) are not addressed. Thus, copyrights, moral rights, utility model rights and from a broader perspective trade secrets, personality rights, goodwill and the rights protecting the names of agricultural products and foodstuffs, namely the protected designation of origin rights (PDO), the protected geographical indication right (PGI) and the speciality guaranteed right (SPG) are disregarded. The reason for disregarding the former six (copyrights, moral rights, utility model rights, trade secrets, personality rights and goodwill) is that they are not found in European unitary versions whereas the reason for disregarding the latter three (PDO, PGI and SPG) is, despite being found in European unitary versions that they are subject to the forum rules in the BR and therefore do not fit in with the study. 1.35

As an exception the above IP rights are addressed if they contribute to the overall purpose of the study. Any such purpose is met for copyrights and personality rights due to the CJEU's judgments in, inter alia, *Pinckney*,[92] *Hi Hotel*,[93] *Shevill*[94] and *e-Date*[95] which all concern interpretations of the *forum delicti* rule being a key element of the present study cf. section 3(c) and so those judgments are referred to, inter alia, in Chapter 9.

1.36 Limit 2 relates to the litigations. Following this limit, actions other than the ones mentioned in section 3(b) are not addressed. Thus, administrative actions on opposition and validity as well as court actions, which do not involve an element of infringement such as validity actions or non-infringement actions testing a 'freedom to operate' and finally actions for preliminary injunctions and possible confirmatory actions are disregarded. As an exception the above actions are addressed if they contribute to the overall purpose of the study. Any such purpose is met *partly* for the CPV given that invalidity of any such right must be brought with the CPVO[96] and *partly* for the EUTM and the CD given that invalidity of any such rights cannot be raised in a non-infringement action meaning that the EUIPO comes into play.[97]

1.37 Limit 3 relates to the jurisdiction rules. Following this limit, forum rules other than the ones mentioned in section 3(c) are not addressed. Thus, the explicit forum agreements' rule (allowing the parties to agree on jurisdiction), the implicit forum agreements' rule (allowing the defendant to establish jurisdiction by appearing before a court out of his/her own motion) and the annexed jurisdiction rule (allowing IP infringement actions to be brought where the criminal action is pending) are disregarded. The reason for disregarding the forum agreements' rules is *that* any such agreements would make the study redundant provided that the parties keep themselves within the limits of the rules[98] since otherwise the agreements would be void and *that* the explicit forum agreement rule would require a contractual obligation between the parties e.g. by way of a forum law clause in a license agreement, which is not covered by the scope of the study cf. section 3(b). The reason for

92 Case C-170/12, *Peter Pinckney.*

93 Case C-387/12, *Hi Hotel.*

94 Case C-68/93, *Fiona Shevill.*

95 Joined cases C-509/09, *e-Date Advertising GmbH v X* and case C-161/10, *Olivier Martinez and Robert Martinez v MGN Ltd.*

96 Chapter 11, section C.3.

97 Ibid., sections C.2(a) and C.2(b).

98 One limit is that a forum agreement cannot waive art. 24(4) Brussels I Regulation cf. arts 25 and 26 Brussels I Regulation and another limit is that a forum agreement cannot waive the exclusive jurisdiction of EUTM or CD courts cf. art. 97(4) cf. 94(2)(b) EUTMR and arts 82(4) cf. 79(3)(b) CDR.

disregarding the annexed jurisdiction rule is *that* any such rule is not compatible with a plaintiff's approach cf. section 4 since in criminal actions the 'plaintiff' is always the rightholder and never the infringer and *that* the rule is rarely used in practical life since the rightholder usually fears that the infringer may not be able to pay both compensation and a fine and so focus lies with the former.

Limit 4 relates to the nature of the invalidity claim. Following this limit, the ways invalidity are raised in infringement or non-infringement proceedings i.e. by way of a claim, counterclaim or possibly by way of a defence as well as the grounds for claiming invalidity[99] is not addressed. Only the option of claiming/not claiming invalidity and the body competent to hear invalidity are addressed. **1.38**

Limit 5 relates to the Member States' and third states' own international forum rules. Following this limit, the numbers and natures of the Member States' own international forum rules,[100] which allow e.g. a US defendant to be sued in a Member State as well as the numbers and natures of third states' own international forum rules, which allow e.g. a US defendant to be sued in his/her home state are not addressed including the conditions under which they apply. The rules are merely referred to as such. The reason is that they vary widely.[101] **1.39**

Limit 6 relates to the competence of the UPC. Following this limit, the competence of the UPC for European patents, which the proprietors can escape from for a limited period of time if they continue to litigate before national courts,[102] is not addressed. The reason is *that* litigating a European patent before the UPC expresses a 'third path' since invalidity of any such patent designating more than Contracting Member States e.g. the entire EU is subject to a combination of rules namely the rules in the AUPC for Contracting (EU) Member States and the rules in the BR for non-Contracting (EU) Member States[103] and *that* accordingly any such 'third path' does not fit in with the study. The UPC's competence for European patents is, however, addressed if it contributes to the overall purpose of the study. Any such purpose **1.40**

---

99 Section 3(b) for examples.

100 Art. 6 Brussels I Regulation.

101 Kono, *supra* note 2.

102 Art. 83(1) AUPC.

103 Non-paper from the Commission Services regarding the Compatibility of the Draft Agreement on the Unified Patent Court with the Union Aquis (14191/11 LIMITE PI 114 COUR 50) of 20 September 2011, pp. 3 and 7.

is met, inter alia, in order to interpret the extent of jurisdiction under the AUPC and the *forum delicti* rule under the AUPC cf. Chapters 5 and 9.

1.41 Limit 7 relates to the stay of procedure rules. Following this limit, the rules on same actions (*lis pendens*) and the rules on related actions including the impact of such rules in IP litigation – e.g. by way of the so-called 'torpedos' where non-infringement actions are brought against the rightholder at slow moving courts in order to forestall an action on the merits – are not addressed unless they contribute to the overall purpose of the study. Any such purpose is met, inter alia, in regards to the central division rule in the AUPC cf. Chapter 10 and in regards to the *forum delicti* rules in the EUTMR and CDR cf. Chapter 9.

(b) Applicable law limits

1.42 Applicable law relates to the second stage of the infringement procedures. Such issues being limit 8 are not addressed unless they contribute to the overall purpose of the study. Any such purpose is met for the rules in the Rome II Regulation given that the applicable law rules must be interpreted in line with the forum law rules in the Brussels I Regulation[104] and so the Rome II Regulation rules are referred to, inter alia, in Chapter 9.

(c) Substantive IP law limits

1.43 Substantive IP law relates to the third stage of the infringement procedures. Such issues being limit 9 are not addressed unless they contribute to the overall purpose of the study. Any such purpose is met for the WIPO Joint Recommendation[105] and the CJEU's judgment in *L'Oréal*[106] since they both address when an infringer is subject to the IP laws of a forum state with a potential IP infringement to follow thus illustrating the interconnection with the jurisdiction rules and so they are referred to, inter alia, in Chapter 9.

(d) Recognition and enforcement limits

1.44 Recognition and enforcement relates to the final stage of the infringement procedures. Such issues being limit 10 are not addressed unless they contribute to the overall purpose of the study. Any such purpose is met in order to

---

104 Recital (7) Rome II Regulation.

105 WIPO Joint Recommendation Concerning Provisions on the Protection of Marks, and other Industrial Property Rights in Signs, on the Internet. The Recommendation was adopted by the Assembly of the Paris Union for the Protection of Industrial Property and the General Assembly of the World Intellectual Property Organization (WIPO) at the 36th Series of Meetings of the Assemblies of the Member States of WIPO September 24–October 3, 2001.

106 Case C-324/09, *L'Oréal SA and Others v eBay International AG and others*.

illustrate possible impacts of CJEU judgments, inter alia, *Wintersteiger*.[107] For the purpose of the present limit the term 'enforcement' addresses the meaning within Chapter III, section 2 Brussels I Regulation, which is not to be confused with the term 'effective enforcement' addressed in Chapter 4 section B. In sum, the limits of the study can be illustrated as in Table 1.3 below:

Table 1.3 Limits of the study

Jurisdiction limits	Limit 1	• Copyrights • Moral rights • Utility model rights • Trade secrets • Personality rights • Goodwill • Protected designation of origin rights (PDO) • Protected geographical indication rights (PGI) • Speciality guaranteed rights (SPG)
	Limit 2	• Actions at administrative authority level o Actions on opposition o Actions on validity • Actions at court level o Actions not involving an element of infringement ▪ Actions on validity ▪ Actions testing a 'freedom to operate' o Actions for preliminary injunction and possible confirmatory actions
	Limit 3	• The explicit forum agreements' rule • The implicit forum agreements' rule • The annexed jurisdiction rule
	Limit 4	• Nature of an invalidity claim • Nature of an invalidity counterclaim • Nature of an invalidity defence
	Limit 5	• Member States' own international forum rules • Third states' own international forum rules
	Limit 6	• UPC's competence for European patents
	Limit 7	• Stay of procedure rules on same actions (lis pendens) • Stay of procedure rules on related actions
Applicable law limits	Limit 8	Not addressed
Substantive law limits	Limit 9	
Recognition and enforcement limits	Limit 10	

B. STRUCTURE

The book is divided overall into four parts, which are subdivided into 12 chapters as outlined below. **1.45**

Part I is titled 'Introduction' and encompasses the present Chapter 1. The chapter sets the limits for the study. **1.46**

107 Case C-523/10, *Wintersteiger* cf. Chapter 9 section B.1(a)(ii), Principle 2: Proximity.

1.47 Part II is titled 'Number of jurisdiction rules' and encompasses two chapters. In Chapter 2 the jurisdiction framework is examined (general level) and from the findings in that chapter the jurisdiction rules are outlined in Chapter 3 (specific level). Accordingly, Chapters 2–3 will provide the answer to the number of international jurisdiction rules available to the plaintiff.

1.48 Part III is named 'Nature of jurisdiction rules' and encompasses eight chapters. In Chapter 4 the principles on which the jurisdiction rules are based are outlined (general level). Then, the jurisdiction rules as such are addressed (specific level). Thus, in Chapter 5 the defendant's domicile rule is examined; in Chapter 6 the establishment rule is examined; in Chapter 7 the plaintiff's domicile rule is examined; in Chapter 8 the multiple defendants' rule is examined; in Chapter 9 the *forum delicti* rule is examined; in Chapter 10 the central division rule is examined and finally in Chapter 11 the exclusive jurisdiction rule is examined.[108] Accordingly, Chapters 4–11 will provide the answer to the nature of the international jurisdiction rules available to the plaintiff.

1.49 Part IV is titled 'Conclusion' and encompasses one chapter. In Chapter 12 a conclusion is drawn. Accordingly, Chapter 12 will provide the answer to the study.

108 The reason for addressing the forum rules in the above order which differs from the order in the BR where the defendant's domicile is addressed first (art. 4 Brussels I Regulation), *forum delicti* second (art. 7.2 Brussels I Regulation) and establishment third (art. 7.5 Brussels I Regulation) is twofold, i.e. *that* the defendant's domicile and establishment rules are interrelated given that the latter is known as the 'small' defendant's domicile rule cf. Chapter 6 and *that* Chapters 5–9 reflect the structure from arts 97 EUTMR, 82 CDR and 101 CPVR. The exclusive jurisdiction rule is addressed primarily in Chapter 11 which, however, does not exclude that the effect of raising invalidity under the respective forum rules addressed in Chapters 5–10 is briefly outlined. A general reference is made in those chapters to Chapter 11.

Part II

NUMBER OF JURISDICTION RULES

2

JURISDICTION FRAMEWORK

A. INTRODUCTION

From Chapter 1[1] it follows that the number of international jurisdiction rules available to the plaintiff must be identified. A precondition for being capable of doing so is to identify the jurisdiction framework, which is therefore the purpose of the present Chapter 2. **2.01**

A distinction is drawn between the jurisdiction framework governing a national IP right (section B) and the jurisdiction framework governing a corresponding European unitary IP right (section C). In the end a conclusion is drawn, inter alia, by way of a table (section D). **2.02**

1 Section A.3(c).

B. THE JURISDICTION FRAMEWORK GOVERNING A NATIONAL IP RIGHT

2.03 The jurisdiction framework governing a national IP right does not depend on the IP right in question but rather on whether the defendant is domiciled in the EU (section 1), in the EFTA (section 2) or outside the EU/EFTA (section 3).[2]

1. Defendant is domiciled in the EU

2.04 If the defendant is domiciled in the EU,[3] regardless of nationality and of the domicile of the plaintiff,[4] the Brussels Convention has originally been applicable.[5] The Brussels Convention distributed international jurisdiction between the courts of the Member States in civil and commercial matters, including IP matters.[6] However, the Brussels I Regulation replaced the Brussels Convention on 1 March 2002.[7] The former must be interpreted in line with the latter[8] except where they differ.[9] Originally, the Brussels I Regulation did not apply to Denmark due to its civil law opt out.[10] On 20 September 2005, however, a parallel agreement was signed between Denmark and the EU[11] meaning that the Brussels I Regulation entered into force in Denmark on 1 July 2007.[12] Now, therefore, the Brussels I Regulation applies in every Member State.[13] Whereas the legal basis for the Brussels Convention was art. 220 Treaty of Rome found in Part Six under the heading 'General and

---

2 The reason for the distinction between EU, EFTA and non-EU/EFTA defendants is – despite that the former two are subject to parallel rules cf. sections B.1 and B.2 – that any such distinction must, with variations, also be drawn under the European unitary IP rights cf. section C.

3 List of Member States at 1 January 2017: Austria, Belgium, Bulgaria, Cyprus, Croatia, Czech Republic, Denmark, Estonia, Finland, France, Germany, Greece, Hungary, Ireland, Italy, Latvia, Lithuania, Luxembourg, Malta, Netherlands, Poland, Portugal, Romania, Slovakia, Slovenia, Spain, Sweden and the United Kingdom i.e. 28 in total.

4 Case C-412/98, *Group Josi Reinsurance Company SA v Universal General Insurance Company* (UGIC), para. 78.

5 Ulrich Magnus and Peter Mankowski, *Brussels I Regulation*, European Commentaries on Private International Law, 2nd revised edn, Sellier European Law Publishers, 2012, pp. 14–16 with references.

6 Ibid., pp. 54 *et seq.* and Peter Arnt Nielsen, International Privat- og Procesret, Jurist- og Økonomforbundets Forlag, 1997, pp. 143 *et seq.*

7 Magnus and Mankowski, ibid., pp. 16–20 with references.

8 Case 167/00, *Verein für Konsumenteninformation v Karl Heinz Henkel*, para. 49.

9 Magnus and Mankowski, *supra* note 5, p. 32.

10 Ibid., p. 10 at note 22 with references.

11 Council Decision 2006/325/EC OJ L 120/22 of 27 April 2006 concerning the Conclusion of the Agreement between the European Community and the Kingdom of Denmark on Jurisdiction and the Recognition and Enforcement of Judgments in Civil and Commercial Matters cf. L 299/62, Agreement between the European Community and the Kingdom of Denmark on Jurisdiction and the Recognition and Enforcement of Judgments in Civil and Commercial Matters. The Danish Implementation Act has no. 1563 of 20 December 2006.

12 OJ 2007 L 94/70 cf. Peter Arnt Nielsen, *Brussels I and Denmark*, IPRax, 2007, pp. 506 *et seq.*

13 Magnus and Mankowski, *supra* note 5, pp. 25–31.

Final Provisions'[14] the legal basis for the Brussels I Regulation is arts 61(c) and 67 Treaty of the European Community found in Title IV under the heading 'Visas, Asylum, Immigration and other Policies related to the Free Movement of Persons'.[15] On 14 December 2010 the Commission published its proposal relating to the recast of the Brussels I Regulation[16] this was significantly revised by the European Parliament on 20 November 2012[17] before being finally adopted by the Council on 12 December 2012.[18] It has been applicable since 10 January 2015 in the Member States[19] including in Denmark.[20] The legal basis for the Brussels I Regulation is arts 67(4) and 81(2) TFEU found in Title V under the heading, 'Area of Freedom, Security and Justice'.[21] The legal

14 Art. 220 Treaty of Rome of 25 March 1957 obliged the Member States to enter into negotiations 'with a view to securing for the benefit of their nationals [...] the simplification of formalities governing the reciprocal recognition and enforcement of judgments of courts or tribunals and the arbitration awards'.

15 Art. 61(c) Treaty of the European Community of 10 November 1997 obliges the Council to adopt 'measures in the field of judicial cooperation in civil matters [...]'. Such measures include:

> (a) improving and simplifying [...] the system for cross-border service of judicial and extrajudicial documents [...], the recognition and enforcement of decisions in civil and commercial cases, including decisions in extrajudicial cases; (b) promoting the compatibility of the rules applicable in the Member States concerning the conflict of laws and of jurisdiction; (c) eliminating obstacles to the good functioning of civil proceedings, if necessary by promoting the compatibility of the rules on civil procedure applicable in the Member States.

16 Proposal for a Regulation of the European Parliament and of the Council on Jurisdiction and the Recognition and Enforcement of Judgments in Civil and Commercial Matters, 2010/0383. The proposal followed an extensive consultation of the public, Member States, institutions and experts cf. p. 4 of the proposal with references. A number of studies were carried out prior to the revision, inter alia, a 2007 study on residual jurisdiction conducted by Professor Arnaud Nuyts of the University of Brussels available at http://ec.europa.eu/justice_home/doc_centre/civil/studies/doc_civil_studies_en.htm, a 2007 study on the practical application of the Regulation conducted by Professor Burkhard Hess of the University of Heidelberg available at http://ec.europa.eu/justice_home/doc_centre/civil/studies/doc_civil_studies_en.htm and a 2010 study on data collection and impact analysis conducted by the Centre for Strategy & Evaluation Services available at http://ec.europa.eu/justice_home/doc_centre/civil/studies/doc_civil_studies_en.htm. See also Peter Arnt Nielsen, 'The Recast of the Brussels I Regulation', in Michael Joachim Bonell, Marie-Louise Holle and Peter Arnt Nielsen (eds) *Liber Amicorum Ole Lando*, DJØF Publishing, 2012, pp. 257–6; Peter Arnt Nielsen, 'Forslaget til ny Domsforordning, Ugeskrift for Retsvæsen', U.2012B212 and Peter Arnt Nielsen, 'The State of Play of the Recast of the Brussels I Regulation' (2012) 81(4) *Nordic Journal of International Law* 585–603.

17 European Parliament legislative Resolution of 20 November 2012 on the Proposal for a Regulation of the European Parliament and of the Council on Jurisdiction and the Recognition and Enforcement of Judgments in Civil and Commercial Matters, COM(2010)0748.

18 Council Regulation 1215/2012 of 12 December 2012 on Jurisdiction and the Recognition and Enforcement of Judgments in Civil and Commercial Matters see Peter Arnt Nielsen, 'The New Brussels I Regulation' (2013) 50(2) *Common Market Law Review* 503–28; Peter Arnt Nielsen, Den nye Domsforordning, Ugeskrift for Retsvæsen, U.2013B83 and Peter Arnt Nielsen, 'The Recasted Brussels I Regulation' (2014) *Nordic Journal of International Law* 61–71.

19 Art. 81 Brussels I Regulation.

20 Draft Law amending the Law on the Brussels I Regulation (Implementation of the revised Regulation on Jurisdiction and the Recognition and Enforcement of Judgments in Civil and Commercial Matters) of 4 April 2013, 2012/1 LF 202.

21 Art. 67(4) TFEU obliges the Union to facilitate access to justice, in particular through the principle of mutual recognition of judicial and extrajudicial decisions in civil matters whereas art. 81(2) obliges the European Parliament and the Council to adopt measures, particularly when necessary for the proper

basis corresponds to the one under the former Brussels I Regulation[22] despite the different numbers of the provisions, due to the entry into force of the Treaty of Lisbon.[23] Basically, therefore, the legal basis for the Brussels I Regulation is the 'free movement of judgments'.[24] The legal basis is referred to, inter alia, in Chapter 9.

2. Defendant is domiciled in the EFTA

2.05 If the defendant is domiciled in the EFTA,[25] regardless of nationality, the 1988 Lugano Convention has traditionally been applicable.[26] The Lugano Convention distributes international jurisdiction between the courts of EU and EFTA Member States in civil and commercial matters, including IP matters.[27] However, the 2007 Lugano Convention has to a large extent replaced the 1988 Lugano Convention.[28] Thus, the 2007 Lugano Convention entered into force in the EU, Norway and Denmark on 1 January 2010, in Switzerland on 1 January 2011 and in Iceland on 1 May 2011 with Liechtenstein remaining the only Member State still covered by the 1988 Lugano Convention.[29] For the purpose of the present study no distinction is drawn between Iceland, Norway and Switzerland (which are subject to the new 2007 Lugano Convention) and Liechtenstein (which is subject to the old 1988 Lugano Convention).

2.06 The provisions of the Brussels I Regulation and the Lugano Conventions are, despite different numbers of the articles,[30] overall similar[31] and must be

---

functioning of the internal market, aimed at ensuring '(a) the mutual recognition and enforcement between Member States of judgments and of decisions in extrajudicial cases; [...] (c) the compatibility of the rules applicable in the Member States concerning conflict of laws and of jurisdiction and [...] (e) effective access to justice'.

22 Council Regulation 44/2001 of 22 December 2000 on Jurisdiction and the Recognition and Enforcement of Judgments in Civil and Commercial Matters, preamble.

23 Treaty of Lisbon amending the Treaty on the European Union and the Treaty establishing the European Community signed at Lisbon on 13 December 2007.

24 Recital (6) Brussels I Regulation.

25 List of Member States by 1 January 2017: Iceland, Liechtenstein, Norway and Switzerland.

26 Magnus and Mankowski, *supra* note 5, pp. 19 *et seq.*

27 Ibid.

28 Ibid. p. 20.

29 Ibid.

30 The defendant's domicile rule is found in art. 4 Brussels I Regulation and in art. 2 Lugano Convention, the *forum delicti* rule is found in art. 7(2) Brussels I Regulation and in art. 5(3) Lugano Convention, the establishment rule is found in art. 7(5) Brussels I Regulation and in art. 5(5) Lugano Convention, the multiple defendants' rule is found in art. 8(1) Brussels I Regulation and in art. 6(1) Lugano Convention and the exclusive jurisdiction rule is found in art. 24(4) Brussels I Regulation and in art. 22(4) Lugano Convention.

31 For an overview of the differences between the Brussels I Regulation and the Lugano Conventions see Magnus and Mankowski, *supra* note 5, p. 17.

interpreted in the same way.[32] For that reason the numbers in the Brussels I Regulation are referred to unless reference is made specifically to the Lugano Convention in which event that convention is referred to.

3. Defendant is domiciled outside the EU/EFTA

If, finally, the defendant is domiciled outside the EU/EFTA, regardless of nationality, the Member States' own international forum rules apply.[33] For the reasons in Chapter 1 section A.5(a) (limit 5) any such rules, including the conditions under which they may apply, are not examined for the purpose of the present study. **2.07**

C. THE JURISDICTION FRAMEWORK GOVERNING A EUROPEAN UNITARY IP RIGHT

The jurisdiction framework governing a corresponding European unitary IP right depends on whether the IP right in question is an EUTM (section 1), a CD (section 2), a CPV (section 3) or a UP (section 4). **2.08**

1. European Union Trademark

In disputes concerned with infringement and invalidity of an EUTM[34] the international jurisdiction rules in the EUTMR apply. The rules, which are found in Title X EUTMR concerning 'Jurisdiction and Procedure in Legal Actions Relating to EU Trade Marks',[35] are known as the 'cascade' rules.[36] The 'cascade' rules are a unitary and prioritized set of forum rules, which apply whatever the domicile of the defendant.[37] According to the 'cascade' rules action must be brought at the defendant's EU domicile or, failing that, EU establishment.[38] If the defendant is neither domiciled nor established in the EU action must be brought at the plaintiff's EU domicile or, failing that, EU **2.09**

32 Art. 1 to Protocol No. 2 Lugano Convention cf. Magnus and Mankowski, ibid., p. 21 and Nielsen, *supra* note 5, p. 134.
33 Art. 6 BR.
34 Art. 96 EUTMR.
35 Arts 94 EUTMR *et seq.*
36 Art. 97 EUTMR cf. *Conflict of Laws in Intellectual Property, The CLIP Principles and Commentary*, European Max Planck Group on Conflicts of Laws in Intellectual Property, Oxford University Press, 2013, p. 192 (2:605.N08).
37 Proposal for a European Parliament and Council Regulation on the Community Design presented by the Commission COM (93) 342 final COD 463 Brussels, 3 December 1993, p. 38. The reasoning applies *mutatis mutandis* under the EUTMR cf. the wording '[the forum rules in the CDR] entirely correspond to the parallel provisions relating to the Community Trade Mark', p. 38.
38 Art. 97(1) EUTMR cf. Chapters 5 and 6.

establishment.[39] If neither the defendant nor the plaintiff are domiciled or established in the EU action must be brought in Spain.[40] Alternatively action can, with variations, be brought at *forum delicti*.[41] The justification for the 'cascade' rules is twofold, namely *first* to limit conflicts of jurisdiction between courts of different Member States and *second* to limit the number of fora available to the plaintiff.[42]

2.10 Given, however, *that* defendants domiciled in the EU are usually subject to the rules in the Brussels I Regulation;[43] *that* defendants domiciled in the EFTA are usually subject to the rules in the Lugano Convention[44] and *that* defendants domiciled outside the EU/EFTA are usually subject to the Member States' own international forum rules[45] the question is whether any one of these also apply under the EUTMR and in that case to what extent. The three situations are dealt with individually below in sections (a)–(c).

(a) Defendant is domiciled in the EU

2.11 If the defendant is domiciled in the EU it follows from art. 94(1) EUTMR that 'unless otherwise specified in this Regulation the Union rules on jurisdiction and the recognition and enforcement of judgments in civil and commercial matters shall apply [...]'.[46] Thus, the Brussels I Regulation, being a Union rule, applies as 'fall back' to the EUTMR meaning that the former applies where the latter is silent, which in turn is supported by the principle of lex specialis,[47] the Explanatory Memorandum,[48] writings of legal scholars[49] and by the AG.[50] The reason for the current wording of art. 94(1) EUTMR dates back to the 1975 Community Patent Convention, which established an

39 Art. 97(2) EUTMR cf. Chapter 7.
40 Art. 97(3) EUTMR.
41 Art. 97(5) EUTMR cf. Chapter 9.
42 *Supra* note 37.
43 Section B.1.
44 Section B.2.
45 Section B.3.
46 Art. 94(1) EUTMR.
47 Art. 67 Brussels I Regulation.
48 Bulletin of the European Communities Supplement 5/80, New Trade Mark System for the Community, proposed Directive and Regulation prepared by the Commission of the European Communities (COM 80 635 final 19 November 1980), p. 76.
49 Annette Kur, 'Are there any Common Principles of Private International Law with regard to Intellectual Property' in Stefan Leible and Ansgar Ohly (eds) *Intellectual Property and Private International Law* Mohr Siebeck, 2009, p. 3 and James J. Fawcett and Paul Torremans, *Intellectual Property and Private International Law*, Second Edition, Oxford Private International Law Series, OUP, 2011 at 8.08 and 8.14.
50 Opinion of Advocate General Tanchev in case C-617/15, *Hummel Holding A/S v Nike Inc. and Nike Retail BV*, para. 33.

EU wide patent right[51] similarly to the EU-wide EUTM right.[52] Thus, the 1975 Community Patent Convention read, 'Unless otherwise specified in this Convention [the Brussels Convention] shall apply'.[53] The amended 1989 version of the text,[54] which also established an EU-wide patent right,[55] similarly read, 'Unless otherwise specified in this Convention [the Brussels Convention] shall apply'.[56] Finally, the Protocol on Litigation accompanying the 1989 version of the text also read, 'Unless otherwise specified in this Protocol [the Brussels Convention] shall apply [....]'.[57] Thus, both the 1975 and 1989 versions of the Community Patent Convention referred to the Brussels Convention remaining applicable in the background. This model was copied in to the original CTMR, which read, 'Unless otherwise specified in this Regulation [the Brussels Convention] shall apply'.[58] When the former CTMR was adopted the reference to the Brussels Convention was replaced with a reference to the Brussels I Regulation,[59] which in the EUTMR has been replaced with a reference to the, 'Union rules on jurisdiction and the recognition and enforcement of judgments in civil and commercial matters'.[60]

The 'fall back' nature of the Brussels I Regulation means that the defendant's domicile, *forum delicti* and establishment rules in arts 4, 7(2) and 7(5) Brussels I Regulation do not apply[61] since they have 'sister' provisions in the 'cascade'.[62] **2.12**

51 Art. 2(2) Convention for the European Patent for the Common Market (Community Patent Convention) (76/76/EEC) of 15 December 1975.

52 Art. 1(2) EUTMR.

53 Art. 68 Community Patent Convention.

54 Agreement relating to Community Patents on 15 December 1989 (89/695/EEC) cf. corresponding Convention for the European Patent for the Common Market (Community Patent Convention) and implementing regulations.

55 Art. 2(2) Community Patent Convention No L 401/10.

56 Art. 66 ibid.

57 Art. 13(1) Protocol on the Settlement of Litigation Concerning the Infringement and Validity of Community Patents of 30 December 1989 (Protocol of Litigation).

58 Art. 90(1) Council Regulation (EC) No 40/94 of 20 December 1993 on the Community Trade Mark.

59 Art. 94(1) Council Regulation (EC) No 207/2009 of 26 February 2009 on the Community Trade Mark.

60 Art. 94(1) EUTMR cf. Proposal for a Regulation amending Council Regulation (EC) No 207/2009 on the Community Trade Mark 2013/0088 (COD) published on 27 March 2013 by the Commission pp. 34 *et seq.*

61 Art. 94(2)(a) EUTMR.

62 The 'sister' provision to art. 4 Brussels I Regulation is found in art. 97(1) EUTMR cf. Chapter 5. Art. 4 Brussels I Regulation can in effect be subsumed in art. 97(1) EUTMR since also the latter is subject to the definition of 'domicile' within the meaning of arts 62 and 63 Brussels I Regulation cf. art. 94(1) EUTMR. The 'sister' provision to art. 7(2) Brussels I Regulation is found in art. 97(5) EUTMR cf. Chapter 9. Art. 7(2) Brussels I Regulation can in effect not be subsumed in art. 97(5) EUTMR since non-infringement actions can be brought under the former cf. case C-133/11, *Folien Fischer AG and Fofitec AG v Ritrama SpA*, para. 56 but not under the latter. Finally, the 'sister' provision to art. 7(5) Brussels I Regulation is found in art. 97(1) EUTMR cf. Chapter 6. As to whether art. 7(5) Brussels I Regulation in effect can be subsumed in art. 97(1) EUTMR one can argue both ways. Supporting that art. 7(5) Brussels I Regulation can be subsumed in art. 97(1) EUTMR it is argued that it is a requirement under the former that the dispute has arisen out of the operation of the establishment. Supporting the opposite result namely that art. 7(5) Brussels I Regulation cannot be subsumed in art. 97(1) EUTMR it is argued that the former requires an EU domicile by contrast

Given that art. 24(4) Brussels I Regulation has not been exempted[63] the question is whether it applies as 'fall back' under the EUTMR.

2.13 Supporting that art. 24(4) Brussels I Regulation applies as 'fall back' under the EUTMR it is argued, inter alia, *that* art. 8(1) Brussels I Regulation which has not been exempted in the EUTMR either[64] applies as 'fall back'[65] and *that* the reason for not exempting art. 24(4) Brussels I Regulation may be deliberate taking into account the position for, inter alia, RCDs where invalidity, due to the missing substantial law examination,[66] is frequently raised[67] and where under the CDR art. 24(4) Brussels I Regulation has therefore been exempted[68] since otherwise a large number of cases would be pending in Spain where the RCD is registered[69] contrary to the position for EUTMs where invalidity is not so frequently raised[70] and where under the EUTMR art. 24(4) Brussels I Regulation has therefore not been exempted.

2.14 Supporting the opposite result namely that art. 24(4) Brussels I Regulation does not apply as 'fall back' under the EUTMR it is argued, inter alia, and in the absence of information in the Explanatory Memorandum[71] *that* applying it would conflict with the principle of *lex specialis*[72] since rules on exclusive jurisdiction if invalidity is raised are already found in art. 96(d) EUTMR[73] and in art. 99(2) cf. 56 EUTMR;[74] *that* arts 24(4) Brussels I Regulation and 96(d) EUTMR would conflict since the former would point at the courts of Spain being the place where the EUTM is registered[75] whereas the latter in principle points at every EUTM court in every Member State; *that* art. 24(4) Brussels I Regulation and arts 99(2) cf. 56 EUTMR would also conflict since the former would point at the courts of Spain whereas the latter points at EUIPO in

---

to the latter where an EU domicile renders the provision inapplicable. The former interpretation seems the likely one meaning that art. 7(5) Brussels I Regulation can in effect be subsumed in art. 97(1) EUTMR. One can, however, also argue the opposite. For further reading see Fawcett and Torremans, *supra* note 49 at 8.14 and Guy Tritton, *Intellectual Property in Europe*, Thomson, 3rd edn, Sweet & Maxwell, 2008 at 14–083.

63 Art. 94(2)(a) EUTMR.

64 Art. 94(2)(a) EUTMR.

65 Fawcett and Torremans, *supra* note 49 at 8.25–8.26 and Chapter 8 section C.1.

66 Art. 45 CDR *et seq.*

67 EUIPO.eu for statistics.

68 Art. 79(3)(a) CDR.

69 Art. 72 CDR.

70 EUIPO.eu for statistics.

71 Bulletin of the European Communities Supplement 5/80, New Trade Mark System for the Community, proposed Directive and Regulation prepared by the Commission of the European Communities (COM 80 635 final 19 November 1980), pp. 76–7.

72 Art. 67 Brussels I Regulation.

73 Art. 96(d) EUTMR applies if invalidity is raised in an infringement action cf. Chapter 11.

74 Arts 99(2) cf. 56 EUTMR apply if invalidity is raised in a non-infringement action cf. Chapter 11.

75 Art. 87 EUTMR.

Spain; *that* the reason for art. 8(1) Brussels I Regulation to be applicable despite not being exempted is that no 'sister' provision is found in the EUTMR and finally *that* writings of legal scholars[76] and case law[77] support that art. 24(4) Brussels I Regulation does not apply as 'fall back' under the EUTMR.

In sum and in particular taking into account the principle of *lex specialis* and case law art. 24(4) Brussels I Regulation does not apply as 'fall back' under the EUTMR. It follows, therefore, that arts 4, 7(2), 7(5) and 24(4) Brussels I Regulation do not apply as 'fall back' under the EUTMR. By contrast, however, art. 8(1) Brussels I Regulation applies as 'fall back' under the EUTMR and the same goes for arts 62 and 63 Brussels I Regulation for the purpose of defining 'domicile' within the meaning of art. 97(1) and (2) EUTMR.[78] **2.15**

(b) Defendant is domiciled in the EFTA

If the defendant is domiciled in the EFTA neither the original CTMR adopted in 1993,[79] the former CTMR adopted in 2009[80] nor the current EUTMR adopted in 2015[81] refer to the Lugano Conventions adopted in 1988[82] and 2007[83] even though the latter two were prior in time. The question is therefore whether the Lugano Convention applies under the EUTMR and in that case to what extent.[84] To answer that question an overall distinction must be drawn between whether a EUTM action[85] can be brought in the EU **2.16**

76 European Max-Planck Group for Conflict of Laws in Intellectual Property, Exclusive Jurisdiction and Cross-Border IP (Patent) Infringement Suggestions for Amendment of the Brussels Regulation of 20 December 2006, p. 8 at note 17; Magnus and Mankowski, *supra* note 5, pp. 429–30 and 433 and Tritton, *supra* note 62 at 14–084.

77 Case C-230/15, *Brite Strike Technologies Inc. v Brite Strike Technologies SA*, para. 62.

78 Chapters 5 and 7. Furthermore reliance can be placed on art. 7(5) Brussels I Regulation when defining 'establishment' within the meaning of art. 97(1) and (2) EUTMR cf. Fawcett and Torremans, *supra* note 49 at 8.16 and Chapters 6 and 7.

79 Council Regulation (EC) No 40/94 of 20 December 1993 on the Community Trade Mark.

80 Council Regulation (EC) No 207/2009 of 26 February 2009 on the Community Trade Mark.

81 Council Regulation (EC) No 2015/2424 of 16 December 2015 on the Community Trade Mark.

82 Convention on Jurisdiction and the Enforcement of Judgments in Civil and Commercial Matters signed in Lugano on 16 September 1988.

83 Convention on Jurisdiction and the Enforcement of Judgments in Civil and Commercial Matters signed in Lugano on 30 October 2007.

84 The Brussels I Regulation referred to in art. 94(1) EUTMR obviously does not apply *mutatis mutandis* to EFTA defendants since that would contradict the interrelation between the Brussels I Regulation and the Lugano Convention cf. art. 64 of the 2007 Lugano Convention.

85 Art. 96 EUTMR.

based on the rules in the Lugano Convention[86] and whether a EUTM action can be brought in the EFTA based on the rules in the Lugano Convention.[87]

2.17 As regards whether a EUTM action can be brought in the EU based on the rules in the Lugano Convention the principle of *lex specialis* applies given that every Member State is party to both the Lugano Convention and the EUTMR.[88] Following the principle, which has not been codified in the Lugano Convention[89] but equally applies as a general principle of law,[90] the Lugano Convention applies as 'fall back' meaning, and in line with the reasoning in section C.1(a) whereas consistency is created vis-à-vis the Brussels I Regulation, inter alia, *that* the *forum delicti* and exclusive jurisdiction rules in arts 5(3) and 22(4) Lugano Convention do not apply since they have 'sister' provisions in the 'cascade'[91] and *that* the establishment rule in art. 5(5) Lugano Convention does not apply provided that the establishment is located in the EU since in that case a 'sister' rule is also found in the 'cascade'.[92] If, by contrast, the establishment is located in the EFTA art. 5(5) Lugano Convention points at an EFTA Member State in line with art. 2 Lugano Convention, and so the question is whether a EUTM action can be brought in the EFTA based on, inter alia, those two provisions cf. below.

2.18 As regards whether a EUTM action can be brought in the EFTA based on the rules in the Lugano Convention two questions must be addressed. The first is whether the Lugano Convention applies in any such situation and, provided

86 Changing slightly the example in Chapter 1 section 2 so that Frox is based in Germany whereas Frogs is based in Switzerland the question could be whether Frox, besides being able to bring a non-infringement action under art. 97(2) EUTMR, provided that national law so permits, could also bring any such action at a EUTM court under e.g. art. 5(3) Lugano Convention following case C-133/11, *Folien Fischer*, para. 56.

87 Changing slightly the example in Chapter 1 section 2 so that Frox is based in Switzerland whereas Frogs is based in Liechtenstein the question could be whether Frogs, besides being able to bring an infringement action under art. 97(3) or 97(5) EUTMR, could also bring any such action at a non-EUTM court under e.g. art. 2 Lugano Convention.

88 Magnus and Mankowski, *supra* note 5, p. 20 (as regards the Lugano Convention) and Jens Schovsbo, Morten Rosenmeier and Clement Salung Petersen, *Immaterialret*, Jurist- og Økonomforbundets Forlag, 2015, pp. 535 *et seq.* (as regards the EUTMR).

89 *Infra* note 116.

90 Ruth Nielsen og Christina D. Tvarnø, Retskilder og Retsteorier, Jurist- og Økonomforbundets Forlag, 2011, pp. 224 *et seq.*

91 The 'sister' provision to art. 5(3) Lugano Convention is found in art. 97(5) EUTMR cf. Chapter 9 whereas the 'sister' provisions to art. 22(4) Lugano Convention are found in arts 96(d), 99(2) cf. 56 EUTMR cf. Chapter 11. Given and for the reasons *supra* note 62; *that* art. 5(3) Lugano Convention in effect cannot be subsumed in art. 97(5) EUTMR and *that* art. 5(3) Lugano Convention has not been exempted in the EUTMR one could argue that art. 5(3) Lugano Convention also applies. The effect would be cf. the example *supra* note 86, inter alia, that a non-infringement action of a EUTM could be brought under art. 5(3) Lugano Convention following case C-133/11, *Folien Fischer*, para. 56. Any such interpretation seems unlikely given that inconsistency would be created vis-à-vis the Brussels I Regulation.

92 The 'sister' provision to art. 5(5) Lugano Convention is found in art. 97(1) EUTMR cf. Chapter 6. For the reasons *supra* note 62 art. 5(5) Lugano Convention can be subsumed in art. 97(1) EUTMR.

that the Lugano Convention is found to apply, the second is the extent to which the Lugano Convention applies.

With respect to the first question one can argue both that the Lugano Convention applies and that it does not apply. **2.19**

Supporting that the Lugano Convention applies and that, therefore, a EUTM action can be brought in the EFTA it is argued, inter alia, *that* EFTA courts determine their jurisdiction under their own national laws being, inter alia, the Lugano Convention;[93] *that* any such interpretation is confirmed by case law from national EFTA courts;[94] *that* writings of legal scholars support the application of the Lugano Convention[95] and *that* the narrow term, 'Application of Regulation (EC) No 44/2001' used in the former CTMR[96] does not argue against an EUTM action to be brought in the EFTA since the term may have been used merely because EFTA Member States are not parties to the EUTMR[97] any which argument is confirmed by the fact that the broader term, 'Application of the Brussels and Lugano Conventions' was used in EPLA[98] whereto EFTA Member States could be parties.[99] **2.20**

Supporting the opposite result namely that the Lugano Convention does not apply and that therefore a EUTM action cannot be brought in the EFTA it is **2.21**

93 Section 2.B.

94 Handelsgericht Zurich, decision of 16 October 2006 referred in GRUR int. 2007, pp. 258 *et seq.* The case concerned two EFTA parties i.e. a Liechtenstein plaintiff suing a Swiss defendant for EUTM infringement in Zürich, Switzerland under art. 2 Lugano Convention. The question was whether the Swiss court was competent considering that under art. 97(3) EUTMR action must be brought in Spain if neither the defendant nor the plaintiff are domiciled or established in the EU or at *forum delicti* under art. 97(5) EUTMR cf. Chapter 9. The Swiss court found that it was competent under art. 2 Lugano Convention ruling that:

> Die [Gemeinschaftsmarkenverordnung] regelt die Zuständigkeit der Gerichte innerhalb der EU. Die Zuständigkeit der Schweizer Gerichte betrifft das nicht. Diese bestimmen ihre Zuständigkeit nach ihrem Recht, inklusive der einschlägigen Staatsverträge und dies fürht [...] über Art. 2 Lugano [Übereinkommen] [...] zur örtlichen Zuständigkeit der Gerichte in Zürich.

95 Vincenzo Scordamaglia, 'Jurisdiction and Procedure in Legal Actions relating to Community Trademarks' in Mario Franzosi, *European Community Trade Mark, Commentary to the European Community Regulation*, Kluwer Law International, 1997, pp. 390 *et seq.* and Eike Scharper, Durchsetzung der Gemeinschaftsmarke, Carl Heymanns Verlag, 2006 at note 83. For a different view see (probably) Benedetta Ubertazzi, *Exclusive Jurisdiction in Intellectual Property*, Max Planck Institut für Ausländisches und Internationales Privatrecht, Mohr Siebeck, 2012, p. 74.

96 Art. 94(1) Council Regulation (EC) No 207/2009 of 26 February 2009 on the Community Trade Mark.

97 Birger Stuevold Lassen and Are Stenvik, *Kjennetegnsrett*, 3rd edn, Universitetsforlaget, 2011, p. 38.

98 Art. 38 Draft Agreement on the Establishment of a European Patent Litigation System (EPLA), WPL/10/05, Munich 7 December 2005.

99 Ibid., preamble. Against any such interpretation it is argued, however, art. 101(1) CPVR where the Lugano Convention is referred to even though EFTA Member States are not parties to the CPVR cf. Evaluation of the Community Plant Variety Right *Aquis* – Final Report to the Directorate General for Health and Consumer Affairs (European Commission), April 2011, p. 49 and section C.3.

argued, inter alia, *that* the EUTMR sets up a system with EUTM courts[100] having exclusive jurisdiction;[101] *that* applying the Lugano Convention could contrast any such exclusive jurisdiction;[102] *that* it may be deliberate that the Lugano Convention does not apply given that there is an interplay between exclusivity and the forum rules referred to in the sense that where a system is set up with EU/EFTA courts having exclusive jurisdiction[103] the Lugano Convention, which indirectly incorporates the Brussels I Regulation[104] is referred to[105] because applying the Brussels I Regulation would not contrast any exclusivity whereas if a system is set up with EU courts having exclusive jurisdiction[106] the Brussels I Regulation, which does not indirectly incorporate the Lugano Convention[107] is referred to[108] because applying the Lugano Convention could contrast any such exclusivity; *that* applying the Lugano Convention creates an incompatible interrelationship with the EUTMR since under the EUTMR action must, if not at *forum delicti*,[109] be brought at the plaintiff's EU domicile or, failing that, EU establishment if the defendant is domiciled in the EFTA[110] or in Spain if both the defendant and the plaintiff are domiciled in the EFTA[111] whereas under the Lugano Convention action can be brought, inter alia, at the defendant's EFTA domicile[112] and *that* even though the EUTMR has replaced the narrower 'Regulation (EC) No 44/2001'[113] with the broader 'Union rules on jurisdiction and the recognition and enforcement of judgments in civil and commercial matters'[114] the Lugano Convention still does not apply given that it is not a Union rule.[115]

2.22 Balancing the interests, and despite the exclusivity of EUTM courts and the conflict between the forum rules in the EUTMR and the forum rules in the Lugano Convention, it seems likely that the Lugano Convention applies which is due to, inter alia, the Lugano Convention being part of national laws of EFTA Member States and case law from national EFTA courts.

---

100 Art. 95 EUTMR.
101 Art. 96 EUTMR.
102 *Supra* note 94.
103 Art. 101(4) CPVR.
104 Art. 64 of the 2007 Lugano Convention.
105 Art. 101(1) CPVR.
106 Arts 95 and 96 EUTMR cf. similarly arts 80 and 81 CDR.
107 An equivalent to art. 64 of the 2007 Lugano Convention is not found in the Brussels I Regulation.
108 Arts 94(1) EUTMR cf. similarly 79(1) CDR.
109 Art. 97(5) EUTMR cf. Chapter 9.
110 Art. 97(2) EUTMR cf. Chapter 7.
111 Art. 97(3) EUTMR.
112 Art. 2 Lugano Convention cf. Scordamaglia, *supra* note 95, p. 390 and *supra* note 94.
113 Art. 94(1) Council Regulation (EC) No 207/2009 of 26 February 2009 on the Community Trade Mark.
114 Art. 94(1) EUTMR cf. proposal for a Regulation amending Council Regulation (EC) No 207/2009 on the Community trademark 2013/0088 (COD) published on 27 March 2013 pp. 34 *et seq.*
115 Magnus and Mankowski, *supra* note 5, p. 21 and Nielsen, *supra* note 6, p. 134.

The next question, therefore, is how the Lugano Convention applies if an EUTM action is brought in the EFTA. One option is to apply the Lugano Convention in full along the 'cascade' rules in the EUTMR and another option is to apply the Lugano Convention as 'fall back' to the 'cascade' rules in the EUTMR. **2.23**

Supporting that the Lugano Convention applies in full along the 'cascade' rules in the EUTMR it is argued, inter alia, *that* the Lugano Convention does not restrict its own application;[116] *that* the principle of *lex specialis* does not argue against a full application of the Lugano Convention since EFTA Member States are not parties to the EUTMR;[117] *that* applying art. 2 Lugano Convention would not create a 'double application' of the defendant's domicile rule since art. 97(1) EUTMR does not apply when the defendant is domiciled in the EFTA but only when the defendant is domiciled in the EU;[118] *that* applying art. 5(5) Lugano Convention would not create a 'double application' of the establishment rule either since art. 97(1) EUTMR does not apply when the establishment is located in the EFTA but only when the establishment is located in the EU;[119] *that* applying art. 22(4) Lugano Convention would also not create a 'double application' since art. 96(d) EUTMR does not apply before an EFTA court given that EFTA Member States are not parties to the EUTMR[120] and *that* under another European unitary IP right – the CPVR – the Lugano Convention explicitly applies in full along the 'cascade' rules[121] where action is brought in the EFTA.[122] **2.24**

Supporting the opposite result, namely that the Lugano Convention applies as 'fall back' to the 'cascade' rules in the EUTMR it is argued, inter alia, *that* any such application would correspond to the application of the Brussels I Regulation[123] and the application of the Lugano Convention if action is brought in the EU;[124] *that* applying the Lugano Convention in full would contrast the justification for the 'cascade' rules which is, inter alia, to limit the number of available fora;[125] *that* applying art. 5(3) Lugano Convention would create a 'double application' of the *forum delicti* rule taking into account that **2.25**

---

116 Art. 64(2)(a) of the 2007 Lugano Convention reads that 'this Convention shall *in any event* be applied [...] in matters of jurisdiction, where the defendant is domiciled in the territory of a State where this Convention [...] applies' (emphasis added).

117 Lassen and Stenvik, *supra* note 97, p. 38.

118 Chapter 5 section C.1(a).

119 Chapter 6 section C.1(a).

120 *Supra* note 117.

121 Art. 101(1) CPVR.

122 Section C.3(b).

123 Art. 94(1) EUTMR.

124 See above.

125 *Supra* note 42.

the 'sister' rule in art. 97(5) EUTMR also applies when the defendant is domiciled in the EFTA;[126] *that* any such 'double application' must be avoided *since* the two rules have different impacts;[127] *since* therefore the two rules would create a risk of *forum delicti* forum shopping and *since* any such risk has been dealt with in the Brussels I Regulation and in the Lugano Convention if action is brought in the EU following the principle of *lex specialis*.

2.26 Balancing the interests it seems likely that the Lugano Convention applies in full along the 'cascade' rules in the EUTMR meaning *that* art. 2 Lugano Convention applies; *that* art. 5(5) Lugano Convention applies if the establishment is located in the EFTA; *that* art. 5(3) Lugano Convention applies as a place of action[128] but not as a place(s) of effect(s)[129] given that the EUTMR is not protected outside the EU;[130] *that* art. 22(4) Lugano Convention applies per analogy[131] if invalidity is raised[132] with the effect that the EUIPO, which is located in the Member State where the EUTM is registered[133] must address any such question[134] and *that* arts 59 and 60 Lugano Convention apply for the purpose of defining 'domicile' within the meaning of art. 2 Lugano Convention.

2.27 In sum, therefore, an overall distinction must be drawn between whether an EUTM action can be brought in the EU based on the rules in the Lugano Convention and whether an EUTM action can be brought in the EFTA based on the rules in the Lugano Convention. With respect to the former the

126 Fawcett and Torremans, *supra* note 49 at 8.39 and Chapter 9.

127 The *forum delicti* rules in arts 5(3) Lugano Convention and 97(5) EUTMR differ, inter alia, *since* non-infringement actions can be brought under the former cf. case C-133/11, *Folien Fischer*, para. 56 and Chapter 9 but not under the latter.

128 Case C-523/10, *Wintersteiger AG v Products 4U Sondermaschinenbau GmbH*, para. 37 where a place of action was defined as the place where the defendant is established cf. Chapter 9. Any such place often coincides with art. 2 Lugano Convention.

129 Ibid., para. 29 where a place(s) of effect(s) was defined as the place where the trademark is registered cf. Chapter 9.

130 Art. 1(2) EUTMR cf. *Conflict of Laws in Intellectual Property, The CLIP Principles and Commentary*, *supra* note 36, p. 71 (2:202.C07).

131 The reason that art. 22(4) Lugano Convention applies per analogy is twofold, namely *that* the provision is concerned with registered national IP rights and not European unitary IP rights cf. Fawcett and Torremans, *supra* note 49 at 8.10 and *that* the provision points at the courts of the Member State where the IP right is registered and not the authority having registered the IP right such as EUIPO.

132 Handelsgericht Zurich, *supra* note 94, pp. 258 *et seq.* where during the proceedings the Swiss defendant argued invalidity of the Liechtenstein plaintiff's EUTM. The court stated after having referred to art. 22(4) Lugano Convention and case C-4/03, *Gesellschaft für Antriebstechnik GmbH & Co. KG v. Lamellen und Kupplungsbau Beteiligungs KG (Gat LuK)* cf. Chapter 11 that 'Das Verfahren am Handelsgericht ist deshalb zu sistieren, um der Bekl. [Beklagte] Gelegenheit zu geben, im Sinne von Art. 5[6] GMV [Gemeinschaftsmarkenverordnung] einen Antrag auf Erklärung des Verfalls oder der Nichtigkeit der Streitmarken einzubringen'.

133 Art. 87 EUTMR.

134 Art. 56 EUTMR.

Lugano Convention applies as 'fall back' to the 'cascade' rules in the EUTMR meaning, inter alia, that arts 5(3), 5(5), 6(1) and 22(4) Lugano Convention do not apply. With respect to the latter the Lugano Convention applies in full along the 'cascade' rules in the EUTMR meaning, inter alia, that arts 2, 5(3), 5(5), 6(1), 22(4), 59 and 60 Lugano Convention apply.

(c) Defendant is domiciled outside the EU/EFTA

If, finally, the defendant is domiciled outside the EU/EFTA one could argue that the Brussels I Regulation itself incorporates the Member States' own international forum rules[135] and that, therefore, a reference to the Brussels I Regulation[136] is also a reference to such rules, which equally apply. Any such interpretation is not correct *since* art. 6 Brussels I Regulation has been explicitly exempted in the EUTMR;[137] *since* the Explanatory Memorandum excludes the Member States' own international forum rules by speaking of 'a completely unitary set of rules concerning jurisdiction [...] covering also those cases which, under the [Brussels I Regulation] would be left to the various non-harmonized rules of private law of the Member States';[138] *since* the risk of forum shopping would increase if the Member States' own international forum rules applied taking into account that the numbers and natures of such rules vary from Member State to Member State[139] and *since* writings of legal scholars support that the Member States' own international forum rules do not apply.[140] **2.28**

In sum therefore the Member States' own international forum rules do not apply under the EUTMR meaning that action may not be brought in the EU against non-EU/EFTA defendants based on such rules. Thus, a complete set of rules against non-EU/EFTA defendants is established[141] except that the EUTMR does not exclude a EUTM action to be brought against such defendants at their home non-EU/EFTA domicile.[142] If invalidity is raised at any such place third states' own international forum rules apply. **2.29**

---

135 Art. 6 Brussels I Regulation.

136 Art. 94(1) EUTMR.

137 Art. 94(2)(a) EUTMR.

138 Proposal for a European Parliament and Council Regulation on the Community Design presented by the Commission COM (93) 342 final COD 463 Brussels, 3 December 1993, p. 38. The reasoning applies *mutatis mutandis* under the EUTMR cf. the wording '[the forum rules in the CDR] entirely correspond to the parallel provisions relating to the Community Trade Mark', p. 38.

139 Toshiyuki Kono, *Intellectual Property and Private International Law, Comparative Perspectives*, Hart Publishing, 2012.

140 Scordamaglia, *supra* note 95, p. 379.

141 Memorandum amending Regulation (EU) No 1215/2012 on Jurisdiction and the Recognition and Enforcement of Judgments in Civil and Commercial Matters COM(2013) 554 final, 2013/0268 (COD), p. 6.

142 *Supra* note 140, p. 390. For a different view see (probably) Ubertazzi, *supra* note 95, p. 74.

2.30 Overall the 'cascade' rules in Title X EUTMR[143] apply to disputes concerned with infringement and invalidity of an EUTM.[144] For the purpose of the present study it follows *that* the Brussels I Regulation applies as 'fall back' (meaning arts 8.1, 62 and 63); *that* the Lugano Convention applies as 'fall back' in the EU (meaning no rules); *that* the Lugano Convention applies in full in the EFTA (meaning arts 2, 5.3, 5.5, 6.1, 22.4, 59 and 60); *that* the Member States' own international forum rules do not apply and *that* action may be brought in a third state following their own international forum rules.

2. Community Design

2.31 In disputes concerned with infringement and invalidity of a CD[145] the international jurisdiction rules in the CDR apply. The rules, which are found in Title IX CDR concerning 'Jurisdiction and Procedure in Legal Actions Relating to Community Designs',[146] apply whatever the domicile of the defendant.[147] The rules, also known as 'cascade' rules, 'entirely follow the corresponding provisions relating to the Community [...] Trade Mark [since it is] extremely important for the users to be presented with rules, which are as unitary as possible'.[148] Thus, what applies under the EUTMR applies *mutatis mutandis* under the CDR including to the unregistered CD.[149]

2.32 Similar to the EUTMR[150] the question is whether the Brussels I Regulation, the Lugano Convention and the Member States' own international forum rules also apply and in that case to what extent. The three situations are dealt with individually below in sections (a)–(c).

(a) Defendant is domiciled in the EU

2.33 If the defendant is domiciled in the EU it follows from art. 79(1) CDR that 'unless otherwise specified in this Regulation [the Brussels Convention] shall apply [...]'.[151] Thus, the Brussels Convention,[152] which has been superseded

143 Art. 97 EUTMR.
144 Art. 96 EUTMR.
145 Art. 81 CDR.
146 Arts 79 CDR *et seq.*
147 Art. 82 CDR cf. proposal for a European Parliament and Council Regulation on the Community Design presented by the Commission COM (93) 342 final COD 463 Brussels, 3 December 1993, p. 38.
148 Proposal for a European Parliament and Council Regulation ibid., pp. 37–8.
149 Fawcett and Torremans, *supra* note 49 at 8.112 and 8.116.
150 Section C.1.
151 Art. 79(1) CDR.
152 It is surprising that the Brussels Convention and not the Brussels I Regulation is referred to given that the former Brussels I Regulation (44/2001) was adopted on 22 December 2000 with effect from 1 March 2002 cf. art. 76 Brussels I Regulation (44/2001) whereas the CDR was adopted almost one year later on 12 December 2001 with effect from 6 March 2002 cf. art. 111(1) CDR.

by the Brussels I Regulation[153] applies as 'fall back' to the CDR in the same way as the Brussels I Regulation applies as 'fall back' to the EUTMR[154] meaning that arts 4, 7(2), 7(5) and 24(4) Brussels I Regulation do not apply[155] contrary to arts 8(1), 62 and 63 Brussels I Regulation, which do apply.[156] By contrast to the EUTMR[157] art. 24(4) Brussels I Regulation has been explicitly exempted in the CDR.[158] The reason seems to be a clarification in light of the experience with the former CTMR[159] rather than an intended interconnection with the fact that invalidity of, inter alia, a RCD is frequently raised, which in turn could support the application of the same provision under the EUTMR, which would be wrong.[160]

(b) Defendant is domiciled in the EFTA

If the defendant is domiciled in the EFTA the CDR also does not refer to the Lugano Convention. What applies under the EUTMR applies *mutatis mutandis* under the CDR meaning that an overall distinction must be drawn between actions brought in the EU and actions brought in the EFTA. With respect to the former the Lugano Convention applies as 'fall back' to the 'cascade' rules in the CDR meaning, inter alia, that arts 5(3), 5(5), 6(1) and 22(4) Lugano Convention do not apply. With respect to the latter the Lugano Convention applies in full along the 'cascade' rules in the CDR meaning, inter alia, that arts 2, 5(3), 5(5), 6(1), 22(4),[161] 59 and 60 Lugano Convention apply. **2.34**

(c) Defendant is domiciled outside the EU/EFTA

If finally the defendant is domiciled outside the EU/EFTA the Member States' own international forum rules have also been explicitly exempted in the CDR.[162] Thus, action may not be brought in the EU against non-EU/EFTA defendants based on such rules. In line with the EUTMR, therefore, a **2.35**

153 Art. 68 Brussels I Regulation.

154 Proposal for a European Parliament and Council Regulation on the Community Design presented by the Commission COM (93) 342 final COD 463 Brussels, 3 December 1993, p. 38; Kur, *supra* note 49, p. 3; David Stone, *European Union Design Law, A Practitioners Guide*, Oxford University Press, 2012 at 21.179; Tritton, *supra* note 62 at 14–087 and Fawcett and Torremans, *supra* note 49 at 8.108.

155 Art. 79(3)(a) CDR.

156 Chapters 5, 7 and 8. Furthermore reliance can be placed on art. 7(5) Brussels I Regulation when defining 'establishment' within the meaning of art. 82(1) and (2) CDR cf. Fawcett and Torremans, *supra* note 49 at 8.116 and Chapters 6 and 7.

157 Art. 94(2)(a) EUTMR.

158 Art. 79(3)(a) CDR.

159 Fawcett and Torremans, *supra* note 49 at 8.114.

160 Case C-230/15, *Brite Strike Technologies Inc.*, para. 62 and section C.1(a).

161 Art. 22(4) Lugano Convention only applies per analogy cf. *supra* notes 131–2 to the registered CD and not to the unregistered CD given *that* art. 22(4) Lugano Convention is merely concerned with registered IP rights and *that* EUIPO is not concerned with the unregistered CD cf. art. 52 CDR. If, therefore, invalidity of an unregistered CD is raised before an EFTA court invalidity can be addressed there.

162 Art. 79(3)(a) CDR.

complete set of rules against non-EU/EFTA defendants is established[163] except that the CDR does also not exclude a CD action to be brought against such defendants at their home non-EU/EFTA domicile.[164] If invalidity is raised at any such place third states' own international forum rules apply.

2.36 Overall the 'cascade' rules in Title IX CDR[165] apply to disputes concerned with infringement and invalidity of a CD.[166] For the purpose of the present study it follows *that* the Brussels I Regulation applies as 'fall back' (meaning arts 8.1, 62 and 63); *that* the Lugano Convention applies as 'fall back' in the EU (meaning no rules); *that* the Lugano Convention applies in full in the EFTA (meaning arts 2, 5.3, 5.5, 6.1, 22.4, 59 and 60); *that* the Member States' own international forum rules do not apply and *that* action may be brought in a third state following their own international forum rules.

3. Community Plant Variety

2.37 In disputes concerned with infringement[167] but not invalidity[168] of a CPV the international jurisdiction rules in the CPVR apply. The rules, which are found in Part Six CPVR concerning 'Civil Law Claims, Infringements, Jurisdiction',[169] apply whatever the domicile of the defendant.[170] The rules, also known as 'cascade' rules, are slightly different compared to the ones in the EUTMR and CDR,[171] but serve a similar purpose. According to the 'cascade' rules action must be brought at the defendant's EU/EFTA domicile or, failing that, EU/EFTA establishment.[172] If the defendant is neither domiciled nor established in the EU/EFTA action must be brought at the plaintiff's EU domicile or, failing that, EU establishment.[173] If the defendant is neither domiciled nor established in the EU/EFTA and the plaintiff is neither domiciled nor established in the EU action must be brought in France.[174] Alternatively action can be brought at *forum delicti*.[175]

163 Memorandum amending Regulation (EU) No 1215/2012 on Jurisdiction and the Recognition and Enforcement of Judgments in Civil and Commercial Matters COM(2013) 554 final, 2013/0268 (COD), p. 6.
164 *Supra* note 142.
165 Art. 82 CDR.
166 Art. 81 CDR.
167 Art. 94 CPVR.
168 Art. 20 CPVR.
169 Arts 94 CPVR *et seq.*
170 Art. 101 CPVR.
171 Fawcett and Torremans, *supra* note 49 at 8.145 and sections C.1 and C.2.
172 Art. 101(2)(a) CPVR cf. Chapters 5 and 6.
173 Art. 101(2)(b) CPVR cf. Chapter 7.
174 Art. 101(2)(c) CPVR.
175 Art. 101(3) CPVR cf. Chapter 9.

Similar to the EUTMR[176] and CDR[177] the question is whether the Brussels I Regulation, the Lugano Convention and the Member States' own international forum rules also apply and in that case to what extent. The three situations are dealt with individually below in sections (a)–(c). **2.38**

(a) Defendant is domiciled in the EU

If the defendant is domiciled in the EU the Brussels I Regulation is not referred to in the CPVR. Two questions therefore arise. The first is whether the Brussels I Regulation applies under the CPVR and, provided that it does, the second is the extent to which the Brussels I Regulation applies. **2.39**

With respect to the first question one could argue both that the Brussels I Regulation applies and that it does not apply. Supporting that it does not apply it is argued, inter alia, *that* it is not referred to by contrast to the EUTMR and CDR[178] and *that* the 'cascade' rules can do the job alone without help from the Brussels I Regulation.[179] Supporting the opposite result namely that the Brussels I Regulation applies it is argued, inter alia, *that* EU courts determine their jurisdiction under their own national laws being, inter alia, the Brussels I Regulation;[180] *that* the Brussels I Regulation is indirectly incorporated into the CPVR via the Lugano Convention[181] which is referred to;[182] *that* the Explanatory Memorandum supports any such interpretation by reading that 'the relevant *international* and national rules of jurisdiction [are referred to]'[183] and *that* legal scholars support that the Brussels I Regulation similarly applies.[184] Balancing the interests the Brussels I Regulation applies under the CPVR, which is due to, inter alia, the Brussels I Regulation being part of national laws of the Member States. **2.40**

With respect to the second question, therefore, one could argue both that the Brussels I Regulation applies in full along the 'cascade' rules in the CPVR and that it merely applies as 'fall back' to the 'cascade' rules in the CPVR. Supporting the former it is argued, inter alia, *that* no provisions in the Brussels **2.41**

---

176 Section C.1.
177 Section C.2.
178 Arts 94(1) EUTMR and 79(1) CDR.
179 Art. 101(2)–(3) CPVR.
180 Section B.1.
181 Art. 64 of the 2007 Lugano Convention.
182 Art. 101(1) CPVR cf. section C.3(b).
183 Proposal for a Council Regulation (EEC) on Community Plant Variety Rights, presented by the Commission COM(90) 347 final, 30 August 1990, p. 5 (emphasis added).
184 Gert Würtenberger, Paul Van Der Kooij, Bart Kiewiet and Martin Ekvad, *European Community Plant Variety Protection*, Oxford University Press, 2006 at 7.58 and Fawcett and Torremans, *supra* note 49 at 8.149 and 8.167.

I Regulation have been exempted in the CPVR by contrast to the EUTMR and CDR where a large number of provisions in the Brussels I Regulation have been exempted[185] and *that* legal scholars argue that the Brussels I Regulation applies in full.[186]

2.42 Supporting the latter it is argued inter alia, *that* the principle of lex specialis applies[187] given that all Member States are parties to both the Brussels I Regulation and the CPVR;[188] *that* the principle excludes the application of arts 4, 7(2), 7(5) and 24(4) Brussels I Regulation *since* the former three have 'sister' provisions in the 'cascade'[189] and *since* the latter has a 'sister' provision in art. 20 CPVR, which conflicts within art. 24(4) Brussels I Regulation given that art. 20 CPVR points at the CPVO in France whereas art. 24(4) Brussels I Regulation would point at the courts of France being the place where the CPVR is registered;[190] *that* writings of legal scholars and case law support that art. 24(4) Brussels I Regulation does not apply under the CPVR[191] and *that* a 'fall back' application of the Brussels I Regulation would create consistency vis-à-vis the EUTMR and CDR.[192] Balancing the interests and taking into account the principle of *lex specialis* it seems likely that the Brussels I Regulation applies as 'fall back' to the CPVR.

2.43 In sum, therefore, arts 4, 7(2), 7(5) and 24(4) Brussels I Regulation do not apply whereas art. 8(1) Brussels I Regulation does apply. By contrast to the EUTMR and CDR arts 62 and 63 Brussels I Regulation do not apply either for the purpose of defining 'domicile' within the meaning of art. 101(2)(a) and

---

185 Arts 94(2)(a) EUTMR and 79(3)(a) CDR.

186 Fawcett and Torremans, *supra* note 49 at 8.150 and 8.167.

187 Art. 67 Brussels I Regulation.

188 Magnus and Mankowski, *supra* note 5, pp. 25–31 (as regards the Brussels I Regulation) and Jens Schovsbo and Morten Rosenmeier, *Immaterialret*, Jurist- og Økonomforbundets Forlag, 2015, pp. 388 *et seq.* (as regards the CPVR).

189 The 'sister' provision to art. 4 Brussels I Regulation is found in art. 101(2)(a) CPVR cf. Chapter 5. Art. 4 Brussels I Regulation can in effect be subsumed in art. 101(2)(a) CPVR since also the latter is subject to the definition of 'domicile' within the meaning of arts 62 and 63 cf. art. 102(3) CPVR and *supra* note 62. The 'sister' provision to art. 7(2) Brussels I Regulation is found in art. 101(3) CPVR cf. Chapter 9. Art. 7(2) Brussels I Regulation can also in effect be subsumed in art. 101(3) CPVR since non-infringement actions can be brought under both. Finally and for the reasons *supra* note 62 art. 7(5) Brussels I Regulation can also be subsumed in art. 101(2)(a) CPVR.

190 Art. 87 CPVR.

191 Case C-230/15, *Brite Strike Technologies Inc.*, para. 62; European Max-Planck Group for Conflict of Laws in Intellectual Property, Exclusive Jurisdiction and Cross Border IP (Patent) Infringement Suggestions for Amendment of the Brussels I Regulation of 22 December 2006 p. 8 found on ip.mpg.de and Magnus and Mankowski, *supra* note 5, p. 433.

192 Arts 94(1) EUTMR and 79(1) CDR.

(b) CPVR since the CPVR itself refers to the 'sister' provisions in the Lugano Convention.[193]

(b) Defendant is domiciled in the EFTA

If the defendant is domiciled in the EFTA it follows from art. 101(1) CPVR that 'the Lugano Convention as well as the complementary provisions of [the CPVR] shall apply'.[194] Similar to the EUTMR and CDR[195] an overall distinction must be drawn between whether a CPV action[196] can be brought in the EU based on the rules in the Lugano Convention and whether a CPV action can be brought in the EFTA based on the rules in the Lugano Convention. **2.44**

As regards whether a CPV action can be brought in the EU based on the rules in the Lugano Convention the answer is affirmative given the explicit reference to the Lugano Convention.[197] The next question, therefore, is whether the Lugano Convention applies in full along the 'cascade' rules in the CPVR or whether it merely applies as 'fall back' to the 'cascade' rules in the CPVR. Legal scholars disagree.[198] **2.45**

Supporting that the Lugano Convention applies in full along the 'cascade' rules in the CPVR it is argued, inter alia, *that* the CPVR reads, 'the Lugano Convention [...] shall apply'[199] meaning that the CPVR does not restrict the applicability of the Lugano Convention contrary to the EUTMR and CDR, which both restrict the applicability of the Brussels I Regulation;[200] *that* the CPVR is listed as 'complementary' to the Lugano Convention[201] meaning that **2.46**

193 Art. 102(3) CPVR. Given that the defendant may be domiciled in the EU under art. 101(2)(a) CPVR it would not be correct to apply the definition of 'domicile' within the meaning of arts 59 and 60 Lugano Convention as prescribed in art. 102(3) CPVR to such defendants. The correct would be to apply the definition of domicile within the meaning of arts 62 and 63 Brussels I Regulation. Any one, however, leads to the same result given that the Lugano Convention must be interpreted in line with the Brussels I Regulation cf. *supra* note 32.

194 Art. 101(1) CPVR.

195 Sections C.1(b) and C.2(b).

196 Art. 94 CPVR.

197 Art. 101(1) CPVR cf. Scordamaglia, *supra* note 95, p. 391; Fawcett and Torremans, *supra* note 49 at 8.147 and Tritton, *supra* note 62 at 6–060 *et seq.*

198 Supporting that the Lugano Convention applies in full along the 'cascade' rules in the CPVR see Fawcett and Torremans, ibid., at 8.148 and 8.179 and Tritton, ibid., at 6–060. Supporting the opposite result namely that the Lugano Convention merely applies as 'fall back' to the 'cascade' rules in the CPVR see Würtenberger et al., *supra* note 184 at 7.58.

199 Art. 101(1) CPVR.

200 Arts 94(1) EUTMR and 79(1) CDR.

201 Art. 101(1) CPVR. In other versions the word 'complementary' is also used i.e. 'sowie die ergänzenden Vorschriften' (DE), 'de même que les dispositions complémentaires' (FR), 'supplerende bestemmelser' (DK) and 'kompletterande bestämmelserna' (SV).

the CPVR merely supplements the Lugano Convention contrary to the EUTMR and CDR where the set-up is turned around since the Brussels I Regulation merely supplements the EUTMR and CDR;[202] *that* the CPVR excludes no provisions in the Lugano Convention relevant for infringement purposes[203] contrary to the EUTMR and CDR, which exclude a large number of provisions in the Brussels I Regulation relevant for such purposes[204] and *that* therefore the CPVR leaves a wider scope for the Lugano Convention than the EUTMR and CDR leave for the Brussels I Regulation.

2.47 Supporting the opposite result namely that the Lugano Convention applies as 'fall back' to the 'cascade' rules in the CPVR it is argued, inter alia, *that* the CPVR reads that proceedings 'shall be brought' according to the 'cascade' rules[205] meaning that the Lugano Convention merely supplements the CPVR; *that* the principle of *lex specialis* applies given that all Member States are parties to both the Lugano Convention and the CPVR;[206] *that* applying the Lugano Convention in full would lead to a 'double application' of the exclusive jurisdiction rule, which would conflict *since* art. 22(4) Lugano Convention would point at the courts in France considering that the CPV is registered there[207] whereas art. 20 CPVR points at the CPVO in France; *that* legal scholars support that art. 22(4) Lugano Convention does not apply under the CPVR;[208] *that* a 'fall back' interpretation is the only one consistent with the EUTMR and CDR[209] as well as the wording of the Commission when drafting the CDR whereas it is 'extremely important for the users to be presented with rules which are as unitary as possible'.[210]

2.48 Balancing the interests and despite the wording of art. 101(1) CPVR the Lugano Convention most likely applies as 'fall back' to the 'cascade' rules in the CPVR meaning *that* the *forum delicti* and exclusive jurisdiction rules in arts 5(3) and 22(4) Lugano Convention do not apply since they have 'sister' provisions in the 'cascade';[211] *that* there is no need to apply arts 59 and 60 Lugano Convention as 'fall back' since there is a specific reference to those

---

202 Arts 94(1) EUTMR and 79(1) CDR.

203 Art. 102(1) CPVR.

204 Arts 94(2)(a) EUTMR and 79(3)(a) CDR.

205 Art. 101(2) CPVR.

206 Magnus and Mankowski, *supra* note 5, p. 20 (as regards the Lugano Convention) and Schovsbo, Rosenmeier and Petersen, *supra* note 88, pp. 388 *et seq.* (as regards the CPVR).

207 Art. 87 CPVR.

208 *Supra* note 191.

209 Sections C.1(b) and C.2(b).

210 Proposal for a European Parliament and Council Regulation on the Community Design presented by the Commission COM (93) 342 final COD 463 Brussels, 3 December 1993, p. 37.

211 The 'sister' provision to art. 5(3) Lugano Convention is found in art. 101(3) CPVR cf. Chapter 9. The former can be subsumed in the latter since non-infringement actions can be brought under both. The 'sister'

provisions in the CPVR[212] and *that* the establishment rule in art. 5(5) Lugano Convention does not apply provided that the establishment is located in the EU since in that case a 'sister' rule is found in the 'cascade'.[213] If, by contrast, the establishment is located in the EFTA art. 5(5) Lugano Convention points at an EFTA Member State in line with arts 2 and 6(1) Lugano Convention, and so the question is whether a CPV action can be brought in the EFTA based on, inter alia, those three provisions cf. below.

As regards whether a CPV action can be brought in the EFTA based on the rules in the Lugano Convention it follows from art. 101(1) CPVR itself *that* the Lugano Convention applies[214] which in turn is confirmed by the facts *that* EFTA courts determine their jurisdiction under their own national laws being, inter alia, the Lugano Convention[215] and *that* any such interpretation is confirmed by case law from national EFTA courts.[216] In line with the EUTMR and CDR,[217] therefore, the Lugano Convention most likely applies in full given *that* the Lugano Convention does not restrict its own application;[218] *that* the principle of *lex specialis* does not speak against any such result since EFTA Member States are not parties to the CPVR;[219] *that* applying art. 2 Lugano Convention would fill the gap in art. 101(2)(a) CPVR[220] where jurisdiction is vested at the defendant's EFTA domicile even though EFTA Member States are not parties to the CPVR;[221] *that* applying art. 5(5) Lugano Convention would also fill a gap in art. 101(2)(a) CPVR provided that the defendant is domiciled in the EFTA;[222] *that* art. 5(3) Lugano Convention applies as a place of action[223] but not as a place of **2.49**

provision to art. 22(4) Lugano Convention is found in art. 20 CPVR cf. Chapter 11. As stated above the two provisions conflict.

212 Art. 102(3) CPVR.

213 The 'sister' provision to art. 5(5) Lugano Convention is found in art. 101(2)(a) CPVR cf. Chapter 6. For the reasons *supra* note 62 art. 5(5) Lugano Convention can be subsumed in art. 101(2)(a) CPVR.

214 Art. 101(1) CPVR.

215 Section B.2.

216 *Supra* note 94.

217 Sections C.1(b) and C.2(b).

218 Art. 64(2)(a) of the 2007 Lugano Convention.

219 Evaluation of the Community Plant Variety Right *Aquis*, *supra* note 99, p. 49.

220 Fawcett and Torremans, *supra* note 49 at 8.154.

221 Evaluation of the Community Plant Variety Right *Aquis*, *supra* note 99, p. 49.

222 Art. 5(5) Lugano Convention does, however, not fill a gap if the defendant is not domiciled in the EFTA, but merely established in the EFTA cf. art. 101(2)(a) CPVR. In any such situation and taking into account that EFTA Member States are not parties to the CPVR cf. *supra* note 219 art. 101(2)(a) CPVR seems to be without effect.

223 Case C-523/10, *Wintersteiger*, para. 37 where a place of action was defined as the place where the defendant is established cf. Chapter 9. Any such place often coincides with art. 2 Lugano Convention.

effect[224] given that the CPVR is not protected outside the EU;[225] *that* art. 22(4) Lugano Convention applies per analogy[226] if invalidity of a CPV is raised[227] with the effect that the CPVO, which is located in the Member State where the CPVR is registered,[228] must address any such question[229] and *that* arts 59 and 60 Lugano Convention apply for the purpose of defining 'domicile' within the meaning of art. 2 Lugano Convention.

2.50 In sum therefore an overall distinction must be drawn between whether a CPV action can be brought in the EU based on the rules in the Lugano Convention and whether a CPV action can be brought in the EFTA based on the rules in the Lugano Convention. With respect to the former the Lugano Convention applies as 'fall back' to the 'cascade' rules in the CPVR meaning, inter alia, that arts 5(3), 5(5), 6(1), 22(4), 59 and 60 Lugano Convention do not apply. With respect to the latter the Lugano Convention applies in full along the 'cascade' rules in the CPVR meaning, inter alia, that arts 2, 5(3), 5(5), 6(1), 22(4), 59 and 60 Lugano Convention apply.

(c) Defendant is domiciled outside the EU/EFTA

2.51 If finally the defendant is domiciled outside the EU/EFTA the Member States' own international forum rules apply. Supporting that is argued, inter alia, *that* art. 4 Lugano Convention has not been exempted in the CPVR[230] contrary to art. 6 Brussels I Regulation in the EUTMR and CDR[231] and *that* the Explanatory Report reads that 'the relevant international and *national* rules of jurisdiction [are referred to]'.[232] Action may, therefore, be brought in the EU/EFTA against non-EU/EFTA defendants based on such rules. By contrast to the EUTMR and CDR a complete set of rules against non-EU/EFTA defendants is therefore not established.[233] Whether a CPV action against non-EU/EFTA defendants may also be brought at their home domicile can be argued both ways.

224 Ibid., para. 29 where a place of effect was defined as the place where the IP right is registered cf. Chapter 9.

225 Art. 2 CPVR cf. *Conflict of Laws in Intellectual Property, The CLIP Principles and Commentary*, *supra* note 36, p. 71 (2:202.C07).

226 *Supra* note 131.

227 *Supra* note 132.

228 Art. 87 CPVR.

229 Art. 20 CPVR.

230 Art. 102(1) CPVR.

231 Arts 94(2)(a) EUTMR and 79(3)(a) CDR.

232 Proposal for a Council Regulation (EEC) on Community Plant Variety Rights, presented by the Commission COM(90) 347 final, 30 August 1990, p. 5 (emphasis added).

233 Sections C.1(c) and C.2(c).

Supporting that action may not be brought outside the EU/EFTA it is argued, inter alia, that the CPVR refers to 'the competent courts'[234] being courts in a 'Member State'[235] or courts in a 'Contracting Party to the Lugano Convention'[236] thereby excluding non-EU/EFTA courts. **2.52**

Supporting the opposite result, namely that action may be brought outside the EU/EFTA it is argued, inter alia, the position under the EUTMR where a court outside the framework of the EUTMR – an EFTA court – found itself competent under the Lugano Convention,[237] which is not referred to in the EUTMR, in a situation where both the plaintiff and the defendant were based in the EFTA and where according to the 'cascade' rules action should, if not at *forum delicti*,[238] be brought in Spain;[239] *that* therefore a court outside the framework of the CPVR – a non-EU/EFTA court – can also be competent under its own international forum rules, which are not referred to in the CPVR, in a situation where both the plaintiff and the defendant are based outside the EU/EFTA and where according to the 'cascade' rules action must, if not at *forum delicti*,[240] be brought in France[241] and *that* a non-EU/EFTA court in a CPV situation would not jeopardize exclusivity to the same extent as an EFTA court would do in a EUTM situation since the CPVR merely speaks of 'competent courts'[242] whereas the EUTMR speaks of 'EU trade mark courts'.[243] **2.53**

Balancing the interests it seems likely that a CPV action can be brought at a non-EU/EFTA court. If invalidity is raised before any such court third states' own international forum rules apply. **2.54**

Overall the 'cascade' rules in Part Six CPVR[244] apply to disputes concerned with infringement of a CPV.[245] For the purpose of the present study it follows *that* the Brussels I Regulation applies as 'fall back' (meaning art. 8.1); *that* the Lugano Convention applies as 'fall back' in the EU (meaning art. 6.1); *that* the Lugano Convention applies in full in the EFTA (meaning arts 2, 5.3, 5.5, 6.1, 22.4, 59 and 60); *that* the Member States' own international forum rules apply **2.55**

---

234 Art. 101(4) CPVR.
235 Art. 101(2)(b) and (3) CPVR.
236 Art. 101(2)(a) CPVR.
237 *Supra* note 94.
238 Art. 97(5) EUTMR.
239 Art. 97(3) EUTMR.
240 Art. 101(3) CPVR.
241 Art. 101(2)(c) CPVR.
242 Art. 101(4) CPVR.
243 Arts 95 and 96 EUTMR.
244 Art. 101(1) CPVR.
245 Art. 94 CPVR.

and *that* action may be brought in a third state following their own international forum rules.

4. Unitary Patent

2.56 In disputes concerned with infringement and invalidity of a UP[246] the international jurisdiction rules in the AUPC apply.[247] The overall structure of the rules have been subject to a development in the drafting process from fully excluding the application of both the Brussels I Regulation and the Lugano Convention[248] to include the application of both in the AUPC.[249] In the adopted version of the AUPC the international jurisdiction rules are found in Chapter VI AUPC concerning 'International jurisdiction and competence'.[250]

---

246 Art. 32 AUPC.

247 Torsten Bjørn Larsen, *Rules of Jurisdiction in the Agreement on a Unified Patent Court*, Nordiskt Immateriellt Rättsskydd, 2014, pp. 358 *et seq.* and Pedro Alberto De Miguel Asensio, 'The Unified Patent Court Agreement and the Amendment to the Brussels I Regulation (Recast)', in *The EU Patent Protection Lights and Shades of the New System*, A Cura di Constanza Honorati G Giappichelli Editore – Torino 2014, pp. 153 *et seq.*

248 Draft Agreement on the European Union Patent Judiciary of 14 May 2008 (9124/08 PI 24 COUR 19) chapter IV concerning 'jurisdiction, allocation of cases and effects of decisions' (arts 15 and 16) cf. Draft Agreement on the European Union Patent Judiciary of 30 June 2008 (11270/08 PI 32 COUR 32) chapter IV concerning 'jurisdiction, allocation of cases and effects of decisions' (arts 15 and 16) cf. Draft Agreement on the European Union Patent Court and draft Statute of 4 November 2008 (14970/08 PI 78 COUR 52) chapter IV concerning 'jurisdiction and effects of decisions' (arts 15–16) cf. Draft Agreement on the European and Community Patents Court and draft Statute of 8 January 2009 (5072/09 PI 1 COUR 1) chapter IV concerning 'jurisdiction and effects of decisions' (arts 15–16) cf. Draft Agreement on the European and Community Patents Court and draft Statute, revised Presidency text of 23 March 2009 (7928/09 PI 23 COUR 29) chapter IV concerning 'jurisdiction and effects of decisions' (arts 15–16) cf. Draft Agreement on a Unified Patent Court and draft Statute, Presidency text of 14 June 2011 (11533/11 PI 68 COUR 32) chapter IV concerning 'jurisdiction and effects of decisions' (arts 15–16) cf. Draft Agreement on a Unified Patent Court and draft Statute, revised Presidency text of 2 September 2011 (13751/11 PI 108 COUR 48) chapter IV concerning 'jurisdiction and effects of decisions' (arts 15–16).

249 Draft Agreement on a Unified Patent Court and draft Statute, revised Presidency text of 7 October 2011 (15289/11 PI 127 COUR 56) chapter IV concerning 'competence, jurisdiction and effects of decisions' art. 15b cf. Draft Agreement on a Unified Patent Court and draft Statute, revised Presidency text of 19 October 2011 (15539/11 PI 133 COUR 59) chapter IV concerning 'competence, jurisdiction and effects of decisions' art. 15b cf. Draft Agreement on a Unified Patent Court and draft Statute, revised Presidency text of 26 October 2011 (16023/11 PI 141 COUR 62) chapter IV concerning 'competence, jurisdiction and effects of decisions' art. 15b cf. Draft Agreement on a Unified Patent Court and draft Statute, revised Presidency text of 11 November 2011 (16741/11 PI 155 COUR 64) chapter IV concerning 'competence, jurisdiction and effects of decisions' art. 15b cf. Draft Agreement on the creation of a Unified Patent Court, guidance for future work of 24 November 2011 (17539/11 PI 168 COUR 71) art. 15b cf. Draft Agreement on a Unified Patent Court and draft Statute, consolidated text of 27 September 2012 (14268/12 PI 133 COUR 66) chapter IV concerning 'international jurisdiction and competence' art. -15(ex 15b) cf. Draft Agreement on a Unified Patent Court and draft Statute, consolidated text of 12 October 2012 (14750/12 PI 120 COUR 67) chapter IV concerning 'international jurisdiction and competence' art. -15(ex 15b) cf. Draft Agreement on a Unified Patent Court and draft Statute, consolidated text of 14 November 2012 (16222/12 PI 146 COUR 74) chapter IV concerning 'international jurisdiction and competence' art. -15(ex 15b).

250 Arts 31 AUPC *et seq.*

The rules apply whatever the domicile of the defendant.[251] UPC competence is subject to two provisions in Chapter VI AUPC.

The first provision is art. 31 AUPC. The provision is found under the heading 'International jurisdiction' and reads as follows: 'The international jurisdiction of the Court shall be established in accordance with Regulation (EU) No 1215/2012[252] or, where applicable, on the basis of the Convention on jurisdiction and the recognition and enforcement of judgments in civil and commercial matters (Lugano Convention).'[253] **2.57**

The second provision is art. 33 AUPC. The provision is found under the heading 'Competence of the divisions of the Court of First Instance'. The provision is found in the AUPC given that the Court of First Instance may, when the AUPC comes into effect[254] count a large number of divisions throughout the Contracting Member States (likely) distributed between three central divisions,[255] presumably six regional divisions[256] and presumably 20 or more local divisions.[257] **2.58**

Given, therefore, that art. 31 AUPC is concerned with the 'International jurisdiction' and art. 33 AUPC is concerned with the 'Competence of the divisions of the Court of First Instance' the question is how they exactly interrelate, or simply put: What does it mean when art. 31 AUPC speaks of the international jurisdiction to be established '*in accordance with* [the Brussels I Regulation or, where applicable, the Lugano Convention]'?[258] **2.59**

Does it mean that the Brussels I Regulation or, where applicable, the Lugano Convention *directly* points out the jurisdiction of a division of the Court of **2.60**

---

251 Art. 33 AUPC.

252 Section B.1.

253 Section B.2.

254 Art. 89 AUPC.

255 Art. 7(2) cf. Annex II AUPC whereas the UPC has its seat in Paris (dealing with, inter alia, electronic patents) with sections in London (dealing with, inter alia, chemical patents) and in Munich (dealing with, inter alia, mechanical patents) i.e. three central divisions in total.

256 Art. 7(5) AUPC whereas a regional division shall be set up for two or more Contracting Member States if they so request, which may be one covering DK, EE, FI, LT, LV, SE (RD-North); one covering CZ, HU, SK (RD-East); one covering CY, GR, RO (RD-Southeast); one covering IE, NL, UK (RD-West); one covering AT, DE (RD-Centre) and one covering PT and IT (RD-South) i.e. six regional divisions in total.

257 Art. 7(3) AUPC whereas a local division shall be set up in a Contracting Member State if it so requests. An additional division shall also be set up in a Contracting Member State for every 100 patent cases it conducts per calendar year if it so requests cf. art. 7(4) AUPC. A maximum of four local divisions can be hosted in a Contracting Member State. If the majority of Contracting Member States request for a local division and every Contracting Member State conducting more than 100 patent cases per year (most likely Germany and/or the United Kingdom) so request, the number of local divisions may exceed 20.

258 Emphasis added.

First Instance (option 1) or does it mean that the Brussels I Regulation or, where applicable, the Lugano Convention merely *activates* the overall international jurisdiction of the UPC and accordingly the forum rules in art. 33 AUPC, which then apply to the distribution of local jurisdiction between the different divisions of the Court of First Instance (option 2)?

2.61 The two options differ since applying option 1 the CJEU would ultimately and in effect lay down the jurisdiction of the Court of First Instance due to their competence to interpret the Brussels I Regulation[259] but not the Lugano Convention.[260] By contrast applying option 2 the CJEU would ultimately only be competent to lay down the international jurisdiction of the UPC but not the local jurisdiction of the Court of First Instance since art. 33 AUPC is not Community law.[261]

2.62 Supporting that the Brussels I Regulation or, where applicable, the Lugano Convention *directly* points out the jurisdiction of a division of the Court of First Instance (option 1) it is argued, inter alia, *that* art. 31 AUPC having the heading 'International jurisdiction', requires any such jurisdiction to be 'established *in accordance with* the Brussels I Regulation, or where applicable, the Lugano Convention'[262] contrary to art. 33 AUPC, which does not speak of international jurisdiction and *that* under the EUTMR, CDR and CPVR the Brussels I Regulation and the Lugano Convention also *directly* determine the international jurisdiction.[263]

2.63 Supporting the opposite result namely that the Brussels I Regulation or, where applicable, the Lugano Convention merely *activates* the overall international jurisdiction of the UPC and thereby the forum rules in art. 33 AUPC, which then apply to the distribution of local jurisdiction between the different divisions of the Court of First Instance (option 2), it is argued, inter alia, *that* art. 31 AUPC uses the term 'Court' meaning the UPC[264] whereas art. 33 AUPC uses the term 'Court of First Instance'; *that* given the fact that the UPC is established by way of one supranational court[265] with a large number of divisions located throughout the Contracting Member States[266] jurisdiction

259 Art. 21 cf. Recital (10) AUPC.
260 Magnus and Mankowski, *supra* note 5, p. 21.
261 Opinion 1/09 of 8 March 2011 of the CJEU, para. 7.
262 Emphasis added.
263 Arts 94(1) EUTMR, 97(1) CDR and 101(1) CPVR.
264 Art. 2(a) AUPC.
265 Opinion 1/09 of 8 March 2011 of the CJEU, para. 71.
266 *Supra* notes 255–7.

must fall in two steps[267] contrary to other European unitary IP rights, which are established by way of a large number of national courts, and where jurisdiction can fall in one step;[268] *that* applying option 1 could render art. 33 AUPC superfluous[269] or failing that lead to legal uncertainty which must be avoided[270] *since* infringement actions could be brought at two defendant's domicile and two *forum delicti* rules,[271] *since* non-infringement actions could be brought at *forum delicti* under the BR[272] but not at any such place under the AUPC[273] and *since* invalidity should be brought in the Member State where the patent is registered under the BR[274] but not at any such place under the AUPC;[275] *that* applying option 1 a problem would further arise if the Contracting Member State being pointed out would neither have a local division nor participate in a regional division, which there is no obligation to[276] since then the BR would not be able to do the job alone but would need the help of the AUPC[277] which, in turn, would run counter to the purpose of the BR[278] and finally *that* the Commission non-papers support that the Brussels I Regulation, or where applicable, the Lugano Convention merely *activates* the overall jurisdiction of the UPC by reading:

> As such, the jurisdiction rules of the [BR] apply [...]. The UPC will have jurisdiction any time when a national court of a participating Member State would have jurisdiction based on the [BR]. The UPC would not have jurisdiction when no national court of a participating Member State has jurisdiction pursuant to the [BR].

---

267 The first step is to find out whether the UPC as a supranational court is competent and the second step is to find out which division of the Court of First Instance is competent. The first step is concerned with international jurisdiction and is determined by art. 31 AUPC whereas the second step is concerned with local jurisdiction and is determined by art. 33 AUPC.

268 The one step is to find out which national court is competent, which is determined by arts 97 and 94(1) EUTMR; by arts 82 and 79(1) CDR and by art. 101 CPVR.

269 If arts 4 Brussels I Regulation (defendant's domicile) or 7(2) Brussels I Regulation (*forum delicti*) directly determined the jurisdiction of a division of the Court of First Instance following art. 31 AUPC then arts 33(1)(b) AUPC (defendant's domicile) and 33(1)(a) AUPC (*forum delicti*) could be superfluous.

270 Recital (5) AUPC.

271 Legal uncertainty would arise since art. 4 Brussels I Regulation may be subject to limited forum jurisdiction cf. Chapter 5 section B.1(a), which art. 33(1)(b) AUPC can most likely not cf. art. 34 AUPC cf. Chapter 5 section C.4(a) and since art. 7(2) Brussels I Regulation is subject to limited forum jurisdiction cf. Chapter 9 section B.1(a)(i), which art. 33(1)(a) AUPC is most likely not cf. art. 34 AUPC cf. Chapter 9 section C.4(a).

272 Art. 7(2) BR and case C-133/11, *Folien Fischer*, para. 56 cf. Chapter 9 section B.1(b).

273 Art. 33(4) AUPC cf. Chapter 9 section C.4(b).

274 Art. 24 (4) BR and case C-4/03, *Gat LuK*, para. 32 cf. Chapter 11 section B.

275 Art. 33(3) AUPC cf. Chapter 11 section C.4.

276 Art. 7(3) and (5) AUPC.

277 Art. 33(1)(last sentence) AUPC whereas failing a local or regional division proceedings must be brought at the central division.

278 Recital (6) Brussels I Regulation.

> The rules of the [BR] do not apply to the internal allocation of competences between the various divisions of the UPC, which will be regulated by the UPC Agreement itself.[279]

2.64 In sum the purpose of art. 31 AUPC is not to *directly* determine the jurisdiction of a division of the Court of First Instance. Rather the purpose of art. 31 AUPC is merely to *activate* the overall international jurisdiction of the UPC and thereby the forum rules in art. 33 AUPC, which then apply to the distribution of local jurisdiction between the different divisions of the Court of First Instance.

2.65 The test to be carried out within the meaning of art. 31 AUPC is therefore whether an international jurisdiction rule points at the courts of a Contracting Member State or not. If it points at the courts of a Contracting Member State it triggers UPC jurisdiction meaning art. 33 AUPC, which then applies. If it does not point at the courts of a Contracting Member State UPC jurisdiction is not triggered and art. 33 AUPC does not apply.

2.66 In line with the EUTMR, CDR and CPVR[280] a distinction is drawn between defendants domiciled in the EU, in the EFTA and outside the EU/EFTA. Considering the supranational character of the UPC[281] the distinction addresses *when* the defendants are subject to UPC jurisdiction following art. 31 AUPC and not *where* the defendants can be sued following art. 33 AUPC. The three situations are dealt with individually below in sections (a)–(c).

(a) Defendant is domiciled in the EU

2.67 If the defendant is domiciled in the EU the UPC will have jurisdiction any time a national court of a Contracting Member State has jurisdiction under the Brussels I Regulation cf. the below example:

> Slightly changing the facts of the example in Chapter 1 section 2 Frogs GmbH based in Munich, Germany owns a UP, which has been infringed by an Italian company, Frox SpA, based in Palermo, Italy. Products based on the protected technique are marketed and sold, inter alia, in the UK by the Italian company's establishment in Madrid, Spain. Frogs GmbH wants to bring an infringement action against Frox SpA.

---

279 Non-Paper from the Commission Services regarding the Compatibility of the Draft Agreement on the Unified Patent Court with the Union Aquis (14191/11 LIMITE PI 114 COUR 50) of 20 September 2011, pp. 3, 6 and 7 and Draft Agreement on the Unified Patent Court (17407/11 LIMITE PI 166, COUR 74) of 2 December 2011 with attached Non-Paper of 30 November 2011 from the Commission regarding the Relationship of the Draft Agreement on the Unified Patent Court with Regulation (EC) NO 44/2001 Brussels I, p. 3.

280 Sections C.1–C.3.

281 *Supra* note 265.

Outside the scope of the AUPC the Italian courts would have jurisdiction following art. 4 Brussels I Regulation, the UK courts would have jurisdiction following art. 7(2) Brussels I Regulation and the Spanish courts would have jurisdiction following art. 7(5) Brussels I Regulation. With respect to Italy and the UK jurisdiction would lie with the courts of a Contracting Member State and therefore the UPC also has jurisdiction. The legal basis for this is art. 31 AUPC. The specific rules of jurisdiction available to Frogs GmbH, however, do not follow from art. 31 AUPC but rather from art. 33 AUPC. With respect to Spain jurisdiction would lie with the courts of a non-Contracting Member State and therefore the UPC does not have jurisdiction either cf. art. 31 AUPC.[282]

(b) *Defendant is domiciled in the EFTA*

If the defendant is domiciled in the EFTA the UPC will have jurisdiction any time a national court of a Contracting Member State has jurisdiction under the Lugano Convention cf. the below example: **2.68**

Slightly changing the facts of the example in Chapter 1 section 2 Frogs GmbH based in Munich, Germany owns a UP, which has been infringed by a Norwegian company, Frø A/S, based in Oslo, Norway. Products based on the protected technique are produced in Oslo, but no products have yet been marketed in a Contracting Member State. Frø A/S, however, has plans to do so in the UK in the future, which in turn is confirmed by marketing plans. Frogs GmbH wants to bring an infringement action against Frø A/S. Outside the scope of the AUPC the Norwegian courts would have jurisdiction following art. 2 Lugano Convention. Since jurisdiction would lie with the courts of a non-Contracting Member State the UPC does not have jurisdiction either. Frø A/S, however, has plans to market their products in the UK in the future and so jurisdiction would lie with the courts of a Contracting Member State following art. 5(3) Lugano Convention. The UPC would, therefore, also have jurisdiction. The legal basis for that is again art. 31 AUPC cf. the term 'or, where applicable, [the Lugano Convention]'. The specific rules of jurisdiction available to Frogs GmbH, however, do not follow from art. 31 AUPC but rather from art. 33 AUPC.

(c) *Defendant is domiciled outside the EU/EFTA*

If, finally, the defendant is domiciled outside the EU/EFTA the Contracting Member States' own international forum rules[283] do not apply since they 'would create an unequal access to justice in a unified jurisdictional system **2.69**

---

282 The example is in line with the one given by the Commission in the non-paper *supra* note 279 reading that:

> if proceedings are brought on the basis of Article 2 [4] Brussels I Regulation against a defendant domiciled in Member State X, which is a participating Member State, the UPC shall have jurisdiction. If proceedings are brought on the basis of Article 5(3) [7.2] Brussels I Regulation, i.e. at the place where the harmful event occurred which is situated in Member State Y participating in the UPC Agreement, the UPC will have jurisdiction.

283 Art. 6 Brussels I Regulation.

which could not be justified on any objective reason'.[284] Rather, and in order to create a complete set of rules against non-EU/EFTA defendants as in the EUTMR and CDR,[285] the provisions in Chapter II Brussels I Regulation apply to such defendants.[286] Where the UPC would not have jurisdiction under any such extension UPC competence is ensured under an asset-based forum rule.[287] As a result UPC competence 'will be ensured in situations where the defendant is not domiciled in an EU Member State as access is ensured where the defendant is domiciled in an EU Member State'.[288]

Slightly changing the facts of the example in Chapter 1 section 2 Frogs GmbH based in Munich, Germany owns a UP, which has been infringed by a US company, Frocs Inc., based in New York, US. Products based on the protected technique are marketed in France. Frogs GmbH wants to bring an infringement action against Frocs Inc. Given that the Brussels I Regulation is extended to cover non-EU/EFTA defendants (US defendant) and jurisdiction under art. 7(2) Brussels I Regulation would lie with the courts of a Contracting Member State (France) the UPC also has jurisdiction. The legal basis for this is arts 31 AUPC cf. 71(b)(2) Brussels I Regulation. The specific rules of jurisdiction available to Frogs GmbH, however, do not follow from arts 31 AUPC cf. 71(b)(2) Brussels I Regulation but rather from art. 33 AUPC.

2.70 Overall, the Brussels I Regulation and the Lugano Convention are used differently under the AUPC than under the EUTMR, CDR and CPVR.

2.71 The first difference is that the AUPC refers to both the Brussels I Regulation and, where applicable, to the Lugano Convention[289] whereas the EUTMR and CDR merely refer to the Brussels I Regulation[290] and the CPVR merely refers to the Lugano Convention.[291] Thus, the references are different.

2.72 The second difference is that the Brussels I Regulation or, where applicable, the Lugano Convention merely *activates* the rules of jurisdiction under the

284 Proposal for a Regulation of 27 July 2013 amending Regulation (EU) No 1215/2012 on Jurisdiction and the Recognition and Enforcement of Judgments in Civil and Commercial Matters COM(2013) 554 final, 2013/0268 (COD), p. 6.

285 Sections C.1(c) and C.2(c).

286 Art. 71(b)(2) Regulation (EU) No 542/2014 of the European Parliament and of the Council of 15 May 2014 amending Regulation (EU) No 1215/2012 as regards the Rules to be applied with respect to the Unified Patent Court and the Benelux Court of Justice cf. Jan Brinkhof and Ansgar Ohly, 'Towards a Unified Patent Court in Europe' in Ansgar Ohly and Justine Pila (eds) *The Europeanization of Intellectual Property Law, Towards a European Legal Methodology* , Oxford University Press, 2013, p. 211.

287 Art. 71(b)(3) Regulation (EU) No 542/2014, ibid cf. Asensio, *supra* note 247, pp. 153–69 at 158 *et seq.*

288 Proposal for a Regulation of 27 July 2013 amending Regulation (EU) No 1215/2012 on Jurisdiction and the Recognition and Enforcement of Judgments in Civil and Commercial Matters COM(2013) 554 final, 2013/0268 (COD) cf. p. 7 cf. Recital (6) Regulation (EU) No 542/2014, ibid.

289 Art. 31 AUPC.

290 Arts 94(1) EUTMR and 79(1) CDR.

291 Art. 101(1) CPVR.

AUPC whereas the Brussels I Regulation and the Lugano Convention apply *directly* under the EUTMR, CDR and CPVR. The difference between the two is that the second model opens up for yet another forum for the plaintiff leading to more forum shopping[292] compared to the first model.

The third difference is that all forum rules in the Brussels I Regulation or, where applicable, in the Lugano Convention pointing at the courts of a Contracting Member State apply under the AUPC (full application) whereas under the EUTMR, CDR and CPVR only such rules apply, which do not have 'sister' provisions in the 'cascade' ('fall back' application) unless action is brought in the EFTA. **2.73**

The fourth difference is the way non-EU/EFTA defendants are addressed. Under the AUPC a complete set of rules is established, inter alia, since the provisions of the Brussels I Regulation are extended to cover non-EU/EFTA defendants. Under the EUTMR and CDR a complete set of rules is also established vis-à-vis such defendants since art. 6 Brussels I Regulation has been exempted. Under the CPVR any such complete set of rules is, however, not established given that art. 4 Lugano Convention applies. **2.74**

D. CONCLUSION

The jurisdiction framework depends on whether a national IP right or a corresponding European unitary IP right has been infringed. **2.75**

If a national IP right has been infringed different rules apply depending on the domicile of the defendant. If the defendant is domiciled in the EU the Brussels I Regulation applies. If the defendant is domiciled in the EFTA the Lugano Convention applies. If, finally, the defendant is domiciled outside the EU/EFTA the Member States' own international forum rules apply. The rules in the Brussels I Regulation and in the Lugano Convention are overall similar and must be interpreted in the same way. **2.76**

If a corresponding European unitary IP right has been infringed different rules also apply depending on the domicile of the defendant. If the defendant is domiciled in the EU the 'cascade' rules in Title X EUTMR, Title IX CDR and Part Six CPVR apply with the Brussels I Regulation acting as 'fall back' whereas only Chapter VI AUPC applies. If the defendant is domiciled in the EFTA the 'cascade' rules in Title X EUTMR, Title IX CDR and Part Six **2.77**

292 Chapter 4 section C.3.

CPVR apply with the Lugano Convention acting as 'fall back' in the EU and in full in the EFTA whereas only Chapter VI AUPC applies. If, finally, the defendant is domiciled outside the EU/EFTA the 'cascade' rules in Title X EUTMR and Title IX CDR apply, Chapter VI AUPC apply whereas Part Six CPVR and the Member States' own international forum rules apply. Where other than the 'cascade' rules apply the plaintiff is not obliged to exhaust the 'cascade' rules first since otherwise the other rules would be inapplicable given that the 'cascade' rules can do the job alone. Neither the EUTMR, CDR, CPVR nor the AUPC can prevent action to be brought in a third state.

2.78 The jurisdiction framework governing a national IP right and a corresponding European unitary IP right can be illustrated as in the table below. Third states' own international forum rules are coloured differently since they fall outside the European jurisdiction framework. The specific international forum rules available to the plaintiff, taking into account the above findings, are outlined in the following Chapter 3.

Table 2.1 Jurisdiction framework overview

	Domicile of the defendant	IP right	Jurisdiction framework	
			Source 1	Source 2
National IP rights	In EU	Trademarks Designs Plant varieties Patents	Brussels I Regulation	N/A
	In EFTA		Lugano Convention	N/A
	Outside EU/EFTA		Member States' own international forum rules	N/A
European unitary IP right	In EU	European Union Trademark	Title X EUTMR	Brussels I Regulation applies as 'fall back'
		Community Design	Title IX CDR	Brussels I Regulation applies as 'fall back'
		Community Plant Variety	Part Six CPVR	Brussels I Regulation applies as 'fall back'
		Unitary Patent	Chapter VI AUPC	N/A
	In EFTA	European Union Trademark	Title X EUTMR	Lugano Convention applies as 'fall back' in the EU Lugano Convention applies in full in the EFTA
		Community Design	Title IX CDR	Lugano Convention applies as 'fall back' in the EU Lugano Convention applies in full in the EFTA
		Community Plant Variety	Part Six CPVR	Lugano Convention applies as 'fall back' in the EU Lugano Convention applies in full in the EFTA
		Unitary Patent	Chapter VI AUPC	N/A
	Outside EU/EFTA	European Union Trademark	Title X EUTMR	N/A Third States' own international forum rules
		Community Design	Title IX CDR	N/A Third States' own international forum rules
		Community Plant Variety	Part Six CPVR	Member States' own international forum rules Third States' own international forum rules
		Unitary Patent	Chapter VI AUPC	N/A Third States' own international forum rules

3

JURISDICTION RULES

A. INTRODUCTION

3.01 From Chapter 1[1] it follows that the number of international jurisdiction rules available to the plaintiff must be identified. The purpose of Chapter 3 is to meet any such objective taking into account the findings from Chapter 2.[2] Thus, the number of international jurisdiction rules are addressed and compared at the present stage, which leads to identifying the advantages for the plaintiff.[3] The nature of the international jurisdiction rules referred to are by contrast not addressed at the present stage but rather in Chapters 4–11.

3.02 A distinction is drawn between the international jurisdiction rules applying to a national IP right (section B) and the international jurisdiction rules applying to a corresponding European unitary IP right (section C). In the end a conclusion is drawn, inter alia, by way of a table (section D).

1 Section A.3(c).

2 Torsten Bjørn Larsen, Dansk Immaterialret Bind II, Sanktioner og Håndhævelse, Værneting i Immaterialrets-sager om Krænkelse og Ugyldighed, GAD's Forlag, 2015, pp. 173 *et seq.*

3 More jurisdiction rules is an advantage for the plaintiff cf. Chapter 1 section A.4 (factor 1).

B. THE INTERNATIONAL JURISDICTION RULES APPLYING TO A NATIONAL IP RIGHT

The international jurisdiction rules applying to a national IP right do not depend on the IP right in question but rather on whether the defendant is domiciled in the EU (section 1), in the EFTA (section 2) or outside the EU/EFTA (section 3).[4] **3.03**

1. Defendant is domiciled in the EU

If the defendant is domiciled in the EU the Brussels I Regulation applies.[5] Under the Brussels I Regulation infringement actions may be brought at the defendant's domicile,[6] establishment,[7] at *forum delicti*[8] or following the multiple defendants' rule[9] (four options). Non-infringement actions may be brought at the same fora[10] (four options). If invalidity is raised in infringement or non-infringement actions a distinction must be drawn between registered and unregistered IP rights. Invalidity of the former must be addressed by the courts of the Member State where the IP right is registered[11] whereas invalidity of the latter can be addressed by the courts of the Member State where the infringement or non-infringement action is pending.[12] **3.04**

4 The reason for the distinction between EU, EFTA and non-EU/EFTA defendants is – despite that the former two are subject to parallel rules cf. sections B.1 and B.2 – that any such distinction must, with variations, also be drawn for European unitary IP rights cf. section C.

5 Chapter 2 section 2.1.

6 Art. 4 Brussels I Regulation and Chapter 5 section B.1(a).

7 Art. 7(5) Brussels I Regulation and Chapter 6 section B.1(a).

8 Art. 7(2) Brussels I Regulation and Chapter 9 section B.1(a).

9 Art. 8(1) Brussels I Regulation and Chapter 8 section B.1(a).

10 Art. 4 Brussels I Regulation and Chapter 5 section B.1(b); art. 7(5) Brussels I Regulation and Chapter 6 section B.1(b); art. 7(2) Brussels Regulation and Chapter 9 section B.1(b) and art. 8(1) Brussels I Regulation and Chapter 8 section B.1(b).

11 Art. 24(4) Brussels I Regulation and Chapter 11 section B. Art. 24(4) Brussels I Regulation applies regardless of whether invalidity is raised in infringement or non-infringement actions cf. *Conflict of Laws in Intellectual Property, The CLIP Principles and Commentary*, European Max Planck Group on Conflicts of Laws in Intellectual Property, Oxford University Press, 2013, p. 176 (2:602.N04).

12 James J. Fawcett and Paul Torremans, *Intellectual Property and Private International Law*, 2nd Edition, Oxford Private International Law Series, 2011 at 7.224 *et seq*. Given that under arts 4 and 7(5) Brussels I Regulation 'domicile' and 'establishment' are the connecting factors whereas under art. 7(2) Brussels I Regulation the 'harmful event' (infringement) is the connecting factor one could argue that invalidity of an unregistered IP right can only be addressed under arts 4 and 7(5) Brussels I Regulation and not under art. 7(2) Brussels I Regulation. Any such interpretation seems unlikely given that the infringement or non-infringement action brought under art. 7(2) Brussels I Regulation would then be split up in the sense that infringement could be addressed under art. 7(2) Brussels I Regulation whereas invalidity should be addressed under arts 4 or 7(5) Brussels I Regulation cf. ibid., at 7.227–7.230.

2. Defendant is domiciled in the EFTA

3.05 If the defendant is domiciled in the EFTA the Lugano Convention applies.[13] Section B.1 applies *mutatis mutandis.*

3. Defendant is domiciled outside the EU/EFTA

3.06 If finally the defendant is domiciled outside the EU/EFTA the Member States' own international forum rules apply.[14] If invalidity of an IP right registered in a Member State is raised, however, art. 24(4) BR comes into play given that the provision applies regardless of domicile.[15] The Member States' own international forum rules do not prevent action against non-EU/EFTA defendants to be brought in their home state subject to third states' own international forum rules. For the reasons in Chapter 1 section A.5(a) (limit 5) the above rules including the conditions under which they may apply are not examined for the purpose of the present study.

3.07 The international jurisdiction rules available to the plaintiff can be illustrated as in Figure 3.1 below. Third states' own international forum rules are coloured differently since they fall outside the European jurisdiction framework.

C. THE INTERNATIONAL JURISDICTION RULES APPLYING TO A EUROPEAN UNITARY IP RIGHT

3.08 The international jurisdiction rules applying to a European unitary IP right depend on whether the IP right in question is an EUTM (section 1), a CD (section 2), a CPV (section 3) or a UP (section 4).

1. European Union Trademark

3.09 The international jurisdiction rules available to the plaintiff[16] can be derived from two sources. The first is the 'cascade' rules in Title X EUTMR. The second is the Brussels I Regulation, which applies as 'fall back' (meaning art. 8.1), the Lugano Convention, which applies as 'fall back' in the EU (meaning

13 Chapter 2 section B.2.

14 Art. 6 BR.

15 Chapter 11 section B.

16 For the purpose of the present section arts 62 and 63 BR, which also apply cf. Chapter 2 section C.1, are not considered international jurisdiction rules.

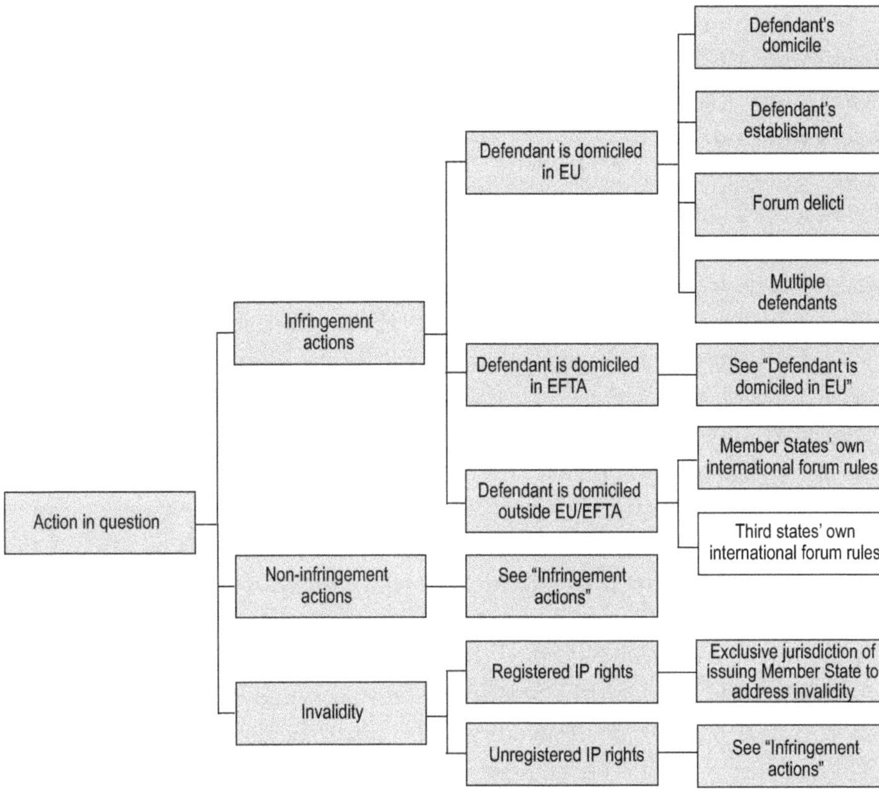

Figure 3.1 The international jurisdiction rules applying to a national IP right

no rules) and in full in the EFTA (meaning arts 2, 5.3, 5.5, 6.1 and 22.4).[17] The available forum rules depend on the action in question.

As regards infringement actions[18] a distinction must be drawn between whether the defendant is domiciled in the EU, in the EFTA or outside the EU/EFTA. If the defendant is domiciled in the EU the plaintiff may bring an action at the defendant's EU domicile,[19] at *forum delicti*,[20] or following the multiple defendants' rule[21] (three options). If the defendant is domiciled in the EFTA the plaintiff may bring an action at the defendant's EU establishment[22] or, failing that, at the plaintiff's EU domicile or, failing that, **3.10**

17 Chapter 2 section C.1.
18 Art. 96(a) EUTMR.
19 Art. 97(1) EUTMR and Chapter 5 section C.1(a).
20 Art. 97(5) EUTMR and Chapter 9 section C.1(a).
21 Art. 94(2)(a) EUTMR cf. art. 8(1) Brussels I Regulation and Chapter 8 section C.1(a).
22 Art. 97(1) EUTMR and Chapter 6 section C.1(a).

EU establishment,[23] or, failing that, in Spain,[24] at *forum delicti*,[25] at the defendant's EFTA domicile,[26] at the defendant's EFTA establishment,[27] at *forum delicti* ('place of action') in the EFTA[28] or following the multiple defendants' rule in the EFTA[29] (six options). If finally the defendant is domiciled outside the EU/EFTA, the plaintiff may bring an action at the defendant's EU establishment[30] or, failing that, at the plaintiff's EU domicile or, failing that, EU establishment,[31] or, failing that, in Spain,[32] at *forum delicti*[33] but nowhere else in the EU since the Member States' own international forum rules do not apply.[34] By contrast action can be brought in a third state under its own international forum rules (> two options).

3.11 As regards non-infringement actions[35] the above forum rules, lacking CJEU case law,[36] most likely apply *mutatis mutandis* except from *forum delicti*[37] unless *forum delicti* is in the EFTA in which event a non-infringement action can be brought there.[38] The effect is that non-infringement actions as a main rule must be brought at the home domicile/establishment of the rightholder.[39]

3.12 If invalidity is raised a distinction must be drawn between whether invalidity is raised at an EUTM court or not. If invalidity is raised at an EUTM court a sub distinction must be drawn between infringement actions, where the EUTM court is exclusively competent[40] and non-infringement actions where the EUIPO is exclusively competent.[41] If, by contrast, invalidity is not raised at an EUTM court a sub distinction must be drawn between EFTA courts, where art. 22(4) Lugano Convention applies per analogy making the EUIPO

23 Art. 97(2) EUTMR and Chapter 7 section C.1(a).
24 Art. 97(3) EUTMR.
25 Art. 97(5) EUTMR and Chapter 9 section C.1(a).
26 Art. 2 Lugano Convention and Chapter 5 section B.1(a).
27 Art. 5(5) Lugano Convention and Chapter 6 section B.1(a).
28 Art. 5(3) Lugano Convention and Chapter 9 section B.1(a).
29 Art. 6(1) Lugano Convention and Chapter 8 section B.1(a).
30 Art. 97(1) EUTMR and Chapter 6 section C.1(a).
31 Art. 97(2) EUTMR and Chapter 7 section C.1(a).
32 Art. 97(3) EUTMR.
33 Art. 97(5) EUTMR and Chapter 9 section C.1(a).
34 Art. 94(2)(a) EUTMR.
35 Art. 96(b) EUTMR.
36 Overall Functioning of the European Trade Mark System presented by Max Planck Institute for Intellectual Property and Competition Law Munich of 15 February 2011 at 3.132 (p. 157) and curia.eu visited on 1 January 2017.
37 Art. 97(5) EUTMR.
38 Art. 5(3) Lugano Convention and Chapter 9 section B.1(b).
39 *Conflict of Laws in Intellectual Property, The CLIP Principles and Commentary*, *supra* note 11, p. 192 (2:605.N08).
40 Art. 96(d) EUTMR and Chapter 11 section C.1.
41 Arts 99(2) cf. 56 EUTMR and Chapter 11 section C.2.

exclusively competent[42] and third states' courts where their own international forum rules apply.

The international jurisdiction rules available to the plaintiff can be illustrated as in Figure 3.2 below. For the reason in section B.3 third states' own forum rules are coloured differently. 3.13

2. Community Design

The international jurisdiction rules available to the plaintiff[43] can be derived from two sources. The first one is the 'cascade' rules in Title IX CDR. The second one is the Brussels I Regulation, which applies as 'fall back' (meaning art. 8.1), the Lugano Convention, which applies as 'fall back' in the EU (meaning no rules) and in full in the EFTA (meaning arts 2, 5.3, 5.5, 6.1 and 22.4).[44] The available forum rules depend on the action in question. 3.14

As regards infringement[45] and non-infringement[46] actions section C.1 similarly applies. 3.15

If invalidity is raised a distinction must be drawn between whether invalidity is raised at a CD court or not. If invalidity is raised at a CD court a sub distinction must be drawn between infringement actions, where the CD court is exclusively competent[47] and non-infringement actions where another sub distinction must be drawn between registered CDs where the EUIPO is exclusively competent[48] and unregistered CDs where neither the CD courts[49] nor the EUIPO[50] are competent meaning that an infringer must wait until an infringement action is brought against him/her before invalidity can be raised. If, by contrast, invalidity is not raised at a CD court a sub distinction must be drawn between EFTA courts, where another sub distinction must be drawn between registered CDs where art. 22(4) Lugano Convention applies per analogy making the EUIPO exclusively competent[51] and unregistered CDs 3.16

42 Chapter 11 section C.1.
43 For the purpose of the present section arts 62 and 63 BR, which also apply cf. Chapter 2 section C.2, are not considered international jurisdiction rules.
44 Chapter 2 section C.2.
45 Art. 81(a) CDR.
46 Art. 81(b) CDR.
47 Art. 81(d) CDR and Chapter 11 section C.2(a).
48 Arts 84(4) cf. 52 CDR and Chapter 11 section C.2(b).
49 Art. 84(4) CDR.
50 Art. 52 CDR.
51 Chapter 11 section C.2.

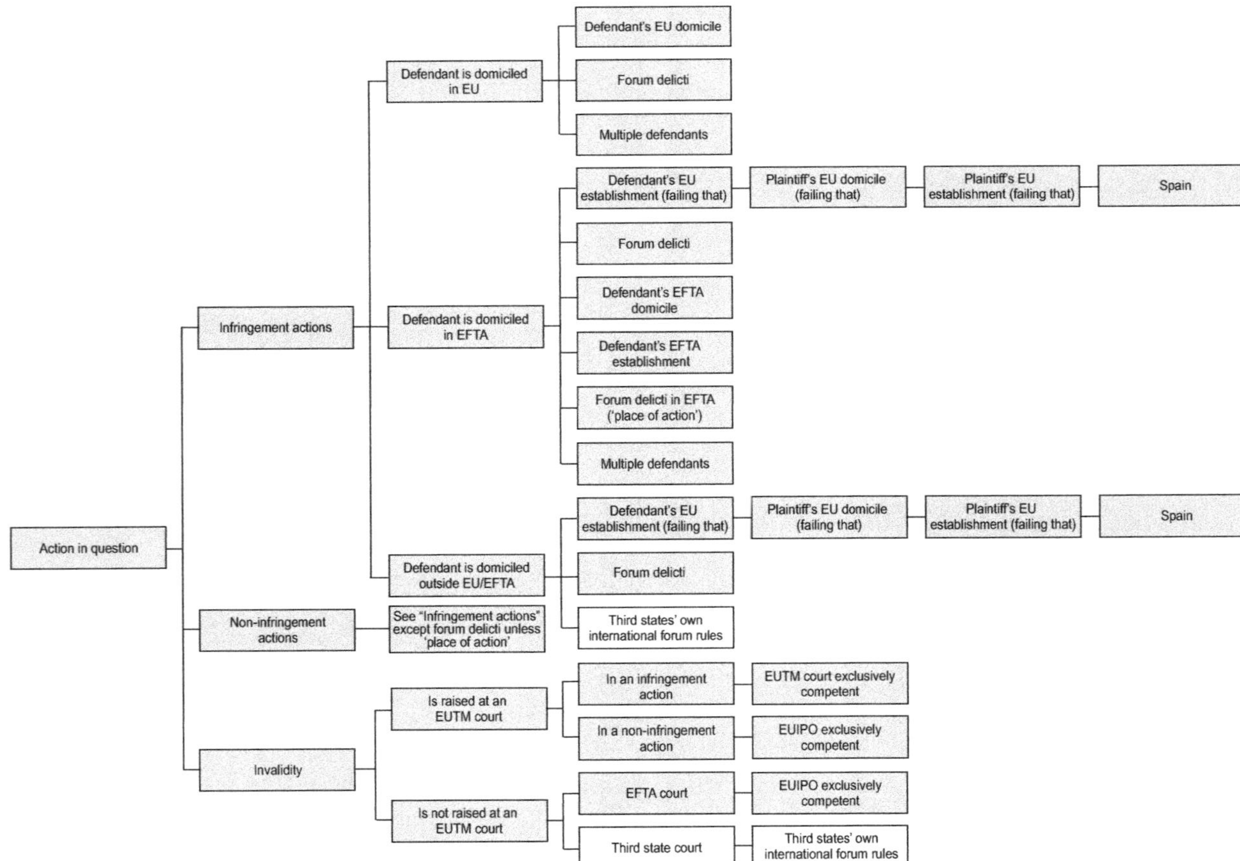

Figure 3.2 The international jurisdiction rules applying to the EUTM

where the EFTA court is competent and third states' courts where their own international forum rules apply.

The international jurisdiction rules available to the plaintiff can be illustrated as in Figure 3.3 below. For the reason in section B.3 third states' own forum rules are coloured differently. **3.17**

3. Community Plant Variety

The international jurisdiction rules available to the plaintiff[52] can be derived from two sources. The first one is the 'cascade' rules in Part Six CPVR. The second one is the Brussels I Regulation, which applies as 'fall back' (meaning art. 8.1), the Lugano Convention, which applies as 'fall back' in the EU (meaning art. 6.1) and in full in the EFTA (meaning arts 2, 5.3, 5.5, 6.1 and 22.4) and the Member States' own international forum rules.[53] The available forum rules depend on the action in question. **3.18**

As regards infringement actions[54] a distinction must be drawn between whether the defendant is domiciled in the EU, in the EFTA or outside the EU/EFTA. If the defendant is domiciled in the EU the plaintiff may bring an action at the defendant's EU domicile,[55] at *forum delicti*[56] or following the multiple defendants' rule[57] (three options). If the defendant is domiciled in the EFTA the plaintiff may bring an action at the defendant's EFTA domicile,[58] at *forum delicti*,[59] at the defendant's EFTA establishment,[60] at *forum delicti* in the EFTA[61] or following the multiple defendants' rule in the EFTA[62] (five options). If finally the defendant is domiciled outside the EU/EFTA the plaintiff may bring an action at the defendant's EU establishment[63] or, failing that, at the plaintiff's EU domicile or, failing that, EU establishment[64] or, **3.19**

52 For the purpose of the present section arts 59 and 60 Lugano Convention, which also apply cf. Chapter 2 section C.3, are not considered international jurisdiction rules.
53 Chapter 2 section C.3.
54 Art. 94 CPVR.
55 Art. 101(2)(a) CPVR and Chapter 5 section C.3(a).
56 Art. 101(3) CPVR and Chapter 9 section C.3(a).
57 Art. 101(1) CPVR cf. art. 8(1) Brussels I Regulation and Chapter 8 section C.3(a).
58 Arts 101(2)(a) CPVR cf. 2 Lugano Convention and Chapter 5 sections C.3(a) cf. B.1(a).
59 Art. 101(3) CPVR and Chapter 9 section C.3(a).
60 Art. 5(5) Lugano Convention and Chapter 6 section B.1(a).
61 Art. 5(3) Lugano Convention and Chapter 9 section B.1(a).
62 Art. 101(1) CPVR cf. art. 6(1) Lugano Convention and Chapter 8 section C.3(a).
63 Art. 101(2)(a) CPVR and Chapter 6 section C.3(a). For the reasons *supra* Chapter 2 note 222 action cannot be brought at the defendant's EFTA establishment under art. 101(2)(a) CPVR if the defendant is not domiciled in the EFTA.
64 Art. 101(2)(b) CPVR and Chapter 7 section C.3(a).

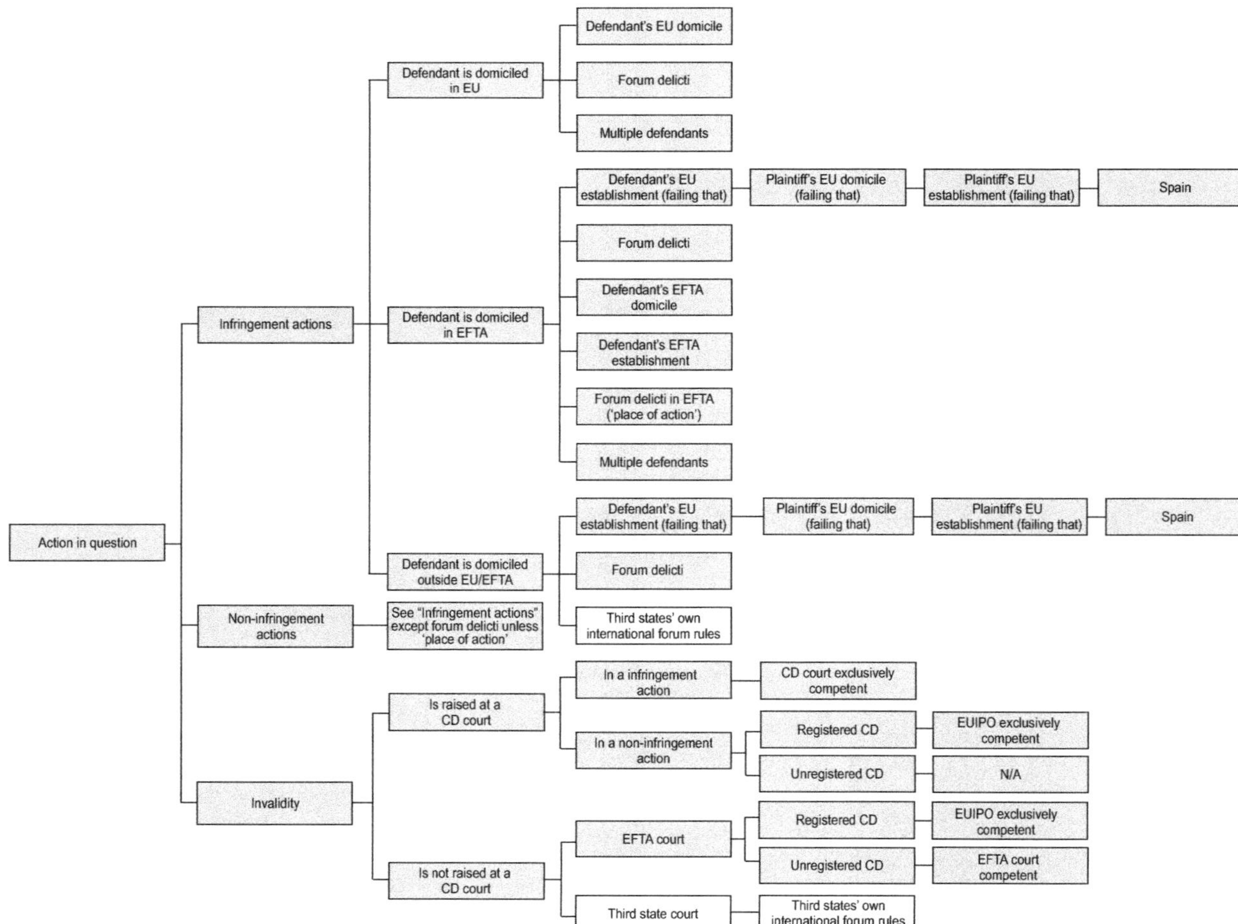

Figure 3.3 The international jurisdiction rules applying to the CD

failing that, in France,[65] at *forum delicti*[66] or following the Member States' or third states' own international forum rules (> three options).

As regards non-infringement actions the question is whether any such actions can at all be brought with the 'competent courts'.[67] **3.20**

Supporting that non-infringement actions cannot be brought with the 'competent courts' it is argued, inter alia, *that* such actions are not mentioned in the CPVR[68] contrary to the EUTMR and CDR where any such actions are explicitly covered by the exclusive competence of the EUTM and CD courts,[69] *that* a specific legal basis is therefore absent; *that* art. 94 CPVR seems to be restricted to infringement actions cf. the wording 'whosoever [infringes a CPV] may be sued by the holder to enjoin such infringement'[70] cf. 'actions for infringement may be brought by the holder'[71] *that* the courts are competent only 'in respect of the claims referred to in Article 94 [...]'[72] and *that* threatened infringement actions – which may serve a similar purpose as non-infringement actions namely to address a possible infringement at an early stage – are also excluded.[73] **3.21**

Supporting the opposite result namely that non-infringement actions can be brought with the 'competent courts' it is argued, inter alia, *that* art. 94 CPVR merely defines infringing activities by referring to acts, which require the authorization of the rightholder thus leaving a scope of activities, which are non-infringing[74] and which could be subject to a non-infringement action, inter alia, acts which are subject to the farmers' privilege[75] and acts performed for non-commercial or experimental purposes;[76] *that* the procedural law remedies available to the infringer would be unnecessarily restricted, which in turn could run counter the principle of equality of arms being a feature of art. 6(1) ECHR[77] if non-infringement actions could not be brought and *that* **3.22**

---

65 Art. 101(2)(c) CPVR.
66 Art. 101(3) CPVR and Chapter 9 section C.3(a).
67 Art. 101(4) CPVR.
68 Arts 94–100 CPVR.
69 Arts 96(b) EUTMR and 81(b) CDR.
70 Art. 94 CPVR.
71 Art. 104 CPVR.
72 Art. 101(1) CPVR.
73 Fawcett and Torremans, *supra* note 12 at 8.146.
74 Gert Würtenberger, Paul Van Der Kooij, Bart Kiewiet and Martin Ekvad, *European Community Plant Variety Protection*, Oxford University Press, 2006 at 7.12.
75 Art. 14 CPVR.
76 Art. 15 CPVR.
77 Jacobs, White and Ovey, The European Convention on Human Rights, 5th edn, Oxford University Press, 2010, p. 261 notes 91–94 with references.

non-infringement actions can also be brought under the EUTMR, CDR and the AUPC.[78]

3.23 Balancing the interests it seems likely that non-infringement actions can be brought with the 'competent courts'. Given that no forum rules are explicitly excluded for the purpose of bringing non-infringement actions by contrast to the EUTMR and CDR[79] the above forum rules apply *mutatis mutandis*.

3.24 If invalidity is raised the situation differs from the ones under the EUTMR and CDR.[80] The reason is that the CPVR does not include any rules on counterclaims[81] contrary to the EUTMR and CDR[82] given that invalidity must be brought with the CPVO[83] with appeal to the Board[84] and further to the CJEU.[85] Thus, a distinction must be drawn between whether invalidity is raised at a 'competent court' making the CPVO exclusively competent following arts 20 CPVR[86] or 22(4) Lugano Convention per analogy[87] or whether invalidity is raised at a non-competent court where any such question is subject to third states' own international forum rules.

3.25 The international jurisdiction rules available to the plaintiff can be illustrated as in Figure 3.4 below. For the reason in section B.3 third states' own forum rules are coloured differently.

4. Unitary Patent

3.26 The international jurisdiction rules available to the plaintiff can be derived from one source only, namely Chapter VI AUPC. The available forum rules depend on the action in question.

---

78 Arts 96(b) EUTMR, 81(b) CDR and 32(1)(b) AUPC.

79 Arts 97(5) EUTMR and 82(5) CDR.

80 Sections C.1 and C.2.

81 Fawcett and Torremans, *supra* note 12 at 8.179 and Würtenberger et al, *supra* note 74 at 7.09.

82 Arts 96(d) EUTMR and 81(d) CDR.

83 Art. 20 cf. Würtenberger et al, *supra* note 74 at 2.01 and 7.09–10.

84 Art. 67 CPVR.

85 Art. 73 CPVR.

86 Art. 20 CPVR is the legal basis if invalidity is raised at a 'competent court' in the EU and Chapter 11 section C.3.

87 Art. 22(4) Lugano Convention is the legal basis if invalidity is raised at a 'competent court' in the EFTA and Chapter 11 section C.3.

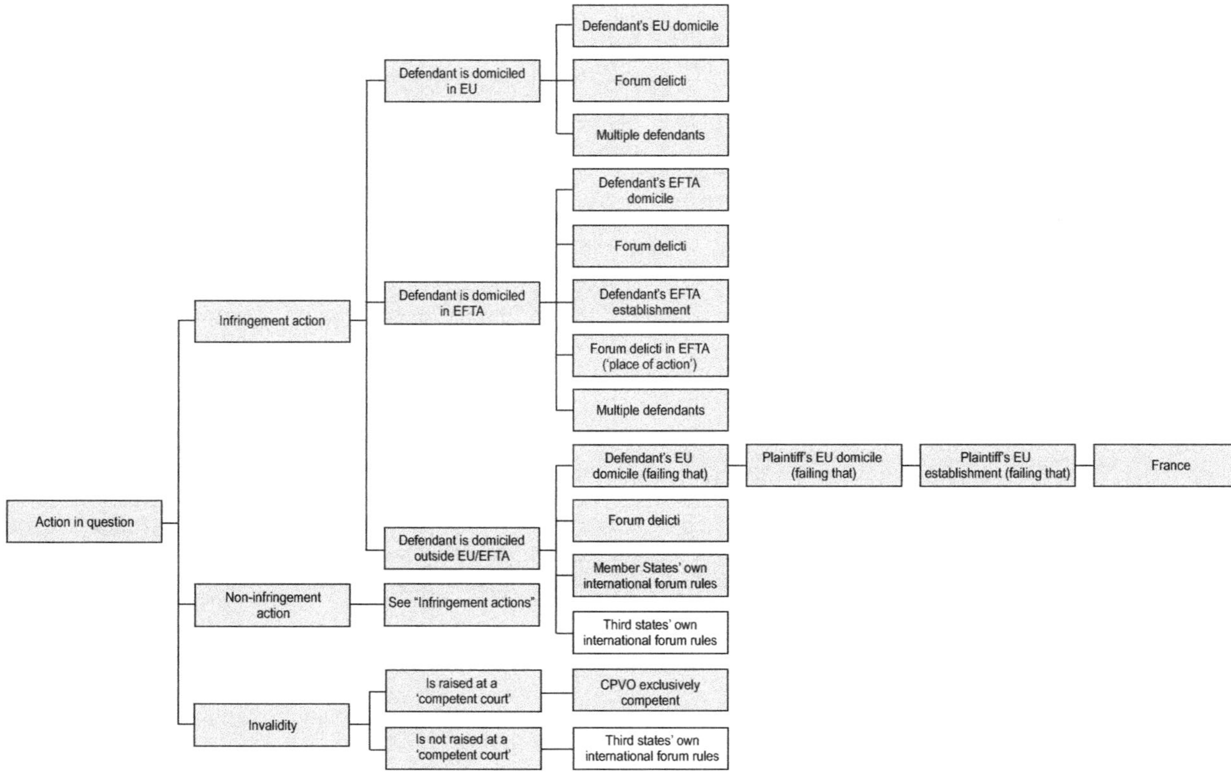

Figure 3.4 The international jurisdiction rules applying to the CPV

3.27 As regards infringement actions[88] different rules apply depending on the residence[89] of the defendant. If the defendant is resident of a Contracting Member State the plaintiff may bring an action at *forum delicti*,[90] at the defendant's residence or principal place of business or, failing that, place of business[91] or following the multiple defendants' rule[92] (three options). If the defendant is not resident of a Contracting Member State the plaintiff may bring an action at *forum delicti*[93] or at the central division in Paris, London or Munich depending on the subject matter.[94] The AUPC, however, cannot prevent action being brought in a third state if its own international forum rules so permit (> two options).

3.28 As regards non-infringement actions[95] a distinction must be drawn between whether an infringement action between the same parties relating to the same patent is pending or not. If any such action is pending the non-infringement action must be brought at the same forum[96] (three options) whereas the non-infringement action, if any such infringement action is not pending, must be brought at the central division[97] in Paris, London or Munich[98] (one option). As above the AUPC cannot prevent action to be brought in a third state if its own international forum rules so permit.

3.29 If invalidity is raised the court has three options. It may at its own discretion and after having heard the parties decide the case (meaning that the court will decide both infringement and invalidity),[99] bifurcate (meaning that invalidity will be referred to the central division and that infringement will be either suspended or proceeded with)[100] or send the case away to the central division if the parties agree (meaning that the central division will decide both infringement and invalidity).[101] If the case is brought in a third state invalidity is subject to the international forum rules of the third state.

---

88 Art. 32(1)(a) AUPC.

89 The AUPC uses the term 'residence' rather than 'domicile' as in the BR, EUTMR, CDR and CPVR cf. Chapter 5 section C.4.

90 Art. 33(1)(a) AUPC and Chapter 9 section C.4(a).

91 Art. 33(1)(b) AUPC and Chapter 5 section 3.4.1 and Chapter 6 section C.4(a).

92 Art. 33(1)(b) and Chapter 8 section C.4(a).

93 Art. 33(1) (third part) AUPC and Chapter 9 section C.4(a).

94 Art. 33(1) cf. Annex II AUPC and Chapter 10 section C.

95 Art. 32(1)(b) AUPC.

96 Art. 33(4) (second part) AUPC.

97 Art. 33(4) (first part) AUPC and Chapter 10 section C.

98 Annex II AUPC.

99 Art. 33(3)(a) AUPC and Chapter 11 section C.4.

100 Art. 33(3)(b) AUPC and Chapter 11 section C.4.

101 Art. 33(3)(c) AUPC and Chapter 11 section C.4.

3.30 The international jurisdiction rules available to the plaintiff can be illustrated as in Figure 3.5 below. For the reason in section B.3 third states' own forum rules are coloured differently.

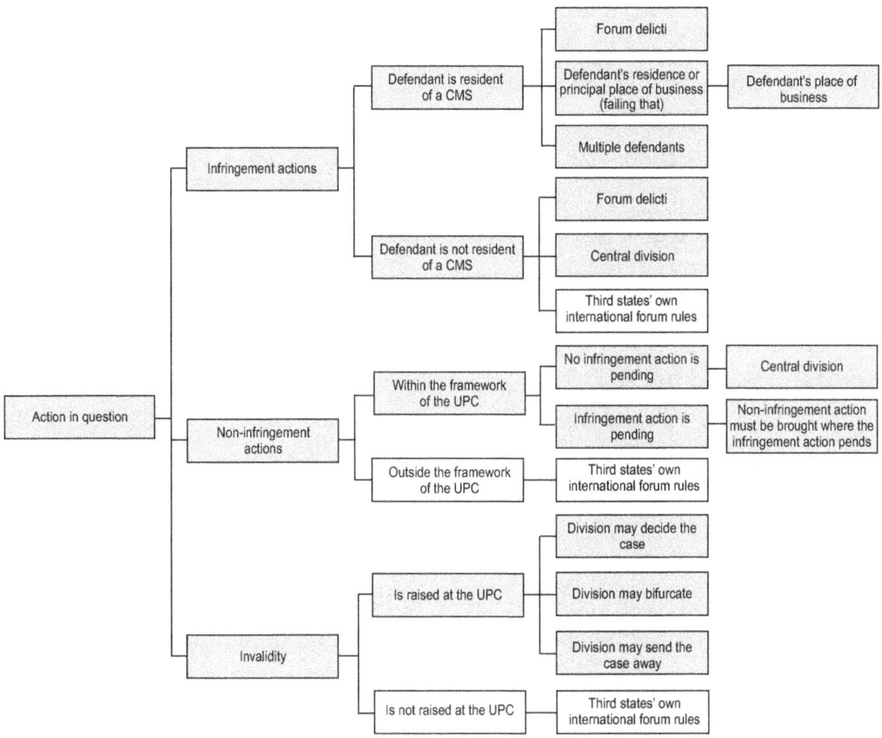

Figure 3.5 The international jurisdiction rules applying to the UP

D. CONCLUSION

3.31 A distinction is drawn between the international jurisdiction rules available to the plaintiff in trademark, design, plant variety and patent cases (see Table 3.1 below).[102]

3.32 In *trademark* cases a distinction must be drawn between infringement, non-infringement and invalidity actions. As regards infringement actions the plaintiff can choose between four 'national rules' and three 'EUTM rules' (if the defendant is domiciled in the EU), four 'national rules' and six 'EUTM

102 For the purpose of the present section the term 'national rules' refers to the overall number of international jurisdiction rules available to the plaintiff if a national IP right has been infringed whereas the terms 'EUTM rules', 'CPV rules' and 'UP rules' refer to the overall number of international jurisdiction rules available to the plaintiff if a EUTM, CPV or a UP has been infringed.

rules' (if the defendant is domiciled in the EFTA) and > two 'EUTM rules' whereas the number of 'national rules' has not been examined (if the defendant is domiciled outside the EU/EFTA). As regards non-infringement actions the plaintiff can choose between four 'national rules' and two 'EUTM rules' (if the defendant is domiciled in the EU), four 'national rules' and five 'EUTM rules' (if the defendant is domiciled in the EFTA) and > one 'EUTM rule' whereas the number of 'national rules' has not been examined (if the defendant is domiciled outside the EU/EFTA). If invalidity is raised in an infringement or in a non-infringement action the plaintiff is subject to one 'national rule' for registered and unregistered trademarks alike[103] and one 'EUTM rule'.[104]

3.33 In sum – and generally speaking – a national trademark is advantageous to the plaintiff if the defendant is domiciled in the EU since more forum rules are available whereas the EUTM is advantageous to the plaintiff if the defendant is domiciled in the EFTA since more forum rules are available. If the defendant is domiciled outside the EU/EFTA a conclusion cannot be drawn given that the Member States' own international forum rules have not been examined.

3.34 In *design* cases a distinction must also be drawn between infringement, non-infringement and invalidity actions. The above applies *mutatis mutandis.*

3.35 In *plant variety* cases a distinction must also be drawn between infringement, non-infringement and invalidity actions. As regards infringement actions the plaintiff can choose between four 'national rules' and three 'CPV rules' (if the defendant is domiciled in the EU), four 'national rules' and five 'CPV rules' (if the defendant is domiciled in the EFTA) and > three 'CPV rules' whereas the number of 'national rules' has not been examined (if the defendant is domiciled outside the EU/EFTA). As regards non-infringement actions the plaintiff can choose between four 'national rules' and three 'CPV rules' (if the defendant is domiciled in the EU), four 'national rules' and five 'CPV rules' (if the defendant is domiciled in the EFTA) and > three 'CPV rules' whereas the number of 'national rules' has not been examined (if the defendant is domiciled

103 With respect to a registered national trademark invalidity must be addressed by the courts of the Member State where the trademark is registered whereas for an unregistered national trademark invalidity can be addressed by the court where the action is pending regardless of forum. The term one 'national rule' for unregistered trademarks, therefore, refers to the forum where the action is pending and not to the number of jurisdiction rules available, which exceeds one.

104 If invalidity is raised in an infringement action the EUTM court where the action is pending is competent. The term 1 'EUTM rule', therefore, refers to the forum where the action is pending and not to the number of jurisdiction rules available, which exceeds 1. If invalidity is raised in the EFTA or in a non-infringement action the EUIPO is competent.

outside the EU/EFTA). If invalidity is raised the plaintiff is subject to one 'national rule' and one 'CPV rule'.[105]

In sum – and generally speaking – a national plant variety is advantageous to **3.36** the plaintiff if the defendant is domiciled in the EU since more forum rules are available whereas the CPV is advantageous to the plaintiff if the defendant is domiciled in the EFTA since more forum rules are available. If the defendant is domiciled outside the EU/EFTA a conclusion cannot be drawn given that the Member States' own international forum rules have not been examined.

In *patent* cases a distinction must also be drawn between infringement, **3.37** non-infringement and invalidity actions. As regards infringement actions the plaintiff can choose between four 'national rules' and three 'UP rules' (if the defendant is domiciled in the EU respectively in a CMS), four 'national rules' and > two 'UP rules' (if the defendant is domiciled in the EFTA respectively outside a CMS) and > two 'UP rules' whereas the number of 'national rules' has not been examined (if the defendant is domiciled outside the EU/EFTA). As regards non-infringement actions the plaintiff can choose between four 'national rules' and one 'UP rule' (if the defendant is domiciled in the EU respectively in a CMS), four 'national rules' and one 'UP rule' (if the defendant is domiciled in the EFTA respectively outside a CMS) and one 'UP rule' whereas the number of 'national rules' has not been examined (if the defendant is domiciled outside the EU/EFTA). If invalidity is raised the plaintiff is subject to one 'national rule' and three 'UP rules'.

In sum – and generally speaking – a national patent is advantageous to the **3.38** plaintiff if the defendant is domiciled in the EU/EFTA since more forum rules are available. If the defendant is domiciled outside the EU/EFTA a conclusion cannot be drawn given that the Member States' own international forum rules have not been examined. If invalidity is raised the UP is advantageous to the plaintiff since more forum rules are available.[106]

Overall, the number of international jurisdiction rules available to the plaintiff **3.39** as well as the advantages for him/her can be illustrated as below. Two reservations apply:

---

105 If invalidity is raised in the EU art. 20 CPVR applies whereas art. 22(4) Lugano Convention applies by analogy if invalidity is raised in the EFTA.

106 The advantage for the plaintiff can, however, not be exaggerated since it is not up to the plaintiff to choose between the three rules. Rather it is up to the local or regional division, after having heard the parties, to decide where invalidity must be addressed cf. Chapter 11 section C.4.

3.40 One reservation is that some jurisdiction rules may overlap and therefore point at the same forum in a specific action e.g. may a 'place of action' coincide with the defendant's domicile. Another reservation is that a jurisdiction rule may be inapplicable in a specific action e.g. if the defendant has no establishment.

3.41 The number in brackets in the column 'advantages for the plaintiff' equals the factor overall identified as an advantage for the plaintiff in Chapter 1 section A.4.

Table 3.1 Jurisdiction rules overview

<table>
<tr><th colspan="3">GENERAL</th><th colspan="3">INTERNATIONAL JURISDICTION RULES AVAILABLE TO THE PLAINTIFF</th><th>CONCLUSION</th></tr>
<tr><th>IP right</th><th>Version</th><th>Domicile of the defendant</th><th>Infringement actions</th><th>Non-infringement actions</th><th>Invalidity</th><th>Advantages for the plaintiff</th></tr>
<tr><td rowspan="6">Trade Marks</td><td rowspan="3">National trademarks</td><td>In the EU</td><td>4</td><td>4</td><td>1</td><td rowspan="6">A national trademark is advantageous
→ To the plaintiff if the defendant is domiciled in the EU since more forum rules are available (1)
The EUTM is advantageous
→ To the plaintiff if the defendant is domiciled in the EFTA since more forum rules are available (1)</td></tr>
<tr><td>In the EFTA</td><td>4</td><td>4</td><td>1</td></tr>
<tr><td>Outside the EU/EFTA</td><td colspan="3">N/A</td></tr>
<tr><td rowspan="3">European Union Trademark (EUTM)</td><td>In the EU</td><td>3</td><td>2</td><td>1</td></tr>
<tr><td>In the EFTA</td><td>6</td><td>5</td><td>1</td></tr>
<tr><td>Outside the EU/EFTA</td><td>> 2</td><td>> 1</td><td>1</td></tr>
<tr><td rowspan="4">Designs</td><td>National designs</td><td colspan="4">What applies to national trademarks applies mutatis mutandis to national designs</td><td rowspan="4">Ibid.</td></tr>
<tr><td rowspan="3">Community Design (CD)</td><td>In the EU</td><td>3</td><td>2</td><td>1</td></tr>
<tr><td>In the EFTA</td><td>6</td><td>5</td><td>1</td></tr>
<tr><td>Outside the EU/EFTA</td><td>> 2</td><td>> 1</td><td>1</td></tr>
<tr><td rowspan="4">Plant Varieties</td><td>National plant varieties</td><td colspan="4">What applies to national trademarks applies mutatis mutandis to national plant varieties
(Except from its unregistered version which does not exist for plant varieties)</td><td rowspan="4">A national plant variety is advantageous
→ To the plaintiff if the defendant is domiciled in the EU since more forum rules are available (1)
The CPV is advantageous
→ To the plaintiff if the defendant is domiciled in the EFTA since more forum rules are available (1)</td></tr>
<tr><td rowspan="3">Community Plant Variety (CPV)</td><td>In the EU</td><td>3</td><td>3</td><td>1</td></tr>
<tr><td>In the EFTA</td><td>5</td><td>5</td><td>1</td></tr>
<tr><td>Outside the EU/EFTA</td><td>> 3</td><td>> 3</td><td>1</td></tr>
<tr><td rowspan="3">Patents</td><td>National patents</td><td colspan="4">What applies to national trademarks applies mutatis mutandis to national patents
(Except from its unregistered version which does not exist for patents)</td><td rowspan="3">A national patent is advantageous
→ To the plaintiff if the defendant is domiciled in the EU/EFTA since more forum rules are available (1)
A UP is advantageous
→ To the plaintiff if invalidity is raised since more forum rules are available</td></tr>
<tr><td rowspan="2">Unitary Patent (UP)</td><td>In a CMS</td><td>3</td><td>1</td><td>3</td></tr>
<tr><td>Outside a CMS</td><td>> 2</td><td>1</td><td>3</td></tr>
</table>

Part III

NATURE OF JURISDICTION RULES

4

GENERAL PRINCIPLES

A. INTRODUCTION

From Chapter 1[1] it follows that the nature of the international jurisdiction rules available to the plaintiff must be identified. Before doing so[2] the principles[3] underlying those rules[4] must be briefly outlined.[5] It is the purpose of this chapter to meet such an objective. **4.01**

1 Section A.3(c).

2 Chapters 5–11.

3 The terms 'principles' and 'general principles' are used synonymously for the purpose of the present study.

4 Marcus Norrgård, 'The European Principles of Intellectual Property Enforcement: Harmonisation through Communication'? in Ansgar Ohly (ed.) *Common Principles of European Intellectual Property Law*, Mohr Siebeck, 2012, p. 204 states that the term 'principles' may have different meanings. For the purpose of the present study the term 'principles' mean any such, *which* underlie – contribute to the interpretation of – the international jurisdiction rules and *which* are therefore referred to in Chapters 5–11.

5 The reason that the principles are briefly outlined is twofold, namely *that* it is outside the scope of the present study to undertake a thorough analysis of any such principles and *that* any such principles have already been subject to a thorough analysis in the legal literature cf., inter alia, Norrgård, ibid., p. 203; Annette Kur, 'Are There Any Common Principles of Private International Law with Regard to Intellectual Property' in Stefan Leible and Ansgar Ohly (eds), *Intellectual Property and Private International Law*, Mohr Siebeck, 2009, p. 1; Jannet A Pontier and Edwige Burg, *EU Principles on Jurisdiction and Recognition and Enforcement of Judgments in Civil and Commercial Matters according to the Case Law of the European Court of Justice*, TMC Asser Press, The Hague, 2004; Marcus Norrgård, Immaterialrättens Territorialitet, JFT, 2005, p. 572; Richard Fentiman, 'Choice of Law and Intellectual Property' in Josef Drexl and Annette Kur (eds), *Intellectual Property and Private International Law, Heading for the Future*, Hart Publishing, 2005, p. 129; Alexander Peukert, 'Territoriality and Extraterritoriality in Intellectual Property Law, Beyond Territoriality: Transnational Legal Authority in an Age of Globalization', in Günther Handl, Joachim Zekoll and Peer Zumbansen (eds), *Beyond Territoriality: Transnational Legal Authority in an Age of Globalization*, Queen Mary Studies in International Law, Brill Academic Publishing, Leiden/Boston, 2012, p. 189 and Graeme B. Dinwoodie, Developing a Private International Intellectual Property Law: The Demise of Territoriality? (2009) 51(2) *William and Mary Law Review* 713.

4.02 A distinction is drawn between the principles of effective enforcement of IP rights (section B); the principles of private international law (section C) and the principles of IP law (section D). In the end a conclusion is drawn, inter alia, by way of a table (section E).

B. PRINCIPLES OF EFFECTIVE ENFORCEMENT OF IP RIGHTS

4.03 The principles of effective enforcement of IP rights can be sub divided into a group of general procedural principles and a group of specific IP procedural principles.[6] The latter are derived from the former.[7]

4.04 From the general procedural principles it follows that excessive lengths of legal proceedings may violate the right to a fair trial in the ECHR[8] as interpreted by the ECtHR.[9] A fair trial is also guaranteed in the Charter[10] being part of EU law[11] and is acknowledged in CJEU case law as a 'principle of effective judicial protection'[12] and by the European Commission in a non-binding green paper as 'an obligation which is met by the Member States through the provision of swift and inexpensive legal proceedings'.[13] Thus, the general procedural principles provide for cost-effective, swift and fair proceedings.

4.05 From the specific IP procedural principles, which underlie both a national IP right and a European unitary IP right[14] it follows as a 'general obligation'[15] *that* procedures shall be available so as to permit 'effective action against any act of infringement'[16] and *that* the procedures 'shall not be unnecessarily complicated or costly or entail unreasonable time limits or unwarranted delays'.[17] Thus, the specific IP procedural principles also provide for cost-effective, swift and fair proceedings.

---

6 The distinction is a sub distinction of the overall group 'procedural principles' used by Norrgård, *supra* note 4, p. 206.

7 Ibid.

8 Art. 6 ECHR.

9 Norrgård, *supra* note 4, p. 207 note 8 with references and Jacobs, White and Ovey, *The European Convention on Human Rights*, Oxford University Press, 5th edn, 2010, p. 272 with references.

10 Art. 47 Charter.

11 Art. 6 TFEU.

12 Case C-432/05, *Unibet (London) Ltd. and Unibet (International) Ltd. v Justitiekanslern*, para. 37 cf. case C-7/98, *Dieter Krombach v André Bamberski*, paras 25–27.

13 Green Paper on Alternative Dispute Resolution in Civil and Commercial Matters, COM (2002) 196 final, p. 8.

14 Art. 2 and Recital (13) ED cf. arts 1(2), 15, 25 and 27 TRIPS and Daniel Gervais, *The TRIPS Agreement, Drafting History and Analysis*, Sweet & Maxwell, 2012, p. 177.

15 Arts 41 TRIPS and 3 ED.

16 Art. 41(1) TRIPS.

17 Arts 41(2) TRIPS and 3(1) ED.

Overall, therefore, trademark, design, plant variety and patent rights must be enforced in a cost-effective, swift and fair way.[18] **4.06**

C. PRINCIPLES OF PRIVATE INTERNATIONAL LAW

The principles of private international law encompass predictability (section 1), proximity, (section 2), avoiding forum shopping (section 3) and avoiding 'pollution'[19] (section 4). The principles are interconnected e.g. *if* forum shopping is restricted predictability is strengthened;[20] *if* 'pollution' is restricted predictability is strengthened[21] and *if* sufficient proximity is present predictability is strengthened.[22] The principles are non-exhaustive.[23] **4.07**

1. Predictability

Predictability is one private of the international law principles.[24] Predictability meets legal certainty.[25] The principle is laid down in Recital (15) Brussels I Regulation whereas 'the rules of jurisdiction *should* be highly predictable'[26] any wording has been softened compared to Recital (11) of the former Brussels I **4.08**

18 Norrgård, *supra* note 4, pp. 206–207 and Norrgård, *supra* note 5, p. 445.

19 For the purpose of the present study avoiding 'pollution' means that a court must be able to decide jurisdiction without considering the substance of the case.

20 Case C-269/95 *Francesco Benincasa v Dentalkit Srl*, para. 26.

21 Ibid., para. 27.

22 Recital (16) Brussels I Regulation.

23 A *fifth* principle of private international law would be procedural efficiency cf. Kur, *supra* note 5, p. 6. Any such principle coincides with the principle of effective enforcement of IP rights, which is addressed in section B. A *sixth* principle of private international law would be the principle of party autonomy cf. Kur, ibid. Any such principle is not addressed given that party autonomy is excluded from the present study cf. Chapter 1 section A.5(a) (limit 3). A *seventh* principle of private international law would be avoiding irreconcilable judgments cf. Recital (21) Brussels I Regulation. Any such principle is not addressed either given that *lis pendens* and related actions are also excluded from the present study cf. Chapter 1 section A.5(a) (limit 7). An *eighth* principle of private international law would be protection of the weaker party cf. Kur, ibid., p. 7. Any such principle is not addressed given that it is only randomly referred to in the study.

24 Kur, ibid. pp. 6–7 and Peter Arnt Nielsen, *International Privat- og Procesret*, Jurist- og Økonomforbundets Forlag, 1997, p. 29.

25 Case C-26/91, *Jakob Handte & Co. GmbH v Traitements Mécano-Chimiques des Surfaces (TMCS) SA*, para. 19; case C-256/00, *Besix SA v Wasserreinigungsbau Alfred Kretzschmar GmbH & Co. KG (WABAG) Planungs- und Forschungsgesellschaft Dipl. Ing. W. Kretzschmar GmbH & KG (Plafog)*, paras. 24–26; case C-288/92, *Custom Made Commercial Ltd. v Stawa Metallbau GmbH*, para. 18; case C-440/97, *GIE Groupe Concorde and Others v The Master of the vessel 'Suhadiwarno Panjan' and Others*, para. 23; case C-281/02, *Andrew Owusu v N.B. Jackson, trading as 'Villa Holidays Bal-Inn Villas' and Others*, para. 38 and Report on the Convention on Jurisdiction and the Enforcement of Judgments in Civil and Commercial Matters, signed at Brussels 27 September 1968, by P. Jenard, Director in the Belgium Ministry of Foreign Affairs and External Trade, p. 15.

26 In the German, French, Swedish and Danish versions of the text the word *should* is also used cf. 'sollten', 'devraient', 'bör' and 'bør' (emphasis added).

Regulation[27] which read 'the rules of jurisdiction *must* be highly predictable'.[28] Predictability is not met if jurisdiction is conferred on wholly unforeseeable places.[29] The predictability principle has, it seems, developed over time from early CJEU case law to be interpreted one-sidedly as to 'enable a normally well-informed defendant reasonably to predict before which courts, other than those of the State in which he is domiciled, he may be sued'[30] or in the words of the AG to enable 'the defendant [to] be in a position to know precisely [...] before which court or courts it risks being sued'[31] (predictability relates to the defendant) into in later CJEU case law to be interpreted two-sidedly as to 'allow the claimant to easily identify the court before which he may bring an action and the defendant reasonably to foresee the court before which he may be sued'[32] (predictability relates to the plaintiff and to the defendant).

4.09 The predictability principle most likely also applies outside the scope of the BR given that it expresses general considerations and common sense.[33]

2. Proximity

4.10 Proximity is another private international law principle.[34] Proximity requires a distinction between the defendant's domicile rule[35] and the special jurisdiction rules.[36]

27 Regulation 44/2001 of 22 December 2000 on Jurisdiction and the Recognition and Enforcement of Judgments in Civil and Commercial Matters.

28 In the German, French and Swedish versions of the text the word *must* is also used cf. 'müssen', 'doivent' and 'måste' whereas in the Danish version of the text the word *should* is used cf. 'bør' (emphasis added).

29 Opinion of Advocate General Cosmas in case C-51/97, *Réunion européenne SA and Others v Spliethoff's Bevrachtingskantoor BV and the Master of the vessel Alblasgracht V002*, para. 56 and judgment of the CJEU, para. 34; Opinion of Advocate General Jacobs in case C-18/02, *Danmarks Rederiforening, acting on behalf of DFDS Torline A/S v LO Landsorganisationen i Sverige, acting on behalf of SEKO Sjöfolk Facket för Service och Kommunikation*, para. 56 and case C-364/93, *Antonio Marinari v Lloyds Bank plc and Zubaidi Trading Company*, para. 19.

30 Case C-26/91, *Jakob Handte & Co. GmbH*, para. 18; case C-440/97, *GIE Groupe Concorde and Others*, para. 24 and case C-256/00, *Besix SA*, para. 26.

31 Opinion of Advocate General Darmon (first opinion) in case C-68/93, *Fiona Shevill, Ixora Trading Inc., Chequepoint SARL and Chequepoint International Ltd. v Presse Alliance SA*, para. 75.

32 Case C-18/02, *Danmarks Rederiforening*, , para. 20; Joined cases C-509/09, *e-Date Advertising GmbH v X and case C-161/10, Olivier Martinez and Robert Martinez v MGN Ltd.*, para. 50 and case C-327/10, *Hypoteční banka a.s. v Mike Lindner*, para. 44.

33 Opinion of Advocate General Jääskinen in case C-360/12, *Coty Prestige Lancaster Group GmbH v First Note Perfumes NV*, para. 35.

34 Jannet A Pontier and Edwige Burg, *EU Principles on Jurisdiction and Recognition and Enforcement of Judgments in Civil and Commercial Matters according to the Case Law of the European Court of Justice*, TMC Asser Press, The Hague, 2004, pp. 160 *et seq.* and Nielsen, *supra* note 24, p. 28.

35 Art. 4 BR.

36 Chapter II Section 2 BR.

For the defendant's domicile rule proximity is the domicile itself[37] whereas for the special jurisdiction rules it is either 'a close connection between the court and the action or [a] sound administration of justice' cf. Recital (16) Brussels I Regulation. **4.11**

The way the CJEU has applied Recital (16) Brussels I Regulation to the special jurisdiction rules has, it seems, developed.[38] In early 1976 case law a court was competent 'having regard to the existence [...] of a particular close connecting factor between the dispute and the court [...] with a view to the efficacious conduct of the proceedings'[39] (meaning that the efficacious proceedings was the connecting factor, which justified jurisdiction). In later 1988–2004 case law jurisdiction could be 'based on the existence of a particularly close connecting factor between the dispute and [the court] for reasons relating to the sound administration of justice and the efficacious conduct of proceedings'[40] (meaning that the sound administration of justice and efficacious proceedings were the connecting factors, which justified jurisdiction). In recent 2002–09 case law jurisdiction can be **4.12**

> based on the existence of a particularly close connecting factor between a dispute and the courts [...] which justifies the attribution of jurisdiction to those courts for reasons relating to the sound administration of justice and the efficacious conduct of proceedings. The courts [...] are usually the most appropriate for deciding the case, in particular on the grounds of proximity and ease of taking evidence[41]

(meaning that the sound administration of justice, efficacious proceedings, proximity or easy access to evidence are the connecting factors, which justify jurisdiction). The development can be illustrated as in Figure 4.1 below.

From Figure 4.1 it follows, inter alia, *that* the grounds justifying jurisdiction are alternatives in Recital (16) Brussels I Regulation whereas the grounds are subordinate to a close connection in CJEU case law; *that* therefore a close connection is not *as such* a connecting factor in CJEU case law contrary to **4.13**

---

37 Ulrich Magnus and Peter Mankowski, *Brussels I Regulation* European Commentaries on Private International Law, 2nd revised edn, Sellier European Law Publishers, 2012, p. 80.

38 Case law referred to *infra* notes 39–41 is based on arts 7(2) and 7(5) BR.

39 Case 21/76, *Handelskwekerij G.J. Bier BV v Mines de potasse d'Alsace SA*, para. 11 and case 33/78, *Somafer SA v Saar-Ferngas AG*, para. 7.

40 Case C-220/88, *Dumez France SA and Tracoba SARL v Hessische Landesbank and Others*, para. 17; case C-68/93, *Fiona Shevill*, para. 19; case C-364/93, *Antonio Marinari*, para. 10; case C-51/97, *Réunion européenne SA*, para. 27 and case C-168/02, *Rudolf Kronhofer v Marianne Maier and Others*, para. 15.

41 Case C-167/00, *Verein für Konsumenteninformation v Karl Heinz Henkel*, para. 46; Opinion of Advocate General Jacobs in case C-18/02, *Danmarks Rederiforening* , para. 40 and case C-189/08, *Zuid-Chemie BV v Philippo's Mineralenfabriek NV/SA*, para. 24.

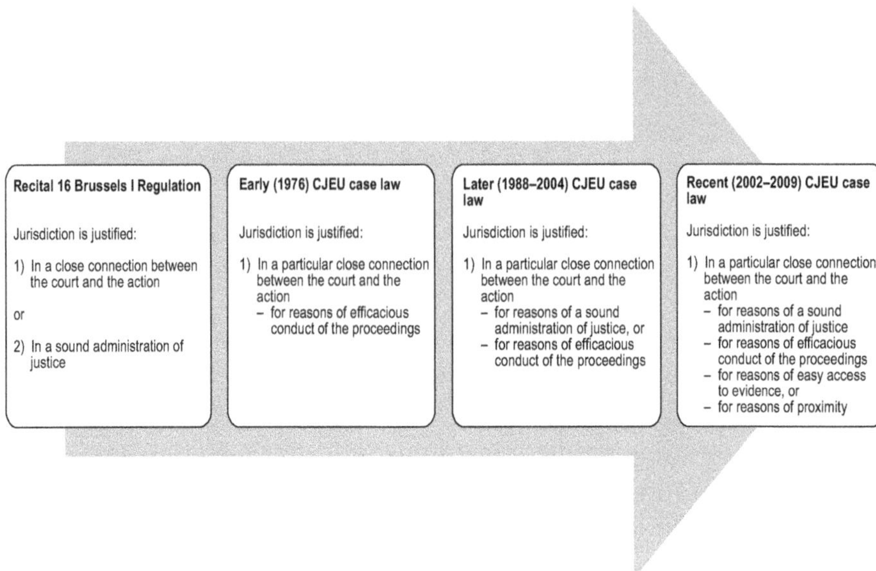

Figure 4.1 Proximity principle development

Recital (16) Brussels I Regulation;[42] *that* the CJEU seems to justify a close connection with more and more subordinate grounds i.e. efficient proceedings in early 1976 case law to efficient proceedings and sound administration of justice in later 1998–2004 case law and efficient proceedings, sound administration of justice, easy access to evidence and proximity in recent 2002–09 case law; *that* the reasons given by the CJEU overlap to some extent e.g. may easy access to evidence overlap with a sound administration of justice and finally *that* Recital (16) Brussels I Regulation speaks of a 'close' connection between the court and the action whereas CJEU case law speaks of a 'particular close' connecting factor between the court and the action thus strengthening the requirement.[43] Despite the apparent disharmony between Recital (16) Brussels I Regulation and CJEU case law this is not the case since behind the recital lies the general principle of private international law to search for proximity.[44]

42 Magnus and Mankowski, , *supra* note 37, p. 106.

43 European Parliament Resolution of 7 September 2010 on the Implementation and Review of Council Regulation No 44/2001 similarly strengthened the requirement given that it spoke of a 'sufficient, substantial or significant link' cf. 2009/2140(INI), P7 TA(2010)0304, Recital Q and point 25.

44 Report by P. Jenard *supra* note 25, p. 22; Magnus and Mankowski, *supra* note 37, p. 105 with references; Nielsen, n 24, p. 150 and Ketilbjørn Hertz, *Jurisdiction in Contract and Tort under the Brussels Convention*, DJØF Publishing Copenhagen, 1998, p. 87.

The proximity principle most likely also applies outside the scope of the BR given that it expresses general considerations and common sense.[45] **4.14**

3. Avoiding forum shopping

Avoiding forum shopping is a third private international law principle.[46] Forum shopping has at least two meanings. One is whether the plaintiff can shop between different forum rules[47] and another is whether the plaintiff can shop between different fora within one and the same forum rule.[48] Whereas the former is accepted[49] the latter seems, with exceptions,[50] apparently to not be accepted, considering the wording of the CJEU where it must be avoided 'so far as possible, creating a situation in which a number of courts have jurisdiction in respect of one and the same [legal relationship]'[51] since otherwise the risk of irreconcilable judgments would increase,[52] which in turn could jeopardize predictability.[53] Even though it has not been stressed in case law and despite any clear definition in the legal literature[54] it seems to be a requirement that the legal relationships (e.g. delicts) arise out of the *same* legal matter since legal relationships (e.g. delicts) arising out of *different* legal matters terminologically speaking cannot be subject to forum shopping.[55] **4.15**

The avoiding forum shopping principle most likely also applies outside the scope of the BR given its character as a general principle.[56] **4.16**

---

45 Opinion of Advocate General Jääskinen in case C-360/12, *Coty Prestige Lancaster Group GmbH*, para. 35.

46 Nielsen, *supra* note 24, pp. 95–6.

47 Chapter 1 section A.4 (factor 1).

48 Chapter 1 section A.4 (factor 2).

49 Chapter 3.

50 Case 21/76, *Handelskwekerij G. J. Bier BV*, para. 25 and Kur, *supra* note 5, p. 8 and Pontier and Burg, *supra* note 34, p. 100.

51 Case 14/76, *De Bloos, SPRL v Société en Commandite par Actions Bouyer*, para. 9; case C-220/88, *Dumez France SA and Tracoba SARL*, para. 18; case C-125/92, *Mulox IBC Ltd. v Hendrick Geels*, para. 21 cf. Opinion of Advocate General Darmon (first opinion) in case C-68/93, *Fiona Shevill*, para. 57 and Pontier and Burg, *supra* note 34, p. 98.

52 Case C-220/88, *Dumez France SA and Tracoba SARL*, para. 18.

53 Case C-256/00, *Besix SA*, paras 24–26 and *supra* section C.1.

54 James C. Fawcett and Paul Torremanns, *Intellectual Property and Private International Law*, 2nd edn, Oxford University Press, 2011 at 5.252 *et seq.* and Magnus and Mankowski, *supra* note 37, pp. 564 *et seq.*

55 Case 21/76, *Handelskwekerij G. J. Bier BV* and case C-68/93, *Fiona Shevill* are both examples of delicts arising out of the same legal matter. In *Bier* the harm to the plantations was due to polluted water being discharged into the Rhine (one same legal matter) and in *Shevill* the harm to the plaintiff's honour was due to infringement of her personality right (one same legal matter). By contrast case C-523/10, *Wintersteiger AG* is an example of delicts arising out of different legal matters due to the territoriality principle underlying trademark rights cf. Chapter 9 section B.1(a)(ii) Principle 3: Avoiding forum shopping.

56 *Supra* note 46.

4. Avoiding 'pollution'

4.17 Avoiding 'pollution' is a fourth private international law principle.[57] Following the principle the BR must be interpreted in a way that enables the courts to decide jurisdiction without considering the substance of the case[58] since otherwise the procedural and the substantial law stages would be 'polluted', which would run counter to predictability.[59]

4.18 The avoiding 'pollution' principle most likely also applies outside the scope of the BR given its character as a general principle.[60]

D. PRINCIPLES OF IP LAW

4.19 The principles of IP law cover territoriality.[61] Following the principle an IP right is limited to the state/region that has granted it and the IP right can only cover activities that have occurred there.[62] The principle is reflected in international conventions,[63] agreements,[64] treaties,[65] in applicable law rules[66]

57 Pontier and Burg, *supra* note 34, p. 108.

58 Case C-269/95, *Francesco Benincasa*, para. 27; case C-288/92, *Custom Made Commercial Ltd*, para. 20 and case 34/82, *Martin Peters Bauunternehmung GmbH v Zuid Nederlandse Aannemers Vereniging*, para. 17.

59 Section C.1.

60 Nielsen, n 24, pp. 25 *et seq.*

61 Kur, *supra* note 5, p. 6; Norrgård, *supra* note 5, pp. 572 *et seq.*; Richard Fentiman, 'Choice of Law and Intellectual Property' in Josef Drexl and Annette Kur (eds) *Intellectual Property and Private International Law, Heading for the Future*, Hart Publishing, 2005, pp. 132 *et seq.*; Peukert, *supra* note 5, pp. 189 *et seq.*; Dinwoodie, *supra* note 5, p. 713; Benedetta Ubertazzi, *Exclusive Jurisdiction in Intellectual Property*, Max Planck Institut für Ausländisches und Internationales Privatrecht, Mohr Siebeck, 2012, pp. 138 *et seq.*; M. Virgos Soriano and F.J. Garcimartin Alférez, Derecho Procesal Civil Internacional Litigación Internacional, Thomson-Civitas, 2007, pp. 194–5 and Jürgen Basedow, Toshiyuki Kono and Axel Metzger, *Intellectual Property in the Global Arena, Jurisdiction, Applicable Law and the Recognition of Judgments in Europe, Japan and the US*, MatIPR 49, Mohr Siebeck, 2010, pp. 68–9.

62 Peukert, ibid., pp. 189–90 and 194.

63 Art. 5(2) Berne Convention for the Protection of Literary and Artistic Works of September 9, 1886 completed at Paris on May 4, 1896 revised at Berlin on November 13, 1908 completed at Berne on March 20, 1914 revised at Rome on June 2, 1928 at Brussels on June 26, 1948 at Stockholm on July 14, 1967 and at Paris on July 24, 1971 and amended on September 28, 1979 speaking of the 'laws of the country where protection is claimed' and arts 2, 3 and 64 Convention on the Grant of European Patents of 5 October 1973 as revised by the act revising art. 63 EPC of 17 December 1991 and the act revising the EPC of 29 November 2000.

64 Preamble TRIPS speaking of 'taking into account differences in national legal systems'.

65 Preamble Patent Corporation Treaty done at Washington on June 19, 1970 as amended on September 28, 1979 as modified on February 3, 1984 and on October 3, 2001 speaking of 'desiring to simplify and render more economical the obtaining of protection for inventions where protection is sought in several countries'.

66 Art. 8 cf. Recital (26) Rome II Regulation.

and is recognized by the CJEU.[67] The principle underlies both a national IP right[68] and a European unitary IP right.[69]

E. CONCLUSION

The principles, which all most likely underlie both a national IP right and a European unitary IP right and which, with variations, contribute to the interpretation of the international jurisdiction rules in Chapters 5–11 count principles of effective enforcement of IP rights, principles of private international law and principles of IP law. **4.20**

The principles of effective enforcement of IP rights require trademark, design, plant variety and patent rights to be enforced in a cost-effective, swift and fair way. **4.21**

The principles of private international law include predictability, proximity, avoiding forum shopping and avoiding 'pollution'. Predictability requires the plaintiff to identify where to bring an action and the defendant to foresee where it will be sued. Proximity requires a nexus between the action and the court in terms of either a domicile or a subject matter. Avoiding forum shopping requires the number of competent courts in respect of one and the same legal relationship to be limited and avoiding 'pollution' requires the courts to be able to decide jurisdiction without considering the substance of the case. **4.22**

The principles of IP law count territoriality meaning that the IP right in question is limited to the state/region that has granted it and that the IP right can only cover activities that have occurred there. The above can be illustrated as in Table 4.1 below. **4.23**

67 Case C-192/04, *Lagardère Active Broadcast v Société pour la perception de la rémunération équitable (SPRE) and Gesellschaft zur Verwertung von Leistungsschutzrechten mbH (GVL)*, para. 46; case C-4/03, *Gesellschaft für Antriebstechnik mbH & Co. KG v Lamellen und Kupplungsbau Beteiligungs KG*, para. 31; case C-539/03, *Roche Nederland BV and Others v Frederick Primus and Milton Goldenberg*, para. 31; case C-523/10, *Wintersteiger AG*, para. 25; case C-170/12, *Peter Pinckney v KDG Mediatech AG*, para. 39 and case C-387/12, *Hi Hotel HCF SARL v Uwe Spoering*, para. 39.

68 Ibid.

69 Arts 1(2) EUTMR, 1(3) CDR, 2 CPVR and 3(2) UPR cf. 2(f) AUPC.

Table 4.1 General principles overview

	SCOPE	IMPACT
Principles of effective enforcement of IP rights	• Underlies a national IP right • Underlies a European unitary IP right	• IP rights must be enforced in a cost-effective way • IP rights must be enforced in a swift way • IP rights must be enforced in a fair way
Principles of private international law	• Underlies a national IP right • Underlies a European unitary IP right	• IP jurisdiction must be predictable • IP jurisdiction must be proximate • IP jurisdiction must avoid forum shopping • IP jurisdiction must avoid 'pollution'
Principles of IP law	• Underlies a national IP right • Underlies a European unitary IP right	• IP rights are limited to the state/region of grant

5

DEFENDANT'S DOMICILE RULE

A. INTRODUCTION

From Chapter 1[1] it follows that the nature of the international jurisdiction rules available to the plaintiff must be identified. The purpose of Chapter 5 is to meet any such objective for the defendant's domicile rule[2] also known as *actor sequitur forum rei*[3] or *forum domicilii*.[4] Thus, the various versions of the **5.01**

1 Section A.3(c).

2 The defendant's domicile rule is one of the jurisdiction rules covered by the present study cf. Chapter 1 section A.3(c).

3 Toshiyuki Kono, *Studies in Private International Law, Intellectual Property and Private International Law, Comparative Perspectives*, Hart Publishing, 2012, p. 24.

4 Marcus Norrgård, 'Gemenskapsvarumärket och de Nationella Domstolarnas Internationella Behörighet, Nordiskt Immateriellt Rättsskydd (NIR)', 3/1998, p. 455 at 457.

rule are addressed and compared at the present stage, which leads to identify the advantages for the plaintiff.[5]

5.02 A distinction is drawn between the defendant's domicile rule applying to a national IP right (section B) and the defendant's domicile rule applying to a corresponding European unitary IP right (section C). In the end a conclusion is drawn, inter alia, by way of a table (section D).

B. THE DEFENDANT'S DOMICILE RULE APPLYING TO A NATIONAL IP RIGHT

5.03 Different defendant's domicile rules apply to a national IP right. The application depends on whether the defendant is domiciled in the EU/EFTA (section 1) or outside the EU/EFTA (section 2).[6]

1. Defendant is domiciled in the EU/EFTA

5.04 If the defendant is domiciled in the EU/EFTA art. 4 BR applies. Below a distinction is drawn between applying the rule to infringement actions (section a); to non-infringement actions (section b) and to invalidity actions (section c).[7]

(a) Art. 4 BR to infringement actions

5.05 Art. 4 BR states that: '[…] persons domiciled in a Member State [State bound by the Lugano Convention] shall, whatever their nationality, be sued in the courts of that Member State [State bound by the Lugano Convention]'.[8]

5.06 The provision expresses a basic principle[9] as also laid down in the recital to the Brussels I Regulation[10] that defendants must be sued where they are domiciled. The justification is twofold, namely to protect the defendant[11] and to

5 The factors defining the advantages for the plaintiff are overall identified in Chapter 1 section A.4.

6 The reason for the distinction between defendants domiciled in the EU/EFTA and defendants domiciled outside the EU/EFTA is that parallel rules govern the former defendants cf. Chapter 2 sections B.1–B.2.

7 The three kinds of actions are overall defined in Chapter 1 section A.3(b).

8 Art. 4 BR.

9 Ulrich Magnus and Peter Mankowski, *Brussels I Regulation*, 2nd revised edn, Sellier European Law Publishers, 2012, p. 78 and *Conflict of Laws in Intellectual Property, The CLIP Principles and Commentary*, European Max Planck Group on Conflicts of Laws in Intellectual Property, Oxford University Press, 2013, p. 56 (2:101.C01) with references.

10 Recital (15) Brussels I Regulation.

11 Case 220/84, *AS-Autoteile Service GmbH v Pierre Malhé*, para. 15; case C-26/91, *Jakob Handte v Traitements Mécano-chimiques des Surfaces*, para. 14; case C-412/98, *Group Josi Reinsurance Company SA v Universal*

allow the plaintiff to bring unrestricted claims at any such place.[12] Exceptions to the rule must be interpreted strictly[13] any which requirement, however, seems to have been softened in case law[14] and in the Brussels I Regulation.[15]

The provision applies when the defendant is domiciled in the EU/EFTA regardless of his/her nationality[16] and regardless of the domicile of the plaintiff.[17] Infringement actions[18] and threatened infringement actions[19] can both be brought under the provision. The provision is subject to unlimited full **5.07**

General Insurance Company (UGIC), para. 35 and case C-256/00, *Besix SA v Wasserreinigungsbau Alfred Kretzschmar GmbH & Co. KG (WABAG) and Planungs- und Forschungsgesellschaft Dipl. Ing. W. Kretzschmar GmbH & KG (Plafog)*, para. 52 cf. Report on the Convention on Jurisdiction and the Enforcement of Judgments in Civil and Commercial Matters (signed at Brussels 27 September 1968) by P. Jenard, Director in the Belgium Ministry of Foreign Affairs and External Trade, at 18; Jan Kropholler, Europäisches Zivilprocessrecht, 9th edn, 2011, pp. 117 *et seq*; James J. Fawcett and Paul Torremans, *Intellectual Property and Private International Law*, 2nd edn, Oxford Private International Law Series, 2011 at 5.07; Annette Kur, 'Jurisdiction and Enforcement of Foreign Judgments – the General Structure of the MPI Proposal' in Josef Drexl and Annette Kur (eds) *Intellectual Property and Private International Law – Heading for the Future*, Hart Publishing 2005, pp. 21 and 31; *Conflict of Laws in Intellectual Property, The CLIP Principles and Commentary*, *supra* note 9, p. 56 (2:101.C01) and Kono, *supra* note 3, p. 23.

12 Annette Kur and Thomas Dreier (eds), *European Intellectual Property Law, Text, Cases and Materials*, Edward Elgar, 2013, p. 486; Magnus and Mankowski, ibid., p. 78; Fawcett and Torremans, ibid., at 5.08; *The CLIP Principles and Commentary*, ibid., p. 58 (2:201.N01); Kono, ibid., p. 24 note 110 with references and case C-68/93, *Fiona Shevill, Ixora Trading Inc., Chequepoint SARL and Chequepoint International Ltd. v Presse Alliance SA*, paras 25–26.

13 Chapters 6, 8 and 9.

14 Case C-523/10, *Wintersteiger AG v Products 4U Sondermaschinenbau GmbH* where the CJEU widened the scope of art. 7(2) BR by allowing actions to be brought where a trademark is registered cf. para. 29 and Chapter 9 section B.1(a) and joined cases C-509/09, *e-Date Advertising GmbH v X* and C-161/10, *Olivier Martinez and Robert Martinez v MGN Ltd.* where the CJEU in an online personality rights case also widened the scope of art. 7(2) BR by allowing actions to be brought at the courts of the plaintiff's own domicile – the 'centre of interest' – having unlimited full jurisdiction cf. para. 52.

15 According to Recital (15) Brussels I Regulation 'the rules of jurisdiction *should* be [...] founded on the principle that jurisdiction is generally based on the defendant's domicile. Jurisdiction *should* always be available on this ground save in a few well-defined situations [...]' whereas in Recital (11) of the former Brussels I Regulation (44/2001) 'the rules of jurisdiction *must* be [...] founded on the principle that jurisdiction is generally based on the defendant's domicile and jurisdiction *must* always be available on this ground save in a few well-defined situations [...]'. Thus, the word 'must' under the former Brussels I Regulation (44/2001) has been replaced with the word 'should' under the current Brussels I Regulation indicating a softening of the use of the defendant's domicile as the basic principle.

16 Case C-327/10, *Hypoteční banka a.s. v Udo Mike Lindner*, para. 31 cf. Magnus and Mankowski, *supra* note 9, p. 78.

17 Case C-412/98, *Group Josi Reinsurance Company SA v Universal General Insurance Company (UGIC)*, para. 78.

18 Fawcett and Torremans, *supra* note 11 at 5.07 note 24 with references and Kono, *supra* note 3, p. 24.

19 The possibility of bringing threatened infringement actions does not follow explicitly from arts 4 BR as opposed to 7(2) BR. Given art. 4 BR's nature as a basic principle cf. *supra* note 9 threatened infringement actions must be permitted. Any such interpretation corresponds, with variations, to its 'sister' rules in arts 97(1) cf. 96(a) EUTMR cf. section C.1(a); arts 82(1) cf. 81(a) CDR cf. section C.2(a) and arts 33(1)(b) cf. 32(1)(a) AUPC cf. section C.4(a) but contrasts arts 101(2)(a) cf. 94 CPVR where threatened infringement actions are not permitted cf. Fawcett and Torremans, ibid. at 8.146 and section C.3(a).

jurisdiction[20] unless the plaintiff chooses otherwise. The principle of *forum non-conveniens* does not apply.[21]

5.08 The term 'domicile' is separately defined for natural and legal persons.

5.09 Domicile for natural persons is not subject to an autonomous definition in the BR.[22] Rather a conflicts rule is provided for where the court where the action is brought must apply its own internal law to determine whether the defendant is domiciled there.[23]

5.10 Domicile for legal persons is by contrast subject to an autonomous definition.[24] The definition lists three exhaustive, equal and non-hierarchical alternatives.[25] The first one is 'statutory seat' meaning the Member State where the legal person is incorporated.[26] The second one is 'central administration'[27] meaning the Member State where the primary functions of the legal person are found (i.e. the management and control centre),[28] excluding Member States where the secondary functions are found (i.e. the accounting or tax departments).[29] The third one is 'principal place of business'[30] meaning the Member State where the main business activities are located.[31]

5.11 If all three places are located within the same Member State (e.g. Germany) the legal person can be sued there.[32] If only one of the places are located in a

---

20 *Supra* note 12.

21 Case C-281/02, *Andrew Owusu v N.B. Jackson, trading as 'Villa Holidays Bal-Inn Villas' and Others*, paras. 37–43 cf. Kur and Dreier, *supra* note 12, pp. 488 *et seq.*

22 Art. 62 BR.

23 Case C-327/10, *Hypoteční banka a.s.*, para. 40 cf. Magnus and Mankowski, *supra* note 9, pp. 807–8; Jan Kropholler and J Hein, *Europäisches Zivilprocessrecht*, 9th edn, 2011, pp. 693 *et seq.*; James Fawcett and Janeen M Carruthers, *Cheshire, North and Fawcett, Private International Law*, Oxford University Press, 2008, pp. 210–11 and Fawcett and Torremans, *supra* note 11 at 8.15.

24 Art. 63 BR cf. Recital (15) Brussels I Regulation.

25 Magnus and Mankowski, *supra* note 9, p. 811 and Kropholler and Hein, *supra* note 23, pp. 698 *et seq.*

26 Art. 63(1)(a) BR cf. Magnus and Mankowski, ibid., p. 811. For Member States where the concept of 'statutory seat' is unknown, i.e. UK and Ireland, art. 63(2) BR applies.

27 Art. 63(1)(b) BR.

28 Bundesgerichtshof 27 June 2007, XII ZB, 114/06 [2008], NJW-RR 551 at 11 and Queen's Bench Division, Commercial Court in case 889457 *Alberta Inc. v Katanga Mining Ltd*, [2008] EWHC 2679 (Comm) at 23.

29 *Conflict of Laws in Intellectual Property, The CLIP Principles and Commentary*, *supra* note 9, p. 170 (2:601.C06) note 7 referring to Bundesarbeitsgericht 23 January 2008, 5 AZR 60/07 [2008] NJW 2797 at 2798 [16].

30 Natural persons can also be sued at their 'principal place of business' but the legal basis is not arts 63(1)(c) BR but rather 7(5) BR cf. Magnus and Mankowski, *supra* note 9, p. 280 and Chapter 6 section B.1(a).

31 Art. 63(1)(c) BR cf. Magnus and Mankowski, ibid., p. 812. Art. 63(1)(c) BR contrasts art. 2:601(3) CLIP Principles which does not refer to the place where the main business activities are located but rather to the place from which the external activities are conducted cf. *Conflict of Laws in Intellectual Property, The CLIP Principles and Commentary*, *supra* note 9, p. 86 (2:203.C05) and p. 171 (2:601.C07).

32 Magnus and Mankowski, ibid., p. 811.

Member State (e.g. Germany) while the remaining two are located outside the Member States (e.g. in China and in the US) the legal person can be sued in the Member State.[33] If all three places are located in three different Member States the legal person can, at the plaintiff's discretion, be sued in any one of these.[34] An establishment does not constitute a domicile for the purpose of art. 63 BR cf. Chapter 6.

Applying the example in Chapter 1 section 2 Frogs GmbH may bring an infringement action against Frox SpA within the meaning of arts 4 cf. 63 BR in Italy (where Frox SpA has its statutory seat) or in the Netherlands (where Frox SpA has its management and control centre) or in France (where Frox SpA has its principal place of business). The courts in any of these places are subject to unlimited full jurisdiction unless Frogs GmbH chooses otherwise.

(b) *Art. 4 BR to non-infringement actions*

The possibility of bringing non-infringement actions does not follow from art. 4 BR. Given art. 4 BR's nature as a basic principle[35] such actions must be permitted, which in turn is supported by scholarly reports,[36] by legal scholars[37] and by corresponding European unitary IP rights where non-infringement actions, with variations, may also be brought at the defendant's domicile.[38] **5.12**

(c) *Art. 4 BR to invalidity actions*

If invalidity is raised during the infringement or non-infringement actions brought under art. 4 BR a distinction must be drawn between registered national IP rights where invalidity leads to split adjudication given that art. 24(4) BR and *Gat LuK*[39] apply and unregistered national IP rights where invalidity leads to joint adjudication given that art. 24(4) BR and *Gat LuK* do not apply. Art. 24(4) BR and *Gat LuK* are addressed in Chapter 11 section B. **5.13**

---

33 Ibid.

34 Explanatory Report on the Convention on Jurisdiction and the Recognition and Enforcement of Judgments in Civil and Commercial Matters, signed in Lugano on 30 October 2007, by Professor Fausto Pocar, p. 8 (at 28).

35 *Supra* note 9.

36 Arts 2:602 cf. 2:101 CLIP Principles and §§ 213 cf. 201 ALI Principles.

37 *Conflict of Laws in Intellectual Property, The CLIP Principles and Commentary, supra* note 9, p. 176 (2:602.N04).

38 Arts 97(1) cf. 96(b) EUTMR cf. section C.1(b); arts 82(1) cf. 81(b) CDR cf. section C.2(b); art. 101(2)(a) CPVR cf. section C.3(b) and, under certain circumstances, arts 33(4) cf. 33(1)(b) AUPC cf. section C.4(b).

39 Case C-4/03, *Gesellschaft für Antriebstechnik mbH & Co. KG v Lamellen und Kupplungsbau Beteiligungs KG.*

2. Defendant is domiciled outside the EU/EFTA

5.14 If the defendant is domiciled outside the EU/EFTA third states' own international forum rules apply.[40] For the reasons in Chapter 1 section A.5(a) (limit 5) any such rules, including the conditions under which they may apply are not examined for the purpose of the present study.

C. THE DEFENDANT'S DOMICILE RULE APPLYING TO A EUROPEAN UNITARY IP RIGHT

5.15 Four different defendant's domicile rules apply depending on the corresponding European unitary IP right in question. If a EUTM has been infringed the defendant's domicile rule in the EUTMR applies (section 1); if a CD has been infringed the defendant's domicile rule in the CDR applies (section 2); if a CPV has been infringed the defendant's domicile rule in the CPVR applies (section 3) and if a UP has been infringed the defendant's domicile rule in the AUPC applies (section 4).

1. The defendant's domicile rule in the EUTMR

5.16 The defendant's domicile rule is found in art. 97(1) EUTMR. The CJEU has yet to interpret the provision[41] and no case is pending.[42] Below a distinction is drawn between applying the rule to infringement actions (section a); to non-infringement actions (section b) and to invalidity actions (section c).[43]

(a) Art. 97(1) EUTMR to infringement actions

5.17 Art. 97(1) EUTMR allows[44] infringement actions[45] to be brought in: '[...] the courts of the Member State in which the defendant is domiciled [...]'.[46]

---

40 Changing the example in Chapter 1 section 2 so that Frox is based in the US whereas Frogs is still based in Germany, Frogs may bring an action against Frox in the US being the defendant's domicile.

41 Study on the Overall Functioning of the European Trade Mark System presented by Max Planck Institute for Intellectual Property and Competition Law Munich of 15 February 2011 at 3.126 (p. 156).

42 Curia.eu visited on 1 January 2017.

43 The three kinds of actions are overall defined in Chapter 1 section A.3(b).

44 The reason for using the term 'allows', contrary to art. 97(1) EUTMR using the term 'shall', is that infringement actions may also be brought under the *forum delicti* rule in art. 97(5) EUTMR cf. Chapter 9 section C.1(a) meaning that two alternatives are available to the plaintiff. In addition to that 'fall back' rules may apply cf. Chapter 3 section C.1.

45 Art. 96(a) EUTMR.

46 Art. 97(1)(first part) EUTMR. art. 97(1)(second part) EUTMR adds '[...] or if he is not domiciled in any of the Member States, in which he has an establishment'. The addition is addressed in Chapter 6 section C.1(a).

The provision is modelled on the corresponding provisions in the 1975 Community Patent Convention[47] and in the protocol to the amended 1989 version.[48] The reason for adopting the provision is that it expresses a general rule[49] and so the underlying justifications equal the ones behind its 'sister' provision in art. 4 BR, which therefore apply *mutatis mutandis* cf. section B.1(a). 5.18

Compared to its 'sister' provision in art. 4 BR the provision is similar *since* it also speaks of 'domicile' and *since* it is also subject to unlimited full jurisdiction[50] unless the plaintiff chooses otherwise[51] but different *since* jurisdiction is allocated at the defendant's EU[52] and not EU/EFTA[53] domicile and *since* bringing threatened infringement actions requires that national law so permits,[54] which is not a requirement under art. 4 BR.[55] 5.19

The term 'domicile' is not defined in the EUTMR.[56] Given the lack of CJEU case law[57] one could argue that 'domicile' must be interpreted independently, which is supported by the fact that art. 4 BR, where the term 'domicile' is used cf. section B.1(a), has been exempted in the EUTMR.[58] Any such interpretation seems, however, unlikely given that the BR acts as 'fall back' where the EUTMR is silent[59] meaning that arts 62 and 63 BR apply. Thus, the term 5.20

47 Art. 69(1)(first sentence) Convention for the European Patent for the Common Market (Community Patent Convention) (76/76/EEC) of 15 December 1975 which, however, does not speak of 'domicile' but rather of 'residence' in line with art. 33(1)(b) AUPC cf. section C.4(a).

48 Art. 15(1) Protocol on the Settlement of Litigation Concerning the Infringement and Validity of Community Patents of 30 December 1989 (Protocol of Litigation).

49 Bulletin of the European Communities Supplement 5/80, New Trade Mark System for the Community, proposed Directive and Regulation prepared by the Commission of the European Communities (COM 80 635 final 19 November 1980), p. 76.

50 Art. 98(1)(a) EUTMR.

51 Case C-235/09, *DHL Express France SAS v Chronopost SA*. The reason that e.g. an art. 97(1) EUTMR court, despite art. 98(1)(a) EUTMR, may hand down territorially limited judgments is due to either factual differences in the Member States or due to the plaintiff having limited his/her claims cf. para. 48. The case is commented by Annette Kur in (2012) 2 *Common Market Law Review* 753–66 cf. *Conflict of Laws in Intellectual Property, The CLIP Principles and Commentary*, *supra* note 9, p. 189 (2:605.C11) at note 13; Joel Smith and Julian Gauld, 'The Territorial Effect of Sanctions under the Community Trade Marks Regulation: The ECJ delivers its Judgment in DHL v Chronopost' (2011) 33(9) *European Intellectual Property Review* 588–90 and Gert Würtenberger, 'The Enforcement of Judgments of Community Trade Mark Courts' (2012) 7(5) *Journal of Intellectual Property Law and Practice* 273–377. The case is in line with prior national case law see, inter alia, OLG Düsseldorf, 8 November 2005, Az. I-20 U 110/04, Rodeo.

52 Art. 97(1) EUTMR speaks of 'courts of the Member State'.

53 *Supra* note 8.

54 Art. 96(a) EUTMR. The Member State referred to is the Member State where the action is brought cf. Overall Functioning of the European Trade Mark System, *supra* note 41 at 3.131 (p. 157).

55 *Supra* note 19.

56 Fawcett and Torremans, *supra* note 11 at 8.15.

57 *Supra* note 41.

58 Art. 94(2)(a) EUTMR.

59 Chapter 2 section C.1.

'domicile' in art. 97(1) EUTMR must be construed by applying arts 62 and 63 BR[60] and so the above in section B.1(a) applies *mutatis mutandis*.

(b) Art. 97(1) EUTMR to non-infringement actions

5.21 Art. 97(1) EUTMR also allows[61] non-infringement actions[62] to be brought at the defendant's EU domicile. It requires, however, that national law so permits.[63]

5.22 Assuming that national law does not so permit a situation could potentially arise where the plaintiff, under the existing legal framework, would not be able to bring a non-infringement action against his/her EU defendant.

> Applying the example in Chapter 1 section 2 Frox SpA may bring a non-infringement action against Frogs GmbH in Germany under art. 97(1) EUTMR provided that national German law so permits, cf. art. 96(b) EUTMR. Assuming that national German law does not allow for non-infringement actions no other forum rules are available for Frox SpA given *that* arts 97(2) and (3) EUTMR do not apply since the defendant is domiciled in the EU; *that* art. 97(5) EUTMR does not apply since non-infringement actions cannot be brought under *forum delicti* and *that* no other forum rules in the Brussels I Regulation, which apply as 'fall back' cf. art. 94(1) EUTMR seem helpful since arts 4, 7(2) and 7(5) Brussels I Regulation have all been exempted cf. art. 94(2)(a) EUTMR. Under such circumstances, therefore, Frox SpA may not be able to bring a non-infringement action against Frogs GmbH.

(c) Art. 97(1) EUTMR to invalidity actions

5.23 A distinction must be drawn between invalidity in infringement actions brought under art. 97(1) EUTMR which leads to joint adjudication given that art. 96(d) EUTMR applies and invalidity in non-infringement actions brought under art. 97(1) EUTMR which leads to either split or joint adjudication given that arts 99(2) cf. 56 EUTMR apply. Arts 96(d) and 99(2) cf. 56 EUTMR are addressed in Chapter 11 section C.1.

---

60 Art. 94(1) EUTMR cf. arts 62 and 63 BR cf. Bulletin of the European Communities Supplement 5/80, New Trade Mark System for the Community, proposed Directive and Regulation prepared by the Commission of the European Communities (COM 80 635 final 19 November 1980), p. 76 and Fawcett and Torremans, *supra* note 11 at 8.15.

61 The reason for using the term 'allows', contrary to art. 97(1) EUTMR using the term 'shall', is that non-infringement actions may also be brought under the 'fall back' rules cf. Chapters 2 and 3 section C.1. With respect to defendants domiciled in the EU cf., however, the example below.

62 Art. 96(b) EUTMR.

63 Art. 96(b) EUTMR.

2. The defendant's domicile rule in the CDR

The defendant's domicile rule is found in art. 82(1) CDR. The CJEU has yet to interpret the provision[64] and no case is pending.[65] Below a distinction is drawn between applying the rule to infringement actions (section a); to non-infringement actions (section b) and to invalidity actions (section c).[66] **5.24**

(a) Art. 82(1) CDR to infringement actions

Art. 82(1) CDR allows[67] infringement actions[68] to be brought in: '[...] the courts of the Member State in which the defendant is domiciled [...]'.[69] **5.25**

Compared to its 'sister' provision in the EUTMR[70] art. 82(1) CDR is equal *since* it also speaks of EU domicile; *since* it is also subject to unlimited full jurisdiction[71] unless the plaintiff chooses otherwise[72] and *since* the option of bringing threatened infringement actions also require that national law so permits.[73] Thus, section C.1(a) applies *mutatis mutandis* including to the unregistered CD.[74] **5.26**

(b) Art. 82(1) CDR to non-infringement actions

Art. 82(1) CDR also allows[75] non-infringement actions[76] to be brought at the defendant's EU domicile. In line with its 'sister' provision in the EUTMR[77] it requires that national law so permits.[78] Thus, section C.1(b) applies *mutatis mutandis* including to the unregistered CD.[79] **5.27**

---

64 Curia.eu visited on 1 January 2017.

65 Ibid.

66 The three kinds of actions are overall defined in Chapter 1 section A.3(b).

67 The reason for using the term 'allows', contrary to art. 82(1) CDR using the term 'shall', is that infringement actions may also be brought under the *forum delicti* rule in art. 82(5) CDR cf. Chapter 9 section C.2(a) meaning that two alternatives are available to the plaintiff. In addition to that 'fall back' rules may apply cf. Chapter 3 section C.2.

68 Art. 81(a) CDR.

69 Art. 82(1)(first part) CDR. Art. 82(1)(second part) CDR adds '[...] or if he is not domiciled in any of the Member States, in which he has an establishment'. The addition is addressed in Chapter 6 section C.2(a).

70 Art. 97(1) EUTMR.

71 Art. 83(1) CDR.

72 Case C-235/09, *DHL Express France SAS*, para. 48 applies *mutatis mutandis* under the CDR cf. *supra* note 51.

73 Art. 81(a) CDR.

74 Fawcett and Torremans, *supra* note 11 at 8.116.

75 The reason for using the term 'allows', contrary to art. 82(1) CDR using the term 'shall', is that non-infringement actions may also be brought under the 'fall back' rules cf. Chapters 2 and 3 section C.2. With respect to defendants domiciled in the EU cf., however, the example in section C.1(b).

76 Art. 81(b) CDR.

77 Art. 97(1) EUTMR.

78 Art. 81(b) CDR.

79 Fawcett and Torremans, *supra* note 11 at 8.116.

(c) Art. 82(1) CDR to invalidity actions

5.28 A distinction must be drawn between invalidity in infringement actions brought under art. 82(1) CDR, which leads to joint adjudication given that art. 81(d) CDR applies and invalidity in non-infringement actions brought under art. 82(1) CDR, which leads to either split or joint adjudication given that arts 84(4) cf. 52 CDR apply. Arts 81(d) and 84(4) cf. 52 CDR are addressed in Chapter 11 section C.2.

3. The defendant's domicile rule in the CPVR

5.29 The defendant's domicile rule is found in art. 101(2)(a) CPVR. The CJEU has yet to interpret the provision[80] and no case is pending.[81] Below a distinction is drawn between applying the rule to infringement actions (section a); to non-infringement actions (section b) and to invalidity actions (section c).[82]

(a) Art. 101(2)(a) CPVR to infringement actions

5.30 Art. 101(2)(a) CPVR allows[83] actions in respect of claims for infringement[84] to be brought in: 'the courts of the Member State or another Contracting Party to the Lugano Convention in which the defendant is domiciled or has its seat [...]'.[85]

5.31 The reason for adopting the provision is unspoken in the Explanatory Memorandum[86] but given that art. 101(2)(a) CPVR also expresses a general rule[87] the justifications in section B.1(a) apply *mutatis mutandis.*

5.32 Compared to its 'sister' provisions in the EUTMR and CDR[88] art. 101(2)(a) CPVR is similar *since* it also allows for unlimited full jurisdiction[89] unless the

---

80 Curia.eu visited on 1 January 2017.

81 Ibid.

82 The three kinds of actions are overall defined in Chapter 1 section A.3(b).

83 The reason for using the term 'allows', contrary to art. 101(2) CPVR using the term 'shall', is that infringement actions may also be brought under the *forum delicti* rule in art. 101(3) CPVR cf. Chapter 9 section 3.3.1 meaning that two alternatives are available to the plaintiff. In addition to that 'fall back' rules may apply cf. Chapters 2 and 3 section C.3.

84 Art. 94 CPVR.

85 Art. 101(2)(a)(first part) CPVR. Art. 101(2)(a)(second part) CPVR adds '[...] or, in the absence of such, has an establishment'. The addition is addressed in Chapter 6 section C.3(a).

86 Proposal for a Council Regulation on Community Plant Variety Rights presented by the Commission COM(90)347 (90/C 244/01) Brussels 6 September 1990.

87 Gert Würtenberger, Paul Van Der Kooij, Bart Kiewiet and Martin Ekvad, *European Community Plant Variety Protection*, Oxford University Press, 2006 at 7.62 and Fawcett and Torremans, *supra* note 11 at 8.152 *et seq.*

88 Arts 97(1) EUTMR and 82(1) CDR.

89 Art. 101(2)(last sentence) CPVR.

plaintiff chooses otherwise[90] and *since* it also speaks of 'domicile' but different *since* jurisdiction can be allocated at the defendant's EFTA domicile,[91] which the EUTMR and CDR do not allow for;[92] *since* threatened infringement actions are not permitted[93] contrary to the EUTMR and CDR where bringing such actions requires that national law so permits[94] and *since* it refers to 'seat' which the EUTMR and CDR do not speak of cf. below.

The terms 'domicile' and 'seat' are not defined in the CPVR but must be construed in line with arts 52 and 53 of the 1988 Lugano Convention[95] which applied at the time.[96] Given, however, *that* the 1988 Lugano Convention has been replaced by the 2007 Lugano Convention[97] and *that* under the latter 'seat' is now 'statutory seat, central administration or principal place of business' a legal person can be sued at any of the latter three within the meaning of art. 101(2)(a) CPVR.[98] Thus, section B.1(a) applies *mutatis mutandis*. **5.33**

(b) Art. 101(2)(a) CPVR to non-infringement actions

Art. 101(2)(a) CPVR also allows[99] non-infringement actions[100] to be brought at the defendant's EU/EFTA domicile or seat. Thus, section C.3(a) applies *mutatis mutandis*. **5.34**

(c) Art. 101(2)(a) CPVR to invalidity actions

If invalidity of a CPV is raised during the infringement or non-infringement actions brought under art. 101(2)(a) CPVR the CPVO comes into play given **5.35**

90 Case C-235/09, *DHL Express France SAS*, para. 48 applies *mutatis mutandis* under the CPVR cf. *supra* note 51.

91 The fact that jurisdiction can be allocated at the defendant's EFTA domicile following art. 101(2)(a) CPVR raises a problem given that EFTA Member States are not parties to the CPVR, cf. Evaluation of the Community Plant Variety Right *Aquis* – Final Report to the Directorate General for Health and Consumer Affairs (European Commission), April 2011, p. 49, section 4.5.7.2 and accordingly EFTA courts may not find themselves competent on the basis of its provisions, inter alia, art. 101(2)(a) CPVR. The problem is addressed in Chapter 2 section C.3(b).

92 Arts 97(1) EUTMR and 82(1) CDR.

93 Fawcett and Torremans, *supra* note 11 at 8.146.

94 Arts 96(a) EUTMR and 81(a) CDR.

95 Art. 102(3) CPVR.

96 The CPVR was passed on 27 July 1994 whereas the Lugano Convention was passed on 16 September 1988.

97 Chapter 2 section B.2.

98 Art. 69(6) Lugano Convention cf. Fawcett and Torremans, *supra* note 11 at 8.155.

99 The reason for using the term 'allows', contrary to art. 101(2) CPVR using the term 'shall', is that non-infringement actions may also be brought under the *forum delicti* rule in art. 101(3) CPVR cf. Chapter 9 section C.3(b). In addition to that 'fall back' rules may apply cf. Chapters 2 and 3 section C.3.

100 Non-infringement actions are not explicitly mentioned in Part Six CPVR. For the reasons in Chapter 3 section C.3 non-infringement actions must, however, be covered by the CPVR.

their exclusivity to address invalidity,[101] which in turn leads to either split or joint adjudication. Art. 20 CPVR is addressed in Chapter 11 section C.3.

4. The defendant's domicile rule in the AUPC

5.36 The defendant's domicile rule is found in art. 33(1)(b) AUPC.[102] Below a distinction is drawn between applying the rule to infringement actions (section a); to non-infringement actions (section b) and to invalidity actions (section c).[103]

(a) Art. 33(1)(b) AUPC to infringement actions

5.37 Art. 33(1)(b) AUPC allows[104] infringement actions[105] to be brought before: 'the local division hosted by the Contracting Member State where the defendant [...] has its residence or principal place of business [...]'.[106]

5.38 The reason for adopting the provision is unspoken in the drafting history[107] but given that art. 33(1)(b) AUPC expresses a general principle the justifications in section B.1(a) apply *mutatis mutandis* except from allowing the plaintiff to bring unrestricted claims, which for the reasons below is generally permitted under the AUPC[108] and is therefore not a special art. 33(1)(b) AUPC characteristic.

5.39 Compared to its European unitary IP 'sister' provisions[109] art. 33(1)(b) AUPC is different *since* jurisdiction must be allocated in a Contracting Member

---

101 Art. 20 CPVR.

102 Torsten Bjørn Larsen, *Rules of Jurisdiction in the Agreement on a Unified Patent Court*, Nordisk Immateriellt Rättsskydd, 4/2014, pp. 357–74 at 361 *et seq.* and Torsten Bjørn Larsen, *A Bundle of National Patents v a European Patent with Unitary Effect – Jurisdictional Comparison, Intellectual Property and General Legal Principles – Is IP a Lex Specialis?* Edward Elgar Publishing, 2015, pp. 208 *et seq.*

103 The three kinds of actions are overall defined in Chapter 1 section A.3(b).

104 The reason for using the term 'allows', contrary to art. 33(1) AUPC using the term 'shall', is that infringement actions may also be brought under the *forum delicti* rule in art. 33(1)(a) AUPC cf. Chapter 9 section C.4(a) meaning that two alternatives are available to the plaintiff.

105 Art. 32(1)(a) AUPC.

106 As an alternative action can be brought at the regional division in which that Contracting Member State participates. If a Contracting Member State neither hosts a local division nor participates in a regional division action shall be brought at the central division cf. art. 33(1) (last sentence). If the defendant does not have a residence or a principal place of business in a Contracting Member State action must be brought at *forum delicti* or at the central division cf. art. 33(1) (second last sentence). In line with the BR cf. section B.1(a) the plaintiff is irrelevant when determining jurisdiction following art. 33(1)(b) AUPC. Art. 33(1)(b) AUPC also adds 'or in the absence of residence or principal place of business, its place of business'. The addition is addressed in Chapter 6 section C.4(a).

107 Chapter 2 notes 248–9.

108 Art. 34 AUPC.

109 Arts 97(1) EUTMR, 82(1) CDR and 101(2)(a) CPVR.

State[110] and not in the EU[111] or in the EU/EFTA;[112] *since* it speaks of 'residence' whereas its 'sister' provisions speak of 'domicile';[113] *since* 'residence' is not subject to a definition contrary to 'domicile';[114] *since* it is subject to unlimited full jurisdiction[115] cf. below contrary to its 'sister' provisions where the plaintiff may choose from unlimited full and limited forum jurisdiction[116] and finally *since* threatened infringement actions are permitted[117] contrary to the EUTMR/CDR where bringing such actions requires that national law so permits[118] and the CPVR where such actions are not permitted.[119]

The terms 'residence' and 'principal place of business' have not been defined in the AUPC. **5.40**

'Residence' is the first term. 'Residence' is not new.[120] On a general level the term '[habitual] residence' is used in personal and familiy civil procedure,[121] in the Hague Conventions[122] and was discussed in the *Jenard* report but rejected since it would 'represent a divergence from that [...] under the laws of the **5.41**

---

110 The reason that the AUPC speaks of Contracting Member States is that not every EU Member State is party to the AUPC cf. Chapter 1 note 28.

111 Arts 97(1) EUTMR and 82(1) CDR.

112 Art. 101(2)(a) CPVR.

113 Arts 97(1) EUTMR, 82(1) CDR and 101(2)(a) CPVR.

114 Arts 97(1) cf. 94(1) EUTMR cf. 62 and 63 BR; arts 82(1) cf. 79(1) CDR cf. 62 and 63 BR and arts 101(2)(a) cf. 102(3) CPVR cf. arts 59 and 60 Lugano Convention.

115 Art. 34 AUPC.

116 Arts 98(1)(a) EUTMR, 83(1) CDR and art. 101(2)(last sentence) CPVR cf. case C-235/09, *DHL Express France SAS*, para. 48 and *supra* note 51.

117 Arts 33(1)(b) cf. 32(1)(a) AUPC.

118 Arts 97(1) cf. 96(a) EUTMR and arts 82(1) cf. 81(a) CDR cf. sections C.1(a) and C.2(a).

119 Fawcett and Torremans, *supra* note 11 at 8.146.

120 For a distinction between 'residence' and 'domicile' cf. Toshiyuki Kono, 'Intellectual Property Rights, Conflict of Laws and International Jurisdiction: Applicability of ALI Principles in Japan' (2005) 30(3) *Brooklyn Journal of International Law* 865 at 870. The distinction seems to have lost some significance in IP, inter alia, *since* 'residence' for legal persons in art. 69(5) Convention for the European Patent for the Common Market (Community Patent Convention) (76/76/EEC) of 15 December 1975 should be defined in line with 'domicile' within the meaning of art. 53 Brussels Convention (now art. 63 BR) and *since* 'habitual residence' for legal persons in art. 2:601(2) CLIP Principles, with one variation must also be defined in line with art. 63 BR cf. *Conflict of Laws in Intellectual Property, The CLIP Principles and Commentary*, *supra* note 9, pp. 169 *et seq.* (2:601.C04) cf. p. 58 (2:101.C05).

121 Art. 3(1) Council Regulation (EC) No 1347/2000 of 29 May 2000 on Jurisdiction and the Recognition and Enforcement of Judgments in Matrimonial Matters and in Matters of Parental Responsibility for Children of both Spouses and art. 8(1) Council Regulation (EC) No 2201/2003 of 27 November 2003 concerning Jurisdiction and the Recognition and Enforcement of Judgments in Matrimonial Matters and the Matters of Parental Responsibility, repealing Regulation (EC) No 1347/2000.

122 Art. 3 Preliminary Draft Convention on Jurisdiction and Foreign Judgments in Civil and Commercial Matters adopted by the Special Commission (1999) and arts 1 and 4 Hague Convention on Choice of Court Agreements (2005).

Contracting States, the majority of which use domicile as a basis of protection'[123] and similarly discussed in the *Pocar* report but also rejected since it would be 'more appropriate to personal and family relations[124] rather than to those of a commercial nature'.[125] On an IP level the term '[habitual] residence' is, however, new given that it is not used in existing European unitary IP law[126] but only in the 1975 Community Patent Convention,[127] which never came into force,[128] and in scholarly reports.[129]

5.42 With respect to natural persons one could argue that 'residence' within the meaning of art. 33(1)(b) AUPC must be interpreted in line with art. 62 BR. In doing so the court where the action is brought would have to apply its own internal law to determine whether the defendant is resident there.[130] Any such reference to national law seems unlikely, which is supported, inter alia, *by* the supranational character of the UPC,[131] which is subject to its own forum rules[132] and *by* the ROP, which are likely to be interpreted in line with the equivalent terms in the AUPC, and where 'residence' for natural persons when serving the statement of claim and written pleadings on the defendant is defined autonomously as 'his/[her] usual or last known residence [...]'.[133]

5.43 With respect to legal persons one could also argue that 'residence' within the meaning of art. 33(1)(b) AUPC must be interpreted in line with art. 63 BR. In doing so action could be brought at the defendant's 'statutory seat, central

123 Report by P. Jenard, *supra* note 11, p. 15.

124 *Supra* note 121.

125 Report by Professor Fausto Pocar, *supra* note 34 at 24. By contrast the CLIP and ALI Principles finds the flexible term '[habitual] residence' more appropriate than the fixed term 'domicile' in IP due to the increase of virtual companies which may rapidly change location cf. *Conflict of Laws in Intellectual Property, The CLIP Principles and Commentary, supra* note 9, p. 58 (2:101.C05) cf. § 201 ALI Principles reporters note 2.

126 Sections C.1–C.3.

127 Art. 69(1) Convention for the European Patent for the Common Market (Community Patent Convention) (76/76/EEC) of 15 December 1975.

128 Chapter 2 section C.1(a).

129 Art. 2:101 CLIP Principles uses the term 'habitually resident'; § 201 ALI Principles uses the term 'resident' and art. 201 Waseda Project uses the term 'habitually resident'. The reasons for using the terms see *Conflict of Laws in Intellectual Property, The CLIP Principles and Commentary, supra* note 9, p. 58 (2:101.C05).

130 Section B.1(a).

131 Opinion 1/09 of 8 March 2011 of the CJEU, para. 71.

132 Art. 33 AUPC.

133 Arts 271(5)(b) and 278(3)(b) ROP. The reason for the addition i.e. 'last known residence' seems to be two-fold, i.e. to widen the scope of UPC jurisdiction and to allow the plaintiff to more easily enforce an infringement which, taking into account that non-infringement actions must as a main rule be brought at the central division cf. art. 33(4) AUPC, confirms the expected pro-patentee approach of the UPC cf. Clement Salung Petersen and Jens Schovsbo, 'On Law and Policy in a European and European Union Patent Court (EEUPC), What will it do to Patent Law and What will Patent Law do to it?' in Henning Koch, Karsten Hagel-Sørensen, Ulrich Haltern and Joseph H.H. Weiler (eds), *Europe The New Legal Realism*, DJØF Publishing, p. 636 (section IV.4).

administration or principal place of business'.[134] Any such interpretation seems, despite that 'residence' and 'principal place of business' would partly overlap, likely which is supported, inter alia, *by* the ROP where 'residence' for legal persons when serving the statement of claim and written pleadings on the defendant is so defined,[135] *by* the 1975 Community Patent Convention where 'residence' for legal persons should also be interpreted in line with art. 53 Brussels Convention (now art. 63 BR);[136] *by* the Hague Conventions where the term '[...] resident shall be interpreted in line with art. 6[3] BR',[137] *by* scholarly reports[138] and *by* the fact that the UPC, despite recital 6 AUPC speaking of a 'fair balance between [the parties]', is expected to pursue a pro patentee approach[139] which, taking into account that non-infringement actions must as a main rule be brought at the central division,[140] renders likely a broad interpretation of 'residence'.

Thus, it seems likely that 'residence' within the meaning of art. 33(1)(b) AUPC must be defined as 'his/[her] usual or last known residence' for natural persons and as 'statutory seat, central administration or principal place of business' for legal persons. **5.44**

'Principal place of business' is the second term. 'Principal place of business' is not new either. The term is addressed above for legal persons, whereto is referred. The question, however, remains whether a natural person can also be sued at his/her principal place of business.[141] **5.45**

Supporting that a natural person can be sued at his/her principal place of business it is argued, inter alia, *that* 'principal place of business' in art. 33(1)(b) **5.46**

---

134 Section B.1(a).

135 Arts 271(5)(a) and 278(3)(a) ROP.

136 Art. 69(5) Community Patent Convention (76/76/EEC) of 15 December 1975.

137 Art. 3(2) Preliminary Draft Convention on Jurisdiction and Foreign Judgments in Civil and Commercial Matters adopted by the Special Commission (1999) and art. 4(2) Hague Convention on Choice of Court Agreements (2005). Both, however, differ from art. 63 BR in one sense given that they speak of an additional residence for companies in the country of incorporation or formation cf. arts 3(2)(b) and 4(2)(b).

138 Art. 2:601(2) CLIP Principles cf. *Conflict of Laws in Intellectual Property, The CLIP Principles and Commentary*, *supra* note 9, p. 169 (2:601.C04), which however differs from art. 63 BR in one sense given that it defines 'principal place of business' as the place from which the external activities are conducted cf. art. 2:601(3) rather than the place where the main business activities are located and § 201 ALI Principles, which speaks of an additional residence for companies in the country of incorporation or formation cf. § 201(3)(b).

139 Petersen and Schovsbo, *supra* note 133, p. 636 (section IV.4).

140 Art. 33(4) AUPC.

141 Changing the example in Chapter 1 section 2 so that Frox is a natural person with residence in Italy but acting in the course of business in France where the infringement takes place given that the foam shoes are manufactured and sold there could – provided that a principal place of business rule applies to natural persons – be sued in France following art. 33(1)(b) AUPC.

AUPC seems not restricted to legal persons; *that* the principles of predictability and proximity support that action can be brought at the principal place of business;[142] *that* scholarly reports allow natural persons to be sued at their principal place of business;[143] *that* the Rome II Regulation refers to natural persons' principal place of business;[144] *that* the expected pro patentee approach of the UPC[145] renders likely any such broad interpretation, which in turn is supported by the fact that the term 'residence' for natural persons is also defined broadly as 'his/[her] usual or *last known* residence'[146] and finally *that* the BR also allows natural persons to be sued at their principal place of business.[147]

5.47 Supporting the opposite result namely that a natural person cannot be sued at his/her principal place of business it is argued, inter alia, *that* the ROP when serving the statement of claim and written pleadings excludes any such interpretation by speaking exclusively of 'his/[her] usual or last known residence'[148] and *that* the need for suing a natural person at his/her principal place of business may be sparse given that *forum delicti* in art. 33(1)(a) AUPC will likely apply in any such situation.[149]

5.48 Balancing the interests and in particular taking into account the ROP, which are likely to be interpreted in line with the equivalent terms in the AUPC, it seems unlikely that natural persons can be sued at their principal place of business.

5.49 The final question is the extent of jurisdiction under art. 33(1)(b) AUPC. The answer is laid down in art. 34 AUPC having the heading 'territorial scope of decisions': 'Decisions of the Court shall cover, in the case of a European patent, the territory of those Contracting Member States for which the European patent has effect'.[150]

5.50 It follows that the jurisdiction of the UPC when hearing a European patent action brought under art. 33(1)(b) AUPC extends to the Contracting Member

---

142 *Conflict of Laws in Intellectual Property, The CLIP Principles and Commentary*, *supra* note 9, p. 168 (2:601.C02) and Chapter 4 sections C.1-C.2.
143 Art. 2:601(1) CLIP Principles cf. *Conflict of Laws in Intellectual Property, The CLIP Principles and Commentary*, ibid.
144 Art. 23(2) Rome II Regulation.
145 Petersen and Schovsbo, *supra* note 133, p. 636 (section IV.4).
146 Emphasis added.
147 Art. 7(5) BR and Chapter 6 section B.1(a).
148 Arts 271(5)(b) and 278(3)(b) ROP.
149 Chapter 9 section C.4(a).
150 Art. 34 AUPC.

States where the European patent has effect. Thus, the UPC has unlimited full jurisdiction under art. 33(1)(b) AUPC for European patents.

It also follows, however, that the provision does not address the extent of jurisdiction for UP actions brought under art. 33(1)(b) AUPC. From the drafting history behind art. 34 AUPC the extent of jurisdiction for UPs was explicitly addressed as unlimited in the early 2008 Draft,[151] which, with variations, was upheld in the September 2011[152] and in the October 2011[153] drafts. In the November 2012 draft[154] and in the final agreement[155] the extent of jurisdiction for UPs was written out. Despite being silent it seems likely that art. 33(1)(b) AUPC is also subject to unlimited full jurisdiction for UPs *since* its 'sister' European unitary IP rights are also subject to unlimited full jurisdiction;[156] *since* unlimited full jurisdiction was explicitly provided for in the early 2008–2011 drafts; *since* there is nothing in the drafting history indicating a restriction of jurisdiction for UPs; *since* unlimited full jurisdiction for patent rights, which are divided (European patents) even more so supports unlimited full jurisdiction for patent rights, which are united (UP) given that the former is more extensive than the latter; *since* unlimited full jurisdiction contributes to the required efficiency and cost effectiveness of the functioning of the UPC[157] and thus to an effective enforcement of patents[158] and *since* unlimited full jurisdiction removes the risk of diverging decisions being one of the goals behind the AUPC.[159] For the latter two reasons, and despite *Chronopost*,[160] which applies to its 'sister' European unitary IP 5.51

151 In the Draft Agreement on the European Union Patent Judiciary of 14 May 2008 (9124/08 PI 24 COUR 19) the extent of jurisdiction was found in art. 16 under the heading 'territorial effects of decisions', which read, 'Decisions of the Court will have effect, in the case of a Community patent, for the whole territory of the European Union [...]'.

152 In the Draft Agreement on a Unified Patent Court and Draft Statute, revised Presidency Text of 2 September 2011 (13751/11 PI 108 COUR 48) the provision – still found in art. 16 and under the same heading – was revised into 'Decisions of the Court shall have effect, in the case of a European patent with unitary effect, for the territory of the Contracting Member States in which the patent has unitary effect [...]'.

153 In the Draft Agreement on a Unified Patent Court and Draft Statute, revised Presidency text of 19 October 2011 (15539/11 PI 133 COUR 59) the provision – still found in art. 16 and under the same heading – was revised into 'Decisions of the Court shall cover [...]' and in the later Draft Agreement on a Unified Patent Court and draft Statute, revised Presidency text of 26 October 2011 (16023/11 PI 141 COUR 62) the headline of the provision was revised into 'Territorial scope of decisions'.

154 In the Draft Agreement on a Unified Patent Court and draft Statute, consolidated text of 14 November 2012 (16222/12 PI 146 COUR 74) the provision – still found in art. 16 and under the same heading – was revised into 'Decisions of the Court shall cover [...] in the case of a European patent, the territory of those Contracting Member States for which the European patent has effect'.

155 Art. 34 AUPC.

156 Arts 97(1) cf. 98(1)(a) EUTMR; 82(1) cf. 83(1) CDR and 101(2)(a) cf. 101(2)(last sentence) CPVR.

157 Arts 40(3) and 41(3) AUPC.

158 Recital (5) AUPC and Chapter 4 section B.

159 Recital (2) AUPC.

160 *Supra* note 51.

rights,[161] it seems unlikely that the UPC will allow for territorially limited judgments under art. 34 AUPC, which in turn is supported by the wording of art. 33(2)(last sentence) AUPC[162] and by legal scholars.[163]

5.52 Thus, it seems likely that UP actions in line with European patent actions brought under art. 33(1)(b) AUPC are subject to unlimited full jurisdiction, which may not be restricted cf. art. 34 AUPC.[164]

(b) Art. 33(1)(b) AUPC to non-infringement actions

5.53 Art. 33(1)(b) AUPC also applies to non-infringement actions.[165] It requires, however, that an infringement action between the same parties relating to the same patent is already pending before an art. 33(1)(b) AUPC court. In that case the non-infringement action, for reasons of procedural economy, may only be brought there.[166] If, however, an infringement action is not already pending art. 33(1)(b) AUPC does not apply. In that case the non-infringement action must be brought at the central division cf. Chapter 10 section C.

(c) Art. 33(1)(b) AUPC to invalidity actions

5.54 If invalidity of a UP is raised during the infringement or non-infringement actions brought under art. 33(1)(b) AUPC the flexible exclusive jurisdiction rule in art. 33(3) AUPC comes into play, which in turn leads to either split or joint adjudication. Art. 33(3) AUPC is addressed in Chapter 11 section C.4.

D. CONCLUSION

5.55 A distinction is drawn between the application of the defendant's domicile rule in trademark, design, plant variety and patent cases.

5.56 In *trademark* cases the applicable defendant's domicile rules are found in arts 4 BR, 97(1) EUTMR and in third states' own international forum rules, which

---

161 Sections C.1–C.3.

162 Art. 33(2)(last sentence) AUPC reads 'in case an action between the same parties on the same patent is brought before several different divisions, the division first seized shall be competent *for the whole case* and any division seized later shall declare the action inadmissible [...]' (emphasis added).

163 Jan Brinkhof and Ansgar Ohly, 'Towards a Unified Patent Court in Europe' in Ansgar Ohly and Justine Pila (eds) *The Europeanization of Intellectual Property Law, Towards a European Legal Methodology*, Oxford University Press, 2013, p. 211.

164 Whether the *forum delicti* rule in art. 33(1)(a) AUPC is similarly subject to unlimited full jurisdiction for UPs is addressed in Chapter 9 section C.4(a).

165 Art. 33(4) AUPC.

166 Art. 33(4) (second sentence) AUPC.

have not been examined. The justifications behind arts 4 BR and 97(1) EUTMR are similar whereas the scopes and impacts are both similar and different.

They are similar *since* the defendant's domicile is defined in the same way; *since* infringement actions can be brought under both; *since* both are subject to unlimited full jurisdiction unless the plaintiff chooses otherwise and *since* invalidity in non-infringement actions concerning registered trademarks usually leads to split adjudication. **5.57**

They are different *since* the defendant's domicile can be in EU/EFTA under art. 4 BR but only in EU under art. 97(1) EUTMR; *since* threatened infringement actions can be brought under art. 4 BR but only under art. 97(1) EUTMR if national law so permits; *since* non-infringement actions can be brought under art. 4 BR but only under art. 97(1) EUTMR if national law so permits and *since* invalidity in infringement actions concerning registered trademarks leads to split adjudication under art. 4 BR but joint adjudication under art. 97(1) EUTMR. **5.58**

In sum – and generally speaking – art. 4 BR is advantageous to the plaintiff acting as the rightholder since threatened infringement actions can always be brought whereas art. 4 BR is advantageous to the plaintiff acting as the infringer since non-infringement actions can always be brought and since adjudication for registered trademarks is split. Art. 97(1) EUTMR is advantageous to the plaintiff acting as the rightholder since adjudication is joint whereas art. 97(1) EUTMR is advantageous to both since the scope of the defendant's domicile is restricted meaning that action can be brought at their own domiciles if the defendant is domiciled in e.g. EFTA following art. 97(2) EUTMR and Chapter 7. **5.59**

In *design* cases the applicable defendant's domicile rules are found in arts 4 BR, 82(1) CDR and in third states' own international forum rules, which have not been examined. The above applies *mutatis mutandis* including to the unregistered CD. **5.60**

In *plant variety* cases the defendant's domicile rules are found in arts 4 BR, 101(2)(a) CPVR and in third states' own international forum rules, which have not been examined. The justifications behind arts 4 BR and 101(2)(a) CPVR are similar whereas the scopes and impacts are both similar and different. **5.61**

5.62 They are similar *since* the defendant's domicile is defined in the same way; *since* the defendant's domicile can be in EU/EFTA; *since* infringement and non-infringement actions can be brought under both; *since* adjudication is usually split and *since* both are subject to unlimited full jurisdiction unless the plaintiff chooses otherwise.

5.63 They are different *since* threatened infringement actions can be brought under art. 4 BR but not under art. 101(2)(a) CPVR and *since* adjudication is split under art. 4 BR but may be joint under art. 101(2)(a) CPVR.

5.64 In sum – and generally speaking – art. 4 BR is advantageous to the plaintiff acting as the rightholder since threatened infringement actions can be brought whereas art. 4 BR is advantageous to the plaintiff acting as the infringer since adjudication is split. Art. 101(2)(a) CPVR is advantageous to the plaintiff acting as the rightholder since adjudication may be joint.

5.65 In *patent* cases the defendant's domicile rules are found in arts 4 BR, 33(1)(b) AUPC and in third states' own international forum rules, which have not been examined. The justification, scope and impacts of arts 4 BR and 33(1)(b) AUPC are both similar and different.

5.66 They are similar *since* infringement and threatened infringement actions can be brought; *since* adjudication may be split and *since* 'domicile' and 'residence' for legal persons are most likely defined similarly.

5.67 They are different *since* the defendant's domicile can be in EU/EFTA under art. 4 BR but only in a Contracting Member State under art. 33(1)(b) AUPC; *since* the justification behind art. 4 BR is to protect the defendant and to allow the plaintiff to bring unrestricted claims whereas the justification behind art. 33(1)(b) AUPC seems restricted to the former; *since* art. 4 BR is subject to unlimited full jurisdiction unless the plaintiff chooses otherwise whereas art. 33(1)(b) AUPC is subject to unlimited full jurisdiction; *since* non-infringement actions can be brought under art. 4 BR but only under art. 33(1)(b) AUPC if an infringement action between the same parties regarding the same patent is already pending; *since* adjudication is split under art. 4 BR but may be joint under art. 33(1)(b) AUPC and *since* 'domicile' and 'residence' for natural persons are most likely defined differently.

5.68 In sum – and generally speaking – art. 4 BR is advantageous to the plaintiff acting as the infringer since adjudication is split and is advantageous to the plaintiff acting as both the rightholder and the infringer since the extent of jurisdiction is subject to discretion. Art. 33(1)(b) AUPC is advantageous to the plaintiff acting as the rightholder since adjudication may be joint and since natural persons are most likely subject to a broad and unanimous definition.

Overall, the above similarities and differences as well as the advantages for the plaintiff can be illustrated as in Table 5.1 below. As stated in Chapter 3 section D the numbers in brackets refer to the factor identified as an advantage for the plaintiff in Chapter 1 section A.4. **5.69**

Table 5.1 Defendant's domicile rule overview

	GENERAL			JUSTIFICATION	SCOPE				IMPACT				CONCLUSION
										If invalidity is raised			
	Version	Defendant's domicile rule	Wording	Ratio legis	Requirement	Infringement actions	Threatened infringement actions	Non-infringement actions	Places to sue	In infringement actions	In non-infringement actions	Extent of jurisdiction	Advantages for the plaintiff
Trade Marks	National trademarks	Art. 4 BR	'[…] Persons domiciled in a Member State [State bound by the Lugano Convention] shall, whatever their nationality, be sued in the courts of that Member State [State bound by the Lugano Convention]'	• To protect the defendant • To allow for unrestricted claims	Defendant must be domiciled in EU/EFTA	Yes	Yes	Yes	Natural person (not autonomously defined) • At its EU/EFTA domicile Legal person (autonomously defined) • At its EU/EFTA statutory seat, or • At its EU/EFTA central administration, or • At its EU/EFTA principal place of business	• Split adjudication for registered national trademarks • Joint adjudication for unregistered national trademarks		Unlimited or limited	Art. 4 BR is advantageous → To the plaintiff acting as the rightholder since threatened infringement actions can always be brought (8) → To the plaintiff acting as the infringer since non-infringement actions can always be brought (9) and since adjudication for registered trademarks is split (6–7) Art. 97(1) EUTMR is advantageous → To the plaintiff acting as the rightholder since adjudication is joint (6–7) → To the plaintiff acting as both the rightholder and the infringer since the scope of the defendant's domicile is restricted (3)
	European Union Trademark (EUTM)	Art. 97(1) EUTMR	'[Be sued] in the courts of the Member State in which the defendant is domiciled […]'	• To protect the defendant • To allow for unrestricted claims	Defendant must be domiciled in EU	Yes Art. 96(a) EUTMR	Yes But requires that national law so permits cf. art. 96(a) EUTMR	Yes But requires that national law so permits cf. art. 96(b) EUTMR	Natural person (not autonomously defined) • At its EU domicile Legal person (autonomously defined) • At its EU statutory seat, or • At its EU central administration, or • At its EU principal place of business	Joint adjudication Art. 96(a) and (d) EUTMR	Joint/split adjudication Arts 99(2) cf. 56 EUTMR	Unlimited Art. 98(1)(a) EUTMR or Limited *Chronopost*	
Designs	National designs	Art. 4 BR	What applies to national trademarks applies *mutatis mutandis* to national designs										*Ibid.*
	Community Design (CD)	Art. 82(1) CDR	'[Be sued] in the courts of the Member State in which the defendant is domiciled […]'	• To protect the defendant • To allow for unrestricted claims	Defendant must be domiciled in EU	Yes Art. 81(a) CDR	Yes But requires that national law so permits cf. art. 81(a) CDR	Yes But requires that national law so permits cf. art. 81(b) CDR	Natural person (not autonomously defined) • At its EU domicile Legal person (autonomously defined) • At its EU statutory seat, or • At its EU central administration, or • At its EU principal place of business	Joint adjudication Art. 81(a) and (d) CDR	Invalidity of a RCD leads to joint/split adjudication Arts 84(4) cf. 52 CDR Invalidity of an UCD cannot be raised	Unlimited Art. 83(1) CDR or Limited *Chronopost*	

	GENERAL			JUSTIFICATION	SCOPE				IMPACT				CONCLUSION
										If invalidity is raised			
	Version	Defendant's domicile rule	Wording	Ratio legis	Requirement	Infringement actions	Threatened infringement actions	Non-infringement actions	Places to sue	In infringement actions	In non-infringement actions	Extent of jurisdiction	Advantages for the plaintiff
Plant Varieties	National plant varieties	Art. 4 BR	What applies to national trademarks applies *mutatis mutandis* to national plant varieties (Except from its unregistered version which does not exist for plant varieties)										Art. 4 BR is advantageous → To the plaintiff acting as the rightholder since threatened infringement actions can be brought (8) → To the plaintiff acting as the infringer since adjudication is split (6–7) Art. 101(2)(a) CPVR is advantageous → To the plaintiff acting as the rightholder since adjudication may be joint (6–7)
	Community Plant Variety (CPV)	Art. 101(2)(a) CPVR	'[Be sued] in the courts of the Member State or another Contracting Party to the Lugano Convention in which the defendant is domiciled or has his seat […]'	● To protect the defendant ● To allow for unrestricted claims	Defendant must be domiciled in EU/EFTA	Yes Art. 94 CPVR	No Art. 94 CPVR	Yes Art. 94 CPVR	Natural person (not autonomously defined) ● At its EU/EFTA domicile Legal person (autonomously defined) ● At its EU/EFTA statutory seat, or ● At its EU/EFTA central administration, or ● At its EU/EFTA principal place of business	● Joint/split adjudication Art. 20 CPVR		Unlimited Art. 101(2) CPVR or Limited *Chronopost*	
Patents	National patents	Art. 4 BR	What applies to national trademarks applies *mutatis mutandis* to national patents (Except from its unregistered version which does not exist for patents)										Art. 4 BR is advantageous → To the plaintiff acting as the infringer since adjudication is split (6–7) → To the plaintiff acting as both the rightholder and the infringer since the extent of jurisdiction is subject to discretion (4) Art. 33(1)(b) AUPC is advantageous → To the plaintiff acting as the rightholder since adjudication may be joint (6–7) and since natural persons are subject to a broad definition (2)
	Unitary Patent (UP)	Art. 33(1)(b) AUPC	'[Be sued in the courts of] the Contracting Member State where the defendant […] has its residence, or principal place of business […]'	● To protect the defendant	Defendant must have a residence or principal place of business in a CMS	Yes Art. 32(1)(a) AUPC	Yes Art. 32(1)(a) AUPC	(Yes) Art. 33(4) AUPC	Natural person (autonomously defined) ● At its CMS usual or last known residence Legal person (autonomously defined) ● At its CMS statutory seat, or ● At its CMS central administration, or ● At its CMS principal place of business	● Joint adjudication Art. 33(3)(a) and (c) AUPC ● Split adjudication Art. 33(3)(b) AUPC		Unlimited Art. 34 AUPC	

6

ESTABLISHMENT RULE

A. INTRODUCTION

6.01 From Chapter 1[1] it follows that the nature of the international jurisdiction rules available to the plaintiff must be identified. The purpose of Chapter 6 is to meet any such objective for the establishment rule[2] also known as *forum*

1 Section A.3(c).

2 The establishment rule is one of the jurisdiction rules covered by the present study cf. Chapter 1 section A.3(c). The term 'establishment rule' seems not as established as the terms 'defendant's domicile rule' cf. Chapter 5 and '*forum delicti* rule' cf. Chapter 9 since in the legal literature sometimes the forum rule is referred to, inter alia, as the 'special jurisdiction based on an establishment' cf. Ulrich Magnus and Peter Mankowski, *Brussels I Regulation*, European Commentaries on Private International Law, 2nd revised edn, Sellier European Law Publishers, 2012, p. 277; sometimes as 'the domicile of the branch' cf. Marta Pertegás Sender, *Cross-Border Enforcement of Patent Rights*, Oxford Private International Law Series, 2002 at 3.56; sometimes as 'company branch offices' cf. Report on the Convention on Jurisdiction and the Enforcement of Judgments in Civil and Commercial Matters signed in Lugano on 30 October 2007 by Professor Fausto Pocar (2009/C 319/01) at 68 and sometimes as the 'branch, agency or other establishment' cf. art. 2:207

negotii.[3] Thus, the various versions of the rule are addressed and compared at the present stage, which leads to identify the advantages for the plaintiff.[4]

A distinction is drawn between the establishment rule applying to a national IP right (section B) and the establishment rule applying to a corresponding European unitary IP right (section C). In the end a conclusion is drawn, inter alia, by way of a table (section D). **6.02**

B. THE ESTABLISHMENT RULE APPLYING TO A NATIONAL IP RIGHT

Different establishment rules apply to a national IP right. The application depends on whether the defendant is domiciled in the EU/EFTA (section 1) or outside the EU/EFTA (section 2).[5] **6.03**

1. Defendant is domiciled in the EU/EFTA

If the defendant is domiciled in the EU/EFTA art. 7(5) BR applies. Below a distinction is drawn between applying the rule to infringement actions (section a); to non-infringement actions (section b) and to invalidity actions (section c).[6] **6.04**

(a) Art. 7(5) BR to infringement actions

Art. 7(5) BR states that: **6.05**

> A person domiciled in a Member State [bound by this Convention] may be sued in another Member State [bound by this Convention] as regards a dispute arising out of the operations of a branch, agency or other establishment, in the courts for the place where the branch, agency or other establishment is situated.[7]

CLIP Principles and *Conflict of Laws in Intellectual Property, The CLIP Principles and Commentary*, European Max Planck Group on Conflicts of Laws in Intellectual Property, Oxford University Press, 2013, p. 120 (2:207.C01). The reason for using the term 'establishment rule' is to cover a broad range of wordings under the same umbrella i.e. 'branch, agency or other establishment' used in art. 7(5) BR, 'establishment' used in arts 97(1) EUTMR, 82(1) CDR and 101(2)(a) CPVR and 'place of business' used in art. 33(1)(b) AUPC. The term 'establishment' is also used under the auspices of the 'plaintiff's domicile rules' in arts 97(2) EUTMR, 82(2) CDR and 101(2)(b) CPVR but are for those addressed in Chapter 7.

3 Stig Strömholm, Upphovsrätt och Internationell Privaträtt, Instituttet för Rättsvetenskaplig Forskning [CLXXIV], Norstedts Juridik, 2001, p. 124.

4 The factors defining the advantages for the plaintiff are overall identified in Chapter 1 section A.4.

5 The reason for the distinction between defendants domiciled in the EU/EFTA and defendants domiciled outside the EU/EFTA is that parallel rules govern the former defendants cf. Chapter 2 sections B.1-B.2.

6 The three kinds of actions are overall defined in Chapter 1 section A.3(b).

7 Art. 7(5) BR.

6.06 Art. 7(5) BR is a special jurisdiction rule[8] supplementing art. 4 BR[9] meaning that the plaintiff may choose between the two[10] along with art. 7(2) BR[11] without being restricted through the doctrine of *forum non-conveniens*.[12] Proximity, which is the overall justification for the provision[13] and which follows from the provision itself[14] is that the defendant has established a branch, agency or other establishment for the purposes of doing business being the place where he/she seeks an advantage and where he/she may feel the consequences of being sued.[15] Thus, art. 7(5) BR is, lacking CJEU case law, a small defendant's domicile rule[16] cf. below. It is not a requirement that the IP right is protected in the forum by contrast to the place(s) of registration in art. 7(2) BR.[17] Infringement actions[18] and threatened infringement actions[19] can both be brought under art. 7(5) BR which, lacking CJEU case law, is likely subject to unlimited full jurisdiction[20] unless the plaintiff chooses otherwise. The provision applies when two requirements are met.

6.07 *First*, the defendant must have a branch, agency or other establishment in a EU/EFTA State different from where he/she is domiciled.[21] 'Branch, agency

---

8 Chapter II section 2 BR.

9 Magnus and Mankowski, *supra* note 2, p. 105 and Peter Arnt Nielsen, *International Privat- og Procesret*, Jurist- og Økonomforbundets Forlag, 1997, p. 150.

10 Case 33/78, *Somafer SA v Saar-Ferngas AG*, para. 7 cf. Oberlandesgericht (OLG) Köln, IHR 2005, 167, 168 and Report on the Convention on Jurisdiction and the Enforcement of Judgments in Civil and Commercial Matters signed at Brussels 27 September 1968 by P. Jenard, Director in the Belgium Ministry of Foreign Affairs and External Trade, p. 22.

11 Chapter 9 section B.1(a).

12 Case C-281/02, *Andrew Owusu v N.B. Jackson, trading as 'Villa Holidays Bal-Inn Villas' and Others*, paras. 37–43 cf. Annette Kur and Thomas Dreier, *European Intellectual Property Law, Text, Cases and Materials*, Edward Elgar Publishing, 2013, pp. 488 *et seq.*; Magnus and Mankowski, *supra* note 2, p. 112; and Nielsen, *supra* note 9, p. 151.

13 Recital (16) Brussels I Regulation cf. case 33/78, *Somafer SA*, paras 7 and 8; case 218/86, *SAR Schotte GmbH v Parfums Rothschild SARL*, para. 9 and case C-439/93, *Lloyd's Register of Shipping v Société Campenon Bernard*, para. 21.

14 Art. 7(5) BR reads 'as regards disputes *arising out of* the operations of the branch, agency or other establishment' (emphasis added).

15 Magnus and Mankowski, *supra* note 2, p. 277; Sender, *supra* note 2 at 3.06 and *Conflict of Laws in Intellectual Property, The CLIP Principles and Commentary*, *supra* note 2, p. 120 (2:207.C01 and 2:207.N01).

16 *Anton Durbeck GmbH v Den Norske Bank ASA* [2003] 2 WLR 1296, 1309, UK Court of Appeal per Lord Philips of Worth Matravers M.R cf. Magnus and Mankowski, ibid., p. 277.

17 Chapter 9 section B.1(a).

18 Case 33/78, *Somafer SA*, para. 13; *IBS Technologies (PVT) Ltd. v APM Technologies SA*, unreported, 7 April 2003 [2003] All ER (D) 105 at 61 cf. James J. Fawcett and Paul Torremans, *Intellectual Property and Private International Law*, 2nd edn, Oxford Private International Law Series, 2011 at 5.112 and *Conflict of Laws in Intellectual Property, The CLIP Principles and Commentary*, *supra* note 2, p. 120 (2:207.C03).

19 Fawcett and Torremans, ibid. at 5.114.

20 Magnus and Mankowski, *supra* note 2; Fawcett and Torremans, *supra* note 18 at 5.114; Sender, *supra* note 2 at 3.61; *Conflict of Laws in Intellectual Property, The CLIP Principles and Commentary*, *supra* note 2, p. 120 (2:207.C03) and *IBS Technologies (PVT) Ltd.* [61]. For a different view see Toshiyuki Kono, *Intellectual Property and Private International Law, Comparative Perspectives*, Hart Publishing, 2012, p. 25.

21 Art. 7 (first sentence) BR.

or other establishment', where the former two are merely illustrations of the latter[22] and for that reason hereinafter referred to as 'establishment', is defined autonomously[23] and requires *that* the establishment has a fixed permanent place of business[24] where, and despite meeting the external business requirement,[25] a website does not qualify;[26] *that* the establishment is subject to the direction and control of the parent where a subsidiary company, unless it acts on behalf of its parent as if it was an establishment,[27] does not qualify due to the lack of legal identity;[28] *that* the establishment has a certain autonomy and finally *that* the establishment acts on behalf of and binds the parent.[29]

Secondly, the dispute must arise out of the operation of the establishment. Thus, a connection between the dispute and the establishment is required.[30] Given the sparse CJEU case law one could argue for both a close connection (with the effect that the number of available fora are limited) and a more distant connection (with the effect that the number of available fora are widened). **6.08**

Supporting a close connection it is argued, inter alia, *that* Recital (16) Brussels I Regulation on which art. 7(5) BR is based speaks of a close connection; *that* any such interpretation is confirmed by the sparse CJEU case law requiring **6.09**

22 Case 14/76, *De Bloos, SPRL v Société en commandite par actions Bouyer*, para. 21; Oberlandesgericht (OLG) Rostock, IPRspr. 2009, Nr. 174, p. 453 and Report on the Convention on Jurisdiction and the Enforcement of Judgments in Civil and Commercial Matters done at Lugano on 16 September 1988 by P. Jenard and. G. Möller 90/C 189/07 (Jenard and Möller report) at 43.

23 Case 33/78, *Somafer SA*, para. 8 and Magnus and Mankowski, *supra* note 2, p. 278, note 1672 with references.

24 If the place of business is a principal place of business a distinction must be drawn between legal and natural persons. Legal persons having a principal place of business in the EU/EFTA cannot be sued under art. 7(5) BR but must be sued under art. 63(1)(c) BR cf. Chapter 5 section B.1(a) whereas natural persons having a principal place of business can be sued under art. 7(5) BR cf. Magnus and Mankowski, ibid., p. 280.

25 Magnus and Mankowski, ibid., p. 279.

26 Michael Bogdan, Svensk Jurist Tidning (SvJT), 1998, 825, 832–4; Ulf Maunsbach, Svensk Domstols Behörighet vid Gränseöverskridande Varumärketvister – Särskilt om Internetrelaterade Intrång, Juridiska Fakulteten, Lund Universitet, 2005, p. 161 cf. Recital (19) Directive 2000/31/EC of the European Parliament and of the Council of 8 June 2000 on Certain Legal Aspects of Information Society Services, in particular Electronic Commerce, in the Internal Market (Directive on electronic commerce).

27 Case 218/86, *SAR Schotte GmbH*, paras 15–17.

28 Magnus and Mankowski, *supra* note 2, p. 278 and James J. Fawcett and Paul Torremans, *Intellectual Property and Private International Law*, 2nd edn, Oxford Private International Law Series, 2011 at 5.113.

29 Case 33/78, *Somafer SA*, para. 12; case 139/80, *Blanckaert & Willems PVBA v Luise Trost*, para. 11; case 218/86, *SAR Schotte GmbH*, para. 10; case C-439/93, *Lloyd's Register of Shipping*, para. 18 cf. Magnus and Mankowski, ibid., p. 278; Fawcett and Torremans, ibid. at 5.111; Sender, *supra* note 2 at 3.58 and *Conflict of Laws in Intellectual Property, The CLIP Principles and Commentary*, *supra* note 2, p. 120 (2:207.C02).

30 James Fawcett and Janeen M. Carruthers, *Cheshire, North and Fawcett, Private International Law*, Oxford University Press, 2008, p. 260; Magnus and Mankowski, ibid., p. 285; J. G. Collier, *Conflict of Laws*, 3rd edn, Cambridge University Press, 2011, p. 147; Fawcett and Torremans, ibid. at 5.111–5.112; Sender, *supra* note 2 at 3.59 and *Conflict of Laws in Intellectual Property, The CLIP Principles and Commentary*, *supra* note 2, p. 120 (2:207.C03).

that art. 7(5) BR 'must show without difficulty the special link';[31] *that* art. 7(5) BR as an exception to art. 4 BR must be interpreted strictly,[32] which in turn requires a close connection; *that* otherwise art. 7(5) BR would become just another art. 4 BR[33] and *that* a more distant connection would lead to forum shopping, which must be avoided.[34]

6.10 Supporting a more distant connection it is argued, inter alia, *that* other language versions of art. 7(5) BR are worded more broadly given that they require the dispute to be 'concerned with/ relating to' the operation of the establishment[35] and *that* a more distant connection suffices under other special jurisdiction rules, which similar to art. 7(5) BR are based on a close connection[36] namely art. 7(2) BR as interpreted in *e-Date*; *Wintersteiger*; and *Pinckney*.[37]

6.11 Balancing the interests and considering in particular Recital (16) Brussels I Regulation and the character of the provision as an exception it seems likely that the connection between the dispute and the establishment must be close under art. 7(5) BR. Distributing infringing products from an establishment meets the requirement of a close connection[38] whereas an establishment merely being the registered owner of an IP right does most likely not, which in turn is confirmed by the lack of external business activity in any such situation.[39]

---

31 Case 33/78, *Somafer SA*, para. 11.

32 Ibid., para. 7.

33 Magnus and Mankowski, *supra* note 2, p. 285.

34 Chapter 4 section C.3.

35 The German version speaks of ('wenn es sich um Streitigkeiten [...] handelt'); the French version speaks of ('s'il s'agit d'une contestation relative à l'exploitation'); the Italian version speaks of ('qualora si tratti di controversia concernente l'esercizio'); the Spanish version speaks of ('si se tratar de litigios relativos a la') and the Danish version speaks of ('i sager vedrørende'). Linguistic differences are also found in art. 24(4) BR where by contrast the English version is the broader one given that it speaks of 'in proceedings concerned with' where other versions speak of 'proceedings which have as its object' cf. Chapter 11 section B.1.

36 Recital (16) Brussels I Regulation.

37 Chapter 9 section B.1(a)(ii) Principle 7: Places(s) of effect(s) subject to connecting factors.

38 Fawcett and Torremans, *supra* note 18 at 5.112.

39 Changing the example in Chapter 1 section 2 so that Frogs GmbH would manufacture and market original foam shoes throughout the EU whereas its establishment in Spain would merely be the registered owner of national IP rights in Spain, Frox SpA could most likely not bring a non-infringement action under art. 7(5) BR against Frogs GmbH in Spain given *that* the establishment would not be engaged in external business activity and *that* the dispute would therefore not arise out of the establishment. Frox SpA could, however, bring any such action at the place of registration in Spain following art. 7(2) BR as interpreted in case C-133/11, *Folien Fischer AG, Fofitec AG v Ritrama SpA*, para. 56 cf. case C-523/10, *Wintersteiger AG v Products 4U Sondermaschinenbau GmbH*, para. 29 and Chapter 9 section B.1(b).

Given the lack of CJEU case law one could also question whether art. 7(5) BR is limited to actions brought *at* the establishment or whether art. 7(5) BR also allows action to be brought *from* the establishment. **6.12**

> Applying the example in Chapter 1 section 2 where Frox SpA has an establishment in the UK, which distributes counterfeited foam shoes to Italy, Spain, France and Austria the question would be whether Frox SpA under art. 7(5) BR could bring a non-infringement action *from* the UK against Frogs GmbH claiming non-infringement of their foam shoes.

Supporting that action cannot be brought from the establishment within the meaning of art. 7(5) BR it is argued, inter alia, *that* doing so would contrast the character of the provision as a small defendant's domicile;[40] *that* a *forum actoris* would be created, which is generally met with hostility[41] provided that, which is likely, the provision is subject to unlimited full jurisdiction;[42] *that* companies with an establishment would therefore have an advantage at the expense of companies not having an establishment; *that* art. 7(5) BR could overlap with art. 7(2) BR;[43] *that* the CJEU has avoided overlapping interpretations in prior case law e.g. in *Bier* where art. 7(2) BR was interpreted not to overlap with art. 4 BR[44] and in *Lloyd's* where art. 7(5) BR was interpreted not to overlap with art. 5(1) BR;[45] *that* allowing action to be brought from the establishment would contrast the principle whereas art. 7(5) BR as an exception to art. 4 BR must be interpreted strictly;[46] *that* the *Jenard* report,[47] the *Pocar* report,[48] legal scholars,[49] AGs[50] and scholarly reports[51] all support that action can only be brought at, and not from, the establishment and finally *that* art. 7(5) BR's 'sister' provisions in the EUTMR, CDR, CPVR and AUPC, even though they express *lex specialis*, support any such interpretation.[52] **6.13**

---

40 *Supra* note 16.
41 Chapter 9 section B.1(a)(ii) Principle 6: Place of action and place(s) of effect(s) with references.
42 *Supra* note 20.
43 Magnus and Mankowski, *supra* note 2, p. 286 and Sender, *supra* note 2 at 3.60.
44 Case C-21/76, *Handelskwekerij G. J. Bier BV v Mines de potasse d'Alsace SA*, para. 20.
45 Case C-439/93, *Lloyd's Register of Shipping*, para. 17.
46 *Supra* note 32.
47 Report by P. Jenard, *supra* note 10, p. 26.
48 Report by Professor Fausto Pocar, *supra* note 2 at 68.
49 Magnus and Mankowski, *supra* note 2, pp. 277 and 280; Cheshire, North and Fawcett, *supra* note 30, Fawcett and Carruthers, *supra* note 30, p. 260; Sender, *supra* note 2 at 3.60 and Nielsen, *supra* note 9, p. 168 with references.
50 Opinion of Advocate General Reischl in case 14/76, *De Bloos, SPRL v Société en commandite par actions Bouyer* at 1519 and opinion of Advocate General Reischl in case 139/80, *Blanckaert & Willems PVBA v Luise Trost* at 838.
51 Art. 2:207 CLIP Principles cf. *Conflict of Laws in Intellectual Property, The CLIP Principles and Commentary, supra* note 2, p. 120 (2:207.C01).
52 Arts 97(1) EUTMR, 82(1) CDR, 101(2)(a) CPVR and 33(1)(b) AUPC cf. section C.

6.14 Supporting the opposite result, namely that action can be brought from the establishment within the meaning of art. 7(5) BR it is argued, inter alia, *that* art. 7(5) BR is phrased in general terms since it identifies the parent be sued as the 'person' and the place to sue as where 'the [...] establishment is situated'; *that* none of those exclude that action can be brought from the establishment; *that* given the legal identity between the parent and the establishment the latter may also act as the plaintiff; *that* art. 7(2) BR, which bears a resemblance to art. 7(5) BR as a special jurisdiction rule[53] has (within certain limits) been interpreted as a *forum actoris*;[54] *that* the legal justification was, inter alia, predictability;[55] *that* predictability could similarly justify a forum actoris under art. 7(5) BR;[56] *that* proximity, which art. 7(5) BR is based upon[57] may support the same result;[58] *that* a liberal interpretation of, inter alia, art. 7(5) BR is possible according to the Preamble;[59] *that* art. 5(1) BR[60] and 5(3) BR[61] apply 'both ways'; *that* provisions in the EUTMR, CDR and CPVR, even though they express *lex specialis*, allow action to be brought from the establishment[62] and *that* reasons of consistency support that IP rights whatever nature and territorial scope can be enforced equally.

6.15 Balancing the interests and considering in particular the character of the provision and the risk of creating a forum actoris it seems unlikely that action can be brought from the plaintiff's establishment within the meaning of art. 7(5) BR.

---

53 Chapter II, section 2 BR.

54 Joined cases C-509/09, *e-Date Advertising GmbH v X* and C-161/10, *Olivier Martinez and Robert Martinez v MGN Ltd.*, para. 52.

55 Ibid., para. 50.

56 Applying the example above on page 119 it may be argued that bringing the action in the UK allows both the plaintiff easily to identify the court in which he/she may sue and the defendant reasonably to foresee before which court he/she may be sued cf. Chapter 4 section C.1.

57 *Supra* note 13.

58 Applying the example above on page 119 it may also be argued that the connection between the dispute and the establishment is close in the UK given that the infringing foam shoes have been distributed from the UK.

59 According to Recital (16) of the Brussels I Regulation 'the rules of jurisdiction *should* be [...] founded on the principle that jurisdiction is generally based on the defendant's domicile. Jurisdiction *should* always be available on this ground save in a few well-defined situations [...]' whereas in Recital (11) of the former Brussels I Regulation (44/2001) 'the rules of jurisdiction *must* be [...] founded on the principle that jurisdiction is generally based on the defendant's domicile and jurisdiction *must* always be available on this ground save in a few well-defined situations [...]'. Thus, the word 'must' under the former Brussels I Regulation (44/2001) has been replaced with the word 'should' under the present Brussels I Regulation indicating a softening of the use of the defendant's domicile as the basic principle.

60 Art. 5(1) BR covers both an obligation to pay and an obligation to deliver cf. case 14/76, *De Bloos, SPRL*, paras 9–13.

61 Art. 7(2) BR covers both infringement actions cf. case C-523/10, *Wintersteiger AG* GmbH and non-infringement actions cf. case C-133/11, *Folien Fischer AG*, para. 56 and Chapter 9 sections B.1(a)–B.1(b).

62 Arts 97(2) EUTMR, 82(2) CDR and 101(2)(b) CPVR. The AUPC most likely also allows action to be brought from the establishment but the legal basis for that is not the establishment rule in art. 33(1)(b) AUPC cf. section C.4 but rather the *forum delicti* rule in art. 33(1)(a) AUPC cf. Chapter 9 section C.4(a).

(b) Art. 7(5) BR to non-infringement actions

The possibility of bringing non-infringement actions does not follow from art. 7(5) BR. Such actions must, however, be permitted, which is supported by scholarly reports[63] and, despite their characters as *lex specialis*, by corresponding European unitary IP rights which all, with variations, allow non-infringement actions to be brought at the establishment.[64] **6.16**

(c) Art. 7(5) BR to invalidity actions

If invalidity is raised during the infringement or non-infringement actions brought under art. 7(5) BR a distinction must be drawn between a registered national IP right where invalidity leads to split adjudication given that art. 24(4) BR and *Gat LuK*[65] apply and an unregistered national IP right where invalidity leads to joint adjudication given that art. 24(4) BR and *Gat LuK* do not apply. Art. 24(4) BR and *Gat LuK* are addressed in Chapter 11 section B. **6.17**

2. Defendant is domiciled outside the EU/EFTA

If the defendant is domiciled outside the EU/EFTA the Member States' own international forum rules apply.[66] For the reasons in Chapter 1 section A.5(a) (limit 5) any such rules, including the conditions under which they may apply are not examined for the purpose of the present study. **6.18**

C. THE ESTABLISHMENT RULE APPLYING TO A EUROPEAN UNITARY IP RIGHT

Four different establishment rules apply depending on the corresponding European unitary IP right in question. If a EUTM has been infringed the establishment rule in the EUTMR applies (section 1); if a CD has been infringed the establishment rule in the CDR applies (section 2); if a CPV has been infringed the establishment rule in the CPVR applies (section 3) and if a UP has been infringed the establishment rule in the AUPC applies (section 4). **6.19**

---

63 Arts 2:602 cf. 2:207 CLIP Principles cf. *Conflict of Laws in Intellectual Property, The CLIP Principles and Commentary, supra* note 2, p. 173 (2:602.C01).

64 Arts 97(1) cf. 96(b) EUTMR and section C.1(b); arts 82(1) cf. 81(b) CDR and section C.2(b); arts 101(2)(a) cf. 94 CPVR and section C.3(b) and, under certain circumstances, arts 33(4) cf. 33(1)(b) AUPC and section C.4(b).

65 Case C-4/03, *Gesellschaft für Antriebstechnik mbH & Co. KG v Lamellen und Kupplungsbau Beteiligungs KG.*

66 Art. 6 BR.

1. The establishment rule in the EUTMR

6.20 The establishment rule is found in art. 97(1) EUTMR. The CJEU has yet to interpret the provision,[67] however, one case is pending.[68] Below a distinction is drawn between applying the rule to infringement actions (section a); to non-infringement actions (section b) and to invalidity actions (section c).[69]

(a) Art. 97(1) EUTMR to infringement actions

6.21 If the defendant is not domiciled in the EU[70] art. 97(1) EUTMR allows[71] infringement actions[72] to be brought in: '[the Member State], in which he has an establishment'.[73]

6.22 The provision is as stated in Chapter 5 section C.1(a) modelled on the corresponding provisions in the 1975 Community Patent Convention and in the protocol to the amended 1989 version where it is referred. The reason for adopting the provision is not mentioned in the Explanatory Memoranda[74] but since it qualifies as a small defendant's domicile rule, which is supported by the fact that the defendant's domicile and establishment rules have been merged into one same provision, the underlying justification equals the one behind its 'sister' provision in art. 7(5) BR[75] except that the connection seems more distant given that it is likely not a requirement that the dispute has arisen out of the operation of the establishment cf. below.

6.23 Compared to its 'sister' provision in art. 7(5) BR the provision is both similar and different. It is similar *since* it is also subject to unlimited full jurisdiction[76]

67 Study on the Overall Functioning of the European Trade Mark System presented by Max Planck Institute for Intellectual Property and Competition Law Munich of 15 February 2011 at 3.126 (p. 156).

68 Case C-617/15, *Hummel Holding A/S v Nike Inc. and Nike Retail BV* (pending).

69 The three kinds of actions are overall defined in Chapter 1 section A.3(b).

70 Art. 97(1) (first part) EUTMR.

71 The reason for using the term 'allows', contrary to art. 97(1) EUTMR using the term 'shall', is that infringement actions may also be brought under the *forum delicti* rule in art. 97(5) EUTMR cf. Chapter 9 section C.1(a) meaning that two alternatives are available to the plaintiff. In addition to that 'fall back' rules may apply cf. Chapters 2 and 3 section C.1.

72 Art. 96(a) EUTMR.

73 Art. 97(1)(second part) EUTMR. Art. 97(1)(first part) EUTMR being the defendant's domicile rule is addressed in Chapter 5 section C.1(a).

74 Memorandum on the Creation of an EEC Trade Mark adopted by the Commission on 6 July 1976, SEC(76)2462 July 1976, p. 36; The Need for a European Trademark System, Competence of the European Community to create one, Commission Working Paper, Working Group on the Community Trademark, October 1979, III/D/1294/79-EN, p. 31 and Bulletin of the European Communities Supplement 5/80, New Trade Mark System for the Community, proposed Directive and Regulation prepared by the Commission of the European Communities (COM 80 635 final 19 November 1980) p. 76.

75 Fawcett and Torremans, *supra* note 18 at 8.14.

76 Art. 98(1)(a) EUTMR.

unless the plaintiff chooses otherwise.[77] It is different *since* it speaks of 'establishment' whereas art. 7(5) BR speaks of 'branch, agency or other establishment' cf. below; *since* it does not explicitly require the dispute to have arisen out of the operation of the establishment as opposed to art. 7(5) BR; *since* jurisdiction is allocated in the EU[78] and not in the EU/EFTA;[79] *since* it extends EU competence more than art. 7(5) BR given that it applies (only) if the defendant is domiciled outside the EU[80] cf. below and *since* bringing threatened infringement actions requires that national law so permits,[81] which is not a requirement under art. 7(5) BR.[82]

The term 'establishment' is not defined in the EUTMR.[83] Given the lack of CJEU case law,[84] however, with one case pending[85] one could argue both that the term must be construed independently and in line with art. 7(5) BR. **6.24**

Supporting that 'establishment' must be construed independently it is argued, inter alia, *that* art. 7(5) BR, where the term 'establishment' is used, has been explicitly exempted in the EUTMR;[86] *that* the wording of art. 97(1) EUTMR differs from the wording of art. 7(5) BR and *that* other rules in the EUTMR with different wordings must also be interpreted independently.[87] **6.25**

Supporting the opposite result namely that 'establishment' must be construed in line with art. 7(5) BR it is argued, inter alia, *that* the Explanatory Memorandum where the derogations from the BR are 'often more formal than substantial'[88] meaning that inspiration is likely to be found in art. 7(5) BR when defining 'establishment'; *that* any such interpretation is confirmed by the fact that art. 7(5) BR merely specifies the content of 'establishment'[89] and *that* **6.26**

77 Case C-235/09, *DHL Express France SAS v Chronopost SA*, para. 48 and Chapter 5 note 51.

78 Art. 97(1) EUTMR speaks of 'courts of the Member State'.

79 *Supra* note 21.

80 Extending EU competence more than the provisions in the BR is a general phenomenon under the EUTMR cf. art. 94(2)(c) EUTMR and opinion of Advocate General Tanchev in case C-617/15, *Hummel Holding A/S v Nike Inc. and Nike Retail BV*, para. 77.

81 Art. 96(a) EUTMR.

82 *Supra* note 19.

83 Fawcett and Torremans, *supra* note 18 at 8.16.

84 Curia.eu visited on 1 January 2017.

85 Case C-617/15, *Hummel Holding A/S* (pending).

86 Art. 94(2)(a) EUTMR.

87 Art. 97(5) EUTMR cf. Chapter 9 section C.1(a).

88 Proposal for a European Parliament and Council Regulation on the Community Design presented by the Commission COM (93) 342 final COD 463 Brussels, 3 December 1993, p. 38. The reasoning applies *mutatis mutandis* under the EUTMR cf. the wording '[the forum rules in the CDR] entirely correspond to the parallel provisions relating to the Community Trade Mark'.

89 *Supra* note 22.

legal scholars support that reliance can be placed on art. 7(5) BR when interpreting 'establishment'.[90]

6.27 Balancing the interests and considering the wording of the provision as well as writings of legal scholars it seems likely that 'establishment' in art. 97(1) EUTMR encompasses a branch, agency or other establishment, hereinafter referred to as 'establishment', in line with art. 7(5) BR.

6.28 The impact of establishment in art. 97(1) EUTMR, however, differs from the impact in art. 7(5) BR.

6.29 *First*, art. 7(5) BR can only be invoked if the defendant is domiciled in the EU/EFTA[91] thus being an alternative to the defendant's domicile in art. 4 BR whereas art. 97(1) EUTMR can only be invoked in the exact opposite situation, namely where the defendant is not domiciled in the EU[92] thus not being an alternative to the defendant's domicile but rather a surrogate.[93]

6.30 *Secondly*, art. 7(5) BR can only be invoked if the dispute has arisen out of the operation of the establishment[94] whereas any such requirement does not follow from art. 97(1) EUTMR.[95] Given the lack of CJEU case law[96] one could argue both that an 'arise out of' requirement implicitly applies under art. 97(1) EUTMR and that it does not apply.

6.31 Supporting that any such requirement implicitly applies under art. 97(1) EUTMR it is argued, inter alia, the Explanatory Memorandum whereas the derogations from the BR are 'often more formal than substantial',[97] the principles of predictability[98] and proximity[99] which given their general natures[100] also apply under the EUTMR,[101] scholarly reports,[102] case law

90 Fawcett and Torremans, *supra* note 18 at 8.16.
91 Arts 7(first sentence) cf. 4 cf. 62 and 63 BR.
92 Art. 97(1) EUTMR reads 'or if he is not domiciled in a Member State [...]'.
93 Opinion of Advocate General Tanchev in case C-617/15, *Hummel Holding*, para. 77.
94 *Supra* note 30.
95 Art. 97(1) EUTMR reads '[...] in which he has an establishment' cf. Opinion of Advocate General Tanchev in case 617/15, *Hummel Holding*, para. 69.
96 *Supra* notes 67–8.
97 *Supra* note 88.
98 Chapter 4 section C.1.
99 Chapter 4 section C.2.
100 Chapter 4 sections C.1–C.2.
101 Opinion of Advocate General Jääskinen in case C-360/12, *Coty Prestige Lancaster Group GmbH v First Note Perfumes NV*, para. 34.
102 Arts 2:605 cf. 2:207 CLIP Principles cf. *Conflict of Laws in Intellectual Property, The CLIP Principles and Commentary*, *supra* note 2, p. 120 (2:207.C03).

from Germany[103] and finally that art. 97(1) EUTMR would coincide with art. 97(5) EUTMR[104] if no requirement was applied which in turn would deprive the provision its effect.

Supporting the opposite result, namely that any such requirement does not apply under art. 97(1) EUTMR it is argued, inter alia, the wording of the provision,[105] writings of legal scholars,[106] AG opinions,[107] the fact that art. 97(1) EUTMR need not to be interpreted strictly[108] and that any such requirement would catch fewer situations by the exclusive jurisdiction of EUTM courts, which has not been the intention of the drafters behind the EUTMR taking into account *that* art. 7(5) BR holding any such requirement has been exempted[109] and *that* the applicable 'fall back' provisions in the BR apply even if the defendant is merely established in the EU[110] thus widening the competence of EUTM courts. **6.32**

Balancing the interests and in particular considering the wording of the provision it seems likely not a requirement in art. 97(1) EUTMR that the dispute has arisen out of the operation of the establishment. **6.33**

> Applying the example in Chapter 1 section 2 Frox SpA distributes foam shoes from its establishment in London, UK. If Frogs GmbH decides to enforce its 'Frogs' EUTM against Frox SpA they cannot bring an action under art. 97(1) EUTMR in London since Frox SpA is based in Italy irrespective of whether the London, UK establishment has distributed the shoes or not[111] and they cannot do so under art. 7(5) Brussels I Regulation either since the provision has been explicitly exempted cf. art. 94(2)(a) EUTMR. If, by contrast, Frogs GmbH decides to enforce its national Frogs trademark right they can bring any such action under art. 7(5) Brussels I Regulation in London *since* Frox SpA is based in Italy and *since* the dispute has arisen out of the operation of the establishment given that the infringing foam shoes have been distributed from London, UK.

---

103 Oberlandesgericht Düsseldorf in case I-20 U 175 of 31 January 2012 concerning art. 82(1) CDR which has an identical text and analogous ratio as art. 97(1) EUTMR.
104 Chapter 9 section C.1.
105 Art. 97(1) EUTMR speaks of the courts of the Member State in which the defendant 'has an establishment'.
106 Fawcett and Torremans, *supra* note 18 at 8.18.
107 Opinion of Advocate General Tanchev in case 617/15, *Hummel Holding*, para. 90.
108 Ibid., paras. 79–86.
109 Art. 94(2)(a) EUTMR.
110 Art. 94(2)(c) EUTMR.
111 Frogs GmbH would, however, most likely be able to bring an action in London, UK following art. 97(5) EUTMR cf. Chapter 9 section C.1(a).

(b) Art. 97(1) EUTMR to non-infringement actions

6.34 Art. 97(1) EUTMR also allows[112] non-infringement actions[113] to be brought at the defendant's EU establishment. It requires, however, that national law so permits.[114] Assuming that national law does not so permit the example in Chapter 5 section C.2(a) applies *mutatis mutandis* provided that the defendant's EU domicile is replaced with the defendant's EU etablishment.

(c) Art. 97(1) EUTMR to invalidity actions

6.35 A distinction must be drawn between invalidity in infringement actions brought under art. 97(1) EUTMR which leads to joint adjudication given that art. 96(d) EUTMR applies and invalidity in non-infringement actions brought under art. 97(1) EUTMR which leads to either split or joint adjudication given that arts 99(2) cf. 56 EUTMR apply. Arts 96(d) and 99(2) cf. 56 EUTMR are addressed in Chapter 11 section C.1.

2. The establishment rule in the CDR

6.36 The establishment rule is found in art. 82(1) CDR. The CJEU has yet to interpret the provision[115] and no case is pending.[116] Below a distinction is drawn between applying the rule to infringement actions (section a); to non-infringement actions (section b) and to invalidity actions (section c).[117]

(a) Art. 82(1) CDR to infringement actions

6.37 If the defendant is not domiciled in the EU[118] art. 82(1) CDR allows[119] infringement actions[120] to be brought in: '[...] any Member State in which he has an establishment'.[121]

---

112 The reason for using the term 'allows', contrary to art. 97(1) EUTMR using the term 'shall', is that non-infringement actions may also be brought under the 'fall back' rules cf. Chapters 2 and 3 section C.1.

113 Art. 96(b) EUTMR.

114 Art. 96(b) EUTMR.

115 Curia.eu visited on 1 January 2017.

116 See, however, the pending case C-617/15, *Hummel Holding A/S* concerning the interpretation of the 'sister' provision in art. 97(1) EUTMR.

117 The three kinds of actions are overall defined in Chapter 1 section A.3(b).

118 Art. 82(1) (first part) CDR.

119 The reason for using the term 'allows', contrary to art. 82(1) CDR using the term 'shall', is that infringement actions may also be brought under the *forum delicti* rule in art. 82(5) CDR cf. Chapter 9 section C.2(a) meaning that two alternatives are available to the plaintiff. In addition to that 'fall back' rules may apply cf. Chapters 2 and 3 section C.2.

120 Art. 81(a) CDR.

121 Art. 82(1)(second part) CDR. Art. 82(1)(first part) CDR being the defendant's domicile rule is addressed in Chapter 5 section C.2(a).

Compared to its 'sister' provision in the EUTMR[122] art. 82(1) CDR is, with one slight linguistic variation,[123] equal *since* it also requires that the defendant is not domiciled in the EU; *since* it also allocates jurisdiction at the EU establishment; *since* it is also subject to unlimited full jurisdiction[124] unless the plaintiff chooses otherwise[125] and *since* bringing threatened infringement actions also requires that national law so permits.[126] Thus, section C.1(a) applies *mutatis mutandis* including to the unregistered CD.[127] **6.38**

(b) Art. 82(1) CDR to non-infringement actions

Art. 82(1) CDR also allows[128] non-infringement actions[129] to be brought at the defendant's EU establishment. In line with its 'sister' provision in the EUTMR[130] it requires that national law so permits.[131] Thus, section C.1(b) applies *mutatis mutandis* including to the unregistered CD.[132] **6.39**

(c) Art. 82(1) CDR to invalidity actions

A distinction must be drawn between invalidity in infringement actions brought under art. 82(1) CDR which leads to joint adjudication given that art. 81(d) CDR applies and invalidity in non-infringement actions brought under art. 82(1) CDR which leads to either split or joint adjudication given that arts 84(4) cf. 52 CDR apply. Arts 81(d) and 84(4) cf. 52 CDR are addressed in Chapter 11 section C.2. **6.40**

3. The establishment rule in the CPVR

The establishment rule is found in art. 101(2)(a) CPVR. The CJEU has yet to interpret the provision[133] and no case is pending.[134] Below a distinction is **6.41**

---

122 Art. 97(1) EUTMR.
123 The variation is that art. 97(1) EUTMR speaks of 'in which he has an establishment' whereas art. 82(1) CDR speaks of 'in any Member State in which he has an establishment'. Any one leads to the same result.
124 Art. 83(1) CDR.
125 Case C-235/09, *DHL Express France SAS*, para. 48 applies *mutatis mutandis* under the CDR cf. Chapter 5 note 51.
126 Art. 81(a) CDR.
127 Fawcett and Torremans, *supra* note 18 at 8.116.
128 The reason for using the term 'allows', contrary to art. 82(1) CDR using the term 'shall', is that non-infringement actions may also be brought under the 'fall back' rules cf. Chapters 2 and 3 section C.2.
129 Art. 81(b) CDR.
130 Art. 97(1) EUTMR.
131 Art. 81(b) CDR.
132 Fawcett and Torremans, *supra* note 18 at 8.116.
133 Curia.eu visited on 1 January 2017.
134 See, however, the pending case C-617/15, *Hummel Holding* concerning the interpretation of the 'sister' provision in art. 97(1) EUTMR.

drawn between applying the rule to infringement actions (section a); to non-infringement actions (section b) and to invalidity actions (section c).[135]

(a) Art. 101(2)(a) CPVR to infringement actions

6.42 If the defendant is not domiciled in the EU/EFTA[136] art. 101(2)(a) CPVR allows[137] actions in respect of claims for infringement[138] to be brought in: '[the Member State or another Contracting Party to the Lugano Convention in which he/she] has an establishment'.[139]

6.43 The reason for adopting the provision is not mentioned in the Explanatory Memorandum[140] but given that the defendant's domicile and establishment rules in line with the EUTMR and CDR[141] have been merged into one same provision the justification in section C.1(a) applies *mutatis mutandis*.

6.44 Compared to its 'sister' provisions in the EUTMR and CDR[142] art. 101(2)(a) CPVR is similar *since* it also speaks of 'establishment' and *since* it also allows for unlimited full jurisdiction[143] unless the plaintiff chooses otherwise[144] but is different *since* it applies only if the defendant is not domiciled in the EU/EFTA; *since* jurisdiction – at least according to the provision – can be allocated at the defendant's EFTA establishment[145] and *since* threatened

135 The three kinds of actions are overall defined in Chapter 1 section A.3(b).

136 Art. 101(2)(a) (first part) CPVR.

137 The reason for using the term 'allows', contrary to art. 101(2) CPVR using the term 'shall', is that infringement actions may also be brought under the *forum delicti* rule in art. 101(3) CPVR cf. Chapter 9 section C.3(a) meaning that two alternatives are available to the plaintiff. In addition to that 'fall back' rules may apply cf. Chapters 2 and 3 section C.3.

138 Art. 94 CPVR.

139 Art. 101(2)(a) (second part) CPVR. Art. 101(2)(a)(first part) CPVR being the defendant's domicile rule is addressed in Chapter 5 section C.3(a).

140 Proposal for a Council Regulation on Community Plant Variety Rights presented by the Commission COM(90)347 (90/C 244/01) Brussels 6 September 1990.

141 Arts 97(1) EUTMR and 82(1) CDR.

142 Ibid.

143 Art. 101(2) (last sentence) CPVR.

144 Case C-235/09, *DHL Express France SAS*, para. 48 applies *mutatis mutandis* under the CPVR cf. Chapter 5 note 51.

145 The fact that jurisdiction can be allocated at the defendant's EFTA establishment following art. 101(2)(a) CPVR raises a twofold problem. The first problem, which is general in nature, is that EFTA Member States are not parties to the CPVR cf. Evaluation of the Community Plant Variety Right *Aquis* – Final Report to the Directorate General for Health and Consumer Affairs (European Commission), April 2011, p. 49, section 4.5.7.2 and accordingly EFTA courts may not find themselves competent on the basis of its provisions, inter alia, art. 101(2)(a) CPVR. The second problem, which is specific in nature, is that art. 101(2)(a) CPVR allows for jurisdiction at an EFTA establishment when the defendant is not domiciled in EU/EFTA, which art. 5(5) Lugano Convention does not allow for. Both problems are addressed in Chapter 2 section C.3(b).

infringement actions are not permitted[146] contrary to the EUTMR and CDR where bringing such actions requires that national law so permits.[147]

6.45 The term 'establishment' is not defined in the CPVR. For the reasons in section C.1(a), however, it seems likely that the term must be construed in the same way as the corresponding terms in the EUTMR and CDR,[148] which in turn is supported by legal scholars.[149] Thus, section C.1(a) applies *mutatis mutandis*.

(b) Art. 101(2)(a) CPVR to non-infringement actions

6.46 Art. 101(2)(a) CPVR also allows[150] non-infringement actions[151] to be brought at the defendant's EU/EFTA establishment. Thus, section C.3(a) applies *mutatis mutandis*.

(c) Art. 101(2)(a) CPVR to invalidity actions

6.47 If invalidity of a CPV is raised during the infringement or non-infringement actions brought under art. 101(2)(a) CPVR the CPVO comes into play given their exclusivity to address invalidity,[152] which in turn leads to either split or joint adjudication. Art. 20 CPVR is addressed in Chapter 11 section C.3.

4. The establishment rule in the AUPC

6.48 The establishment rule is found in art. 33(1)(b) AUPC.[153] Below a distinction is drawn between applying the rule to infringement actions (section a); to non-infringement actions (section b) and to invalidity actions (section c).[154]

---

146 Fawcett and Torremans, *supra* note 18 at 8.146.

147 Arts 96(a) EUTMR and 81(a) CDR.

148 Arts 97(1) EUTMR and 82(1) CDR.

149 Fawcett and Torremans, *supra* note 18 at 8.156.

150 The reason for using the term 'allows', contrary to art. 101(2) CPVR using the term 'shall', is that non-infringement actions may also be brought under the *forum delicti* rule in art. 101(3) CPVR cf. Chapter 9 section C.3(b). In addition to that 'fall back' rules may apply cf. Chapters 2 and 3 section C.3.

151 Non-infringement actions are not explicitly mentioned in Part Six CPVR. For the reasons in Chapter 3 section C.3 non-infringement actions must, however, be covered by the CPVR.

152 Art. 20 CPVR.

153 Torsten Bjørn Larsen, *Rules of Jurisdiction in the Agreement on a Unified Patent Court*, Nordisk Immateriellt Rättsskydd, 4/2014, pp. 357–74 at 366 *et seq.* and Torsten Bjørn Larsen, *A Bundle of National Patents v a European Patent with Unitary Effect – Jurisdictional Comparison, Intellectual Property and General Legal Principles – Is IP a Lex Specialis?* Edward Elgar Publishing, 2015, pp. 208 *et seq.*

154 The three kinds of actions are overall defined in Chapter 1 section A.3(b).

(a) Art. 33(1)(b) AUPC to infringement actions

6.49 If the defendant does not have a residence or a principal place of business in a Contracting Member State[155] art. 33(1)(b) AUPC allows[156] infringement actions[157] to be brought before: '[the local division hosted by the Contracting Member State where the defendant has] its place of business [...]'.[158]

6.50 The reason for adopting the provision is unspoken in the drafting history[159] but given that the defendant's residence (which for the reasons in Chapter 5 section C.4(a), and with few variations, is likely to be interpreted as the defendant's domicile) and that the defendant's place of business (which for the reasons below is likely to be interpreted as the defendant's establishment) have been merged into one same provision the justification in section C.1(a) applies *mutatis mutandis*.

6.51 Compared to its 'sister' European unitary IP provisions[160] art. 33(1)(b) AUPC is both similar and different. It is similar *since*, and for the reasons in section C.1(a), it is likely not a requirement that the dispute has arisen out of the operation of the 'place of business' and *since* a 'place of business' is also not an alternative to the defendant's 'residence'.[161] It is different *since* it speaks of 'place of business' whereas its 'sister' provisions speak of 'establishment';[162] *since* jurisdiction must be allocated in a Contracting Member State[163] and not in the EU[164] or in the EU/EFTA;[165] *since* it is subject to unlimited full jurisdiction[166] contrary to its 'sister' provisions where the plaintiff may choose between unlimited full and limited forum jurisdiction[167] and finally *since* threatened infringement actions are permitted[168] contrary to the EUTMR

155 Art. 33(1)(b)(first part) AUPC.

156 The reason for using the term 'allows', contrary to art. 33(1) AUPC using the term 'shall', is that infringement actions may also be brought under the *forum delicti* rule in art. 33(1)(a) AUPC cf. Chapter 9 section C.4(a) meaning that two alternatives are available to the plaintiff cf. Chapters 2 and 3 section C.4.

157 Art. 32(1)(a) AUPC.

158 Art. 33(1)(b)(second part) AUPC. Art. 33(1)(b)(first part) AUPC being the defendant's domicile rule is addressed in Chapter 5 section C.4(a).

159 Chapter 2 notes 248–9.

160 Arts 97(1) EUTMR, 82(1) CDR and 101(2)(a) CPVR.

161 Art. 33(1)(b) AUPC speaks of 'or in the absence of [...]'.

162 Arts 97(1) EUTMR, 82(1) CDR and 101(2)(a) CPVR.

163 The reason that the AUPC speaks of Contracting Member States is that not every EU Member State is party to the AUPC cf. Chapter 1 note 28.

164 Arts 97(1) EUTMR and 82(1) CDR.

165 Art. 101(2)(a) CPVR.

166 Art. 34 AUPC and Chapter 5 section C.4(a).

167 Arts 98(1)(a) EUTMR, 83(1) CDR and art. 101(2)(last sentence) CPVR cf. case C-235/09, *DHL Express France SAS*, para. 48 and Chapter 5 note 51.

168 Arts 33(1)(b) cf. 32(1)(a) AUPC.

and CDR where bringing such actions requires that national law so permits[169] and the CPVR where such actions are not permitted.[170]

Taking into account that 'place of business' and 'establishment' are used as synonyms in the legal literature,[171] in Explanatory Memoranda[172] and in case law[173] it seems likely that art. 33(1)(b) AUPC must be interpreted as an establishment rule. 6.52

An establishment rule has, however, not always been found in the AUPC given that (what is now art. 33(1)(b) AUPC) initially spoke of the place 'where the defendant is domiciled'[174] (one option), which was revised in to the place 'where the defendant [...] has his residence or principal place of business'[175] (two options). First in 2011 the provision was revised in to the place 'where the defendant [...] has his residence, principal place of business or place of business'[176] (three options) and further in to the place 'where the defendant [...] has his residence or principal place of business or, in the absence of residence or principal place of business, place of business'[177] (two

169 Arts 97(1) cf. 96(a) EUTMR and arts 82(1) cf. 81(a) CDR.

170 Fawcett and Torremans, *supra* note 18 at 8.146.

171 Magnus and Mankowski, *supra* note 2, p. 280.

172 Bulletin of the European Communities Supplement 5/80, New Trade Mark System for the Community, proposed Directive and Regulation prepared by the Commission of the European Communities (COM 80 635 final 19 November 1980) p. 76.

173 Case 218/86, *SAR Schotte GmbH v Parfums Rothschild SARL*, paras 15–17.

174 Draft Agreement on the European Union Patent Judiciary of 14 May 2008 (9124/08 PI 24 COUR 19) chapter IV concerning 'jurisdiction, allocation of cases and effects of decisions' art. 15a(5)(b) cf. Draft Agreement on the European Union Patent Judiciary of 30 June 2008 (11270/08 PI 32 COUR 32) chapter IV concerning 'jurisdiction, allocation of cases and effects of decisions' art. 15a(5)(b) cf. Draft Agreement on the European Union Patent Court and draft Statute of 4 November 2008 (14970/08 PI 78 COUR 52) chapter IV concerning 'jurisdiction and effects of decisions' art. 15a(1)(b) cf. Draft Agreement on the European and Community Patents Court and draft Statute of 8 January 2009 (5072/09 PI 1 COUR 1) chapter IV concerning 'jurisdiction and effects of decisions' art. 15a(1)(b) cf. Draft Agreement on the European and Community Patents Court and draft Statute, revised Presidency text of 23 March 2009 (7928/09 PI 23 COUR 29) chapter IV concerning 'jurisdiction and effects of decisions' art. 15a(1)(b) cf. Draft Agreement on a Unified Patent Court and draft Statute, Presidency text of 14 June 2011 (11533/11 PI 68 COUR 32) chapter IV concerning 'jurisdiction and effects of decisions' art. 15a(1)(b) cf. Draft Agreement on a Unified Patent Court and draft Statute, revised Presidency text of 2 September 2011 (13751/11 PI 108 COUR 48) chapter IV concerning 'jurisdiction and effects of decisions' art. 15a(1)(b) and Draft Agreement on a Unified Patent Court and draft Statute, revised Presidency text of 7 October 2011 (15289/11 PI 127 COUR 56) chapter IV concerning 'competence, jurisdiction and effects of decisions' art. 15a(1)(b).

175 Draft Agreement on a Unified Patent Court and draft Statute, revised Presidency text of 19 October 2011 (15539/11 PI 133 COUR 59) chapter IV concerning 'competence, jurisdiction and effects of decisions' art. 15a(1)(b).

176 Draft Agreement on a Unified Patent Court and draft Statute, revised Presidency text of 26 October 2011 (16023/11 PI 141 COUR 62) chapter IV concerning 'competence, jurisdiction and effects of decisions' art. 15a(1)(b).

177 Draft Agreement on a Unified Patent Court and draft Statute, revised Presidency text of 11 November 2011 (16741/11 PI 155 COUR 64) chapter IV concerning 'competence, jurisdiction and effects of decisions' art. 15a(1)(b) cf. Draft Agreement on the creation of a Unified Patent Court, guidance for future work of 24 November 2011 (17539/11 PI 168 COUR 71) art. 15a(1)(b) cf. Draft Agreement on a Unified Patent Court and draft Statute, consolidated text of 27 September 2012 (14268/12 PI 133 COUR 66) chapter IV

options and failing them a place of business comes into play) being the version which, with few variations[178] was passed.[179]

6.53 The term 'place of business' is not defined in the AUPC. It seems, however, likely that the term must be construed broadly given *that* the ROP when serving the statement of claim and written pleadings defines it as 'any place within the Contracting Member States where the [...] legal person has a place of business';[180] *that* any such broad interpretation is confirmed by the fact that it is likely not a requirement that the dispute has arisen out of the operation of the 'place of business'; *that* the expected pro patentee approach of the UPC[181] renders likely a broad interpretation and *that* any such broad interpretation does not necessarily lead to more forum shopping given that the exclusive patent rights,[182] its limitations,[183] remedies and damages[184] and the ROP are the same.

6.54 Finally, and in line with its 'sister' provisions[185] it seems likely not possible to bring an action from the 'place of business' within the meaning of art. 33(1)(b) AUPC, which speaks of the place where the 'defendant has its [...] place of business'.[186]

(b) Art. 33(1)(b) AUPC to non-infringement actions

6.55 Art. 33(1)(b) AUPC also applies to non-infringement actions.[187] It requires, however, that an infringement action between the same parties relating to the same patent is already pending before an art. 33(1)(b) AUPC court. In that

---

concerning 'international jurisdiction and competence' art. 15a(1)(b) cf. Draft Agreement on a Unified Patent Court and draft Statute, consolidated text of 12 October 2012 (14750/12 PI 120 COUR 67) chapter IV concerning 'international jurisdiction and competence' art. 15a(1)(b) and Draft Agreement on a Unified Patent Court and draft Statute, consolidated text of 14 November 2012 (16222/12 PI 146 COUR 74) chapter IV concerning 'international jurisdiction and competence' art. 15a(1)(b).

178 One variation is that the 14 November 2012 draft cf. *supra* note 177 spoke of 'his' residence whereas the final version speaks of 'its' residence and another variation is that the 14 November 2012 draft spoke of 'place of business' whereas the final version speaks of 'its place of business'.

179 Art. 33(1)(b) AUPC.

180 Arts 271(5)(a) and 278(3)(a) ROP.

181 Clement Salung Petersen and Jens Schovsbo, 'On Law and Policy in a European and European Union Patent Court (EEUPC), What will it do to Patent Law and What will Patent Law do to it?' in Henning Koch, Karsten Hagel-Sørensen, Ulrich Haltern and Joseph H. H. Weiler (eds), *Europe The New Legal Realism*, DJØF Publishing p. 636 (section IV.4).

182 Arts 24(b) cf. 25–26 AUPC.

183 Arts 24(b) cf. 27 AUPC.

184 Arts 24(b) cf. 56 AUPC *et seq.*

185 Arts 7(5) BR, 97(1) EUTMR, 82(1) CDR and 101(2)(a) CPVR.

186 One could also argue the opposite considering that the *forum delicti* rule in arts 33(1)(a) cf. 34 AUPC may likely lead to a *forum actoris* cf. Chapter 9 section C.4(a) which would therefore equal art. 33(1)(b) AUPC if action could be brought from the plaintiff's place of business.

187 Art. 33(4) AUPC.

case the non-infringement action may only be brought there.[188] If, however, an infringement action is not already pending art. 33(1)(b) AUPC does not apply. In that case the non-infringement action must be brought at the central division cf. Chapter 10 section C.

(c) Art. 33(1)(b) AUPC to invalidity actions

If invalidity of a UP is raised during the infringement or non-infringement actions brought under art. 33(1)(b) AUPC cf. above the flexible exclusive jurisdiction rule in art. 33(3) AUPC comes into play, which in turn leads to either split or joint adjudication. Art. 33(3) AUPC is addressed in Chapter 11 section C.4. **6.56**

D. CONCLUSION

A distinction is drawn between the application of the establishment rule in trademark, design, plant variety and patent cases. **6.57**

In *trademark* cases the applicable establishment rules are found in arts 7(5) BR, 97(1) EUTMR and possibly in the Member States' own international forum rules, which have not been examined. The natures of arts 7(5) BR and 97(1) EUTMR are both similar and different. **6.58**

They are similar *since* 'establishment' is defined in the same way; *since* infringement actions can be brought under both; *since* both are subject to unlimited full jurisdiction unless the plaintiff chooses otherwise and *since* invalidity in non-infringement actions concerning registered trademarks usually leads to split adjudication. **6.59**

They are different *since* art. 7(5) BR is justified in proximity whereas art. 97(1) EUTMR seems proximate in a slightly more distant way; *since* art. 7(5) BR is an alternative to the defendant's domicile which art. 97(1) EUTMR is not; *since* the defendant's establishment must be in EU/EFTA under art. 7(5) BR but in EU under art. 97(1) EUTMR; *since* art. 7(5) BR requires the dispute to have arisen out of the establishment as opposed to art. 97(1) EUTMR; *since* threatened infringement actions can be brought under art. 7(5) BR but under art. 97(1) EUTMR only if national law so permits; *since* non-infringement actions can be brought under art. 7(5) BR but under art. 97(1) EUTMR only **6.60**

188 Art. 33(4) (second sentence) AUPC.

if national law so permits and *since* invalidity in infringement actions concerning registered trademarks usually leads to split adjudication under art. 7(5) BR but joint adjudication under art. 97(1) EUTMR.

6.61 In sum – and generally speaking – art. 7(5) BR is advantageous to the plaintiff acting as the rightholder since threatened infringement actions can always be brought whereas art. 7(5) BR is advantageous to the plaintiff acting as the infringer since non-infringement actions can always be brought and since adjudication for registered trademarks is split. Art. 97(1) EUTMR is advantageous to the plaintiff acting as the rightholder since adjudication is joint whereas art. 97(1) EUTMR is advantageous to both since the scope of the defendant's establishment is restricted meaning that action can be brought at their own domicile if the defendant is established in e.g. EFTA following art. 97(2) EUTMR and Chapter 7 and since more fora may be available.

6.62 In *design* cases the applicable establishment rules are found in arts 7(5) BR, 82(1) CDR and possibly in the Member States' own international forum rules, which have not been examined. The above applies *mutatis mutandis* including to the unregistered CD.

6.63 In *plant variety* cases the establishment rules are found in arts 7(5) BR, 101(2)(a) CPVR and possibly in the Member States' own international forum rules, which have not been examined. The natures of arts 7(5) BR and 101(2)(a) CPVR are both similar and different.

6.64 They are similar *since* 'establishment' is defined in the same way; *since* infringement actions can be brought under both; *since* non-infringement actions can be brought under both; *since* adjudication is usually split; *since* both rules are subject to unlimited full jurisdiction unless the plaintiff chooses otherwise and *since* the establishment must be in EU/EFTA.

6.65 They are different *since* art. 7(5) BR is justified in proximity whereas art. 101(2)(a) CPVR seems proximate in a slightly more distant way; *since* art. 7(5) BR is an alternative to the defendant's domicile which art. 101(2)(a) CPVR is not; *since* art. 7(5) BR requires the dispute to have arisen out of the establishment as opposed to art. 101(2)(a) CPVR; *since* threatened infringement actions can be brought under arts 7(5) BR but not under 101(2)(a) CPVR and *since* adjudication is split under art. 7(5) BR as opposed to art. 101(2)(a) CPVR where adjudication may be joint.

6.66 In sum – and generally speaking – art. 7(5) BR is advantageous to the plaintiff acting as the rightholder since threatened infringement actions can be brought whereas art. 7(5) BR is advantageous to the plaintiff acting as the infringer since adjudication is split. Art. 101(2)(a) CPVR is advantageous to the plaintiff acting as the rightholder since adjudication may be joint and art. 101(2)(a) CPVR is advantageous to both since more fora may be available.

In *patent* cases the establishment rules are found in arts 7(5) BR, 33(1)(b) AUPC and possibly in the Member States' own international forum rules, which have not been examined. The natures of arts 7(5) BR and 33(1)(b) AUPC are both similar and different. **6.67**

They are similar *since* infringement actions can be brought under both; *since* threatened infringement actions can be brought under both and *since* adjudication may be split under both. **6.68**

They are different *since* art. 7(5) BR speaks of '[...] establishment' whereas art. 33(1)(b) AUPC speaks of 'place of business'; *since* art. 7(5) BR is justified in proximity whereas art. 33(1)(b) AUPC seems proximate in a slightly more distant way; *since* art. 7(5) BR is an alternative to the defendant's domicile which art. 33(1)(b) AUPC is not; *since* the defendant's establishment must be in EU/EFTA under art. 7(5) BR but in a Contracting Member State under art. 33(1)(b) AUPC; *since* art. 7(5) BR requires the dispute to have arisen out of the operation of the establishment as opposed to art. 33(1)(b) AUPC; *since* art. 7(5) BR is subject to unlimited full jurisdiction unless the plaintiff chooses otherwise as opposed to art. 33(1)(b) AUPC, which is subject to unlimited full jurisdiction; *since* non-infringement actions can be brought under art. 7(5) BR but only under art. 33(1)(b) AUPC if an infringement action between the same parties regarding the same patent is already pending and *since* adjudication may be joint under art. 33(1)(b) AUPC as opposed to art. 7(5) BR where adjudication is split. **6.69**

In sum – and generally speaking – art. 7(5) BR is advantageous to the plaintiff acting as the infringer since adjudication is split and is advantageous to both since jurisdiction is subject to discretion. Art. 33(1)(b) AUPC is advantageous to the plaintiff acting as the rightholder since adjudication may be joint and since more fora may be available. **6.70**

Overall, the above similarities and differences as well as the advantages for the plaintiff can be illustrated as shown in Table 6.1 below. As stated in Chapter 3 section D the number in brackets refers to the factor identified as an advantage for the plaintiff in Chapter 1 section A.4. **6.71**

Table 6.1 Establishment rule overview

	GENERAL			JUSTIFICATION	SCOPE				IMPACT				CONCLUSION
										If invalidity is raised			
	Version	Establishment rule	Wording	Ratio legis	Requirements	Infringement actions	Threatened infringement actions	Non-infringement actions	Places to sue	In infringement actions	In non-infringement actions	Extent of jurisdiction	Advantages for the plaintiff
Trade Marks	National trademarks	Art. 7(5) BR	'[…] as regards a dispute arising out of the operations of a branch, agency or other establishment, in the courts for the place where the branch, agency or other establishment is situated'	• Proximity	• Defendant must be domiciled in EU/EFTA • Defendant must have an establishment in EU/EFTA • Dispute must have arisen out of the operation of the establishment	Yes	Yes	Yes	• At the defendant's EU/EFTA establishment	• Split adjudication in regards to a registered national trademark • Joint adjudication in regards to an unregistered national trademark		Unlimited or Limited	Art. 7(5) BR is advantageous → To the plaintiff acting as the rightholder since threatened infringement actions can always be brought (8) → To the plaintiff acting as the infringer since non-infringement actions can always be brought (9) and since adjudication for registered trademarks is split (6–7) Art. 97(1) EUTMR is advantageous → To the plaintiff acting as the rightholder since adjudication is joint (6–7) → To the plaintiff acting as both the rightholder and the infringer since the scope of the defendant's establishment is restricted (3) and since more fora may be available (2)
	European Union Trademark (EUTM)	Art. 97(1) EUTMR	'Member State in which the defendant […] has an establishment'	• Proximity (More distant)	• Defendant must not be domiciled in EU • Defendant must have an establishment in EU	Yes Art. 96(a) EUTMR	Yes But requires that national law so permits cf. art. 96(a) EUTMR	Yes But requires that national law so permits cf. art. 96(b) EUTMR	• At the defendant's EU establishment	Joint adjudication Art. 96(a) and (d) EUTMR	Joint/split adjudication Art. 99(2) cf. 56 EUTMR	Unlimited Art. 98(1)(a) EUTMR or Limited *Chronopost*	
Designs	National designs	Art. 7(5) BR	What applies to national trademarks apply *mutatis mutandis* to national designs										
	Community Design (CD)	Art. 82(1) CDR	'Member State in which the defendant […] has an establishment'	• Proximity (More distant)	• Defendant must not be domiciled in EU • Defendant must have an establishment in EU	Yes Art. 81(a) CDR	Yes But requires that national law so permits cf. art. 81(a) CDR	Yes But requires that national law so permits cf. art. 81(b) CDR	• At the defendant's EU establishment	Joint adjudication Art. 81(a) and (d) CDR	Invalidity of the RCD leads to joint/split adjudication Art. 84(4) cf. 52 CDR Invalidity of the UCD cannot be raised	Unlimited Art. 83(1) CDR or Limited *Chronopost*	*Ibid.*

	GENERAL			JUSTIFICATION	SCOPE				IMPACT				CONCLUSION
	Version	Establishment rule	Wording	Ratio legis	Requirements	Infringement actions	Threatened infringement actions	Non-infringement actions	Places to sue	If invalidity is raised: In infringement actions	If invalidity is raised: In non-infringement actions	Extent of jurisdiction	Advantages for the plaintiff
Plant Varieties	National plant varieties	Art. 7(5) BR	What applies to national trademarks applies *mutatis mutandis* to national plant varieties (Except from its unregistered version which does not exist for plant varieties)										Art. 7(5) BR is advantageous → To the plaintiff acting as the rightholder since threatened infringement actions can be brought (8) → To the plaintiff acting as the infringer since adjudication is split (6–7) Art. 101(2)(a) CPVR is advantageous → To the plaintiff acting as the rightholder since adjudication may be joint (6–7) → To the plaintiff acting as both the rightholder and the infringer since more fora may be available (2)
	Community Plant Variety (CPV)	Art. 101(2)(a) CPVR	'Member State or another Contracting Party to the Lugano Convention in which the defendant […] has an establishment'	• Proximity (More distant)	• Defendant must not be domiciled in EU/EFTA • Defendant must have an establishment in EU/EFTA	Yes Art. 94 CPVR	No	Yes	• At the defendant's EU establishment	• Joint/split adjudication Art. 20 CPVR		Unlimited Art. 101(2) CPVR or Limited *Chronopost*	
Patents	National patents	Art. 7(5) BR	What applies to national trademarks applies *mutatis mutandis* to national patents (Except from its unregistered version which does not exist for patents)										Art. 7(5) BR is advantageous → To the plaintiff acting as the infringer since adjudication is split (6–7) → To the plaintiff acting as both the rightholder and the infringer since the extent of jurisdiction is subject to discretion (4) Art. 33(1)(b) AUPC is advantageous → To the plaintiff acting as the rightholder since adjudication may be joint (6–7) and since more fora may be available (2)
	Unitary Patent (UP)	Art. 33(1)(b) AUPC	'The Contracting Member State where the defendant […] has […] its place of business'	• Proximity (More distant)	• Defendant must not have a residence or a principal place of business in a CMS • Defendant must have a place of business in a CMS	Yes Art. 32(1)(a) AUPC	Yes Art. 32(1)(a) AUPC	(Yes)	• At the defendant's CMS place of business	• Joint adjudication Art. 33(3)(a) and (c) AUPC • Split adjudication Art. 33(3)(b) AUPC		Unlimited Art. 34 AUPC	

7

PLAINTIFF'S DOMICILE RULE

A. INTRODUCTION

7.01 From Chapter 1[1] it follows that the nature of the international jurisdiction rules available to the plaintiff must be identified. The purpose of Chapter 7 is to meet any such objective for the plaintiff's domicile rule[2] also known as *forum actoris* defined as unlimited full jurisdiction before the courts of the plaintiff's domicile.[3] Thus, the various versions of the rule are addressed and compared at the present stage, which leads to identify the advantages for the plaintiff.[4]

7.02 A distinction is drawn between the plaintiff's domicile rule, if any, applying to a national IP right (section B) and the plaintiff's domicile rule applying to a

1 Section A.3(c).

2 The plaintiff's domicile rule is one of the jurisdiction rules covered by the present study cf. Chapter 1 section A.3(c).

3 *Conflict of Laws in Intellectual Property, The CLIP Principles and Commentary*, European Max Planck Group on Conflict of Laws in Intellectual Property, Oxford University Press, 2013, p. 86 (2:203.C04).

4 The factors defining the advantages for the plaintiff are overall identified in Chapter 1 section A.4.

corresponding European unitary IP right (section C). In the end a conclusion is drawn, inter alia, by way of Table 7.1 (section D).

B. THE PLAINTIFF'S DOMICILE RULE APPLYING TO A NATIONAL IP RIGHT

Different plaintiff's domicile rules apply to a national IP right. The application depends on whether the defendant is domiciled in the EU/EFTA (section 1) or outside the EU/EFTA (section 2).[5] **7.03**

1. Defendant is domiciled in the EU/EFTA

If the defendant is domiciled in the EU/EFTA, the BR applies.[6] In the BR a number of plaintiff's domicile rules are found[7] but none of them apply to infringement of IP.[8] Further none of the forum rules, which apply to infringement of IP, inter alia, the *forum delicti* and the establishment rules can be interpreted to that effect.[9] Thus, the BR does not allow actions concerned with infringement of IP to be brought at the plaintiff's own domicile subject to unlimited full jurisdiction.[10] **7.04**

2. Defendant is domiciled outside the EU/EFTA

If the defendant is domiciled outside the EU/EFTA the Member States' own international forum rules[11] apply to actions concerned with infringement of IP. For the reasons in Chapter 1 section A.5(a) (limit 5) any such rules **7.05**

5 The reason for the distinction between defendants domiciled in the EU/EFTA and defendants domiciled outside the EU/EFTA is that parallel rules govern the former defendants cf. Chapter 2 sections B.1–B.2.

6 Chapter 2 sections B.1–B.2.

7 Arts 11(1)(b), 18(1) and 21(1)(b)(i) BR.

8 Ulrich Magnus and Peter Mankowski, *Brussels I Regulation*, European Commentaries on Private International Law, 2nd. revised edn, 2012, pp. 339 *et seq.* concerning art. 11(1)(b) BR; pp. 384 *et seq.* concerning art. 18(1) BR and pp. 400 *et seq.* concerning art. 21(1)(b)(i) BR.

9 With respect to the *forum delicti* rule in art. 7(2) BR see case C-523/10, *Wintersteiger AG v Products 4U Sondermaschinenbau GmbH*, paras 22–25 where a plaintiff's domicile rule was rejected to IP cf. Chapter 9 section B.1(a)(ii) Principle 8: Unlimited full jurisdiction and limited forum jurisdiction. By contrast a plaintiff's domicile rule was applied to online infringement of personality rights, the so-called 'centre of interests' rule see joined cases C-509/09, *e-Date Advertising GmbH v X* and C-161/10, *Olivier Martinez and Robert Martinez v MGN Ltd.*, paras 48–52 cf. Chapter 9 section B.1(a)(i): Principle 8 Unlimited full jurisdiction and limited forum jurisdiction. With respect to the establishment rule in art. 7(5) BR cf. Chapter 6 section B.1(a).

10 Art. 7(2) BR as interpreted in case C-523/10, *Wintersteiger*, para. 29, however, allows action to be brought at the place(s) of registration, which may coincide with the plaintiff's own domicile but the courts at any such place(s) are most likely subject to limited forum jurisdiction cf. Chapter 9 section B.1(a)(ii) Principle 8: Unlimited full jurisdiction and limited forum jurisdiction.

11 Art. 6 BR.

including the conditions under which they may apply are, however, not examined for the purpose of the present study.

C. THE PLAINTIFF'S DOMICILE RULE APPLYING TO A EUROPEAN UNITARY IP RIGHT

7.06 Four different plaintiff's domicile rules apply depending on the corresponding European unitary IP right in question. If a EUTM has been infringed the plaintiff's domicile rule in the EUTMR applies (section 1); if a CD has been infringed the plaintiff's domicile rule in the CDR applies (section 2); if a CPV has been infringed the plaintiff's domicile rule in the CPVR applies (section 3) and if a UP has been infringed the *forum delicti* rule in the AUPC, which is likely to be interpreted as a plaintiff's domicile rule,[12] applies (section 4).

1. The plaintiff's domicile rule in the EUTMR

7.07 The plaintiff's domicile rule is found in art. 97(2) EUTMR.[13] The CJEU has yet to interpret the provision[14] and no case is pending.[15] Below a distinction is drawn between applying the rule to infringement actions (section a); to non-infringement actions (section b) and to invalidity actions (section c).[16]

(a) Art. 97(2) EUTMR to infringement actions

7.08 If the defendant is neither domiciled nor established in the EU[17] art. 97(2) EUTMR allows[18] infringement actions[19] to be brought in: '[...] the courts of the Member State in which the plaintiff is domiciled or, if he is not domiciled in any of the Member States, in which he has an establishment'.[20]

---

12 Chapter 9 section C.4(a).

13 No other plaintiff's domicile rules are found in the EUTMR given that neither the establishment rule in art. 97(1) EUTMR cf. Chapter 6 section C.1 nor the *forum delicti* rule in art. 97(5) EUTMR cf. Chapter 9 section C.1 can be interpreted to that effect.

14 Study on the Overall Functioning of the European Trade Mark System presented by Max Planck Institute for Intellectual Property and Competition Law Munich of 15 February 2011 at 3.126 (p. 156).

15 Curia.eu visited on 1 January 2017.

16 The three kinds of actions are overall defined in Chapter 1 section A.3(b).

17 Art. 97(2)(first part) EUTMR.

18 The reason for using the term 'allows', contrary to art. 97(2) EUTMR using the term 'shall', is that infringement actions may also be brought under the *forum delicti* rule in art. 97(5) EUTMR cf. Chapter 9 section C.1(a) meaning that two alternatives are available to the plaintiff. In addition to that 'fall back' rules may apply cf. Chapters 2 and 3 section C.1.

19 Art. 96(a) EUTMR.

20 Art. 97(2)(second part) EUTMR.

The provision is in line with art. 97(1) EUTMR modelled over the corresponding provisions in the 1975 Community Patent Convention and in the protocol to the amended 1989 version cf. Chapter 5 section C.1(a) to where it is referred. The reason for adopting the provision is not mentioned in the Explanatory Memoranda[21] but may be – despite being a rule, which is usually met with hostility[22] – fourfold. **7.09**

The first reason may be that the provision is merely a 'light' version of the plaintiff's domicile rule given *that* art. 97(2) EUTMR only applies when the defendant has no contact with the EU neither by way of domicile nor establishment meaning that the scope is restricted[23] and *that* art. 97(2) EUTMR is not an alternative to the defendant's domicile rule in art. 97(1) EUTMR as, inter alia, art. 7(2) BR to the defendant's domicile rule in art. 4 BR where interpreting the former as a *forum actoris* would in effect rule out or at least limit the application of the latter[24] which introducing art. 97(2) EUTMR would not lead to vis-à-vis art. 97(1) EUTMR.[25] **7.10**

The second reason may be that the provision aims to ensure that competence is kept within the EU taking into account the exclusivity of EUTM courts.[26] **7.11**

The third reason may be that a plaintiff's domicile rule in itself is predictable for the parties, which was one of the justifications behind introducing any such rule in *e-Date*.[27] **7.12**

---

21 Memorandum on the Creation of an EEC Trade Mark adopted by the Commission on 6 July 1976, SEC(76)2462 July 1976, p. 36; The Need for a European Trademark System, Competence of the European Community to create one, Commission Working Paper, Working Group on the Community Trademark, October 1979, III/D/1294/79-EN, p. 31 and Bulletin of the European Communities Supplement 5/80, New Trade Mark System for the Community, proposed Directive and Regulation prepared by the Commission of the European Communities (COM 80 635 final 19 November 1980), p. 76.

22 Chapter 9 section B.1(a)(ii) Principle 6: Place of action and place(s) of effect(s) with references.

23 Applying the example in Chapter 1 section 2 Frogs GmbH may not bring an infringement action against Frox SpA at his/her domicile in Germany since Frox SpA is based in Italy with an establishment in London. Assuming that Frox was based in the US with an establishment in London Frogs GmbH could still not bring an infringement action in Germany but would have to bring it in the UK. Only if Frox did not have an establishment in London could an action be brought at the plaintiff's domicile in Germany following art. 97(2) EUTMR.

24 Chapter 9 section B.1(a)(ii) Principle 6: Place of action and place(s) of effect(s).

25 One could also argue that art. 97(2) EUTMR is not a 'light' version of the plaintiff's domicile rule since it applies if the plaintiff is not domiciled, but only established, in the EU. Changing the example in Chapter 1 section 2 so that Frogs would be based in the US with an establishment in London whereas Frox would be based in China, Frogs could bring an infringement action against Frox in the UK following art. 97(2) EUTMR.

26 Arts 95 and 96 EUTMR. Any such purpose may, however, be jeopardized given that the Lugano Convention applies as 'fall back' to the EUTMR cf. Chapters 2 and 3 section C.1.

27 Joined cases C-509/09, *e-Date Advertising GmbH v X* and C-161/10, *Olivier Martinez and Robert Martinez v MGN Ltd.*, para. 50.

7.13 The fourth reason may be that the provision establishes *internal* balance within the 'cascade'[28] given that the defendant's domicile rule[29] is disadvantageous to the plaintiff, the plaintiff's domicile rule[30] is disadvantageous to the defendant and the Member State where the IP right is registered rule[31] is disadvantageous to both.

7.14 Compared to art. 97(1) EUTMR[32] the provision is equal *since* actions can also be brought at the EU domicile, or failing that, EU establishment; *since* the terms 'domicile' and 'establishment' must be defined in the same way;[33] *since* bringing threatened infringement actions requires that national law so permits[34] and *since* the provision is also subject to unlimited full jurisdiction[35] unless the plaintiff chooses otherwise.[36]

(b) Art. 97(2) EUTMR to non-infringement actions

7.15 If the defendant is neither domiciled nor established in the EU[37] art. 97(2) EUTMR also allows[38] non-infringement actions[39] to be brought at the plaintiff's EU domicile or failing that EU establishment. It requires, however, that national law so permits.[40]

7.16 Assuming that the defendant is domiciled and established outside the EU/EFTA a situation could potentially arise where the EU plaintiff under the existing EU legal framework would not be able to bring a non-infringement action against his/her defendant.

> Changing the example in Chapter 1 section 2 so that Frogs is based in the US with no establishment in the EU whereas Frox SpA is based in Italy, Frox SpA cannot bring a non-infringement action against Frogs under art. 97(1) EUTMR given that Frogs is domiciled outside the EU. Rather Frox SpA must bring any such action under art. 97(2) EUTMR in Italy provided that Italian law so permits cf. art. 96(b) EUTMR.

---

28 Art. 97 EUTMR cf. similarly arts 82 CDR and 101 CPVR.
29 Art. 97(1) EUTMR cf. similarly arts 82(1) CDR and 101(2)(a) CPVR and Chapter 5 section C.
30 Art. 97(2) EUTMR cf. similarly arts 82(2) CDR and 101(2)(b) CPVR.
31 Arts 97(3) cf. 87 EUTMR cf. similarly arts 82(3) cf. 72 CDR and arts 101(2)(c) cf. 87 CPVR.
32 Chapter 5 section C.1(a).
33 James J. Fawcett and Paul Torremans, *Intellectual Property and Private International Law*, 2nd edn, Oxford Private International Law Series, 2011 at 8.15 and Chapter 5 section C.1(a).
34 Art. 96(a) EUTMR.
35 Art. 98(1)(a) EUTMR.
36 Case C-235/09, *DHL Express France SAS v Chronopost SA*, para. 48, which applies *mutatis mutandis* under art. 97(2) EUTMR cf. Chapter 5 note 51.
37 Art. 97(2) (first part) EUTMR.
38 The reason for using the term 'allows', contrary to art. 97(2) EUTMR using the term 'shall', is that non-infringement actions may also be brought under the 'fall back' rules cf. Chapters 2 and 3 section C.1.
39 Art. 96(b) EUTMR.
40 Ibid.

Assuming that Italian law does not allow for non-infringement actions no other forum rules are available for Frox SpA given that non-infringement actions cannot be brought under *forum delicti* cf. art. 97(5) EUTMR and that the Member States' own international forum rules applicable to defendants domiciled outside the EU/EFTA by way of art. 6 Brussels I Regulation have been explicitly excluded as 'fall back' cf. art. 94(2)(a) EUTMR. Under such circumstances, therefore, Frox SpA may not be able to bring a non-infringement action against Frogs unless the action is brought at e.g. the defendant's domicile in the US. Whether that is possible is addressed in Chapter 2 section C.1(c).

(c) *Art. 97(2) EUTMR to invalidity actions*

A distinction must be drawn between invalidity in infringement actions brought under art. 97(2) EUTMR which leads to joint adjudication given that art. 96(d) EUTMR applies and invalidity in non-infringement actions brought under art. 97(2) EUTMR, which leads to either split or joint adjudication given that arts 99(2) cf. 56 EUTMR apply. Arts 96(d) and 99(2) cf. 56 EUTMR are addressed in Chapter 11 section C.1. **7.17**

2. The plaintiff's domicile rule in the CDR

The plaintiff's domicile rule is found in art. 82(2) CDR.[41] The CJEU has yet to interpret the provision[42] and no case is pending.[43] Below a distinction is drawn between applying the rule to infringement actions (section a); to non-infringement actions (section b) and to invalidity actions (section c).[44] **7.18**

(a) *Art. 82(2) CDR to infringement actions*

If the defendant is neither domiciled nor established in the EU[45] art. 82(2) CDR allows[46] infringement actions[47] to be brought in: '[...] the courts of the Member State in which the plaintiff is domiciled or, if he is not domiciled in any of the Member States, in any Member State in which he has an establishment'.[48] **7.19**

---

41 No other plaintiff's domicile rules are found in the CDR given that neither the establishment rule in art. 82(1) CDR cf. Chapter 6 section C.2 nor the *forum delicti* rule in art. 82(5) CDR cf. Chapter 9 section C.2 can be interpreted to that effect.

42 Curia.eu visited on 1 January 2017.

43 Ibid.

44 The three kinds of actions are overall defined in Chapter 1 section A.3(b).

45 Art. 82(2)(first part) CDR.

46 The reason for using the term 'allows', contrary to art. 82(2) CDR using the term 'shall', is that infringement actions may also be brought under *the forum delicti* rule in art. 82(5) CDR cf. Chapter 9 section C.2(a) meaning that two alternatives are available to the plaintiff. In addition to that 'fall back' rules may apply cf. Chapters 2 and 3 section C.2.

47 Art. 81(a) CDR.

48 Art. 82(2) (second part) CDR.

7.20 Compared to its 'sister' provision in the EUTMR[49] art. 82(2) CDR is, with one variation,[50] equal *since* it also speaks of EU domicile, or failing that, EU establishment; *since* it also allows for unlimited full jurisdiction[51] unless the plaintiff chooses otherwise[52] and *since* bringing threatened infringement actions also requires that national law so permits.[53] Thus, section C.1(c) applies *mutatis mutandis* including to the unregistered CD.[54]

(b) Art. 82(2) CDR to non-infringement actions

7.21 If the defendant is neither domiciled nor established in the EU[55] art. 82(2) CDR also allows[56] non-infringement actions[57] to be brought at the plaintiff's EU domicile, or failing that EU establishment. In line with its 'sister' provision in the EUTMR[58] it requires that national law so permits.[59] Thus, section C.1(b) applies *mutatis mutandis* including to the unregistered CD.[60]

(c) Art. 82(2) CDR to invalidity actions

7.22 A distinction must be drawn between invalidity in infringement actions brought under art. 82(2) CDR which leads to joint adjudication given that art. 81(d) CDR applies and invalidity in non-infringement actions brought under art. 82(2) CDR which leads to either split or joint adjudication given that arts 84(4) cf. 52 CDR apply. Arts 81(d) and 84(4) cf. 52 CDR are addressed in Chapter 11 section C.2.

49 Art. 97(2) EUTMR.

50 The variation is that art. 97(2) EUTMR speaks of '[...] or if he is not domiciled in any of the Member States *in which* he has an establishment' whereas art. 82(2) CDR speaks of '[...] if he is not domiciled *in any Member State in which* he has an establishment'. Any one leads to the same result (emphasis added).

51 Art. 83(1) CDR.

52 Case C-235/09, *DHL Express France SAS*, para. 48 applies *mutatis mutandis* under the CDR cf. Chapter 5 note 51.

53 Art. 81(a) CDR.

54 Fawcett and Torremans, *supra* note 33 at 8.116.

55 Art. 82(2) (first part) CDR.

56 The reason for using the term 'allows', contrary to art. 82(2) CDR using the term 'shall', is that non-infringement actions may also be brought under the 'fall back' rules cf. Chapters 2 and 3 section C.2.

57 Art. 81(b) CDR.

58 Art. 97(2) EUTMR.

59 Art. 81(b) CDR.

60 Fawcett and Torremans, *supra* note 33 at 8.116.

3. The plaintiff's domicile rule in the CPVR

The plaintiff's domicile rule is found in art. 101(2)(b) CPVR.[61] The CJEU has yet to interpret the provision[62] and no case is pending.[63] Below a distinction is drawn between applying the rule to infringement actions (section a); to non-infringement actions (section b) and to invalidity actions (section c).[64] **7.23**

(a) Art. 101(2)(b) CPVR to infringement proceedings

If the defendant is neither domiciled nor established in the EU/EFTA[65] art. 101(2)(b) CPVR allows[66] actions in respect of claims for infringement[67] to be brought in: '[the courts] of the Member State in which the plaintiff is domiciled or has its seat, or in the absence of such, has an establishment'.[68] **7.24**

The justifications behind the rule corresponds to the justifications behind its 'sister' rules in the EUTMR and CDR[69] which therefore apply *mutatis mutandis*. **7.25**

The provision is both similar and different compared to its 'sister' provisions in the EUTMR and CDR.[70] It is similar *since* it also allows the plaintiff to sue at his/her domicile, or failing that at his/her establishment[71] and *since* it is also subject to unlimited full jurisdiction[72] unless the plaintiff chooses otherwise.[73] It is different *since* threatened infringement actions are not permitted[74] contrary to its 'sister' provisions in the EUTMR and CDR where bringing **7.26**

61 No other plaintiff's domicile rules are found in the CPVR given that neither the establishment rule in art. 101(2)(a) CPVR cf. Chapter 6 section C.3 nor the *forum delicti* rule in art. 101(3) CPVR cf. Chapter 9 section C.3 can be interpreted to that effect.

62 Curia.eu visited on 1 January 2017.

63 Ibid.

64 The three kinds of actions are overall defined in Chapter 1 section A.3(b).

65 Art. 101(2)(b) (first part) CPVR.

66 The reason for using the term 'allows', contrary to art. 101(2) CPVR using the term 'shall', is that infringement actions may also be brought under the *forum delicti* rule in art. 101(3) CPVR cf. Chapter 9 section C.3(a) meaning that two alternatives are available to the plaintiff. In addition to that 'fall back' rules may apply cf. Chapters 2 and 3 section C.3.

67 Art. 94 CPVR.

68 Art. 101(2)(b)(second part) CPVR.

69 Arts 97(2) EUTMR and 82(2) CDR.

70 Arts 97(2) EUTMR and 82(2) CDR.

71 Fawcett and Torremans, *supra* note 33 at 8.157–8.158.

72 Art. 101(2) (last sentence) CPVR.

73 Case C-235/09, *DHL Express France SAS*, para. 48, which applies *mutatis mutandis* under the CPVR cf. Chapter 5 note 51.

74 Fawcett and Torremans, *supra* note 33 at 8.146.

such actions requires that national law so permits;[75] *since* it narrows down the scope of the plaintiff's domicile rule compared to the scope of the defendant's domicile rule,[76] which its 'sister' provisions in the EUTMR and CDR do not do[77] and *since* it speaks of 'domicile [or] seat' whereas its 'sister' provisions in the EUTMR and CDR speak of 'domicile', any such difference can, however, be explained.[78]

(b) Art. 101(2)(b) CPVR to non-infringement actions

7.27 If the defendant is neither domiciled nor established in the EU/EFTA[79] art. 101(2)(b) CPVR also allows[80] non-infringement actions[81] to be brought at the plaintiff's EU domicile, seat or failing that establishment. Section C.3(a) applies *mutatis mutandis*.

(c) Art. 101(2)(b) CPVR to invalidity actions

7.28 If invalidity of a CPV is raised during the infringement or non-infringement actions brought under art. 101(2)(b) CPVR the CPVO comes into play given the exclusivity to address invalidity,[82] which in turn leads to either split or joint adjudication. Art. 20 CPVR is addressed in Chapter 11 section C.3.

4. The *forum delicti* rule in the AUPC

7.29 No plaintiff's domicile rule is found in the AUPC *as such*. Given, however, *that* the *forum delicti* rule in art. 33(1)(a) AUPC is likely to be interpreted as the places where the UP has taken effect and *that* the courts are subject to unlimited full jurisdiction[83] art. 33(1)(a) AUPC may in effect turn into a

---

75 Arts 96(a) EUTMR and 81(a) CDR.

76 Art. 101(2)(a) CPVR allows a defendant to be sued in the EU or EFTA whereas art. 101(2)(b) CPVR allows a plaintiff to sue in the EU.

77 Arts 97(1) EUTMR and 82(1) CDR allow a defendant to be sued in the EU whereas arts 97(2) EUTMR and 82(2) CDR similarly allow a plaintiff to sue in the EU.

78 Chapter 5 section C.3(a), which applies *mutatis mutandis*.

79 Art. 101(2)(b)(first part) CPVR.

80 The reason for using the term 'allows', contrary to art. 101(2) CPVR using the term 'shall', is that non-infringement actions may also be brought under the *forum delicti* rule in art. 101(3) CPVR cf. Chapter 9 section C.3(b). In addition to that 'fall back' rules may apply cf. Chapters 2 and 3 section C.3.

81 Non-infringement actions are not explicitly mentioned in Part Six CPVR. For the reasons in Chapter 3 section C.3 non-infringement actions must, however, be covered by the CPVR.

82 Art. 20 CPVR.

83 Art. 34 AUPC.

plaintiff's domicile rule. Applying art. 33(1)(a) AUPC to infringement actions, to non-infringement actions[84] and to invalidity actions is addressed in Chapter 9.

D. CONCLUSION

A distinction is drawn between the application of the plaintiff's domicile rule in trademark, design, plant variety and patent cases. **7.30**

In *trademark* cases the applicable plaintiff's domicile rules are found in art. 97(2) EUTMR and in the Member States' own international forum rules, which have not been examined. The similarities and differences between the EUTMR and the BR are therefore not addressed. By contrast the effect can be addressed of a plaintiff's domicile rule being found in the EUTMR and not in the BR, which leads to identify the advantages for the plaintiff. **7.31**

If the defendant is domiciled in the EU a plaintiff's domicile rule never comes into play since in that case the Brussels I Regulation does not allow for such a forum[85] and since art. 97(2) EUTMR does not apply.[86] The results therefore match. **7.32**

If the defendant is domiciled in the EFTA a plaintiff's domicile rule comes into play since in that case art. 97(2) EUTMR applies[87] whereas the Lugano Convention does not allow for such a forum.[88] The results therefore differ. **7.33**

If, finally, the defendant is domiciled outside the EU/EFTA a plaintiff's domicile rule comes into play since in that case art. 97(2) EUTMR applies[89] whereas the conditions under which any such rules may apply in the Member States' own international forum rules have not been examined. The results may therefore differ. **7.34**

---

84 Art. 33(1)(a) AUPC only applies to a limited extent to non-infringement actions given that any such as a main rule must be brought at the central division cf. art. 33(4) AUPC and Chapter 10 section C. Thus, the plaintiff acting as the infringer does not benefit from art. 33(1)(a) AUPC to be interpreted as a plaintiff's domicile rule.

85 *Supra* note 9.

86 Art. 97(1) EUTMR applies in any such situation.

87 Provided that the plaintiff is domiciled, or failing that, established in the EU.

88 *Supra* note 9.

89 Provided that the plaintiff is domiciled, or failing that, established in the EU.

7.35 In sum – and generally speaking – art. 97(2) EUTMR is advantageous to the plaintiff acting as both the rightholder and the infringer if the defendant is domiciled in the EFTA and may be advantageous to him/her if the defendant is domiciled outside the EU/EFTA.

7.36 In *design* cases the applicable plaintiff's domicile rules are found in art. 82(2) CDR and in the Member States' own international forum rules, which have not been examined. The above applies *mutatis mutandis*.

7.37 In *plant variety* cases the applicable plaintiff's domicile rules are found in art. 101(2)(b) CPVR and in the Member States' own international forum rules, which have not been examined. The similarities and differences between the CPVR and the BR are therefore not addressed. By contrast the effect can be addressed of a plaintiff's domicile rule being found in the CPVR and not in the BR, which leads to identify the advantages for the plaintiff.

7.38 If the defendant is domiciled in the EU/EFTA a plaintiff's domicile rule never comes into play since in that case the BR does not allow for such a forum[90] and since art. 101(2)(b) CPVR does not apply.[91] The results therefore match.

7.39 If the defendant is domiciled outside the EU/EFTA a plaintiff's domicile rule comes into play since in that case art. 101(2)(b) CPVR applies[92] whereas the conditions under which any such rules may apply in the Member States' own international forum rules have not been examined. The results may therefore differ.

7.40 In sum – and generally speaking – art. 101(2)(b) CPVR may be advantageous to the plaintiff acting as both the rightholder and the infringer if the defendant is domiciled outside the EU/EFTA.

7.41 In *patent* cases no plaintiff's domicile rules are found *as such* except the ones in the Member States' own international forum rules, which have not been examined. Subject to a reservation the *forum delicti* rule in art. 33(1)(a) AUPC is likely to be interpreted as a plaintiff's domicile rule cf. art. 34 AUPC.

---

90 *Supra* note 9.

91 Art. 101(2)(a) CPVR applies in any such situation.

92 Provided that the plaintiff is domiciled, or failing that, established in the EU.

In sum – and generally speaking – art. 33(1)(a) AUPC is advantageous to the plaintiff acting as the rightholder whatever the domicile of the defendant. 7.42

Overall, the above similarities and differences as well as the advantages for the plaintiff can be illustrated as in Table 7.1 below. As stated in Chapter 3 section D the numbers in brackets refers to the factor identified as an advantage for the plaintiff in Chapter 1 section A.4. 7.43

Table 7.1 Plaintiff's domicile rule overview

	GENERAL			JUSTIFICATION	SCOPE				IMPACT				CONCLUSION
	Version	Plaintiff's domicile rule	Wording	Ratio legis	Requirements	Infringement actions	Threatened infringement actions	Non-infringement actions	Places to sue	If invalidity is raised		Extent of jurisdiction	Advantages for the plaintiff
										In infringement actions	In non-infringement actions		
Trade Marks	National trademarks	N/A (Member States' own plaintiff's domicile rules may apply)											Art. 97(2) is advantageous → To the plaintiff acting as both the rightholder and the infringer if the defendant is domiciled in EFTA (3) Art. 97(2) may be advantageous → To the plaintiff acting as both the rightholder and the infringer if the defendant is domiciled outside the EU/EFTA (3)
	European Union Trademark (EUTM)	Art. 97(2) EUTMR	'Member State in which the plaintiff is domiciled [or failing that] has an establishment'	• Rule is a 'light' plaintiff's domicile • Rule ensures EU competence • Rule is predictable • Rule establishes internal balance in the 'cascade'	• Defendant must not be domiciled or established in EU • Plaintiff must be domiciled or, failing that, established in EU	Yes Art. 96(a) EUTMR	Yes But requires that national law so permits cf. art. 96(a) EUTMR	Yes But requires that national law so permits cf. art. 96(b) EUTMR	Natural persons (not autonomously defined) • At its own EU domicile Legal persons (autonomously defined) • At its own EU statutory seat, or • At its own EU central administration, or • At its own EU principal place of business, (or failing any of the latter three) • At its own EU establishment	Joint adjudication Art. 96(a) and (d) EUTMR	Joint/split adjudication Arts 99(2) cf. 56 EUTMR	Unlimited Art. 98(1)(a) EUTMR or limited *Chronopost*	
Designs	National designs	N/A (Member States' own plaintiff's domicile rules may apply)											
	Community Design (CD)	Art. 82(2) CDR	'Member State in which the plaintiff is domiciled [or failing that] has an establishment'	• Rule is a 'light' plaintiff's domicile • Rule ensures EU competence • Rule is predictable • Rule establishes internal balance in the 'cascade'	• Defendant must not be domiciled or established in EU • Plaintiff must be domiciled or, failing that, established in EU	Yes Art. 81(a) CDR	Yes But requires that national law so permits cf. art. 81(a) CDR	Yes But requires that national law so permits cf. art. 81(b) CDR	Natural persons (not autonomously defined) • At its own EU domicile Legal persons (autonomously defined) • At its own EU statutory seat, or • At its own EU central administration, or • At its own EU principal place of business, (or failing any of the latter three) • At its own EU establishment	Joint adjudication Art. 81(a) and (d) CDR	Invalidity of a RCD leads to joint/split adjudication Arts 84(4) cf. 52 CDR Invalidity of an UCD cannot be raised	Unlimited Art. 83(1) CDR or limited *Chronopost*	*Ibid.*

	GENERAL			JUSTIFICATION	SCOPE				IMPACT				CONCLUSION
	Version	Plaintiff's domicile rule	Wording	Ratio legis	Requirements	Infringement actions	Threatened infringement actions	Non-infringement actions	Places to sue	If invalidity is raised: In infringement actions	If invalidity is raised: In non-infringement actions	Extent of jurisdiction	Advantages for the plaintiff
Plant Varieties	National plant varieties	N/A (Member States' own plaintiff's domicile rules may apply)											Art. 101(2)(b) CPVR may be advantageous → To the plaintiff acting as both the rightholder and the infringer if the defendant is domiciled outside the EU/EFTA (3)
	Community Plant Variety (CPV)	Art. 101(2)(b) CPVR	'Member State in which the plaintiff is domiciled or has his seat [or failing that] has an establishment'	• Rule is a 'light' plaintiff's domicile • Rule ensures EU competence • Rule is predictable • Rule establishes internal balance in the 'cascade'	• Defendant must not be domiciled or established in EU/EFTA • Plaintiff must be domiciled or, failing that, established in EU	Yes Art. 94 CPVR	No	Yes	Natural persons (not autonomously defined) • At its own EU domicile Legal persons (autonomously defined) • At its own EU statutory seat, or • At its own EU central administration, or • At its own EU principal place of business, (or failing any of the latter three) • At its own EU establishment	Joint/split adjudication Art. 20 CPVR		Unlimited Art. 101(2) CPVR or limited *Chronopost*	
Patents	National patents	N/A (Member States' own plaintiff's domicile rules may apply)											Art. 33(1)(a) AUPC is advantageous → To the plaintiff acting as the rightholder whatever the domicile of the defendant (3)
	Unitary Patent (UP)	Art. 33(1)(a) AUPC	'Contracting Member State where the [...] infringement has occurred'	Proximity	Chapter 9 Section C.4(a)	Yes Art. 32(1)(a) AUPC	Yes Art 32(1)(a) AUPC	(Yes) Art. 33(4) AUPC	Places where the UP has taken effect	• Joint adjudication Art. 33(3)(a) and (c) AUPC • Split adjudication Art. 33(1)(b) AUPC		Unlimited Art. 34 AUPC	

8

MULTIPLE DEFENDANTS' RULE

A. INTRODUCTION

8.01 From Chapter 1[1] it follows that the nature of the international jurisdiction rules available to the plaintiff must be identified. The purpose of Chapter 8 is to meet any such objective for the multiple defendants' rule.[2] Thus, the various versions of the rule are addressed and compared at the present stage, which leads to identify the advantages for the plaintiff.[3]

8.02 A distinction is drawn between the multiple defendants' rule applying to a national IP right (section B) and the multiple defendants' rule applying to a

1 Section A.3(c).

2 The multiple defendants' rule is one of the jurisdiction rules covered by the present study cf. Chapter 1 section A.3(c).

3 The factors defining the advantages for the plaintiff are overall identified in Chapter 1 section A.4.

corresponding European unitary IP right (section C). In the end a conclusion is drawn, inter alia, by way of Table 8.1 (section D).

B. THE MULTIPLE DEFENDANTS' RULE APPLYING TO A NATIONAL IP RIGHT

Different multiple defendants' rules apply to a national IP right. The application depends on whether the defendant is domiciled in the EU/EFTA (section 1) or outside the EU/EFTA (section 2).[4] 8.03

1. Defendant is domiciled in the EU/EFTA

If the defendants are domiciled in the EU/EFTA art. 8(1) BR applies.[5] Below a distinction is drawn between applying the rule to infringement actions (section a); to non-infringement actions (section b) and to invalidity actions (section c).[6] 8.04

(a) Art. 8(1) BR to infringement actions

Art. 8(1) BR, in which *Kalfelis* has been codified,[7] states that: 8.05

4 The reason for the distinction between defendants domiciled in the EU/EFTA and defendants domiciled outside the EU/EFTA is that parallel rules govern the former defendants cf. Chapter 2 sections B.1–B.2.

5 Case C-645/11, *Land Berlin v Ellen Mirjam Sapir and Others*, para. 55; Gerechtshof Amsterdam, 12.11.2010, *Scor Holding (Switzerland) AG and Others*; Bundesgerichtshof, 30.11.2009, IX ZR 55/09; Oberster Gerichtshof, 21.05.2007, 8 ObA 68/06t; Cour de Cassation, 19.12.2007, *Y et Héritiers v Syndicat de Copropriété Le Syracuse*; Bundesgerichtshof 09.06.2004, 4C84/2004; Bundesgerichtshof, 23.10.2001, XI ZR 83/01; *Canada Trust Co and Others v Stolzenberg and Others* [2000] UKHL 51; [2000] 4 All ER 481; [2000] 3 WLR 1376; Högsta Domstolen, 26.10.1999, *Thessalian Paper Industry Svenska AB i likvidation konkursbo v Peter F och Leif O;* Oberster Gerichtshof, 13.01.1998, 9NdA 4/97 and Høyesteretts kjæremålsutvalg, 17.08.1995, *Kjell Tore Skjevesland v Geveran Trading Co. Ltd.*

6 The three kinds of actions are overall defined in Chapter 1 section A.3(b).

7 Case 189/87, *Athanasios Kalfelis v Bankhaus Schröder, Münchmeyer, Hengst and Co. and Others*, para. 13; case C-51/97, *Réunion européenne SA and Others v Spliethoff's Bevrachtingskantoor BV and the Master of the Vessel Alblasgracht V002*, para. 48; Report on the Convention on Jurisdiction and the Enforcement of Judgments in Civil and Commercial Matters, signed in Brussels, 27 September 1968, by P. Jenard, Director in the Belgium Ministry of Foreign Affairs and External Trade, p. 26; Marcus Norrgård, 'A Spider Without a Web, Multiple Defendants in IP Litigation', in Stefan Leible and Ansgar Ohly (eds) *Intellectual Property and Private International Law*, Mohr Siebeck, 2009, p. 212, note 10; James J. Fawcett and Paul Torremans, *Intellectual Property and Private International Law*, 2nd edn, Oxford Private International Law Series, 2011 at 5.119, note 273; Annette Kur and Thomas Dreier, *European Intellectual Property Law, Text, Cases and Materials*, Edward Elgar Publishing, 2013, p. 498; Ulrich Magnus and Peter Mankowski, *Brussels I Regulation*, 2nd revised edn, European Commentaries on Private International Law Sellier European Law Publishers, 2012, p. 311, note 52; Cristina Gonzalez Beilfuss, 'Is There Any Web for the Spider? Co-Defendants after Roche Nederland, International Litigation' in Arnaud Nuyts (ed.) *Intellectual Property and Information Technology*, Kluwer Law International, 2008, p. 80 and Marta Pertegás Sender, *Cross-Border Enforcement of Patent Rights*, Oxford Private International Law Series, 2002 at 3.26, note 34.

> A person domiciled in a Member State may also be sued [...] where he is one of a number of defendants, in the courts for the place where any one of them is domiciled, provided the claims are so closely connected that it is expedient to hear and determine them together to avoid the risk of irreconcilable judgments resulting from separate proceedings.[8]

8.06 Art. 8(1) BR is a special jurisdiction rule,[9] which must be interpreted strictly[10] meaning, inter alia, that the provision does not apply if the intention is to deprive a defendant of the courts of his/her own domicile[11] – e.g. if the plaintiff and the anchor defendant have secretly colluded that action should be brought at the latter's home domicile[12] – even though any such strict approach has not been upheld consequently.[13] Infringement actions[14] and threatened infringement actions[15] can both be brought under the provision. Art. 8(1) BR supplements the defendant's domicile rule in art. 4 BR and so the plaintiff may choose between the two without being restricted through the doctrine of *forum non-conveniens*.[16]

8.07 Considering the twofold justification for art. 8(1) BR, which is to avoid irreconcilable judgments[17] and to create foreseeability as to where to be sued,[18] art. 8(1) BR allows the plaintiff to consolidate the actions, not only where the

8 Art. 8(1) BR.

9 Magnus and Mankowski, *supra* note 7, p. 308 and Gonzalez Beilfuss, *supra* note 7, p. 80.

10 Case C-98/06, *Freeport plc v Olle Arnoldsson*, para. 35; case C-462/06, *Glaxosmithkline and Laboratoires Glaxosmithkline v Jean-Pierre Rouard*, para. 28; case C-145/10, *Eva-Maria Painer v Standard Verlags GmbH and Others*, para. 74; case 616/10, *Solvay SA v Honeywell Fluorine Products Europe BV and Others*, para. 21; case C-645/11, *Land Berlin*, para. 41; Norrgård, *supra* note 7, p. 212; Magnus and Mankowski, *supra* note 7, p. 309; Kur and Dreier, *supra* note 7, p. 498 and Gonzalez Beilfuss, *supra* note 7, p. 80.

11 Case 189/87, *Athanasios Kalfelis*, para. 9; case C-51/97, *Réunion européenne SA*, para. 47 and case C-103/05, *Reisch Montage AG v Kiesel Baumaschinen Handels GmbH*, para. 32.

12 Opinion of Advocate General Jääskinen in case C-352/13, *CDC Cartel Damage Claims Hydrogen Peroxide SA v Evonik Degussa GmbH and Others*, para. 84 *et seq.* and Annette Kur, 'Enforcement of Unitary Intellectual Property Rights: International Jurisdiction and Applicable Law' (2015) *Journal of Intellectual Property Law & Practice* 476.

13 Case C-98/06, *Freeport plc*, para. 54.

14 Case C-539/03, *Roche Nederland BV and Others v Frederick Primus, Milton Goldenberg*.

15 Chapter 5 section B.1(a) note 19, which applies *mutatis mutandis*.

16 Case C-281/02, *Andrew Owusu v N. B. Jackson, trading as 'Villa Holidays Bal-Inn Villas' and Others*, paras 37–43; Kur and Dreier, *supra* note 7, pp. 488 *et seq.* and Magnus and Mankowski, *supra* note 7, p. 112.

17 Recital (21) Brussels I Regulation; Report by P. Jenard, *supra* note 7, p. 27; case 189/87, *Athanasios Kalfelis*, para. 11; case C-51/97, *Réunion européenne SA*, para. 48; case C-145/10, *Eva-Maria Painer*, para. 77; case 616/10, *Solvay*, para. 19; Magnus and Mankowski, ibid, pp. 297–8 and *Conflict of Laws in Intellectual Property, The CLIP Principles and Commentary*, European Max Planck Group on Conflicts of Laws in Intellectual Property, Oxford University Press, 2013, p. 103.

18 Recital (15) Brussels I Regulation; case C-539/03, *Roche Nederland BV*, paras 36–39; case C-103/05, *Reisch Montage AG*, para. 25; case C-98/06, *Freeport plc*, para. 36; case C-462/06, *Glaxosmithkline and Laboratoires Glaxosmithkline*, para. 33; case C-145/10, *Eva-Maria Painer*, para. 75 and case 616/10, *Solvay SA*, para. 20.

'spider' defendant is domiciled (i.e. where the defendant coordinating the activities is based),[19] but anywhere in the 'web' (i.e. where any one of the defendants are based).[20] Any such interpretation is supported by the wording of the provision speaking of 'the place where any one of them is domiciled'.[21]

The term 'domicile' is – as art. 4 BR – subject to arts 62 and 63 BR.[22] Thus, a distinction must be drawn between natural persons and legal persons within the meaning of art. 8(1) BR and so Chapter 5 section B.1(a) applies *mutatis mutandis*. If action is brought under art. 8(1) BR the court is subject to unlimited full jurisdiction, which cannot be restricted.[23] **8.08**

For art. 8(1) BR to apply the claims must be closely connected.[24] To find out whether the claims are closely connected the court where the action is brought must address 'all the elements of the case'[25] including whether the laws are substantially identical and whether the facts are the same. The two requirements, which are cumulative, are dealt with individually below. **8.09**

The substantially identical law requirement – being the first condition – has been subject to a development. Thus, the EU was for a long time split into two when it came to consolidate actions relating to a European patent. One view was that a European patent was not identical law being the narrow approach taken in Denmark,[26] in Germany[27] and in Britain.[28] Another view was that a European patent was in fact identical law being the broad approach taken in **8.10**

19 Gerechtshof's Gravenhage [1998] Netherlands Internationaal Privaatrecht No 371, 389, 392–393 – *Expandable Grafts Partnership v Boston Scientific*.

20 Opinon of Advocate General Jääskinen in case C-352/13, *CDC Cartel Damage Claims Hydrogen Peroxide SA*, para. 89; Opinion of Advocate General Mengozzi in case C-98/06, *Freeport plc*, para. 52 note 27; Norrgård, *supra* note 7, p. 212;. Fawcett and Torremans, *supra* note 7 at 5.17; Kur, *supra* note 12, p. 475; Magnus and Mankowski, *supra* note 7, p. 308; Gonzalez Beilfuss, *supra* note 7, p. 79; *Conflict of Laws in Intellectual Property, The CLIP Principles and Commentary*, *supra* note 17, p. 115 and Sender, *supra* note 7 at 3.19.

21 *Supra* note 8.

22 Recital (15) Brussels I Regulation and Opinon of Advocate General Jääskinen in case C-352/13, *CDC Cartel Damage Claims Hydrogen Peroxide SA*, para. 56.

23 Kur, *supra* note 12, p. 476.

24 *Supra* note 8.

25 Case 145/10, *Eva-Maria Painer*, para. 83; case 616/10, *Solvay SA*, para. 23; case C-98/06, *Freeport plc*, para. 41 and Opinion of Advocate General Jääskinen in case C-352/13, *CDC Cartel Damage Claims Hydrogen Peroxide SA*, para. 74.

26 *Meyn Food Processing Technology BV v Lindholst & Co. A/S*, Western Division of the Danish High Court of 8 January 2003 published in Ugeskrift for Retsvæsen 2003, p. 898. The case is commented on by Nicolai Lindgreen and Louise Knudsen, Danish High Court Rejects Pan European Injunctions in Patent Cases, European Intellectual Property Review, 2004, p. 182.

27 InstGE 1, 146, 03/28/2002, 4 0 137 InstGE 2, 82, 2 F (unreported).

28 *Fort Dodge v Akzo Nobel*, Court of Appeal, 1998, FSR 222.

the Netherlands[29] and in Britain.[30] In *Roche* the CJEU took a narrow approach ruling that a European patent was not identical law[31] and that accordingly the claims were not closely connected.[32] Art. 8(1) BR did not therefore apply.[33] The effect of *Roche* was that art. 8(1) BR only came into play for identical national IP rights.[34]

8.11 The AG qualified the result in *Roche* as 'rather unsatisfactory'[35] and *Roche* was also heavily criticized by most[36] but not all[37] legal scholars and in the *Hess* report.[38] The points of critique were, inter alia – and despite that the narrow approach in *Roche* could meet foreseeability[39] – *that* the CJEU read territoriality too strictly thus excluding consolidation where the national laws are different due to the lex loci protectionis principle;[40] *that* the analysis carried out by the CJEU where the European patents are independent of each other[41] was not correct due to art. 69 EPC;[42] *that Roche* would lead to fragmented

29 *Chiron Corp. v Akzo Pharma-Organon Technika-UBI*, The Hague District Court, 22 July 1994, IER, No. 24, 150 and Gerechtshof's Gravenhage – *Expandable Grafts Partnership v Boston Scientific.*

30 *Coin Controls Ltd. v Suzo International (UK) Ltd.* [1999] Ch 33; Fawcett and Torremans, *supra* note 7 at 5.120 *et seq*; Gonzalez Beilfuss, *supra* note 7, pp. 81 *et seq.* and Sender, *supra* note 7 at 3.19 *et seq.*

31 Case C-539/03, *Roche Nederland BV*, para. 28.

32 Ibid., para. 32.

33 Ibid,, para. 35.

34 European Max Planck Group on Conflict of Laws in Intellectual Property, *Conflict of Laws in Intellectual Property, The CLIP Principles and Commentary*, *supra* note 17, p. 116, note 65 with further references.

35 Opinion of Advocate General Léger in case C-539/03, *Roche Nederland BV*, para. 69 and Opinion of Advocate General Trstenjak in case 145/10, *Eva-Maria Painer*, para. 81.

36 Norrgård, *supra* note 7, p. 211; Annette Kur, 'A Farewell to Cross-Border Injunctions? The ECJ Decisions GAT v LuK and Roche Nederland v Primus and Goldenberg' (2006) 37(7) IIC 844; Annette Kur and Axel Metzger, 'Exclusive Jurisdiction and Cross Border IP (Patent) Infringement Suggestions for Amendment of the Brussels I Regulation', Intellectuelle Eigendom & Reclamerecht, 2007, Volume 23, Nr. 1, p. 1; Adrian Biggs, 'Jurisdiction over Defences and Connected Claims' (2006) LMCLQ 447; Gonzalez Beilfuss, *supra* note 7, p. 79; Magnus and Mankowski, *supra* note 7, p. 312; Ulf Maunsbach, Gränsöverskridande Patenttvister i ny Gemenskapsrättslig Belysning – en Kommentar til EG-Domstolens Avgöranden i Målen C-4/03 (GAT) och C-539/09 (Roche), Nordiskt Immateriellt Rättsskydd, 2007, p. 240; Lydia Lundstedt, *In the Wake of GAT/LuK and Roche/Primus*, Nordiskt Immateriellt Rättsskydd, 2008, p. 122; Steven Warner and Susie Middlemiss, 'Patent Litigation in Multiple Jurisdictions: An End to Cross-Border Relief in Europe' (2006) *European Intellectual Property Review* 580 and *Conflict of Laws in Intellectual Property, The CLIP Principles and Commentary*, *supra* note 17, p. 105, note 8 with further references.

37 J Adolphsen, 2007, IPRax 15, at 20 and Stefan Leible, Art. 6 Brüssel I-VO in T Rauscher (ed.), Europäisches Zivilprozess und Kollisionsrecht, 2001, para. 8c.

38 Report on the Application of the Brussels I Regulation in the Member States prepared by the Institute of Private International Law at the University of Heidelberg (Burkhard Hess, Thomas Pfeiffer and Peter Schlosser), Study JLS/C4/2005/03, Final Version, September 2007 at 825–33 and at 920–22.

39 Case C-539/03, *Roche Nederland BV*, para. 37 and *supra* note 18.

40 *Conflict of Laws in Intellectual Property, The CLIP Principles and Commentary*, *supra* note 17, p. 111.

41 Case C-539/03, *Roche Nederland BV*, para. 29.

42 Norrgård, *supra* note 7, p. 219; Kur, *supra* note 36, p. 850; Fawcett and Torremans, *supra* note 7 at 11.07 and Gonzalez Beilfuss, *supra* note 7, p. 84.

litigation[43] which not only would contradict effective enforcement[44] but also run counter to the aim to promote a European area of justice in civil and commercial matters;[45] *that Roche* was cost-inefficient[46] and finally *that* the result in *Roche* – as the result in 'the spider in the web'[47] – did not find support in the wording of art. 8(1) BR.[48]

Subsequent art. 8(1) BR case law in *Freeport* was somewhat contradictory in that on the one hand the CJEU cited *Roche* and its identical law requirement[49] while stating on the other that 'different legal bases does not preclude [the] application of [art. 8(1) BR]'.[50] That led the AG to say in *Painer* that 'the [CJEU's] overall approach remains unclear'.[51] In the same *Painer* case, therefore, the CJEU loosened up[52] and stated, without citing *Roche*[53] that 'the identical legal bases [...] is not an indispensable requirement' for triggering art. 8(1) BR.[54] Rather, 'a difference in [the] legal basis between the actions brought against the various defendants does not, in itself, preclude the application of [art. 8(1) BR]'[55] if 'the national laws [are] substantially identical'.[56] Thus, the substantially identical law requirement seems the minimum condition to be met. Below, therefore, it is addressed what national IP rights are to be considered substantially identical. **8.12**

For trademarks a sub distinction must be drawn between registered and unregistered versions. For registered trademarks the substantially identical law requirement is likely met, which is supported by the trademark directive,[57] case **8.13**

43 Fawcett and Torremans, ibid. at 11.06; Report on the Application of the Brussels I Regulation, *supra* note 38 at 828 and Gonzalez Beilfuss, *supra* note 7, p. 85.

44 Norrgård, *supra* note 7, p. 220; Report on the Application of the Brussels I Regulation, *supra* note 38 at 829; Fawcett and Torremans, ibid. at 11.08 and Chapter 4 section B.

45 Fawcett and Torremans, ibid. at 11.09 and Paul Torremans, 'Exclusive Jurisdiction and Cross-Border IP (Patent) Infringement – Suggestions for Amendment of the Brussels I Regulation' (2007) *European Intellectual Property Review* 201.

46 Norrgård, *supra* note 7, p. 221 and Gonzalez Beilfuss, *supra* note 7, p. 85.

47 Gerechtshof's Gravenhage – *Expandable Grafts Partnership v Boston Scientific*.

48 Opinon of Advocate General Trstenjak in case 145/10, *Eva-Maria Painer*, para. 102.

49 Case C-98/06, *Freeport plc*, para. 40.

50 Ibid., para. 47.

51 Opinon of Advocate General Trstenjak in case 145/10, *Eva-Maria Painer* para. 85; Herbert Roth, Das Konnexitätserfordernis im Mehrparteiengerichtsstand des Artikel 6(1) EuGVO, Die Richtige Ordnung – Festschrift für Jan Kroppholler, Mohr Siebeck 2008, p. 887 and Hélène Gaudemet-Tallon, Compétence et Exécution des Jugements en Europe, 4th edn, LGDJ, 2010, pp. 256 and 258.

52 Kur, *supra* note 12, p. 475.

53 Kur and Dreier, *supra* note 7, p. 500, note 28.

54 Case 145/10, *Eva-Maria Painer*, para. 80.

55 Ibid., para. 81.

56 Ibid. para. 82; case C-645/11, *Land Berlin*, para. 44 and Opinion of Advocate General Jääskinen in case C-352/13, *CDC Cartel Damage Claims Hydrogen Peroxide SA*, para. 66.

57 Arts 10, 14 and 15 TD.

law[58] and writings of legal scholars.[59] For unregistered trademarks the situation is different since neither the Explanatory Memorandum behind the original trademark directive,[60] the former trademark directive[61] nor the current trademark directive[62] regulate such marks. Thus, protection is subject to national laws, which are not uniform[63] meaning that the substantially identical law requirement is likely not met for unregistered trademarks.

8.14 For designs the same sub distinction must be drawn. For registered designs, therefore, the substantially identical law requirement is likely met, which is supported by the design directive,[64] case law[65] and writings of legal scholars.[66] For unregistered designs neither the Explanatory Memorandum behind the design directive[67] nor the current design directive[68] regulate such designs. Thus, protection is like unregistered trademarks subject to national laws, which – due to the fact that any such design cannot act as a prior right in invalidity proceedings under neither the design directive[69] nor under the design regulation[70] – are likely not uniform in the Member States. Thus, the substantially identical law requirement is likely not met for unregistered designs.

58 Case C-16/03, *Peak Holding AB v Axolin-Elinor AB (formerly Handelskompaniet Factory Outlet i Löddeköpinge AB)*, para. 30; case C-355/96, *Silhouette International Schmied GmbH & Co. KG v Hartlauer Handelsgesellschaft mbH*, paras. 25 and 29 and joined cases C-414/99 to C-416/99, *Zino Davidoff SA v A & G Imports Ltd. and Levi Strauss & Co. and Others v Tesco Stores Ltd. and Others*, para. 39.

59 Norrgård, *supra* note 7, p. 228 and *Conflict of Laws in Intellectual Property, The CLIP Principles and Commentary*, *supra* note 17, p. 112.

60 Recital (2) Proposal for a first Council Directive to approximate the Laws of the Member States relating to Trade Marks, COM (80) 635 final, 19 November 1980.

61 Recital (5) Directive 2008/95/EC of the European Parliament and of the Council of 22 October 2008 to approximate the Laws of the Member States relating to Trade Marks (Codified Version).

62 Recital (11) TD.

63 Section 3.2.2 Guidelines for Examination in the Office for the Harmonization in the Internal Market (Trade Marks and Designs) on Community Trade Marks, Part C, Opposition, Section 4 Rights under the Article 8(4) CTMR.

64 Arts 12–15 cf. Recital (5) DD.

65 *Supra* note 58, which likely applies *mutatis mutandis*.

66 *Supra* note 59.

67 Section 1.5 and art. 2 Proposal for a European Parliament and Council Directive on the Legal Protection of Designs, COM (93) 344 final, 3 December 1993.

68 Recital (7) DD.

69 Art. 11(1)(d) DD.

70 Art. 25(1)(d) CDR; case R 584/2009-3, *MFB Diffusion SARL v Jinjun YU*, Board of Appeal, 25 January 2010, para. 25 and David Stone, *European Union Design Law, A Practitioner's Guide*, Oxford University Press, 2012, p. 186.

For plant varieties and due to TRIPS[71] all Member States are bound by the UPOV Convention.[72] The Convention harmonizes basic plant variety law, inter alia, the conditions of protection,[73] scope of protection,[74] limitations[75] and exhaustion.[76] Thus, it seems likely that the substantially identical law requirement is met for plant varieties. **8.15**

For patents a sub distinction must be drawn between European patents and purely national patents. For European patents one national part of the same European patent[77] obviously meets the substantially identical law requirement[78] whereas different national parts of the same European patent[79] do not.[80] For purely national patents the substantially identical law requirement is, despite the Paris Convention[81] and TRIPS,[82] not met.[83] **8.16**

In sum, therefore, the laws are substantially identical for registered national trademarks and designs, for national plant varieties and for one same national part of the same European patent. By contrast, the laws are not substantially identical for unregistered national trademarks and designs, for different national parts of the same European patent and for purely national patents. **8.17**

---

71 Art. 27(3) TRIPS.

72 International Convention for the Protection of New Varieties of Plants of December 2, 1961, as revised at Geneva on November 10, 1972, on October 23, 1978, and on March 19, 1991.

73 Arts 5–9 UPOV.

74 Art. 14 UPOV.

75 Art. 15 UPOV.

76 Art. 16 UPOV.

77 Case 616/10, *Solvay SA*, para. 30 and Opinion of Advocate General Villalón in case 616/10, *Solvay SA*, paras 27 and 29.

78 Applying the example in Chapter 1 section 2 the requirement is met if Frox SpA, Frox ApS and Frox AB all market and sell their counterfeit shoes in Germany thus all infringing the German part of the same European patent.

79 Case C-539/03, *Roche Nederland BV*, para. 33; case 616/10, *Solvay SA*, para. 25 and Opinion of Advocate General Villalón in the same case, para. 27 and *Meyn Food Processing Technology BV v Lindholst & Co.* A/S, Western Division of the Danish High Court of 8 January 2003, published in Ugeskrift for Retsvæsen 2003, p. 898.

80 Applying the example in Chapter 1 section 2 the requirement is not met if Frox SpA markets and sells its counterfeit shoes in Italy thus infringing the Italian part of a European patent whereas Frox ApS and Frox AB market and sell their counterfeit shoes in Denmark and Sweden respectively thus infringing the Danish and Swedish parts of the European patent.

81 Art. 4*bis*-Art. 5*quater* Paris Convention for the Protection of Industrial Property of March 20, 1883 as revised at Brussels on December 14, 1900 at Washington on June 2, 1911, at The Hague on November 6, 1925, at London on June 2, 1934, at Lisbon on October 31, 1958, and at Stockholm on July 14, 1967, and as amended on September 28, 1979.

82 Arts 27–34 TRIPS.

83 *Conflict of Laws in Intellectual Property, The CLIP Principles and Commentary, supra* note 17, p. 112 a contrario.

8.18 The same fact requirement[84] – being the second condition – can be divided into two sub requirements i.e. that the defendants must have acted in an identical or similar manner, and in accordance with a common policy elaborated by one of them.[85] Both requirements must be met.[86]

8.19 The former condition i.e. 'in an identical or similar manner' requires the infringement to relate to the same use of an IP right.[87]

8.20 The requirement is e.g. met if a defendant produces goods under a sign and those goods are subsequently brought to the end users by other defendants under the same sign.[88]

8.21 The requirement is e.g. not met *if* the defendants use the same sign for different goods or use different signs; *if* the defendants use the same design for different goods or use different designs or *if* the defendants infringe different parts of the patent claim(s) or of the plant variety claim(s).

8.22 The latter condition i.e. 'in accordance with a common policy elaborated by one of them' is twofold.

8.23 The first part i.e. 'in accordance with a common policy' is linked to the principle of foreseeability.[89] This means that the co-defendants must be able to predict that they can be sued where the anchor defendant is domiciled.[90]

8.24 The requirement is met if the co-defendants' behaviours are linked to the behaviour of the anchor defendant and knew of that behaviour.[91] Since the burden of proof is hard to satisfy the requirement is presumably met,[92] inter alia, *where* defendants belong to a corporate group as the CJEU have ruled in

84 Opinion of Advocate General Trstenjak in case 145/10, *Eva-Maria Painer*, para. 91.

85 Case C-539/03, *Roche Nederland BV*, para. 34 and Norrgård, *supra* note 7, p. 218 note 25.

86 *Conflict of Laws in Intellectual Property, The CLIP Principles and Commentary*, *supra* note 17, p. 106.

87 Ibid.

88 Applying the example in Chapter 1 section 2 the requirement is met if Frox SpA produces counterfeit shoes under the name Frox and those shoes are subsequently sold under the same name by Frox ApS and Frox AB.

89 *Supra* note 18.

90 Opinon of Advocate General Trstenjak in case 145/10, *Eva-Maria Painer*, para. 91 and *Conflict of Laws in Intellectual Property, The CLIP Principles and Commentary*, *supra* note 17, pp. 107 and 109.

91 *Conflict of Laws in Intellectual Property, The CLIP Principles and Commentary*, ibid., p. 107.

92 Ibid.

competition[93] and in tort[94] law cases; *where* the defendants do not belong to such a corporate group but have collaborated in carrying out a joint infringement[95] and *where* the defendants belong to a chain of infringers who interact (concerted behaviour).[96]

The requirement is not met if the defendants have acted independently and without any knowledge of each other (unconcerted behaviour).[97] **8.25**

The second part i.e. 'elaborated by one of them' means that the common policy must have been imposed by a single directing party[98] e.g. a company vis-à-vis its sales offices. Thus, common policies, which have been consensually adopted by all the parties e.g. a company and its sales offices do not meet the requirement and any such parallel infringement cannot be subject to consolidation. This rigid approach, which is somewhat surprising in light of 'the spider in the web' doctrine being rejected,[99] is not found under art. 33(1)(b) AUPC.[100] **8.26**

In sum, therefore, the facts are the same where the defendants have acted in an identical or similar manner in accordance with a common policy elaborated by one of them. The former requires the infringement to relate to the same use of an IP right whereas the latter requires the behaviours of the co-defendants to be linked to the behaviour of the anchor defendant (concerted behaviour) excluding parallel behaviour which have been consensually agreed by all the parties. **8.27**

(b) Art. 8(1) BR to non-infringement actions

The possibility of bringing non-infringement actions does not follow from art. 8(1) BR. Given art. 8(1) BR's justification[101] such actions must be permitted, **8.28**

93 Case C-97/08, *Akzo Nobel NV and Others v Commission of the European Communities*, para. 58; case 48/69, *Imperial Chemical Industries v Commission*, paras. 132–133; case 52/69, *Geigy v Commission*, para. 44; case 6/72, *Europemballage and Continental Can v Commission*, para. 15 and case C-286/98 P. *Stora Kopparbergs Bergslags v Commission*, para. 26.

94 Case C-358/08, *Aventis Pasteur SA v OB*, para. 63 and Opinion of Advocate General Trstenjak in the same case, para. 95.

95 Fawcett and Torremans, *supra* note 7 at 5.143.

96 *Conflict of Laws in Intellectual Property, The CLIP Principles and Commentary*, *supra* note 17, p. 109.

97 Case 145/10, *Eva-Maria Painer*, para. 83 and Opinion of Advocate General Trstenjak in the same case, para. 92; case C-539/03, *Roche Nederland* para. 27; District Court of the Hague in case 05/913, *Bacardi & Company Limited v Bat Beverage GmbH and Others*, 23 August 2007 and *Conflict of Laws in Intellectual Property, The CLIP Principles and Commentary*, *supra* note 17, p. 109.

98 *Conflict of Laws in Intellectual Property, The CLIP Principles and Commentary*, ibid., p. 107.

99 *Supra* note 19.

100 Section C.4.

101 *Supra* notes 17–18.

which in turn is supported by scholarly reports,[102] by writings of legal scholars[103] and by the UP where non-infringement actions may also be brought at the multiple defendants' domiciles.[104]

(c) Art. 8(1) BR to invalidity actions

8.29 If invalidity is raised during the infringement or non-infringement actions brought under art. 8(1) BR a distinction must be drawn between registered national IP rights where invalidity often leads to split adjudication given that art. 24(4) BR and *Gat LuK*[105] apply and unregistered national IP rights where invalidity leads to joint adjudication given that art. 24(4) BR and *Gat LuK* do not apply. Art. 24(4) BR and *Gat LuK* are addressed in Chapter 11 section B.

2. Defendant is domiciled outside the EU/EFTA

8.30 If the defendants are domiciled outside the EU/EFTA third states' own international forum rules apply. For the reasons in Chapter 1 section A.5(a) (limit 5) any such rules, including the conditions under which they may apply are not examined for the purpose of the present study.

C. THE MULTIPLE DEFENDANTS' RULE APPLYING TO A EUROPEAN UNITARY IP RIGHT

8.31 Two different multiple defendants' rules apply depending on the corresponding European unitary IP right in question. If a EUTM has been infringed the EUTMR applies (section 1); if a CD has been infringed the CDR applies (section 2); if a CPV has been infringed the CPVR applies (section 3) and if a UP has been infringed the AUPC applies (section 4).

1. The multiple defendants' rule in the EUTMR

8.32 No multiple defendants' rule is found in the 'cascade' in the EUTMR.[106] Rather art. 8(1) Brussels I Regulation applies as 'fall back' if the defendants are domiciled in the EU;[107] art. 6(1) Lugano Convention applies as 'fall back' if

---

102 Arts 2:602 cf. 2:206 CLIP Principles cf. §§ 213 cf. 206 ALI Principles.

103 *Conflict of Laws in Intellectual Property, The CLIP Principles and Commentary, supra* note 17, p. 176 (2:602.N04).

104 Section C.4(b).

105 Case C-4/03, *Gesellschaft für Antriebstechnik mbH & Co. KG v Lamellen und Kupplungsbau Beteiligungs KG.*

106 Art. 97 EUTMR.

107 Art. 94(2)(a) EUTMR conversely; case C-25/16, *Nintendo Co. Ltd. v BigBen Interactive GmbH, BigBen Interactive S.A* (pending); Bulletin of the European Communities Supplement 5/80, New Trade Mark

the defendants are domiciled in the EFTA[108] whereas multiple defendants' rules in the Member States' own private international laws do not apply if the defendants are domiciled outside the EU/EFTA.[109] Below a distinction is drawn between applying art. 8(1) BR to infringement actions (section a); to non-infringement actions (section b) and to invalidity actions (section c).[110]

(a) Art. 8(1) BR to infringement actions

Art. 8(1) BR applies in infringement actions[111] and in threatened infringement actions if national law so permits.[112] The substantially identical law and same fact requirements must, however, be met.[113] **8.33**

The substantially identical law requirement is most likely met due to the unitary character of the EUTM,[114] which in turn is supported by CJEU case law,[115] writings of legal scholars[116] and German[117] and Dutch[118] case law. The fact that infringement of an EUTM is not fully subject to the EUTMR[119] since the sanctions imposed are governed by national law,[120] which is only harmonized on a minimum level[121] as e.g. stated in Danish case law[122] may not change the conclusion that a EUTM must be considered substantially identical law.[123] **8.34**

System for the Community, proposed Directive and Regulation prepared by the Commission of the European Communities (COM 80 635 final 19 November 1980), p. 76; Fawcett and Torremans, *supra* note 7 at 8.25–8.26; Kur, *supra* note 12, p. 475, note 54 and Chapter 2 section C.1(a).

108 Chapter 2 section C.1(b).

109 Art. 94(2)(a) EUTMR; Proposal for a European Parliament and Council Regulation on the Community Design presented by the Commission COM (93) 342 final COD 463 Brussels, 3 December 1993, p. 38; Vincenzo Scordamaglia, 'Jurisdiction and Procedure in Legal Actions relating to Community Trademarks' in Mario Franzosi (ed.), *European Community Trade Mark, Commentary to the European Community Regulation*, Kluwer Law International, 1997, p. 379 and Chapter 2 section C.1(c).

110 The three kinds of actions are overall defined in Chapter 1 section A.3(b).

111 Arts 96(a) cf. 94(2)(a) EUTMR.

112 Arts 96(a) cf. 94(2)(a) EUTMR.

113 Section B.1(a).

114 Art. 1(2) EUTMR.

115 Case C-616/10, *Solvay SA*, para. 30 and Opinion of Advocate General Jääskinen in case C-352/13, *CDC Cartel Damage Claims Hydrogen Peroxide SA*, para. 67 per analogy.

116 Norrgård, *supra* note 7, pp. 223 and 227; Roland Knaak, GRUR Int., 2007, 391 and *Conflict of Laws in Intellectual Property, The CLIP Principles and Commentary*, *supra* note 17, p. 112 note 40.

117 Bundesgerichtshof in case ZR 11/04, Aufarbeitung von Fahrzeugkomponenten, 14 December 2006, GRUR Int. 2007, 864.

118 District Court of the Hague in case 05/913, *Bacardi & Co. Ltd. v Bat Beverage GmbH and Others*, 23 August 2007.

119 *Conflict of Laws in Intellectual Property, The CLIP Principles and Commentary*, *supra* note 17, p. 110, note 32 with references and illustration 4, p. 112.

120 Art. 102 EUTMR cf. art. 8(2) Rome II Regulation and case C-25/16, *Nintendo Co. Ltd.*

121 Arts 2(1) and 13 ED.

122 Danish Maritime and Commercial Court in case V-151–04, *Hummel A/S v Ellos A/S and Others*, 9 February 2007.

123 See, however, P. Lange, GRUR, 2007, p. 112.

8.35 The same fact requirement is met if the defendants have acted in an identical or similar manner in accordance with a common policy elaborated by one of them and so section B.1(a) applies *mutatis mutandis.*

(b) Art. 8(1) BR to non-infringement actions

8.36 Art. 8(1) BR applies in non-infringement actions if national law so permits[124] and section B.1(b) applies *mutatis mutandis.*

(c) Art. 8(1) BR to invalidity actions

8.37 A distinction must be drawn between invalidity in infringement actions brought under art. Art. 8(1) BR which leads to joint adjudication given that art. 96(d) EUTMR applies and invalidity in non-infringement actions brought under art. 8(1) BR which leads to either split or joint adjudication given that arts 99(2) cf. 56 EUTMR apply. Arts 96(d) and 99(2) cf. 56 EUTMR are addressed in Chapter 3.1.

2. The multiple defendants' rule in the CDR

8.38 No multiple defendants' rule is found in the 'cascade' in the CDR.[125] Rather art. 8(1) Brussels I Regulation applies as 'fall back' if the defendants are domiciled in the EU;[126] art. 6(1) Lugano Convention applies as 'fall back' if the defendants are domiciled in the EFTA[127] whereas multiple defendants' rules in the Member States' own private international laws do not apply if the defendants are domiciled outside the EU/EFTA.[128] Below a distinction is drawn between applying art. 8(1) BR to infringement actions (section a); to non-infringement actions (section b) and to invalidity actions (section c).[129]

---

124 Arts 96(b) cf. 94(2)(a) EUTMR.

125 Art. 82 CDR.

126 Art. 79(3)(a) CDR conversely; case C-25/16, *Nintendo Co. Ltd.;* Proposal for a European Parliament and Council Regulation on the Community Design presented by the Commission COM (93) 342 final COD 463 Brussels, 3 December 1993, p. 38; Annette Kur, 'Are there any Common Principles of Private International Law with regard to Intellectual Property' in Stefan Leible and Ansgar Ohly (eds) *Intellectual Property and Private International Law,* Mohr Siebeck, 2009, p. 3; Stone, *supra* note 70 at 21.179; Guy Tritton, *Intellectual Property in Europe,* 3rd edn, Thomson, 2008 at 14–087; Fawcett and Torremans, *supra* note 7 at 8.108 and Chapter 2 section C.2(a).

127 Chapter 2 section C.2(b).

128 Art. 79(3)(a) CDR and Memorandum amending Regulation (EU) No 1215/2012 on Jurisdiction and the Recognition and Enforcement of Judgments in Civil and Commercial Matters COM(2013) 554 final, 2013/0268 (COD), p. 6 and Chapter 2 section C.2(c).

129 The three kinds of actions are overall defined in Chapter 1 section A.3(b).

(a) Art. 8(1) BR to infringement actions

Art. 8(1) BR applies in infringement actions[130] and in threatened infringement actions if national law so permits.[131] Section C.1(a) applies *mutatis mutandis* given the unitary character of both the registered and the unregistered CD.[132] **8.39**

(b) Art. 8(1) BR to non-infringement actions

Art. 8(1) BR applies in non-infringement actions if national law so permits[133] and section B.1(b) applies *mutatis mutandis.* **8.40**

(c) Art. 8(1) BR to invalidity actions

A distinction must be drawn between invalidity in infringement actions brought under art. 8(1) BR which leads to joint adjudication given that art. 81(d) CDR applies and invalidity in non-infringement actions brought under art. 8(1) BR which leads to either split or joint adjudication given that arts 84(4) cf. 52 CDR apply. Arts 81(d) and 84(4) cf. 52 CDR are addressed in Chapter 11 section C.2. **8.41**

3. The multiple defendants' rule in the CPVR

No multiple defendants' rule is found in the 'cascade' in the CPVR.[134] Rather art. 8(1) Brussels I Regulation applies as 'fall back' if the defendants are domiciled in the EU;[135] art. 6(1) Lugano Convention applies as 'fall back' if the defendants are domiciled in the EFTA[136] and – by contrast to the EUTMR/CDR[137] – multiple defendants' rules in the Member States' own private international laws apply if the defendants are domiciled outside the EU/EFTA.[138] Below a distinction is drawn between applying art. 8(1) BR to **8.42**

130 Arts 81(a) cf. 79(3)(a) CDR.
131 Arts 81(a) cf. 79(3)(a) CDR.
132 Art. 1(2) CDR.
133 Arts 81(b) cf. 79(3)(a) CDR.
134 Art. 101(2) CPVR.
135 Art. 101(1) CPVR; case C-25/16, *Nintendo Co. Ltd.*; Proposal for a Council Regulation (EEC) on Community Plant Variety Rights presented by the Commission COM(90) 347 final, 30 August 1990, p. 5; Gert Würtenberger, Paul Van Der Kooij, Bart Kiewiet and Martin Ekvad, *European Community Plant Variety Protection*, Oxford University Press, 2006 at 7.58 and Chapter 2 section C.3(a).
136 Art. 101(1) CPVR; Magnus and Mankowski, *supra* note 7, p. 20; Proposal for a European Parliament and Council Regulation on the Community Design presented by the Commission COM (93) 342 final COD 463 Brussels, 3 December 1993, p. 37 and Chapter 2 section C.3(b).
137 Arts 94(2)(a) EUTMR and 79(3)(a) CDR.
138 Art. 102(1) CPVR and Proposal for a Council Regulation (EEC) on Community Plant Variety Rights presented by the Commission COM(90) 347 final, 30 August 1990, p. 5 and Chapter 2 section C.3(c).

infringement actions (section a); to non-infringement actions (section b) and to invalidity actions (section c).[139]

(a) Art. 8(1) BR to infringement actions

8.43 Art. 8(1) BR applies in infringement actions[140] but not in threatened infringement actions[141] and with that exception section C.1(a) applies *mutatis mutandis* given the unitary character of the CPV.[142]

(b) Art. 8(1) BR to non-infringement actions

8.44 Art. 8(1) BR applies in non-infringement actions[143] and section B.1(b) applies *mutatis mutandis.*

(c) Art. 8(1) BR to invalidity actions

8.45 If invalidity of a CPV is raised during the infringement or non-infringement actions brought under art. 8(1) BR the CPVO comes into play given their exclusivity to address invalidity,[144] which in turn leads to either split or joint adjudication. Art. 20 CPVR is addressed in Chapter 11 section C.3.

4. The multiple defendants' rule in the AUPC

8.46 No multiple defendants' rule was originally found in the AUPC.[145] A rule came in at a rather late stage.[146] The rule is now found in art. 33(1)(b) AUPC.

---

139 The three kinds of actions are overall defined in Chapter 1 section A.3(b).

140 Arts 94 cf. 101(1) CPVR.

141 Fawcett and l Torremans, *supra* note 7 at 8.146.

142 Art. 2 CPVR.

143 Chapter 3 section C.3.

144 Art. 20 CPVR.

145 Art. 15(a)(5) Draft Agreement on the European Union Patent Judiciary of 14 May 2008 (9124/08 PI 24 COUR 19) Chapter IV concerning 'Jurisdiction, Allocation of Cases and Effects of Decisions'; Art. 15(a)(5) Draft Agreement on the European Union Patent Judiciary of 30 June 2008 (11270/08 PI 32 COUR 32) Chapter IV concerning 'Jurisdiction, Allocation of Cases and Effects of Decisions'; Art. 15(a)(1) Draft Agreement on the European Union Patent Court and Draft Statute of 4 November 2008 (14970/08 PI 78 COUR 52) Chapter IV concerning 'Jurisdiction and Effects of Decisions'; Art. 15(a)(1) Draft Agreement on the European and Community Patents Court and Draft Statute of 8 January 2009 (5072/09 PI 1 COUR 1) Chapter IV concerning 'Jurisdiction and Effects of Decisions'; Art. 15(a)(1) Draft Agreement on the European and Community Patents Court and Draft Statute, Revised Presidency Text of 23 March 2009 (7928/09 PI 23 COUR 29) Chapter IV concerning 'Jurisdiction and Effects of Decisions'; Art. 15(a)(1) Draft Agreement on a Unified Patent Court and Draft Statute, Presidency Text of 14 June 2011 (11533/11 PI 68 COUR 32) Chapter IV concerning 'Jurisdiction and Effects of Decisions' and Art. 15(a)(1) Draft Agreement on a Unified Patent Court and Draft Statute, Revised Presidency Text of 2 September 2011 (13751/11 PI 108 COUR 48) Chapter IV concerning 'Jurisdiction and Effects of Decisions'.

146 Art. 15(a)(1)(b) Draft Agreement on a Unified Patent Court and Draft Statute, Revised Presidency Text of 7 October 2011 (15289/11 PI 127 COUR 56) Chapter IV concerning 'Competence, Jurisdiction and Effects of Decisions'; Art. 15(a)(1)(b) Draft Agreement on a Unified Patent Court and Draft Statute, Revised Presidency Text of 19 October 2011 (15539/11 PI 133 COUR 59) Chapter IV concerning 'Competence,

Below a distinction is drawn between applying art. 33(1)(b) AUPC to infringement actions (section a); to non-infringement actions (section b) and to invalidity actions (section c).[147]

(a) Art. 33(1)(b) AUPC to infringement actions

Art. 33(1)(b) AUPC allows[148] infringement actions[149] and threatened infringement actions[150] to be brought in: **8.47**

> [...] the local division hosted by the Contracting Member State where [...] in the case of multiple defendants, one of the defendants has its residence, or principal place of business, or in the absence of residence or principal place of business, its place of business [...]. An action may be brought against multiple defendants only where the defendants have a commercial relationship and where the action relates to the same alleged infringement.[151]

The multiple defendants' rule in art. 33(1)(b) AUPC only comes into play if the UPC has competence in respect of all of the defendants.[152] The justification for the rule is most likely, lacking information in the drafting history,[153] foreseeability given that any such principle expresses a general consideration and common sense.[154] **8.48**

Jurisdiction and Effects of Decisions'; Art. 15(a)(1)(b) Draft Agreement on a Unified Patent Court and Draft Statute, Revised Presidency Text of 26 October 2011 (16023/11 PI 141 COUR 62) Chapter IV concerning 'Competence, Jurisdiction and Effects of Decisions'; Art. 15(a)(1)(b) Draft Agreement on a Unified Patent Court and Draft Statute, Revised Presidency Text of 11 November 2011 (16741/11 PI 155 COUR 64) Chapter IV concerning 'Competence, Jurisdiction and Effects of Decisions'; Art. 15(a)(1)(b) Draft Agreement on the Creation of a Unified Patent Court, Guidance for Future Work of 24 November 2011 (17539/11 PI 168 COUR 71); Art. 15(a)(1)(b) Draft Agreement on a Unified Patent Court and Draft Statute, Consolidated Text of 27 September 2012 (14268/12 PI 133 COUR 66) Chapter IV concerning 'International Jurisdiction and Competence'; Art. 15(a)(1)(b) Draft Agreement on a Unified Patent Court and Draft Statute, Consolidated Text of 12 October 2012 (14750/12 PI 120 COUR 67) Chapter IV concerning 'International Jurisdiction and Competence' and Art. 15(a)(1)(b) Draft Agreement on a Unified Patent Court and Draft Statute, Consolidated Text of 14 November 2012 (16222/12 PI 146 COUR 74) Chapter IV concerning 'International Jurisdiction and Competence'.

147 The three kinds of actions are overall defined in Chapter 1 section A.3(b).

148 The reason for using the term 'allows', contrary to art. 33(1) AUPC using the term 'shall', is that infringement actions may also be brought under the *forum delicti* rule in art. 33(1)(a) AUPC cf. Chapter 9 section C.4(a) meaning that two alternatives are available to the plaintiff.

149 Art. 32(1)(a) AUPC.

150 Ibid.

151 Art. 33(1)(b) AUPC.

152 Rule 303(1) ROP.

153 *Supra* notes 145–6.

154 Opinion of Advocate General Jääskinen in case C-360/12, *Coty Prestige Lancaster Group GmbH v First Note Perfumes NV*, para. 35 and Chapter 4 section C.1.

8.49 Art 33(1)(b) supplements the defendant's domicile rule in the same provision cf. the wording 'or' and allows – as art. 8(1) BR – the plaintiff to bring the action 'where [...] one of the defendants [are based]'.

8.50 Contrary to art. 8(1) BR using the term 'domicile'[155] art. 33(1)(b) AUPC uses the terms 'residence', 'principal place of business' and 'place of business', none of which have been defined in the AUPC. 'Residence' is likely to be interpreted as 'his/[her] usual or last known residence' for natural persons and as 'statutory seat, central administration or principal place of business' for legal persons.[156] 'Principal place of business' is likely to be interpreted so that only legal persons can be sued at any such place[157] and finally 'place of business', which is subordinate to the former two cf. the wording 'or in the absense of [...]' is likely to be interpreted as any place where the legal person has 'a permanent or temporary place of business'.[158] Given that 'place of business' and 'establishment' are used as synonyms in the legal literature,[159] in Explanatory Memoranda[160] and in case law[161] it seems likely that 'place of business' must be interpreted as meaning that consolidation is possible at one of the defendants' establishments under art. 33(1)(b) AUPC. So read, art. 33(1)(b) AUPC deviates from art. 8(1) BR, which does not allow for consolidation at any such place.[162]

8.51 If action is brought under art. 33(1)(b) AUPC the court is subject to unlimited full jurisdiction, which cannot be restricted.[163]

8.52 For art. 33(1)(b) AUPC to apply – and by contrast to art. 8(1) BR[164] – it is not explicitly required that the claims must be closely connected. The UPC may, however – despite being a court outside the judicial and institutional framework of the EU[165] not bound by case law from the CJEU – likely read any such requirement into the provision. There are more reasons for that: one reason is that a rightholder is free to shop between arts 33(1)(b) AUPC and

155 *Supra* note 8.
156 Chapter 5 section C.4(a).
157 Chapter 5 section C.4(a).
158 Rule 271(5)(a) ROP.
159 Magnus and Mankowski, *supra* note 7, p. 280.
160 Bulletin of the European Communities Supplement 5/80, New Trade Mark System for the Community, proposed Directive and Regulation prepared by the Commission of the European Communities (COM 80 635 final 19 November 1980) p. 76.
161 Case 218/86, *SAR Schotte GmbH v Parfums Rothschild SARL*, paras 15–17.
162 *Supra* note 22.
163 Art. 34 AUPC.
164 *Supra* note 24.
165 Opinion 1/09 of 8 March 2011 of the CJEU, para. 71.

8(1) BR for European patents for an extendable period of seven years.[166] Another reason is that interpreting art. 33(1)(b) AUPC consistent for UPs and European patents would create legal certainty for the users, which is a declared goal under the AUPC.[167] A third reason is that art. 8(1) BR is founded on foreseeability,[168] which expresses a general consideration and common sense[169] and therefore most likely also applies under art. 33(1)(b) AUPC. Thus, it seems likely that consolidation is possible under art. 33(1)(b) AUPC only where the law is substantially identical and where the facts are the same.

The requirement of substantially identical law does not appear from art. **8.53** 33(1)(b) AUPC itself. The reason seems to be that the requirement is most likely met due to the unitary character of the UP[170] and the fact that the sanctions imposed are the same,[171] which is contrary to other European unitary IP rights.[172]

The requirement of same fact, however, explicitly appears from art. 33(1)(b) **8.54** AUPC itself cf. the wording 'an action may be brought against multiple defendants only where the defendants have a commercial relationship and where the action relates to the same alleged infringement'.[173] Both requirements must be met cf. the wording 'and'.

The first sub requirement i.e. that the defendants must have a commercial **8.55** relationship is the equivalent to the requirement of acting in accordance with a common policy elaborated by one of them under art. 8(1) BR.[174] The two requirements are both similar and different. They are similar since both – however in different terms – require the behaviours of the co-defendants to be linked to the behaviour of the anchor defendant, which is not surprising given that both are based on foreseeability.[175] They are different *since* art. 33(1)(b) AUPC requires a commercial relationship whereas art. 8(1) BR requires concerted behaviour[176] and *since* parallel infringements have not to be imposed by a single directing party under art. 33(1)(b) AUPC by contrast to art. 8(1) BR meaning that parallel infringements which have been consensually agreed

166 Art. 83 AUPC.
167 Recital (5) AUPC.
168 *Supra* note 18.
169 *Supra* note 18.
170 Arts 2(f) AUPC and 3(2) UPR.
171 Arts 24(b) cf. 56 AUPC *et seq.*
172 Sections C.1–C.3.
173 Art. 33(1)(b)(second sentence) AUPC.
174 Section B.1(a).
175 *Supra* note 18.
176 Section B.1(a).

by the parties can be consolidated under art. 33(1)(b) AUPC but not under the art. 8(1) BR. Accordingly, and despite that art. 33(1)(b) AUPC has a 'somewhat narrower wording than article 8(1) [BR]' as pointed out by the Drafting Committee[177] the former might turn out to have a broader scope than the latter.

8.56 The second sub requirement i.e. that the action must relate to the same alleged infringement is the equivalent to the requirement of acting in an identical or similar manner under art. 8(1) BR. The two are similar since also art. 33(1)(b) AUPC seems to require the infringement to relate to the same use of the IP right cf. the wording 'same alleged infringement'.

8.57 In sum, therefore, the laws are substantially identical given the unitary character of the UP and the fact that the sanctions imposed are the same. The facts are the same where the defendants have a commercial relationship and where the action relates to the same alleged infringement. The former requires the behaviours of the co-defendants to be linked to the behaviour of the anchor defendant (commercial relationship) including parallel behaviours which have been consensually agreed by all the parties whereas the latter requires the infringement to relate to the same use of an IP right.

(b) Art. 33(1)(b) AUPC to non-infringement actions

8.58 Art. 33(1)(b) AUPC also applies to non-infringement actions.[178] It requires, however, that an infringement action between the same parties relating to the same patent is already pending before an art. 33(1)(b) AUPC court. In that case the non-infringement action, for reasons of procedural economy, may only be brought there.[179] If, however, an infringement action is not already pending art. 33(1)(b) AUPC does not apply. In that case the non-infringement action must be brought at the central division cf. Chapter 10 section C.

(c) Art. 33(1)(b) AUPC to invalidity actions

8.59 If invalidity of a UP is raised during the infringement or non-infringement actions brought under art. 33(1)(b) AUPC the flexible exclusive jurisdiction rule in art. 33(3) AUPC comes into play, which in turn leads to either split or joint adjudication. Art. 33(3) AUPC is addressed in Chapter 11 section C.4.

177 Note to Art. 303(1) Preliminary Set of Provisions for the Rules of Procedure of the Unified Patent Court, 17 Draft of 31 October 2014.
178 Art. 33(4) AUPC.
179 Art. 33(4) (second sentence) AUPC.

D. CONCLUSION

A distinction is drawn between the application of the multiple defendants' rule in trademark, design, plant variety and patent cases. **8.60**

In *trademark* cases the applicable multiple defendants' rule is found in art. 8(1) BR. Even though the rule applies to both national registered trademark rights and to the EUTM a few advantages for the plaintiff can be identified. Thus, in national registered trademark litigation art. 8(1) BR is an advantage for the plaintiff acting as the rightholder *since* threatened infringement actions can always be brought whereas art. 8(1) BR is an advantage for the plaintiff acting as the infringer *since* non-infringement actions can always be brought and *since* adjudication is often split. In EUTM litigation art. 8(1) BR is an advantage for the plaintiff acting as the rightholder *since* adjudication is joint. **8.61**

In *design* cases the applicable multiple defendants' rule is also found in art. 8(1) BR, which applies to both national registered design rights and to the CDR. The above applies *mutatis mutandis* including to the unregistered CD. **8.62**

In *plant variety* cases the applicable multiple defendants' rule is also found in art. 8(1) BR. Even though the rule applies to both national plant variety rights and to the CPVR an advantage for the plaintiff can be identified. Thus, in national plant variety litigation art. 8(1) BR is an advantage for the plaintiff acting as the rightholder *since* threatened infringement actions can always be brought. **8.63**

In *patent* cases the multiple defendants' rules are found in art. 8(1) BR, which, however, as a main rule does not apply to national patent rights and art. 33(1)(b) AUPC, which applies to the UP. Thus, art. 33(1)(b) is an advantage for the plaintiff since yet another forum rule is available to him/her. **8.64**

Overall, the above similarities and differences as well as the advantages for the plaintiff can be illustrated as in Table 8.1 below. As stated in Chapter 3 section D the numbers in brackets refers to the factor identified as an advantage for the plaintiff in Chapter 1 section A.4. **8.65**

Table 8.1 Multiple defendants' rule overview

	GENERAL			JUSTIFICATION	SCOPE				IMPACT				CONCLUSION
	Version	Multiple defendants' rule	Wording	Ratio legis	Requirements	Infringement actions	Threatened infringement actions	Non-infringement actions	Places to sue	If invalidity is raised: In infringement actions	If invalidity is raised: In non-infringement actions	Extent of jurisdiction	Advantages for the plaintiff
Trade Marks	National trademarks	Art. 8(1) BR	'A person domiciled in a Member State may also be sued [...] where he is one of a number of defendants, in the courts for the place where any one of them is domiciled, provided the claims are so closely connected that it is expedient to hear and determine them together to avoid the risk of irreconcilable judgments resulting from separate proceedings'	To avoid irreconcilable judgments To create foreseeability	The claims must be closely connected in the sense that, inter alia: The laws must be substantially identical, which is met for registered trademarks but not for unregistered trademarks, and The facts must be the same	Yes	Yes	Yes	Possible to sue every defendant where any one of them is domiciled: Which for natural persons is at its EU/EFTA domicile (not autonomously defined) Which for legal persons is at its EU/EFTA statutory seat, at its EU/EFTA central administration or at its EU/EFTA principal place of business (autonomously defined)	Often split adjudication for registered national trademarks		Unrestricted	Art. 8(1) BR is advantageous → To the plaintiff acting as the rightholder in national trademark litigation since threatened infringement actions can always be brought [8] → To the plaintiff acting as the infringer in national trademark litigation since non-infringement actions can always be brought [9]
	European Union Trademark (EUTM)	Arts 94(2)(a) EUTMR cf. 8(1) BR	*Ibid.*	*Ibid.*	*Ibid.* (except from unregistered trademarks)	Yes Art. 96(a) EUTMR	Yes But requires that national law so permits cf. art. 96(a) EUTMR	Yes But requires that national law so permits cf. art. 96(b) EUTMR	*Ibid.*	Joint adjudication cf. art. 96(a) and (d) EUTMR	Joint/split adjudication cf. arts 99(2) cf. 56 EUTMR	*Ibid.*	Art. 8(1) BR is advantageous → To the plaintiff acting as the rightholder in EUTM litigation since adjudication is joint [6]
Designs	National designs	Art. 8(1) BR	What applies to national trademarks applies *mutatis mutandis* to national designs (with the exception of unregistered national designs, which do not meet the requirement of substantially identical law)										*Ibid.*
	Community Design (CDR)	Arts 79(3)(a) CDR cf. 8(1) BR	What applies to the European Union Trademark applies *mutatis mutandis* to the Community Design			Yes Art. 81(a) CDR	Yes But requires that national law so permits cf. art. 81(a) CDR	Yes But requires that national law so permits cf. art. 81(b) CDR	*Ibid.*	Joint adjudication cf. art. 81(a) and (d) CDR	Invalidity of a RCD leads to joint/split adjudication cf. arts 84(4) cf. 52 CDR Invalidity of an UCD cannot be raised	*Ibid.*	

	GENERAL			JUSTIFICATION	SCOPE				IMPACT				CONCLUSION
	Version	Multiple defendants' rule	Wording	Ratio legis	Requirements	Infringement actions	Threatened infringement actions	Non-infringement actions	Places to sue	If invalidity is raised		Extent of jurisdiction	Advantages for the plaintiff
										In infringement actions	In non-infringement actions		
Plant Varieties	National plant varieties	Art. 8(1) BR	What applies to national trademarks applies *mutatis mutandis* to national plant varieties										Art. 8(1) BR is advantageous → To the plaintiff acting as the rightholder in national plant variety litigation since threatened infringement actions can always be brought [8]
	Community Plant Variety (CPV)	Arts 101(1) CPVR cf. 8(1) BR	What applies to the European Union Trademark applies *mutatis mutandis* to the Community Plant Variety			Yes Art. 94 CPVR	No	Yes	*Ibid.*	Joint/split adjudication Art. 20 CPVR		*Ibid.*	
Patents	National patents	Art. 8(1) BR	Art. 8(1) BR does as a main rule not apply to national patents										Art. 33(1)(b) is advantageous → To the plaintiff since yet another forum rule is available to him/her (1)
	Unitary Patent (UP)	Art. 33(1)(b) AUPC	'[Infringement actions can be brought before] the local division hosted by the Contracting Member State where […] in the case of multiple defendants, one of the defendants has its residence, or principal place of business, or in the absence of residence or principal place of business, its place of business […]. An action may be brought against multiple defendants only where the defendants have a commercial relationship and where the action relates to the same alleged infringement'	To create foreseeability	The claims must be closely connected in the sense that, inter alia: The laws must be substantially identical, and The facts must be the same meaning that the defendants must have a commercial relationship, and that the actions must relate to the same alleged infringement	Yes Art. 32(1)(a) AUPC	Yes Art. 32(1)(a) AUPC	(Yes) Art. 33(4) AUPC	Possible to sue every defendant where any one of them is domiciled: Which for natural persons is at its CMS usual or last known residence (autonomously defined) Which for legal persons is at its CMS statutory seat, at its CMS central administration, at its CMS principal place of business, or if any of the above three do not apply at its CMS permanent or temporary place of business (autonomously defined)	Joint adjudication Art. 33(3)(a) and (c) AUPC Split adjudication Art. 33(3)(b) AUPC		Unrestricted cf. art. 34 AUPC	

9

FORUM DELICTI RULE

A. INTRODUCTION

9.01 From Chapter 1[1] it follows that the nature of the international jurisdiction rules available to the plaintiff must be identified. The purpose of Chapter 9 is to meet any such objective for the *forum delicti* rule.[2] Thus, the various versions of the rule are addressed and compared at the present stage, which leads to identify the advantages for the plaintiff.[3]

1 Section A.3(c).

2 The *forum delicti* rule is one of the jurisdiction rules covered by the present study cf. Chapter 1 section A.3(c).

3 The factors defining the advantages for the plaintiff are overall identified in Chapter 1 section A.4.

A distinction is drawn between the *forum delicti* rule applying to a national IP right (section B) and the *forum delicti* rule applying to a corresponding European unitary IP right (section C). In the end a conclusion is drawn, inter alia, in Table 9.1 (section D). **9.02**

B. THE *FORUM DELICTI* RULE APPLYING TO A NATIONAL IP RIGHT

Different *forum delicti* rules apply to a national IP right. The application depends on whether the defendant is domiciled in the EU/EFTA (section 1) or outside the EU/EFTA (section 2).[4] **9.03**

1. Defendant is domiciled in the EU/EFTA

If the defendant is domiciled in the EU/EFTA art. 7(2) BR applies. Below a distinction is drawn between applying the rule to infringement actions (section a); to non-infringement actions (section b) and to invalidity actions (section c).[5] **9.04**

(a) Art. 7(2) BR to infringement actions

Art. 7(2) BR states that: **9.05**

> A person domiciled in a Member State [bound by this Convention] may be sued in another Member State [bound by this Convention] [...] in matters relating to tort, delicti or quasi-delict, in the courts for the place where the harmful event occurred or may occur.[6]

The provision is a special jurisdiction rule[7] supplementing art. 4 BR[8] meaning that the plaintiff may choose between the two without being restricted through the doctrine of *forum non-conveniens*.[9] The provision applies in **9.06**

4 The reason for the distinction between defendants domiciled in the EU/EFTA and defendants domiciled outside the EU/EFTA is that parallel rules govern the former defendants cf. Chapter 2 sections B.1-B.2.

5 The three kinds of actions are overall defined in Chapter 1 section A.3(b).

6 Art. 7(2) BR.

7 Chapter II section 2 BR.

8 Ulrich Magnus and Peter Mankowski, *Brussels I Regulation*, 2nd revised edn, European Commentaries on Private International Law, Sellier European Law Publishers, 2012, p. 105 and Peter Arnt Nielsen, International Privat- og Procesret, Jurist- og Økonomforbundets Forlag, 1997, p. 150.

9 Case C-281/02, *Andrew Owusu v N.B. Jackson, trading as 'Villa Holidays Bal-Inn Villas' and Others*, paras. 37–43; Annette Kur and Thomas Dreier, *European Intellectual Property Law, Text, Cases and Materials*, Edward Elgar Publishing, 2013, pp. 488 *et seq.*; Magnus and Mankowski, ibid., p. 112; and Nielsen, ibid., p. 151.

actions not related to a contract within the meaning of art. 7(1) BR[10] whatever the liability.[11] Compared to art. 4 BR, which favours the defendant[12] art. 7(2) BR attempts to strike a balance between the interests of the parties.[13]

9.07 Art. 7(2) BR was applied to industrial property rights in *Wintersteiger*.[14] Prior to that, legal uncertainty existed as to whether an action could be brought under art. 7(2) BR even though the infringement had not been directed to the forum (mere accessibility approach) or whether it was required that the infringement had in fact been directed to the forum (connecting factors approach).[15] Below a distinction is drawn between the facts and reasoning of *Wintersteiger* (section i), the interpretation of *Wintersteiger* (section ii) and the impact of *Wintersteiger* (section iii).[16]

(i) Wintersteiger (facts and reasoning)

9.08 The case concerned an online trademark dispute between an Austrian-based manufacturer of skiing equipment, Wintersteiger AG, which was the owner of numerous Wintersteiger trademark registrations throughout the EU[17] where, however, only the Austrian registration was subject to the preliminary reference[18] and on the other hand a German-based distributor of, inter alia, Wintersteiger skiing equipment, Products 4U GmbH, which had registered the Google AdWord Wintersteiger for the German country level domain

10 Case C-189/87, *Athanasios Kalfelis v Bankhaus Schröder, Münchmeyer, Hengst and Co. and Others*, para. 18; case C-261/90, *Mario Reichert, Hans-Heinz Reichert and Ingeborg Kockler v Dresdner Bank AG*, para. 16; case C-51/97, *Réunion européenne SA and Others v Spliethoff's Bevrachtingskantoor BV and the Master of the vessel Alblasgracht V002*, para. 22; case C-96/00, *Rudolf Gabriel*, para. 33 and case 167/00, *Verein für Konsumenteninformation v Karl Heinz Henkel*, para. 36.

11 Magnus and Mankowski, *supra* note 8, p. 259.

12 Case 220/84, *AS-Autoteile Service GmbH v Pierre Malhé*, para. 15.

13 Magnus and Mankowski, *supra* note 8, p. 106.

14 Case C-523/10, *Wintersteiger AG v Products 4U Sondermaschinenbau GmbH*. The case is commented, inter alia, by Peter Picht, Von eDate zu Wintersteiger – Die Ausformung des Art. 5 Nr. 3 EuGVVO für Internetdelikte durch die Rechtsprechung des EuGH, GRUR Int., 2013, pp. 19–27 and Birgit Clark, 'Off piste? ECJ decides Austrian Supreme Court's 'Adwords' Jurisdiction Question in *Wintersteiger*' (2012) 7(10) *Journal of Intellectual Property Law and Practice* 701–3.

15 Torsten Bjørn Larsen, *Trademark Infringements on the Internet in a Jurisdictional Perspective*, Nordiskt Immateriellt Rättsskydd, 2007, pp. 28 *et seq.*

16 *Wintersteiger* is addressed differently compared to the judgments addressed in Chapters 2–8 and 11. The reason is twofold namely that *forum delicti* is a focus area for the purpose of the present study cf. Chapter 1 section A.3(c) and that *Wintersteiger* seems to influence the way the equivalent *forum delicti* rules in arts 97(5) EUTMR, 82(5) CDR, 101(3) CPVR and 33(1)(a) AUPC must be interpreted cf. section C.

17 Opinion of Advocate General Villalón in case C-523/10, *Wintersteiger AG*, paras 4 and 14.

18 Ibid., para. 15 and judgment of the CJEU paras. 10, 17, 29, 38 and 40.

(.de)[19] but not for the Austrian country level domain (.at).[20] Products 4U GmbH sold its products in Austria.[21]

Based on these facts Wintersteiger AG brought an action under art. 7(2) BR in Austria and claimed that Products 4U GmbH had infringed its Austrian Wintersteiger trademark by placing the Wintersteiger advertisement on google.de.[22] Supporting jurisdiction in Austria, Wintersteiger AG argued *that* google.de could be accessed in Austria and *that* google.de was configured in German being the language spoken in Austria.[23] Wintersteiger AG did not argue that Products 4U GmbH's website products4u.de, which was drafted in, inter alia, German and where the Wintersteiger trademark was used and Wintersteiger products were sold[24] was directed to Austria or accessible there in support of jurisdiction in Austria.[25] Products 4U GmbH contested jurisdiction in Austria since google.de was not directed to Austria, but exclusively to Germany,[26] thus supporting a lack of connection to Austria. Based on these facts the question was whether there had been a harmful event in Austria, which could justify jurisdiction under art. 7(2) BR. **9.09**

The CJEU stated *that* art. 7(2) BR is based on proximity[27] and *that* art. 7(2) BR covers both a place of action and a place(s) of effect(s).[28] The place of **9.10**

19 Ibid., para. 5 and judgment of the CJEU, para. 12.

20 Ibid., para. 12.

21 Ibid., para. 11. From the facts of the case it is not clear whether the products sold by Products4U GmbH in Austria were legally parallel imported Wintersteiger products justifying the subsequent use of the Wintersteiger trademark following case C-337/95, *Parfums Christian Dior SA and Parfums Christian Dior BV v Evora BV*, para. 38 or whether the products were counterfeited Wintersteiger products. Supporting the former, namely that the products were legally parallel imported products argues that the description of the facts in the AG's opinion stating that, 'Wintersteiger neither *supplies* its products to, nor authorizes the sale of, its products by Products 4U' cf. para. 5. Supporting the opposite result namely that the products were counterfeited products argues that the description of the facts in the decision at national court level stating that, 'dieses Zubehör *stammt* weder von der Klägerin, noch ist es von ihr autorisiert' (Oberster Gerichtshof in 17 Ob 8/10s of 10 July 2012, p. 2) and in the CJEU's decision stating that the 'Wintersteiger accessories were 'neither *produced* by, nor are they authorised by, Wintersteiger' cf. para. 11 (emphasis added).

22 Opinion of Advocate General Villalón in case C-523/10, *Wintersteiger AG*, para. 8 and judgment of the CJEU para. 13.

23 Case C-523/10, *Wintersteiger AG*, para. 13.

24 See archive.org for prior versions of products4u.de.

25 The reason may be interconnected with the nature of the Wintersteiger products as either legally parallel imported products or as counterfeited products.

26 Case C-523/10, *Wintersteiger AG v Products 4U Sondermaschinenbau GmbH*, para. 14.

27 Ibid, para. 18 and Chapter 4 section C.2.

28 Ibid., paras 19–20 and section B.1(a)(ii) Principle 6: Place of action and place(s) of effect(s).

action was defined as the place where the advertiser is established[29] whereas the place(s) of effect(s) was defined as the place where the trademark is registered.[30] The former was justified in proximity[31] and the latter in territoriality[32] thereby meeting predictability and proximity.[33]

9.11 As regards the extent of jurisdiction at the place where the advertiser is established and at the place where the trademark is registered the CJEU did not mention *Shevill*[34] contrary to the AG who dismissed *Shevill* in his opinion.[35] Whereas the impact of dismissing *Shevill* in the view of the AG would be to allow the plaintiff to bring an action 'without there being a fragmentation of jurisdiction which jeopardizes the meaning of [the BR]'[36] the impact of not mentioning *Shevill* in the view of the CJEU was different, namely:

> As regards [the place where the advertiser is established] it should be noted that the territorial limitation of the protection of a national mark is not such as to exclude the international jurisdiction of courts other than the courts of the Member State in which that trade mark is registered,[37]
>
> and
>
> [The place where the trademark is registered] have the power to determine all the damage allegedly caused to the proprietor of the protected right because of an infringement of it [...].[38]

(ii) Wintersteiger (interpretation)

9.12 *Wintersteiger* was delivered by a small Chamber and not by the Grand Chamber. This is not surprising in light of the fact that the latter had already addressed online activity in *Pammer*[39] (which concerned the application of the 'directed to' requirement in art. 17(1)(c) BR) and in *eDate*[40] (which concerned

29 Ibid., para. 37.

30 Ibid., para. 29.

31 Ibid., para. 37 and Chapter 4 section C.2.

32 Ibid., para. 25 and Chapter 4 section D.

33 Ibid., para. 27 and section B.1(a)(ii) Principle 1: Predictability and Principle 2: Proximity.

34 Case C-68/93, *Fiona Shevill, Ixora Trading Inc., Chequepoint SARL and Chequepoint International Ltd. v Presse Alliance SA*, para. 33 and section B.1(a)(ii) Principle 8: Unlimited full jurisdiction and limited forum jurisdiction.

35 Opinion of Advocate General Villalón in case C-523/10, *Wintersteiger AG*, paras 18–20 and section B.1(a)(ii) ibid.

36 Opinion of Advocate General Villalón ibid., para. 30 and section B.1(a)(ii) ibid.

37 Case C-523/10, *Wintersteiger AG*, para. 30 and section B.1(a)(ii) ibid.

38 Ibid.

39 Joined cases C-585/08, *Peter Pammer v Reederei Karl Schlüter GmbH & Co. KG*; and C-144/09, *Hotel Alpenhof GesmbH v Oliver Heller* cf. case C-190/11, *Daniela Mühlleitner v Ahmad Yusufi and Wadat Yusufi*.

40 Joined cases C-509/09, *eDate Advertising GmbH v X* and C-161/10, *Olivier Martinez and Robert Martinez v MGN Ltd.*

the application of art. 7(2) BR to an infringement of a personality right). *Wintersteiger* carries weight *since* never before had the CJEU applied art. 7(2) BR to IP.[41]

In *Wintersteiger*, which will be examined below, the CJEU upheld the distinction between a place of action and a place(s) of effect(s)[42] to online infringement of trademark rights[43] and defined the former as the place where the advertiser is established[44] and the latter as the place where the trademark is registered[45] (hereinafter place(s) of registration). Under the former action can be brought at what usually, but not always, coincides with the defendant's domicile.[46] Under the latter action can be brought in Member States where the plaintiff has a trademark registration. It is not required that the infringement is directed to the forum.[47] The place(s) of registration equals art. 24(4) BR and *GatLuk*[48] if invalidity is raised. **9.13**

Below nine non-exhaustive principles where some are general[49] and some are specific[50] are applied to *Wintersteiger* in order to find out whether they are applied loyally by the CJEU or with a 'twist' to industrial property rights.[51] The principles overlap. **9.14**

---

41 James J. Fawcett and Paul Torremans, *Intellectual Property and Private International Law*, 2nd edn, Oxford Private International Law Series, 2011 at 5.32 *et seq.*; Arnaud Nuyts, 'Suing at the Place of Infringement: The Application of Article 5(3) of Regulation 44/2001 to IP Matters and Internet Disputes' in Arnaud Nuyts (ed.), *International Litigation in Intellectual Property and Information Technology*, Kluwer Law International, 2008, p. 107 and Marta Pertegás Sender, *Cross-Border Enforcement of Patent Rights*, Oxford Private International Law Series, 2002 at 3.67.

42 Case C-21/76, *Handelskwekerij G. J. Bier BV v Mines de potasse d'Alsace SA*, para. 19 and section B.1(a)(ii) Principle 6: Place of action and place(s) of effect(s).

43 Case C-523/10, *Wintersteiger AG*, paras 19–20.

44 Ibid., para. 37.

45 Ibid., para. 29.

46 Magnus and Mankowski, *supra* note 8, pp. 243 *et seq.*

47 Case C-523/10, *Wintersteiger AG*, paras 27–29. In the specific case one could argue, inter alia, that google.de, where the Wintersteiger AdWord was registered, was directed at Austria per se since German is the language spoken in Austria and since products were sold in Austria. Following any such argument one could then question whether the place(s) of registration rule applies *mutatis mutandis* if it is clear from the facts of the case that the infringement is *not* directed to the forum and that, therefore, there has been no effect there cf. *Conflict of Laws in Intellectual Property, The CLIP Principles and Commentary*, European Max Planck Group on Conflicts of Laws in Intellectual Property, Oxford University Press, 2013, p. 82 (2:202.N10). The question is dealt with in section B.1(a)(iii).

48 Case C-4/03, *Gesellschaft für Antriebstechnik mbH & Co. KG v Lamellen und Kupplungsbau Beteiligungs KG (Gat LuK)* and Chapter 11 section B.

49 Principles 1–4. These principles correspond to the ones mentioned in Chapter 4 sections C.1-C.4.

50 Principles 5–9.

51 Principles 1–9 are only applied to the place(s) of registration rule being the more controversial rule except from principle 6 concerning a place of action and a place(s) of effect(s) and principle 8 concerning the extent of jurisdiction.

Principle 1: Predictability

9.15 It follows as a general principle[52] *that* art. 7(2) BR must be highly predictable thereby meeting legal certainty; *that* predictability used to relate to the defendant alone but now relates to both the plaintiff and the defendant and *that* predictability is not met if jurisdiction is conferred on wholly unforeseeable places.

9.16 In *Wintersteiger* the CJEU did not cite any prior art. 7(2) BR case law on predictability[53] but merely stated that a place(s) of registration rule is interconnected with territoriality and is therefore predictable.[54] On the surface this may seem correct since the rule uses an objective criterion (i.e. 'registration'[55] in line with 'distribution'[56]) rather than combined with a relative criterion (i.e. 'effect'[57] in line with 'known'[58]), which in turn restricts the discretion of the courts. Going a bit deeper, however, the rule seems not so predictable after all. The reasons are numerous but include, inter alia, and subject to the examination in section B.1(a)(iii) *that* it is not entirely clear from the judgment whether the rule is actually a place(s) of registration rule[59] or a place(s) of de facto protection rule;[60] *that* there is a difference between them since protection seems to require enforceable trademark rights whereas registration does not;[61] *that* the rule may become a wholly unforeseeable place for a defendant who uses an infringing mark/sign online e.g. may Frox SpA consider it rather unforeseeable that they can be sued where the Frogs trademark is registered without them having targeted that particular Member State;[62] *that* the level of unpredictability increases the higher number of national trademark registrations and finally given that an equivalent rule likely applies to unregistered

52 Chapter 4 section C.1.
53 Case C-523/10, *Wintersteiger AG*, para. 27.
54 Ibid., paras 27 cf. 25.
55 Ibid., para. 29.
56 Case C-68/93, *Fiona Shevill*, para. 29.
57 Opinion of Advocate General Villalón in case C-523/10, *Wintersteiger AG*, para. 28.
58 Case C-68/93, *Fiona Shevill*, para. 29.
59 Case C-523/10, *Wintersteiger AG*, para. 29 speaks of 'the courts of the Member State in which the trade mark is *registered*'. Para. 40, being the conclusion, similarly speaks of 'the courts of the Member State in which the trade mark is *registered*.' Other language versions speak of the same place i.e. 'die Gerichte des Mitgliedstaats der *Eintragung der Marke*' (DE), 'les juridictions de l'État membre dans lequel la marque est *enregistrée*' (FR) or 'hvor varemærket er *registreret*' (DK). Emphasis added.
60 Ibid. para. 27 speaks of 'the courts of the Member State in which the right at issue is *protected*'. Other language versions speak of the same place i.e. the place where the '*Recht geschützt ist*' (DE), where '*le droit en cause est protégé*' (FR) or where '*den omhandlede rettighed er beskyttet*' (DK). Emphasis added.
61 Section B.1(a)(iii).
62 Chapter 1 section 2.

trademark rights[63] any such rule may create unpredictability[64] since there is no place where a defendant can look up such rights.

In sum, the place(s) of registration rule seems obviously predictable for the plaintiff since he/she may easily be able to identify the court(s) before which he/she may bring an action. On the contrary the rule seems not predictable for the defendant since, for the reasons above, he/she may not reasonably be able to foresee the court before which he may be sued, which therefore risks being a wholly unforeseeable place. In turn this creates legal uncertainty. So interpreted the place(s) of registration rule not only contrasts early art. 7(2) BR case law, where predictability related to the defendant alone, but also recent art. 7(2) BR case law, where predictability relates to both parties. In *Wintersteiger* predictability seems primarily to relate to the plaintiff. Interestingly, the CJEU did not explicitly argue that the place(s) of registration rule was predictable for the defendant either contrary to the place where the advertiser is established rule, which was predictable for both the defendant and the plaintiff.[65] **9.17**

Principle 2: Proximity

It follows as a general principle[66] *that* art. 7(2) BR is based on proximity and *that* proximity seeks to prevent the defendant from being sued in a wholly unforeseeable place. **9.18**

In *Wintersteiger* the CJEU cited prior case law[67] and stated that a place(s) of registration rule was justified in proximity.[68] On the surface this may seem correct since *sine qua non* a trademark registration there has been no harmful event within the meaning of art. 7(2) BR.[69] However, a place(s) of registration does not seem to be as proximate as in prior art. 7(2) BR case law *since* there, proximity required more than just one basic connecting factor[70] before the court was 'territorially the best placed to assess the [harm] committed in that **9.19**

63 Section B.1(a)(iii).

64 Opinion of AG Jääskinen in case C-170/12, *Peter Pinckney v KDG Mediatech AG*, para. 68 whereas 'I am opposed to such a multiplication of courts with jurisdiction, for reasons to do with [...] foreseeability'. The case concerned copyrights, which bear a resemblance with unregistered trademark rights given that both come into existence without formalities cf. W. R. Cornish and D. Llewelyn, *Intellectual Property: Patents, Copyrights, Trade Marks and Allied Rights*, 6th edn, Thomson, 2007 at 11.32 and Guy Tritton, *Intellectual Property in Europe*, 3rd edn, Sweet & Maxwell, 2008 at 4.001.

65 Case C-523/10, *Wintersteiger AG*, para. 37.

66 Chapter 4 section C.2.

67 Case C-523/10, *Wintersteiger AG*, para. 18.

68 Ibid., para. 27.

69 *Conflict of Laws in Intellectual Property, The CLIP Principles and Commentary*, *supra* note 47, p. 71 (2:202.C07).

70 Case C-68/93, *Fiona Shevill*, para. 29; case C-18/02, *Danmarks Rederiforening, acting on behalf of DFDS Torline A/S v LO Landsorganisationen i Sverige, acting on behalf of SEKO Sjöfolk Facket för Service och Kommunikation*, para. 44 and Principle 7: Place(s) of effect(s) subject to connecting factors.

State',[71] *since* therefore a place(s) of registration whereto only one basic connecting factor ('registration') but no other ('effect')[72] point, does not qualify to be 'territorially the best placed to assess the [infringement] committed in that State'; *since* in the absence of information in *Wintersteiger* a disclaimer on an infringer's website that he/she does not commercially act in certain place(s) of registration may likely not even protect him/her from being sued there;[73] *since* therefore a place(s) of registration may also in this aspect amount to a wholly unforeseeable place; *since* a place(s) of registration may effect the balance of the parties[74] in the sense *that* it allows an infringer to be sued in a case with no merits thus increasing the risk of frivolous lawsuits; *that* the infringer will face a summary judgment if he/she, even in a case with no merits, does not show up at the place(s) of registration; *that* the summary judgment can be recognized and enforced in every Member State including the one where the infringer is domiciled following Chapter III BR[75] and *that* the infringer may be subject to unnecessary and burdensome costs to defend himself/herself even in cases with no merits.

9.20 In sum, the place(s) of registration rule does not seem as proximate as required in prior art. 7(2) BR case law, which becomes clearer given that a disclaimer may likely not even protect a defendant from being sued following the rule. Consequently, the place(s) of registration may risk being wholly unforeseeable for the defendant with possible procedural law consequences to follow.

Principle 3: Avoiding forum shopping

9.21 It follows as a general principle[76] *that* art. 7(2) BR with exceptions[77] must be interpreted to avoid forum shopping since otherwise the risk of irreconcilable judgments would increase and *that* the risk of forum shopping only shows with respect to delicts arising out of the same legal matter.

9.22 In *Wintersteiger* the CJEU did not justify the place(s) of registration rule in avoiding forum shopping.[78] In fact, the CJEU did not mention forum shopping with one word. One could therefore argue that the reason for not

71 Case C-68/93, *Fiona Shevill*, para. 31.

72 Opinion of Advocate General Villalón in case C-523/10, *Wintersteiger AG*, para. 28.

73 Section B.1(a)(iii).

74 Preamble CLIP Principles speaking of 'the need to consider and balance all interests involved' cf. Recitals (16) and (19) Rome II speaking of 'a reasonable balance between the interests of the person claimed to be liable and the person who has sustained damage' and 'a reasonable balance to be struck between the interests at stake'.

75 If, however, the defendant is not served with the documents instituting the proceedings the judgment cannot be recognized cf. art. 45(1)(b) BR.

76 Chapter 4 section C.3.

77 Principle 6: Place of action and place(s) of effect(s).

78 Case C-523/10, *Wintersteiger AG*, paras 25–28.

mentioning forum shopping is that the place(s) of registration rule does not lead to more forum shopping *since* potentially numerous trademark infringements do not arise out of the same legal matter but rather out of different legal matters, which is due to the territorial principle underlying the place(s) of registration rule;[79] *since* accordingly an infringement of e.g. a Danish trademark being one legal matter can only be heard by the courts in one Member State within the meaning of the place(s) of registration rule, namely by the courts in Denmark; *since* therefore there is no risk of irreconcilable judgments; *since* in practical life a place(s) of registration rule is restricted in at least two ways for a plaintiff, who wants to go forum shopping i.e. *first* due to *L'Oréal* as cited in *Wintersteiger*[80] and whereas the mere accessibility of a website in a Member State cannot subject a defendant to the trademark laws potentially a trademark infringement there given that any such requires the website to be directed to the Member State in question[81] and *second* due to the extent of jurisdiction at the place(s) of registration which is likely limited.[82]

Despite the above a place(s) of registration rule nevertheless allows the plaintiff a wide discretion *since* it allows him/her to bring an action in every Member State where his/her trademark is registered and *since* the Member State being picked by the plaintiff is the one which is typically more advantageous to him/her, inter alia, *because* the evidence can be easily obtained and preserved there; *because* the rules on disclosure of documents are beneficial to the plaintiff; *because* the rules on examination of witnesses are beneficial to the plaintiff; *because* the rules on search and seizure are beneficial to the plaintiff; *because* the expenses of litigation are low; *because* the courts are specialized; *because* the courts are effective; *because* the damages awarded by the courts are high; *because* case law and the excepted outcome is predictable or *because* successful decisions have suspensive effects upon appeal.[83] Even though the above discretion awarded to the plaintiff can hardly be characterized as forum shopping since the rights in question are fully independent[84] they bear a clear resemblance with it. **9.23**

79 Ibid., para. 25 and Chapter 4 section D.
80 Ibid., para. 28.
81 Case C-324/09, *L'Oréal SA and Others v eBay International AG and Others*, paras 64–65.
82 Principle 8: Unlimited full jurisdiction and limited forum jurisdiction.
83 Chapter 1 section A.4.
84 Opinion of AG Jääskinen in case C-170/12, *Peter Pinckney*, para. 68, however, speaks of forum shopping with respect to copyrights within the meaning of art. 7(2) BR even though copyrights are also fully independent rights cf. opinion of Advocate General Léger in case C-539/03, *Roche Nederland BV, Roche Diagnostic Systems Inc., NV Roche SA, Hoffmann-La Roche AG, Produits Roche SA, Roche Products Ltd, F. Hoffmann-La Roche AG, Hoffmann-La Roche Wien GmbH, Roche AB v Frederick Primus, Milton Goldenberg*, paras. 97 and 99 and judgment of the CJEU, para. 38.

9.24 In sum, the place(s) of registration rule allows the plaintiff a wide discretion, which bears a clear resemblance with forum shopping.

Principle 4: Avoiding 'pollution'

9.25 It follows as a general principle[85] that art. 7(2) BR must enable the courts to decide jurisdiction without considering the substance of the case since otherwise the procedural and substantial law stages would be 'polluted', which in turn would run counter to predictability.

9.26 In *Wintersteiger* the CJEU did not require connecting factors to locate the place(s) of effect(s).[86] The CJEU's approach limits the risk of 'pollution', which the CJEU itself is well aware of[87] since connecting factors are only used on substantial law level.[88] So ruling, the CJEU adheres to prior case law in both *Marinari* where art. 7(2) BR does not 'link the rules on territorial jurisdiction with [the rules on tort]'[89] and in *eDate* where the CJEU defined a place(s) of effect(s) as the place where the content placed online 'is or has been accessible'[90] thereby also limiting the risk of 'pollution' given that no connecting factors are used. Thus, the impact of the CJEU's approach is that the term 'damage' is broader in procedural law than in substantial law.

9.27 The CJEU could, however, have required connecting factors as recommended by the AG,[91] by legal scholars[92] and in scholarly reports[93] and still not having 'polluted'. The reason is – and despite the fact that the factors used on procedural law level[94] could equal the factors used on substantial law level[95] – that the former assessment would only consider the infringement 'potential'[96] meaning that the assessment would be broad and unspecified and based on the

85 Chapter 4 section C.4.

86 Case C-523/10, *Wintersteiger AG*, paras 27–29 and Principle 7: Place(s) of effect(s) subject to connecting factors.

87 Ibid., para. 26.

88 Ibid., para. 28 referring to case C-324/09, *L'Oréal SA*.

89 Case 364/93, *Antonio Marinari v Lloyds Bank plc and Zubaidi Trading Company*, para. 18.

90 Joined cases C-509/09, *eDate Advertising GmbH* and C-161/10, *Olivier Martinez and Robert Martinez*, para. 51.

91 Opinion of Advocate General Villalón in case C-523/10, *Wintersteiger AG*, paras 28–31.

92 Annette Kur, 'Trademark Conflicts on the Internet: Territoriality Redefined?' in Jürgen Basedow, Josef Drexl, Annette Kur and Axel Metzger (eds) *Intellectual Property and the Conflict of Laws*, Mohr Siebeck, 2005, p. 5 and *Conflict of Laws in Intellectual Property, The CLIP Principles and Commentary*, *supra* note 47, p. 72 (2:202.C08).

93 Art. 2:202 CLIP Principles, § 204 ALI Principles cf. arts 105 Transparency Proposal and 203(2) Waseda Project.

94 Opinion of Advocate General Villalón in case C-523/10, *Wintersteiger AG*, para. 28 whereas 'an effect' must be determined on the basis of the facts of the case taking into account 'a number of criteria'.

95 Case C-324/09, *L'Oréal SA*, paras 64–65 whereas 'targeted at' must be determined on the basis of the facts of the case taking into account 'any relevant factors'.

96 Opinion of Advocate General Villalón in case C-523/10, *Wintersteiger AG*, paras 31 and 37.

claims.[97] So interpreted, the term 'damage' would still be broader in procedural law than in substantial law.[98] Below an example illustrating the CJEU's and the AG's approaches:

> Recalling the facts of the example in Chapter 1 section 2 Frox SpA markets and sells foam shoes, inter alia, online in Italy, Spain, France and Austria under the name Frox. Frogs GmbH owns national trademark rights in the Member States and wants to bring an infringement action against Frox SpA.
>
> The CJEU's decision allows an action to be brought in every Member State where the Frogs trademark is registered. Substantial law-wise an overall assessment must be made given that a defendant can only be subject to the trademark laws of a Member State, potentially an infringement there, provided that the defendant has targeted the Member State which must be determined taking into account any relevant factors including information as to where the defendant is willing to sell a product cf. *L'Oréal*. Taking into account that Frox SpA's focus is Italy, Spain, France and Austria it seems likely that Frox SpA has targeted those Member States and that Frox SpA is subject to the trademark laws of those Member States, potentially infringements there. Thus, the court must make two different assessments, i.e. a broad assessment on procedural law level and a narrow assessment on substantial law level thereby limiting a risk of 'pollution' between the two levels.
>
> If the AG's opinion was followed an action could be brought in every Member State where the Frogs trademark is registered provided that there had been an effect in those Member States which, inter alia, should be determined taking into account a number of criteria including the commercial presence of the defendant where the mark is protected. Taking into account that Frox SpA's focus is Italy, Spain, France and Austria an action could most likely only be brought in those four Member States due to an effect there. Substantial law wise the assessment is similar to the one above. Despite that the two levels are alike there would not be a risk of 'pollution' given that the former assessment would only take account of the infringement potential. The evaluation of the actual infringement would be left to a later stage.

In sum, the place(s) of registration rule limits the risk of 'pollution' as in prior art. 7(2) BR case law. **9.28**

---

97 *Conflict of Laws in Intellectual Property, The CLIP Principles and Commentary*, *supra* note 47, p. 72 (2:202.C09).

98 Ibid.

Principle 5: Narrow interpretation

9.29 It follows as a specific principle that every rule[99] derogating from art. 4 BR[100] 'cannot give rise to an interpretation going beyond the cases expressly envisaged by the [BR]',[101] which for art. 7(2) BR, with exceptions,[102] warrants a narrow interpretation.[103]

9.30 In *Wintersteiger* the CJEU referred to art. 7(2) BR as derogating from art. 4 BR[104] without citing prior case law on a narrow interpretation.[105] Supporting that the place(s) of registration rule nonetheless reflects a narrow interpretation of art. 7(2) BR speaks *that* the rule is likely subject to limited forum jurisdiction[106] whereas supporting a wide interpretation of art. 7(2) BR argues *that* the rule reflects the absolute minimum connection required for IP within the meaning of the provision[107] and *that* the rule opens up for what bears a clear resemblance with forum shopping.[108]

9.31 In sum, the place(s) of registration rule reflects a wide interpretation of art. 7(2) BR given that it widens up the number of available fora.

Principle 6: Place of action and place(s) of effect(s)

9.32 It follows as a specific principle that art. 7(2) BR encompasses a place of action and a place(s) of effect(s)[109] also known as the ubiquity principle.[110] Whereas the place of action is the place giving rise to the damage, which usually, but not always, coincides with the defendant's domicile[111] the place(s) of effect(s) is the place(s) where the event which may give rise to liability resulted in

99 Chapter II section 2 BR.

100 Chapter 5 section B.1.

101 Case C-412/98, *Group Josi Reinsurance Company SA v Universal General Insurance Company (UGIC)*, para. 49; case C-26/91, *Jakob Handte & Co. GmbH v Traitements Mécano-chimiques des Surfaces SA*, para. 14; case C-89/91, *Shearson Lehmann Hutton Inc. v TVB Treuhandgesellschaft für Vermögensverwaltung und Beteiligungen mbH*, paras. 15–16; case C-269/95, *Francesco Benincasa v Dentalkit Srl*, para. 13 and case C-51/97, *Réunion européenne SA*, para. 16.

102 Principle 6: Place of action and place(s) of effect(s).

103 Case C-189/87, *Athanasios*, para. 19; case C-364/93, *Antonio Marinari*, para. 14; case C-168/02, *Rudolf Kronhofer*, para. 14 and case C-189/08, *Zuid-Chemie BV*, para. 22.

104 Case C-523/10, *Wintersteiger*, para. 18.

105 *Supra* note 103.

106 Principle 8: Unlimited full jurisdiction and limited forum jurisdiction.

107 *Supra* note 69.

108 Principle 3: Avoiding forum shopping.

109 Case C-21/76, *Handelskwekerij G. J. Bier BV*, para. 25; case C-220/88, *Dumez France SA*, para. 10; case C-68/93, *Fiona Shevill*, para. 20; case C-364/93, *Antonio Marinari*, para. 11; case C-51/97, *Réunion européenne*, para. 28; case 167/00, *Verein für Konsumenteninformation*, para. 44; case C-18/02, *Danmarks Rederiforening*, para. 40; case C-168/02, *Rudolf Kronhofer*, para. 16 and case C-189/08, *Zuid-Chemie BV*, para. 23.

110 Magnus and Mankowski, *supra* note 8, p. 239.

111 *Supra* note 46.

damage.[112] The plaintiff may sue in either these places.[113] The reason for the ubiquity principle is threefold, namely *that* favouring a place of action would considerably overlap with art. 4 BR thus ruling out the meaning of art. 7(2) BR;[114] *that* favouring a place(s) of effect(s) in situations where a place of action does not overlap with art. 4 BR would exclude action being brought at the place giving rise to the damage[115] and *that* both a place of action and a place(s) of effect(s) meet proximity.[116] Despite the ubiquity principle art. 7(2) BR is restricted[117] given that a place(s) of effect(s) might be located at the plaintiff's own domicile known as a *forum actoris*, which according to art. 7(2) BR case law must be avoided, inter alia, *since* any such place would limit the application of art. 4 BR;[118] *since* only in cases explicitly provided for does the BR confer jurisdiction on a *forum actoris*;[119] *since* the BR is generally hostile towards a *forum actoris*[120] and – with the words of the AG – *since* a *forum actoris* does not meet proximity[121] and *since* it is very easy for the plaintiff to change domicile which would encourage forum shopping.[122] For these reasons and in line with the *Pocar* report[123] the CJEU has consistently rejected places equalling a *forum actoris*[124] such as the place of final delivery,[125] the place where the damage to the victim's assets was ascertained,[126] the place where the victim has claimed to have suffered damage when he/she in fact has suffered damage in another Member State[127] or the place where the victim's assets are concentrated.[128] Sometimes the CJEU has excluded any such places from the scope of art. 7(2) BR by way of a strict reading of the place(s) of effect(s) rule[129] and sometimes

112 Case C-189/08, *Zuid-Chemie BV*, para. 26.
113 Case C-21/76, *Handelskwekerij G. J. Bier BV*, para. 25.
114 Ibid., para. 20.
115 Ibid., para. 21.
116 Ibid., para. 15 and Chapter 4 section C.2.
117 Principle 5: Narrow interpretation.
118 Case C-364/93, *Antonio*, para. 13 and case C-51/97, *Réunion européenne SA*, para. 29.
119 Arts 11(1)(b), 18(1) and 21(1)(b)(i) BR.
120 Art. 3(2) BR cf. case C-220/88, *Dumez France SA*, paras 16 and 19 and case C-168/02, *Rudolf Kronhofer*, para. 20.
121 Opinion of Advocate General Darmon (first opinion) in case C-68/93, *Fiona Shevill*, para. 46 and opinion of Advocate General Darmon (first opinion) in case C-364/93, *Antonio Marinari*, para. 31.
122 Opinion of Advocate General Darmon in case C-220/88, *Dumez France SA*, para. 48.
123 Report on the Convention on Jurisdiction and the Recognition and Enforcement of Judgments in Civil and Commercial Matters, signed in Lugano on 30 October 2007, by Professor Fausto Pocar at 59.
124 Magnus and Mankowski, *supra* note 8, p. 254.
125 Case C-51/97, *Réunion européenne SA* para. 34.
126 Case C-220/88, *Dumez France SA*, para. 22 and case C-51/97, ibid., para. 34.
127 Case C-364/93, *Antonio Marinari*, para. 21.
128 Case C-168/02, *Rudolf Kronhofer*, para. 21.
129 Case C-220/88, *Dumez France SA*, paras 16–22 and case C-51/97, *Réunion européenne SA*, paras 33–34.

the CJEU has done so by way of rejecting a third rule other than a place of action and a place(s) of effect(s) rules.[130]

9.33 In *Wintersteiger* the CJEU upheld the distinction between a place of action and a place(s) of effect(s)[131] to trademark rights in line with that of some national courts[132] and some legal scholars[133] but contrary to scholarly reports.[134] The CJEU defined the former as the place where the advertiser is established[135] in line with *Shevill*[136] and *eDate*[137] and the latter as the place(s) of registration.[138] In so doing the CJEU[139] in line with the AG[140] dismissed the so-called centre of interests' rule,[141] which applies to online infringements of personality rights and where action can be brought at *forum actoris*.[142] Thus, trademark rights did not fall within the term 'wide range of [...] personality rights' as stated in *eDate*.[143] Whereas the AG dismissed the centre of interests' rule arguing *that* trademark rights are based on territoriality (which personality rights are not) and *that* trademark rights are concerned with the commercial exploitation of a product (which personality rights are not)[144] the CJEU did not mention the latter argument in its decision,[145] which makes sense since personality rights may also be concerned with the commercial exploitation of a product given that personality rights cover both a right to privacy and a right to publicity.[146]

---

130 Case C-168/02, *Rudolf Kronhofer*, paras. 18–21. Any such third rule, the so-called 'centre of interests' rule was introduced in joined cases C-509/09, *eDate Advertising* and C-161/10, *Olivier Martinez and Robert Martinez*, para. 48 cf. below.

131 Case C-523/10, *Wintersteiger*, para. 19.

132 *Boss Zigaretten v Hugo Boss*, Oberster Gerichtshof, case 4 Ob 110/01, 2003; *Castellblanch SA v Champagne Louis Roederer SA*, Cour de Cassation, case IL Pr 41, 2004; *GRE Manufacturas and Another v Agrisilos*, Cour de Cassation, case IL Pr 27, 2007; *Carpoint SPA v Microsoft Corporation*, Board of Appeal of the Tribunal of Rome, case ETMR 802, 2000 and *Aredal Foam Systems HB v MSR Dosiertechnik GmbH*, Högsta Domstolen of Sweden, Ö 210–07, 2007.

133 Fawcett and Torremans, *supra* note 48 at 5.48; Klaus Grabinski, Zur Bedeutung des Europäischen Gerichtsstands- und Vollstreckungsübereinkommens (Brüsseler Übereinkommens) und des Lugano-Übereinkommens in Rechtsstreitigkeiten über Patentverletzungen, 2001, 3 GRUR int. 1999 and Pedro De Miguel Asensio, 16, 2007, AIDA 105 at 122–3.

134 Art. 2:202 CLIP Principles cf. *Conflict of Laws in Intellectual Property, The CLIP Principles and Commentary*, *supra* note 47, p. 80 (2:202.N06) cf. p. 69 (2:202.C04).

135 Case C-523/10, *Wintersteiger AG*, para. 37.

136 Case C-68/93, *Fiona Shevill*, para. 24.

137 Joined cases C-509/09, *eDate Advertising* and C-161/10, *Olivier Martinez and Robert Martinez*, para. 52.

138 Case C-523/10, *Wintersteiger AG*, para. 29.

139 Ibid., paras 22–24.

140 Opinion of Advocate General Villalón in ibid., para. 20.

141 Joined cases C-509/09, *eDate Advertising* and C-161/10, *Olivier Martinez and Robert Martinez*, para. 52.

142 Ibid., para. 49 cf. Picht, *supra* note 14, pp. 19 *et seq.*

143 Joined cases C-509/09, *eDate Advertising* and C-161/10, *Olivier Martinez and Robert Martinez*, para. 44.

144 Opinion of Advocate General Villalón in case C-523/10, *Wintersteiger AG*, para. 20.

145 Case C-523/10, *Wintersteiger AG*, para. 25.

146 Thomas Riis, 'Merchandising', in Julebog 1997, Jurist- og Økonomforbundets Forlag (DJØF), 1997, p. 111.

In sum, the CJEU upheld the distinction between a place of action and a place(s) of effect(s) in *Wintersteiger* and rejected a *forum actoris* rule to trademark rights. 9.34

Principle 7: Place(s) of effect(s) subject to connecting factors

It follows as a specific principle that connecting factors are used to locate the place(s) of effect(s). Thus, in *Shevill* the CJEU ruled that the place(s) of effect(s) is 'where the publication is distributed [one connecting factor] when the victim is known in those places [another connecting factor]'[147] and in *DFDS* the CJEU ruled that 'the flag State, that is the State in which the ship is registered [one connecting factor], must be regarded as only one factor, among others [other connecting factors]'.[148] The reason for applying connecting factors to locate the place(s) of effect(s) is to ensure predictability,[149] proximity,[150] and avoiding forum shopping.[151] 9.35

In *Wintersteiger* the CJEU dismissed the need for connecting factors to locate the place(s) of effect(s).[152] The approach dismisses prior offline non-IP case law at CJEU level,[153] prior online IP case law at national court level,[154] the AG's opinion in *Wintersteiger*,[155] scholarly reports[156] and writings by legal 9.36

---

147 Case C-68/93, *Fiona Shevill*, para. 29.

148 Case C-18/02, *Danmarks Rederiforening*, para. 44.

149 Chapter 4 section C.1.

150 Chapter 4 section C.2.

151 Chapter 4 section C.3.

152 Case C-523/10, *Wintersteiger*, paras 27–29.

153 *Supra* notes 147–148.

154 There has been a tendency at national court level from applying a mere accessibility approach to applying a connecting factors approach. Cases illustrating the mere accessibility approach count cases from 1997–2003, inter alia, Concert-Concept, Kammergericht Berlin, CR 685, 1997; *Maritime v Hotel Maritime*, Landgericht 2002 GRUR Int. 163, 2001; *Maritime v Hotel Maritime*, Oberlandesgericht 2002 MMR 822, 2002; *INTEL v Intel S.r.l.*, Oberlandesgericht Karlsruhe, MMR 814, 2002; Oberlandesgericht München, 15.11.2001, MMR 166, 2002, literaturhaus.de; Oberlandesgericht Frankfurt am Main, 03.12.1998 K&R, 138, 1999; Red Bull, OGH, Urteil vom 24.04.2001, 4 Ob 81/01t.; *SG2 v Brokat Informationssysteme GmbH*, TGI Nanterre, 1997 and *Castellblanch v Louis Roederer Champagne*, Cour de Cassation, Premiére Chambre Civil, B 01–03.225, 2004. Cases illustrating the connecting factors approach count cases from 1999–2006, inter alia, *Boss v Boss*, Oberste Gerichtshof Österreich, ÖBl 2001.145, 2001; *Maritime v Hotel Maritime*, Bundesgerichtshof, 13 October 2004, GRUR 2005, 431; *Internet-Fotos*, Oberlandesgericht Köln, 30 Oktober 2007, GRUR-RR 2008, 71; *Normalu*, Cour d'Appel de Paris, 26 April 2006 and *Bonnier Media Ltd. v Smith* [2003] SC 36, 2002 [ETMR] 86 cf. Larsen, *supra* note 15, pp. 28 *et seq.*

155 Opinion of Advocate General Villalón in case C-523/10, *Wintersteiger AG*, paras 27–29. Surprisingly, the AG stated that, 'the Court has consistently rejected the view that the mere fact that harmful information is accessible or is simply circulated on the internet is of sufficient importance to justify the application of the provisions on jurisdiction laid down in Regulation No 44/2001' cf. para. 23, which is exactly the opposite of what the CJEU ruled in *eDate*, para. 51. *eDate* was delivered prior in time i.e. on 25 October 2011 whereas the AG's opinion in *Wintersteiger* was delivered on 12 February 2012.

156 Art. 2:202 CLIP Principles, § 204 ALI Principles cf. arts 105 Transparency Proposal and 203 Waseda Project.

scholars,[157] which all require connecting factors to locate the place(s) of effect(s). By contrast the approach merely follows up on the online approach taken in *eDate.*[158]

9.37 In sum, the place(s) of registration rule does not require connecting factors to the same extent as in existing offline case law on CJEU level (*Shevill* and *DFDS*) but is in line with existing online case law on CJEU level (*eDate*). The offline and online approaches are further examined in section B.1(a)(iii).

Principle 8: Unlimited full jurisdiction and limited forum jurisdiction

9.38 Following the eighth specific principle art. 7(2) BR, lacking information in the provision itself[159] is subject to unlimited full jurisdiction at the place of action[160] and limited forum jurisdiction at the place(s) of effect(s).[161] The reason for limiting the extent of jurisdiction at the place(s) of effect(s), also known as the 'mosaic' rule,[162] is that otherwise a place(s) of effect(s) could equal a *forum actoris*, which must be avoided.[163] The 'mosaic' rule has mostly been welcomed since it limits the risk of forum shopping[164] but it has also been criticized *since* in a personality right context it appears overly burdensome for the plaintiff[165] and *since* courts in different Member States where different parts of the damage occurred may reach different results and in the most unfortunate event reach irreconcilable judgments.[166]

9.39 In *Wintersteiger* the CJEU did not explicitly discuss the extent of jurisdiction at the place(s) of effect(s) defined as the place(s) of registration.[167] The reason seems to be that the preliminary reference[168] concerned only one Austrian

---

157 Kur, *supra* note 92, p. 5; Axel Metzger, 'Jurisdiction in Cases Concerning Intellectual Property Infringements on the Internet' in Stefan Leible and Ansgar Ohly (eds) *Intellectual Property and Private International Law* Mohr Siebeck, 2009, pp. 257–61 and *Conflict of Laws in Intellectual Property, The CLIP Principles and Commentary*, *supra* note 47, p. 72 (2:202.C08 and 2:202.C09).

158 Joined cases C-509/09, *eDate Advertising* and C-161/10, *Olivier Martinez and Robert Martinez*, para. 51.

159 *Conflict of Laws in Intellectual Property, The CLIP Principles and Commentary*, *supra* note 47, p. 90 (2:203.N01).

160 Case C-68/93, *Fiona Shevill*, para. 25 and Principle 6: Place of action and place(s) of effect(s).

161 Ibid., para. 30 and Principle 6, ibid.

162 Magnus and Mankowski, *supra* note 8, p. 240.

163 Principle 6: Place of action and place(s) of effect(s).

164 Magnus and Mankowski, *supra* note 8, pp. 241–2 and Principle 3: Avoiding forum shopping.

165 Annette Kur, 'Jurisdiction and Enforcement of Foreign Judgments – the General Structure of the MPI Proposal' in J. Drexl and A. Kur (eds) IIC Studies, vol. 24, Intellectual Property and Private International Law, Heading for the Future, 2005, p. 29.

166 Nielsen, *supra* note 8, p. 167.

167 Case C-523/10, *Wintersteiger*, para. 29.

168 Opinion of Advocate General Villalón in case C-523/10, *Wintersteiger AG*, para. 8 and judgment of the CJEU, para. 16.

Wintersteiger trademark registration despite the plaintiff's written submissions that he/she was the owner of numerous national Wintersteiger trademark registrations throughout the EU including one in Germany.[169] Given that, it seemed rather obvious that the Austrian courts had jurisdiction to determine any alleged harm in Austria[170] or with the words of the CJEU 'to determine all the damage allegedly caused to the proprietor of the protected right because of an infringement of it'.[171] What seems less obvious, however, is the result, as also pointed out by the AG,[172] if the preliminary reference had in fact concerned more than one Austrian trademark registration. The question would in that case be whether the courts of Austria as one of the place(s) of registration would have unlimited full jurisdiction (no *Shevill* analogy) or only limited forum jurisdiction (*Shevill* analogy).

Supporting that the place(s) of registration would have unlimited full jurisdiction it is argued, inter alia, *that* the term 'all the damage' used in the respective British, German, French, Danish and Swedish versions of *Wintersteiger*[173] has consistently or with slight variations in defamation cases[174] as well as in non-defamation cases[175] been used to equal unlimited full jurisdiction whereas the term 'jurisdiction to rule solely in respect of the harm caused in the State of the court seised' has consistently been used to equal limited forum jurisdiction;[176] *that* therefore and for reasons of consistency the CJEU would most likely have used the term 'jurisdiction to rule solely in 9.40

169 Opinion of Advocate General Villalón, ibid., paras 4 and 14.

170 Ulf Maunsbach, Jurisdiction in Relation to Online Cross-Border Infringements: The Code and the Law' in Dan J. B. Svantesson and Stanley Greenstein (eds), *Internationalization of Law in the Digital Information Society*, Ex Tuto Publishing, 2013, p. 179.

171 Case C-523/10, *Wintersteiger AG*, para. 28.

172 Opinion of Advocate General Villalón in ibid., para. 15.

173 Case C-523/10, *Wintersteiger*, para. 28 speaking of 'all the damage' (UK), 'Gesamten Schaden' (DE), 'l'intégralité du dommage' (FR), 'fulde erstatning' (DK) and 'samlade skada' (SV).

174 Case C-68/93, *Fiona Shevill*, para. 33 speaking of 'all the harm' (UK), 'sämtlicher [...] Schäden' (DE), 'l'intégralité du dommage' (FR), 'erstatning for hele den skade' (DK) and 'samtliga skador' (SV) and joined cases C-509/09, *eDate Advertising* and C-161/10, *Olivier Martinez and Robert Martinez*, para. 52 speaking of 'all of the damage' (UK), 'Gesamten [...] Schäden' (DE), 'l'intégralité des dommages' (FR), 'fuldstændige skade' (DK) and 'hela skadan' (SV).

175 Opinion of Advocate General Poiares Maduro in case C-343/04, *Land Oberösterreich v ČEZ* as, para. 86 at note 68 referring to case C-68/93, *Fiona Shevill*, para. 33 cf. *supra* note 174.

176 Case C-68/93, *Fiona Shevill*, para. 33 speaking of 'jurisdiction to rule solely in respect of the harm caused in the State of the court seised' (UK), '[ü]ber den Ersatz der Schäden zuständig, die in dem Staat des angerufenen Gerichts verursacht worden sind' (DE), 'compétentes pour connaître des seuls dommages causés dans l'État de la juridiction saisie' (FR), 'kompetence til at tage stilling til den skade, der er forvoldt i den stat, for hvis retter sagen er indbragt' (DK) and 'behöriga att pröva enbart de skador som orsakats i respektive domstols stat' (SV) and joined cases C-509/09, *eDate Advertising* and C-161/10, *Olivier Martinez and Robert Martine*, para. 52 speaking of 'jurisdiction only in respect of the damage caused in the territory of the Member State of the court seised' (UK), 'über den Schaden zuständig, der im Hoheitsgebiet des Mitgliedstaats des angerufenen Gerichts verursacht worden ist' (DE), 'compétentes pour connaître du seul dommage causé sur le territoire de l'État membre de la juridiction saisie' (FR), 'kompetence i relation til den skade, der

respect of the harm caused in the State of the court seised [Austria]' if the Austrian courts as the place of registration would only have limited forum jurisdiction; *that* the term 'all the damage' used by the CJEU equals the term 'without there being a fragmentation of jurisdiction' used by the AG[177] as equalling unlimited full jurisdiction; *that* if the term 'all the damage' was interpreted as equalling limited forum jurisdiction there would be no term for equalling unlimited full jurisdiction which in turn would be illogical; *that* unlimited full jurisdiction would provide the plaintiff with a real alternative to the defendant's domicile;[178] *that* unlimited full jurisdiction at the place(s) of registration contributes to procedural economy[179] and an effective enforcement of IP rights;[180] *that* taking into account that Community law must be interpreted in a way that most effectively leads to Community integration the place(s) of registration should be subject to unlimited full jurisdiction given that another interpretation would not in effect create a single area of justice[181] but rather a 'mosaic' area[182] and finally *that* unlimited full jurisdiction is known from the AUPC,[183] the early ALI principles[184] which, however, were amended[185] due to heavy criticism[186] and from the Draft Hague Convention.[187]

9.41 Supporting the opposite result namely that the place(s) of registration would only have limited forum jurisdiction it is argued, inter alia, *that* the *forum delicti* rule as an exception to the defendant's domicile rule must be interpreted narrowly;[188] *that* unlimited full jurisdiction at the place(s) of registration would in effect lead to a *forum actoris*[189] which the CJEU explicitly rejected by dismissing the centre of interests' rule from *eDate*;[190] *that* unlimited full jurisdiction at the place(s) of registration would open up for forum shopping

---

er forårsaget på den medlemsstats område, hvor den ret, som sagen er anlagt for, er beliggende' (DK) and 'behöriga avseende de skador som orsakats i den medlemsstat där den domstol vid vilken talan väckts är belägen' (SV).

177 Opinion of Advocate General Villalón in case C-523/10, *Wintersteiger AG*, para. 30.

178 Sender, *supra* note 41 at 3.115 cf. 3.126.

179 Ibid. at 3.127.

180 Chapter 4 section B.

181 Chapter 2 section B.1.

182 Nielsen, *supra* note 8, p. 168.

183 Arts 33(1)(a) cf. 34 AUPC and section C.4(a).

184 Art. 204(2) American Law Institute, Intellectual Property Principles Governing Jurisdiction, Choice of Law and Judgments in Transnational Disputes, preliminary draft no. 2 of 20 January 2004.

185 Ibid., final draft of 30 March 2007 cf. comments at p. 108.

186 Kur, *supra* note 165, p. 28 and Metzger, *supra* note 157, p. 265.

187 Art. 10(4) Hague Judgments Convention of 1999.

188 Principle 5: Narrow interpretation.

189 Principle 6: Place of action and place(s) of effect(s).

190 Case C-523/10, *Wintersteiger AG*, paras 22–24.

which must be avoided;[191] *that* the *forum delicti* rule despite any clear information in the *Jenard*[192] and *Schlosser*[193] reports does not allow for consolidation of claims[194] contrary to what is possible under art. 8(1) BR[195] but rather the exact opposite, namely splitting up a single claim in to sub claims[196] as done in *Shevill*[197] and *eDate*;[198] *that* the territorial scope of trademark rights following the territorial principle[199] leads to a restriction of jurisdiction at the place(s) of registration,[200] which in turn is confirmed in *Pinckney* and subsequent judgments from the CJEU whereas:

> if that [place(s) of effect(s)] court also had jurisdiction to adjudicate on the damage caused in other Member States, it would substitute itself for the courts of those States even though, in principle, in the light of [territoriality] the latter [would] have jurisdiction to determine [...] the damage caused in their respective Member States[201]

that the territorial principle has also played a role behind the interpretation of other provisions in the BR, inter alia, arts 24(4) BR[202] and 8(1) BR[203] the latter bearing a clear resemblance with art. 7(2) BR as a special jurisdiction rule;[204] *that* the 'sister' *forum delicti* rules in the EUTMR, CDR and CPVR are also subject to limited forum jurisdiction;[205] *that* therefore it would be illogical

---

191 Metzger, *supra* note 157, p. 260; *Conflict of Laws in Intellectual Property, The CLIP Principles and Commentary*, *supra* note 47 p. 86 (2:203.C04) and Principle 3: Avoiding forum shopping.

192 Report on the Convention on Jurisdiction and the Enforcement of Judgments in Civil and Commercial Matters signed at Brussels 27 September 1968 by P. Jenard, Director in the Belgium Ministry of Foreign Affairs and External Trade (Jenard report), p. 22.

193 Report on the Convention on the Association of the Kingdom of Denmark, Ireland and the United Kingdom of Great Britain and Northern Ireland to the Convention on Jurisdiction and the Enforcement of Judgments in Civil and Commercial Matters and the Protocol on its Interpretation by the Court of Justice by Professor Dr. Peter Schlosser (Schlosser report), p. 111.

194 Nuyts, *supra* note 41, p. 129 and Fawcett and Torremanns, *supra* note 41 at 5.70.

195 Chapter 8 section B.1(a).

196 Pocar report, *supra* note 123 at 59.

197 Case C-68/93, *Fiona Shevill*, paras 28–31.

198 Joined cases C-509/09, *eDate Advertising* and C-161/10, *Olivier Martinez and Robert Martinez*, paras 51–52.

199 Opinion of Advocate General Villalón in case C-523/10, *Wintersteiger AG*, para. 20 and judgment of the CJEU para. 25 cf. Chapter 4 section D.

200 Metzger, *supra* note 157, p. 261; Fawcett and Torremanns, *supra* note 41 at 5.95; Th. C.J.A van Engelen, 'Jurisdiction and Applicable Law in Matters of Intellectual Property', (2010) 14(3) EJCL, Nederlandse Vereniging Voor Rechtsvergelijking (Netherlands Comparative Law Association), p. 6; Alexander Peukert, 'Territoriality and Extraterritoriality in Intellectual Property Law', in Gunther Handl and Joachim Zekoll (eds) *Beyond Territoriality: Transnational Legal Authority in an Age of Globalization*, Queen Mary Studies in International Law, Brill Academic Publishing, Leiden/Boston, 2011, p. 6 at note 29 with references.

201 Case C-170/12, *Peter Pinckney*, paras 46 cf. 45; case C-387/12, *Hi Hotel*, paras 39 cf. 38; case C-441/13, *Pez Hejduk v EnergieAgentur NRW GmbH*, paras 36–38 and case C-618/15, *Concurrence SARL v Samsung Electronics France SAS and Amazon Services Europe Sàrl*, para. 31.

202 Case C-4/03, *Gat LuK*, para. 31 and Chapter 11 section B.

203 Case C-539/03, *Roche Nederland BV*, para. 31 and Chapter 8 section B.1(a).

204 Chapter II section 2 BR.

205 Arts 97(5) cf. 98(2) EUTMR, 82(5) cf. 83(2) CDR and 101(3) CPVR cf. sections C.1–C.3.

as also indicated by German courts[206] and legal scholars[207] to allow for unlimited full jurisdiction the motto being 'if fully EU harmonized IP law (EUTMR, CDR and CPVR) is subject to fragmentary enforcement partly EU harmonized IP law (TMD and DD) or even non-EU harmonized IP law (EPC and UPOV) should not lead to unitary enforcement';[208] *that* limited forum jurisdiction at the place(s) of registration corresponds to the applicable law being the law of the protecting country;[209] *that* there is an obligation to ensure such a coherence;[210] *that* if the place(s) of effect(s) defined as the places where the publication is distributed in a case concerning defamation[211] not being subject to a territorial principle[212] are nonetheless considered to be 'territorially the best placed to assess the libel committed in that State'[213] the place(s) of effect(s) defined as the place(s) of registration in a case concerning trademarks[214] in fact being subject to such a principle[215] must logically be territorially even better placed to assess the harm committed in that State;[216] *that* conversely the place(s) of registration are not best placed to assess the harm committed in another State;[217] *that* any such argument is confirmed by the lack of proximity between the place(s) of registration and other Member States;[218] *that* in order to balance the interests of the parties the extent of jurisdiction should be limited given that otherwise the plaintiff would have yet an advantage other than being the first mover;[219] *that* given that the relative strengths of the parties in an IP conflict is usually equal[220] it does not impose

206 District Court Düsseldorf, 25 August 1998, 1999 GRUR Int. 455 confirmed by OLG Düsseldorf, 22 July 1999, IPRax 2001, Shussfadengreifer.

207 Sender, *supra* note 41 at 3.126 cf. 3.124.

208 There is a noticeable difference in the way the territorial principle is applied. For national IP rights protection extends to the border of a given Member State and jurisdiction is likely restricted to the Member State in question cf. art. 7(2) BR. Thus, there is consistency between the scope of protection and the extent of jurisdiction. For European unitary IP rights, however, protection extends to the border of 28 EU Member States cf. arts 1(2) EUTMR, 1(3) CDR and 2 CPVR and jurisdiction is restricted to the Member State in question cf. arts 98(2) EUTMR, 83(2) CDR and 101(3) CPVR. Thus, there is not consistency between the scope of protection and the extent of jurisdiction. Rather the territorial principle is applied in an even stricter manner than for national IP rights cf. opinion of Advocate General Jääskinen in case C-360/12, *Coty Prestige Lancaster Group GmbH*, para. 39.

209 Art. 8(1) and Recital (26) Rome II Regulation.

210 Recital (7) Rome II Regulation.

211 Case C-68/93, *Fiona Shevill.*

212 Opinion of Advocate General Villalón in case C-523/10, *Wintersteiger*, para. 20 and judgment of the CJEU, para. 25.

213 Case C-68/93, *Fiona Shevill*, para. 31.

214 Case C-523/10, *Wintersteiger.*

215 Ibid., para. 25.

216 Case C-170/12, *Peter Pinckney*, para. 46.

217 Fawcett and Torremanns, *supra* note 41 at 5.92.

218 Nuyts, *supra* note 41, p. 128 and *Conflict of Laws in Intellectual Property, The CLIP Principles and Commentary*, *supra* note 47, p. 69 (2:202.CO2).

219 Ibid., p. 87 (2:203.C06).

220 Principle 9: No protection of the weaker party.

an unacceptable burden to be forced to litigate at the defendant's domicile if the plaintiff wants the case addressed in its entirety;[221] *that* limited forum jurisdiction may even be sufficient to end the entire infringement[222] given that a successful judgment can be used as a means of pressure to have the defendant enter into a settlement[223] and finally *that* legal scholars,[224] scholarly reports[225] and art. 7(2) BR case law on national court level regarding infringement of trademarks,[226] patents[227] and copyrights[228] all support restricting the extent of jurisdiction.

Balancing the interests the place(s) of registration is, despite *Wintersteiger* para. 28, likely subject to limited forum jurisdiction. Supporting that it is argued, inter alia, the interplay between the defendant's domicile and *forum delicti* rules, the risk to create a *forum actoris* and increased forum shopping if the rule was subject to unlimited full jurisdiction, the principle of territoriality, the fact that the *forum delicti* rule does not allow for consolidation of claims, the fact that the *forum delicti* rule is also subject to limited forum jurisdiction under the EUTMR, CDR and CPVR, the fact that limited forum jurisdiction corresponds to the applicable law and finally that legal scholars, scholarly reports, CJEU case law and case law on national court level all support restricting the extent of jurisdiction. **9.42**

---

221 *Conflict of Laws in Intellectual Property, The CLIP Principles and Commentary*, *supra* note 47, p. 89 (2:203.C10).

222 Ibid., p. 86 (2:203.C05).

223 Chapter 1 section A.4 (factor 4).

224 Kur, *supra* note 165, p. 29; Metzger, *supra* note 157, p. 260 with references; Nuyts, *supra* note 41, pp. 127 *et seq.*; S. Bariatti, La giurisdizione e l'esecuzione delle sentenze in material di brevetti di invenzione nell'ambito della C.E.E, 1982, RDIPP 518 and Hess, Rechtsfolgen von Patentverletzungen im Europäischen Patentrecht, Duncker und Humblot, 1987, 32. For a different view see Sender, *supra* note 41 at 3.118, 3.126 and 3.127.

225 Art. 2:203(1) CLIP Principles, § 204(2) ALI Principles, arts 105 Transparency Proposal and 203 Waseda Project.

226 *Castellblanch SA v Champagne Louis Roederer SA*, and *Aredal Foam Systems HB v MSR Dosiertechnik GmbH.*

227 President District Court of the Hague, 15 July 1998 (Augustine/Mallinckrodt Medical) 1998, IER 180; District Court of the Hague, 29 September 1999 (*DSM v Orffa*), 1999; District Court of the Hague, 27 February 2008 (*Acco v Nobel*), 2008; District Court of the Hague, 24 March 2010 (*Vacu Products v WMF*), 2010; District Court Düsseldorf, 25 August 1998, 1999 GRUR Int. 455 confirmed by OLG Düsseldorf, 22 July 1999, IPRax 2001, Shussfadengreifer; District Court Düsseldorf, 25 March 1999, Impfstoff II, 1999, GRUR Int. 775 and Suisse Bundesgericht, 23 October 2006, GRUR Int. 2007, 534.

228 Cour de Cassation, 16 July 1997 RIDA 176 (1998), Wegmann; Cour de Cassation, *Saint Tropez A/S v Reuvens II (Societe)*, IL pr. 49; Hoge Raad, Bus Berzelius Umwelt-Service AG v Chemconserve BV Reakt Ltd., 99/245 HR, 2004, IL, pr. 9; *IBS Technologies PVT Ltd. v APM Technologies SA*, unreported, 7 April 2003, All ER (D) 105; Court of Session, *UVG Ambulances Ltd. v Auto Conversion Ltd. (Wilker Auto Conversions)*, 2000, ECDR 479 and Högsta Domstolen of Sweden, 4 July 2012, Ö 2256–10 – Kiki Danielsson.

9.43 In *Wintersteiger* the CJEU did not explicitly discuss the extent of jurisdiction at the place of action defined as the place of establishment of the advertiser.[229] The reason seems to be that the place fully corresponded to the defendant's domicile, namely Germany.[230] Given that, it seemed rather obvious that the German courts had unlimited full jurisdiction or with the words of the CJEU 'that the territorial limitation of the protection of a national mark [under the place(s) of registration rule] is not such as to exclude the international jurisdiction of courts other than the courts of the Member State in which that trade mark is registered'.[231] What seems less obvious, however, is the result if in the rare situation the place where the advertiser was established did not coincide with the place where the defendant was domiciled[232] e.g. because the infringing content was first published in one Member State whereas the defendant was domiciled in another.[233] The question would in that case be whether the courts at the place of establishment of the advertiser would have unlimited full jurisdiction (*Shevill* analogy) or only limited forum jurisdiction (no *Shevill* analogy).

9.44 Supporting that the place of establishment of the advertiser would have unlimited full jurisdiction it is argued, inter alia, *that* the CJEU in line with the AG[234] apparently spoke of unlimited full jurisdiction[235] at 'the place where the event giving rise to the damage occurred'[236] without drawing a distinction as to whether that place would coincide with the defendant's domicile;[237] *that* therefore it seems likely that any such place would be subject to unlimited full jurisdiction even in a situation where the two places did not coincide in line with what the CJEU ruled in *Shevill*[238] and *eDate*;[239] *that* the facts of *Wintersteiger* support unlimited full jurisdiction given that the Wintersteiger

229 Case C-523/10, *Wintersteiger AG*, para. 37.
230 Ibid., paras 11 and 38.
231 Ibid., para. 30.
232 Opinion of Advocate General Villalón in ibid., para. 26; Opinion of AG Jääskinen in case C-170/12, *Peter Pinckney*, para. 58; Metzger, *supra* note 157, p. 260 at note 37 with references and Michael Bogdan, Website Accessibility as Basis for Jurisdiction under the Brussels I Regulation' in View of New Case Law of the ECJ in Nordic Yearbook of Law and Informatics 2010–2012, Internationalization of Law in the Digital Information Society, Dan Jerker B. Svantesson and Stanley Greenstein (eds), Ex Tuto Publishing, 2013, p. 171.
233 *Conflict of Laws in Intellectual Property, The CLIP Principles and Commentary*, *supra* note 47, p. 87 (2:203.C07).
234 Opinion of Advocate General Villalón in case C-523/10, *Wintersteiger AG*, para. 30.
235 Case C-523/10, *Wintersteiger AG*, para. 30.
236 Ibid., heading to paras 30–38.
237 *Conflict of Laws in Intellectual Property, The CLIP Principles and Commentary*, *supra* note 47, p. 92 (2:203.N05) at note 21.
238 Case C-68/93, *Fiona Shevill*, para. 32.
239 Joined cases C-509/09, *eDate Advertising* and C-161/10, *Olivier Martinez and Robert Martinez*, para. 43.

trademark, at least for the purpose of the preliminary reference[240] was not protected in Germany;[241] *that* any such interpretation is also confirmed in *Pinckney* where the AG referred to *Wintersteiger* in support of giving place of action courts unlimited full jurisdiction;[242] *that* some case law at national court level support unlimited full jurisdiction;[243] *that* restricting jurisdiction would fragment the enforcement for trademark rights even more than for personality rights given that personality rights are not subject to a restriction at the place of establishment;[244] *that* restricting jurisdiction would devaluate *forum delicti*;[245] *that* unlimited full jurisdiction at the place of establishment of the advertiser contributes to procedural economy and an effective enforcement of IP rights;[246] *that* some legal scholars[247] and scholarly reports[248] support any such interpretation and finally *that* unlimited full jurisdiction is known from the AUPC.[249]

Supporting the opposite result namely that the place of establishment of the advertiser would only have limited forum jurisdiction it is argued, inter alia, *that* the *forum delicti* rule as an exception to the defendant's domicile must be interpreted narrowly;[250] *that* if the plaintiff wants the case adjudicated in its entirety several fora with unlimited full jurisdiction are open to him/her[251] any one of which there is no reason to extent;[252] *that forum delicti* does not allow for consolidation of claims;[253] *that* trademark rights are subject to a territorial principle leading to a restriction of jurisdiction;[254] *that* territoriality is a general principle[255] and must for that reason apply to both heads of jurisdiction within the meaning of the *forum delicti* rule; *that* this is confirmed by the fact that *Wintersteiger* does not anywhere refer to the 'mosaic' rule in *Shevill*;[256] *that* the **9.45**

240 Opinion of Advocate General Villalón in case C-523/10, *Wintersteiger AG*, para. 15.

241 Ibid., para. 8 and judgment of the CJEU para. 16.

242 Opinion of AG Jääskinen in case C-170/12, *Peter Pinckney*, para. 57 at note 49.

243 *Castellblanch SA v Champagne Louis Roederer SA*, Case No. 01–03.225, 9 December 2003, 2004 and Cour de Cassation, 16 July 1997 RIDA 176 (1998), Wegmann.

244 Case C-68/93, *Fiona Shevill*, para. 25 and joined cases C-509/09, *eDate Advertising* and C-161/10, *Olivier Martinez and Robert Martinez*, para. 52.

245 Sender *supra* note 41 at 3.115 cf. 3.126.

246 Chapter 4 section B.

247 Lydia Lundstedt and Ulf Maunsbach, *Jurisdiction and Applicable Law: A Swedish Perspective on Cross-Border Enforcement of Intellectual Property Rights*, Nordiskt Immateriellt Rättsskydd (NIR), 3/2003, p. 216.

248 § 204(1) ALI Principles cf. arts 105 Transparency Proposal and 203(1) Waseda Project.

249 Arts 33(1)(a) cf. 34 AUPC and section C.4(a).

250 Principle 5: Narrow interpretation.

251 Arts 4 cf. 62 and 63 BR and Chapter 5 section B.1(a).

252 *Conflict of Laws in Intellectual Property, The CLIP Principles and Commentary, supra* note 47, p. 86 (2:203.C05).

253 *Supra* note 194.

254 *Supra* notes 199–200.

255 Chapter 4 section D.

256 Case C-68/93, *Fiona Shevill*, para. 33.

'sister' *forum delicti* rules in the EUTMR, CDR and CPVR are also subject to limited forum jurisdiction;[257] *that* reasons of consistency support that IP rights whatever nature and territorial scope can be enforced equally;[258] *that* limited forum jurisdiction corresponds to the applicable law being the law of the protecting country;[259] *that* there is an obligation to ensure any such coherence;[260] *that* the fact that infringing content was first published in one Member State does not, due to the territoriality principle,[261] guarantee that infringements have occurred in other Member States thereby expressing a lack of proximity to the infringement as a whole;[262] *that* there seems to be no reason why the entire infringement can be more effectively enforced under art. 7(2) BR compared to art. 4 BR[263] and *that* legal scholars,[264] scholarly reports[265] and case law on national court level[266] all support restricting the extent of jurisdiction.

9.46 Balancing the interests the place of establishment of the advertiser seems, despite *Wintersteiger* para. 30, likely to be subject to limited forum jurisdiction. Supporting that it is argued, inter alia, the interplay between the defendant's domicile and the *forum delicti* rules, the principle of territoriality, the fact that *forum delicti* does not allow for consolidation of claims, the fact that *forum delicti* is also subject to limited forum jurisdiction under the EUTMR, CDR and CPVR, that limited forum jurisdiction corresponds to the applicable law and finally that legal scholars, scholarly reports and case law on national court level all support restricting the extent of jurisdiction. If, however, the place of establishment of the advertiser coincides with the defendant's domicile any such place is subject to unlimited full jurisdiction.[267]

9.47 In sum the place(s) of registration and the place where the advertiser is established rules are both likely subject to limited forum jurisdiction.

257 Arts 97(5) cf. 98(2) EUTMR, 82(5) cf. 83(2) CDR and 101(3) CPVR and sections C.1–C.3.

258 Tritton, *supra* note 64 at 14–085.

259 *Supra* note 209.

260 *Supra* note 210.

261 Chapter 4 section D.

262 *Conflict of Laws in Intellectual Property, The CLIP Principles and Commentary, supra* note 47, p. 87 (2:203.C07).

263 Ibid., p. 88 (2:203.C08).

264 Metzger, *supra* note 157, p. 261 at note 42 with references; Fawcett and Torremanns, *supra* note 41 at 5.58 cf. 5.62 and 5.86 and cf. ibid., p. 85 (2:203.C03).

265 Art. 2:203 CLIP Principles.

266 District Court Düsseldorf, 25 August 1998, 1999 GRUR Int. 455 confirmed by OLG Düsseldorf, 22 July 1999, IPRax 2001, Shussfadengreifer and Suisse Bundesgericht, 23 October 2006, GRUR Int. 2007, 534.

267 Magnus and Mankowski, *supra* note 8, p. 247 at note 1379 with references.

Principle 9: No protection of the weaker party

Following the ninth specific principle[268] the purpose of art. 7(2) BR is not to protect the weaker party[269] despite having been so claimed.[270] The reasons number, inter alia, *that* the rule covers a variety of cases[271] with parties having different strengths by contrast to the rules in Chapter II sections 3–5 BR; *that* the weaker party is not necessarily the injured party[272] and *that* protection of the weaker party could generally legitimize a *forum actoris,* which would be wrong.[273] **9.48**

In *Wintesteiger* the CJEU allowed an action to be brought at the place(s) of registration.[274] Even though the rule favours the plaintiff being the rightholder in an infringement action due to the lack of connecting factors[275] the rule neither has the purpose nor the effect of *protecting* him/her given that in the majority of trademark cases the rightholder is not the weaker party but the stronger party[276] or at least the parties have equal strength.[277] *Wintersteiger* exemplifies the latter given that the plaintiff was an Austrian skiing manufacturer and the defendant was a German skiing reseller. **9.49**

In *eDate,* which concerned online infringements of personality rights within the meaning of art. 7(2) BR, the CJEU allowed action to be brought, inter alia, at the place(s) of effect(s) defined as the place(s) where the infringing content is accessible or at the victims own domicile, the so-called centre of interests.[278] Similar to the place(s) of registration rule the place(s) of accessibility and the centre of interests rules both favor the plaintiff being the victim due to the lack of connecting factors or due to the fact that action can be brought at *forum actoris.* Different from the place(s) of registration rule, however, the effect of both rules, contrary to the declared purpose of

268 Protection of the weaker party is a general principle in private international law cf. Annette Kur, 'Are There Any Common Principles of Private International Law with Regard to Intellectual Property' in Stefan Leible and Ansgar Ohly (eds) *Intellectual Property and Private International Law,* Mohr Siebeck, 2009, p. 7 and Chapter 4 section C.

269 Case C-133/11, *Folien Fischer AG, Fofitec AG v Ritrama SpA,* paras 45–46; Opinion of Advocate General Darmon in case C-220/88, *Dumez France SA,* para. 48; Opinion of Advocate General Darmon (first opinion) in case C-364/93, *Antonio Marinari,* paras. 16 and 38; Opinion of Advocate General Léger in case C-168/02, *Rudolf Kronhofer,* para. 34 and opinion of Advocate General Geelhoed in case C-334/00, *Fonderie Officine Meccaniche Tacconi SpA v Heinrich Wagner Sinto Maschinenfabrik GmbH (HWS),* para. 70.

270 Opinion of Advocate General Capotorti in case C-21/76, *Handelskwekerij G. J. Bier BV,* para. 9.

271 Case C-21/76, ibid., para. 18.

272 *Example*: A private blogger publishes dafamatory information about the front singer Bono of the rock band U2. Bono being the injured party (plaintiff) would be the stronger party whereas the private blogger (defendant) would be the weaker party.

273 Principle 6: Place of action and place(s) of effects.

274 Case C-523/10, *Wintersteiger AG,* paras. 27–29.

275 Principle 7: Place(s) of effect(s) subject to connecting factors.

276 Kur, *supra* note 165, p. 29.

277 Ibid.

278 Joined cases C-509/09, *eDate Advertising* and C-161/10, *Olivier Martinez and Robert Martinez,* paras 48 and 51.

art. 7(2) BR,[279] may be to protect the victim as the weaker party given that in the majority of cases the victim is, however not always,[280] the weaker party.[281] By comparison in *Pammer* which concerned the online application of the consumer protection rule in art. 17(1)(c) BR, the CJEU ruled exactly opposite by allowing the consumer, notoriously being the weaker party subject to protection,[282] to bring an action at his/her own domicile only if connecting factors pointed at the consumer's home Member State.[283] Thus, in *eDate* the CJEU basically made it easy for the victim to bring an action under art. 7(2) BR, which does not serve the purpose of protecting the weaker party while at the same time in *Pammer* making it more difficult for the consumer to bring an action under art. 17(1)(c) BR, which by contrast serves such a purpose. Despite the apparent paradox, which however has been softened a bit in *Lokman Emrek*,[284] the results seem justified, *partly* because the provisions are based on two different purposes, i.e. art. 7(2) BR is based on proximity cf. Recital (16) Brussels I Regulation whereas art. 17(1)(c) BR is based on the protection of the consumer as the weaker party cf. Recital (14) Brussels I Regulation and *partly* because art. 17(1)(c) BR itself speaks of 'directed to' cf. *Pammer*, para. 71 which art. 7(2) BR does not cf. *Pinckney* para. 42.[285] Thus, comparing the results in *eDate* and *Pammer* would be the same as comparing apples and oranges. Nonetheless, however, the differences are worth noting.

9.50 In sum, the place(s) of registration rule neither has the purpose nor the effect to protect the weaker party.

(iii) Wintersteiger (impact)

9.51 The impact of *Wintersteiger* is subject to a number of uncertainties. Some are due to the fact that the case has been worded rather ambiguously whereas others are due to the fact specific character of the case.

9.52 The first uncertainty, which was briefly addressed in section B.1(a)(ii)[286] is whether the place(s) of registration rule must be understood as referring to every place(s) where protection can be claimed because the trademark is registered there (the rule would in that case be founded on a registration) or

---

279 *Supra* note 269.

280 *Supra* note 272.

281 In *Shevill* the plaintiff was a British private person (weaker party) whereas the defendant was France Soir (stronger party) and in *eDate* the plaintiffs were a French actor respectively a German convict (weaker parties) whereas the defendants were *Sunday Mirror* respectively an Austian Internet Portal (stronger parties) cf. Kur, *supra* note 165, p. 29.

282 Recital (14) Brussels I Regulation cf. case C-89/91, *Shearson Lehmann Hutton Inc. v TVB Treuhandgesellschaft für Vermögensverwaltung und Beteiligungen mbH*, para. 18; case C-464/01, *Johann Gruber v Bay Wa AG*, para. 34; case C-27/02, *Petra Engler v Janus Versand GmbH*, para. 39 and joined cases C-585/08, *Peter Pammer* and C-144/09, *Hotel Alpenhof*, para. 58.

283 Joined cases C-585/08, *Peter Pammer* and C-144/09, *Hotel Alpenhof*, paras 80–84.

284 Case C-218/12, *Lokman Emrek v Vlado Sabranovic* para. 33.

285 Section B.1(a)(iii).

286 Principle 1: Predictability.

whether the rule must be understood as referring only to the place(s) where the trademark can be enforced because it is valid there (the rule would in that case be founded on *de facto* protection). It follows that there is a difference between the two despite some legal scholars equating them[287] since protection requires enforceable trademark rights whereas registration does not. Applying the latter, therefore, action can be brought in Member States where there is *de facto* no protection, inter alia, *since* the trademark lacks distinctiveness; *since* the trademark has not been used within five years or *since* the trademark has become the common name of the product or service in respect of which it is registered.[288] *Wintersteiger* is worded ambiguously since sometimes the term 'protected' is used[289] and sometimes the term 'registered' is used.[290] Given, however, *that* the term 'registered' is used in the conclusion[291] and *that* art. 7(2) BR lays down, as the sole condition, that a harmful event has occurred or *may occur*[292] it seems likely that the rule merely requires a registration and not *de facto* protection with the effect that unenforceable trademark rights may establish jurisdiction.

The second uncertainty, which was also briefly addressed in section B.1(a)(ii),[293] is whether the place(s) of registration rule applies in a situation where, contrary to *Wintersteiger*,[294] it is clear from the facts of the case that the infringement has had no effect in the forum.[295] The answer is that the place(s) of registration rule most likely applies *mutatis mutandis* in any such situation. The reasons number, inter alia, *that* the CJEU spoke of the 'Member State in which the trade mark is registered'[296] without mentioning connecting factors of any kind; *that* the CJEU did not even mention the connecting factors applied by the AG[297] and *that* in *Pinckney*, which concerned a copyright dispute and where therefore a basic connecting factor (registration) was lacking, jurisdiction was vested in France even though the infringement was not specifically directed to France.[298] **9.53**

287 Bogdan, *supra* note 232, p. 171.
288 Chapter 1 section A.3(b).
289 Case C-523/10, *Wintersteiger AG*, para. 27.
290 Ibid., paras 28 and 29.
291 Ibid., para. 40.
292 Case C-170/12, *Peter Pinckney*, para. 41.
293 *Supra* note 47.
294 Case C-523/10, *Wintersteiger AG*, paras 11–13.
295 *Conflict of Laws in Intellectual Property, The CLIP Principles and Commentary*, *supra* note 47, p. 82 (2:202.N10).
296 Case C-523/10, *Wintersteiger AG*, para. 29.
297 Opinion of Advocate General Villalón in ibid., paras 28–29.
298 Case C-170/12, *Peter Pinckney*, paras 44 cf. 10–11.

9.54 The third uncertainty is whether the place(s) of registration rule applies to other IP rights required to be registered such as national registered design, plant variety and patent rights. The answer is that the place(s) of registration rule most likely applies *mutatis mutandis* given that territoriality, which was the justification for the rule,[299] similarly governs design, plant variety and patent rights, which is supported, inter alia, by TRIPS,[300] legal scholars,[301] the AG in *Wintersteiger*[302] and by the CJEU itself ruling that the place(s) of registration rule applies to 'intellectual property rights, *such as* those [...] in the main proceedings'.[303]

9.55 The fourth uncertainty is whether the place(s) of registration rule applies to IP rights not required to be registered such as national unregistered trademark and design rights. The answer is that the place(s) of registration rule does not apply *mutatis mutandis* given that unregistered rights come into existence without formalities. Rather it may be argued that a place(s) where the trademark or design is continuously used rule applies. Any such rule seems, however, unlikely. The reason is that, even though it would correspond to the place(s) of registration rule when it comes to establish protection, it would conflict with the place(s) of registration rule when it comes to establish jurisdiction *since* it would require a positive action namely to market and sell the products under a specific trademark or design in a particular Member State which, in turn, is not required under the place(s) of registration rule, where the only positive action required to establish jurisdiction is filing an application which has later become a registration and *since* accordingly it would take more to establish jurisdiction for unregistered trademarks and designs than for registered trademarks and designs. A second option, therefore, would be to apply a place(s) protecting unregistered trademarks and designs rule.[304] Any such rule seems likely. The reason is *that* it would correspond to the place(s) of registration rule even though a little less would be required to establish jurisdiction since not even an application has been filed; *that* the CJEU has introduced such a rule to copyrights[305] and *that* art. 7(2) BR lays down, as the sole condition that a harmful event has occurred or *may occur*.

---

299 Case C-523/10, *Wintersteiger AG*, para. 25.

300 Chapter 4 section D.

301 Chapter 4 section D.

302 Opinion of Advocate General Villalón in case C-523/10, *Wintersteiger AG*, para. 20.

303 Case C-523/10, *Wintersteiger AG*, para. 24 (emphasis added).

304 An overview of the Member States protecting unregistered trademarks is given in 'The Manual Concerning Opposition, Part 4, Rights under Article 8(4) CTMR', pp. 24 *et seq*. found on euipo.europa.eu.

305 Case C-170/12, *Peter Pinckney*, paras 43–44; case C-387/12, *Hi Hotel*, para. 35 cf. case C-441/13, *Pez Hejduk v EnergieAgentur NRW GmbH*, para. 29 and case C-618/15, *Concurrence SARL*, para. 30.

The fifth uncertainty is whether the place(s) of registration rule must be read into the 'sister' *forum delicti* rules *in* the EUTMR and CDR both speaking of the place where the 'act of infringement has been committed or threatened',[306] *in* the CPVR speaking of the place where the 'harmful event occurred'[307] and finally *in* the AUPC speaking of the place where the 'actual or threatened infringement has occurred or may occur'.[308] The answers are provided for in section C. **9.56**

The sixth uncertainty, which was briefly addressed in section B.1(a)(ii)[309] is whether the place(s) of registration rule applies despite a disclaimer on the defendant's website that he/she does not do business with the Member State where the IP right is registered. The CJEU did not address the question due to the character of the preliminary reference.[310] Given, however, *that* the use of a disclaimer is usually interconnected with connecting factors in the sense that a disclaimer takes away the connecting factors which would otherwise lead to jurisdiction[311] and *that* the CJEU did not apply connecting factors[312] it seems unlikely that a disclaimer on a defendant's website can protect him/her from being taken to court following the place(s) of registration rule. The same most likely applies under the place(s) protecting unregistered trademarks and designs rule.[313] **9.57**

The seventh uncertainty, which was also briefly addressed in section B.1(a)(ii),[314] is whether the place(s) of registration and the place(s) protecting unregistered trademarks and designs rules apply in an offline context or whether connecting factors are required in any such situations. To be able to address that question the development in art. 7(2) BR case law must be brought in mind. It follows that in early offline art. 7(2) BR case law the CJEU required connecting factors. Thus, in *Shevill* the CJEU ruled that the place(s) of effect(s) is 'where the publication is distributed when the victim is known in those **9.58**

306 Arts 97(5) EUTMR and 82(5) CDR.
307 Art. 101(3) CPVR.
308 Art. 33(1)(a) AUPC.
309 Principle 2: Proximity.
310 Case C-523/10, *Wintersteiger AG*, para. 16.
311 *Conflict of Laws in Intellectual Property, The CLIP Principles and Commentary, supra* note 47, p. 82 (2:202.N12) cf. p. 72 (2:202.C08); *Boss v Boss*, Oberster Gerichtshof, 29 May 2001, case 4 Ob 110/01, 2002, GRUR Int. 344 cf. art. 12 WIPO Joint Recommendation (concerning substantial trademark law) and opinion of Advocate General Trstenjak in joined cases C-585/08, *Peter Pammer* and C-144/09, *Hotel Alpenhof*, paras 91–99 (concerning art. 17(1)(c) BR).
312 Case C-523/10, *Wintersteiger AG*, para. 29.
313 One could, however, also argue opposite taking into account case C-170/12, *Peter Pinckney*, para. 44 a contrario.
314 Principle 7: Place(s) of effect(s) subject to connecting factors.

places'[315] and in *DFDS* the CJEU ruled, 'the flag State, that is the State in which the ship is registered must be regarded as only one factor, among others'.[316] In later online art. 7(2) BR case law the need for connecting factors was restricted. Thus, in *eDate* the CJEU ruled that the place(s) of effect(s) was located where the infringing 'content placed online is or has been accessible'[317] thereby dismissing the second connecting factor ('known') from *Shevill*[318] which, by contrast, was applied by the AG.[319] Similarly in *Wintersteiger* the CJEU ruled that the place(s) of effect(s) was located where 'the trade mark is registered'[320] thereby dismissing the second connecting factor ('effect') which, by contrast, was applied by the AG.[321] Finally, in *Pinckney* the CJEU ruled that the place(s) of effect(s) was located in Member States, which 'protect [...] the copyrights relied on by the plaintiff and [...] the harmful event [...] may occur within the jurisdiction of the court seised' any which requirement is met when it is possible to obtain 'a reproduction of the [infringing] work [...] from an internet site accessible within the jurisdiction of the court seised'[322] thereby dismissing the second connecting factor ('effect') which, by contrast, was applied by the AG.[323] In recent offline art. 7(2) BR case law connecting factors have been re-applied. Thus, in *Hi Hotel*[324] the place(s) of effect(s) was located in Member States, which 'protect [...] the rights of copyright relied on by the applicant and the [...] damage may occur within the jurisdiction of the court seised' any which requirement is met when it is possible to acquire 'a reproduction of the [infringing] work [...] in a bookshop located within the jurisdiction of the court seised'.[325] Thus, in *Shevill* and *DFDS* (offline cases) the CJEU required connecting factors, which were not required to the same extent in *eDate*, *Wintersteiger* and *Pinckney*[326] (online cases) but were re-applied in *Hi Hotel* (offline case). As a general observation, therefore, the CJEU seems to require more connecting factors offline than online in order to be able to bring an action under the place(s) of effect(s) rule.

9.59 The development can be illustrated as in Figure 9.1 below. The AG opinions are coloured in white given that they have been superseded by CJEU rulings.

---

315 Case C-68/93, *Fiona Shevill*, para. 29.
316 Case C-18/02, *Danmarks Rederiforening*, para. 44.
317 Joined cases C-509/09, *eDate Advertising* and C-161/10, *Olivier Martinez and Robert Martinez*, para. 51.
318 *Supra* note 315.
319 Opinion of Advocate General Cruz Villalón in joined cases C-509/09, *eDate Advertising* and C-161/10, *Olivier Martinez and Robert Martinez*, para. 67.
320 Case C-523/10, *Wintersteiger*, para. 29.
321 Opinion of Advocate General Villalón, ibid, para. 28.
322 Case C-170/12, *Peter Pinckney*, paras 43–44.
323 Opinion of AG Jääskinen ibid., paras 64–66.
324 Case C-387/12, *Hi Hotel.*
325 Ibid., paras 35–37.
326 Similarly case C-441/13, *Pez Hejduk.*

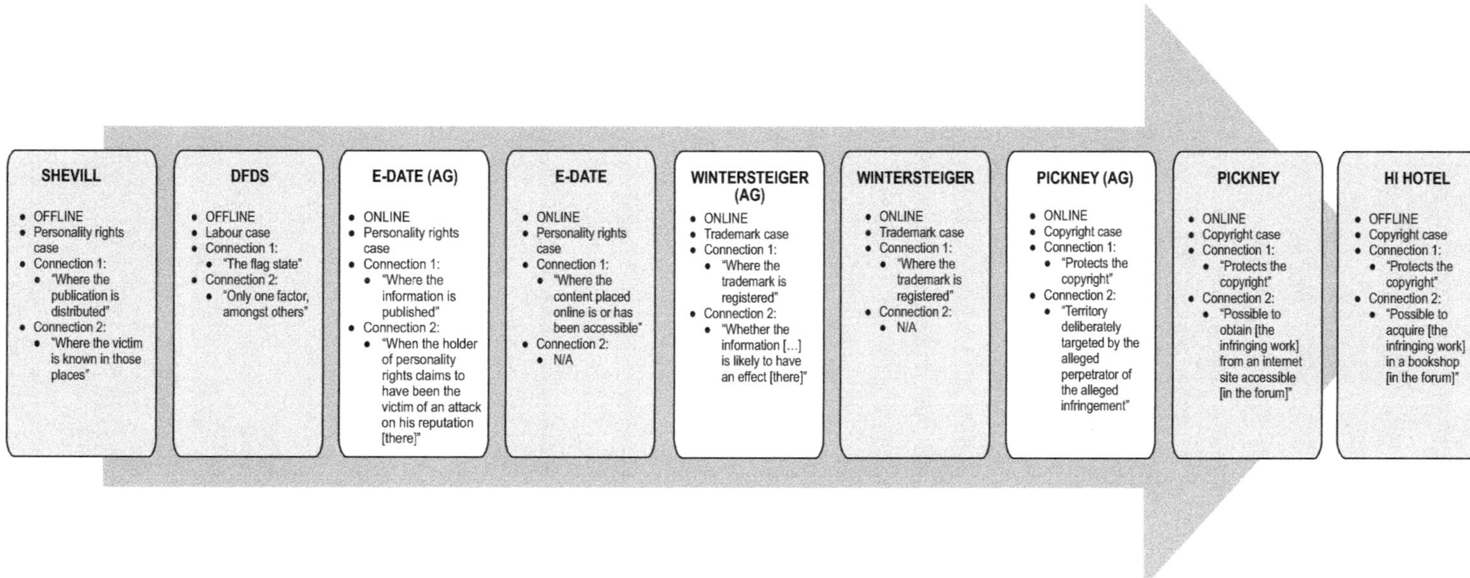

Figure 9.1 Forum delicti *rule development*

9.60 Taking into account the above development a distinction must be drawn as to whether the CJEU will likely require connecting factors offline under the place(s) of registration rule and under the place(s) protecting unregistered trademarks and designs rule.

9.61 As regards the place(s) of registration rule the result seems blurred. Supporting that the CJEU will not require connecting factors offline it is argued, inter alia, *that* the place(s) of registration was justified in territoriality[327] any which principle is general[328] and therefore equally applies offline; *that* therefore, at least in the view of the CJEU, proximity may already for that reason be present and *that* 'unlike Article [17(1)(c) BR] Article [7(2) BR] does not require, *in particular*, that the activity concerned to be 'directed to' the Member State in which the court seised is situated'.[329] Supporting the opposite result namely that the CJEU will require connecting factors offline it is argued, inter alia, the interrelationship between online and offline infringements in *Shevill/eDate* and *Pinckney/Hi Hotel* where the connecting factors, which were not applied online,[330] were applied offline;[331] *that* for reasons of consistency and taking into account that copyrights are similarly subject to territoriality[332] the connecting factors, which were not applied online in *Wintersteiger*[333] must be applied offline; *that* any such interpretation may be confirmed by *L'Oréal* a contrario whereas the connecting factors, which do not apply on online jurisdiction level must apply on online substantial law level;[334] *that* following the motto where online infringements are usually, but not always, more grave than offline infringements[335] it could seem logical to require more from the infringer to take him/her to court in the latter situation; *that* requiring connecting factors offline would not lead to 'pollution'[336] and *that* scholarly reports and legal scholars support connecting factors.[337] Balancing the interests it seems likely that the infringement must have been directed to the forum before an action can be brought under the place(s) of registration rule in an

327 Case C-523/10, *Wintersteiger AG*, para. 25.
328 Chapter 4 section D.
329 Case C-170/12, *Peter Pinckney*, para. 42.
330 Ibid., paras 43–44 and joined cases C-509/09, *eDate Advertising* and C-161/10, *Olivier Martinez and Robert Martinez*, para. 51.
331 Case C-387/12, *Hi Hotel*, paras 35–37 and case C-68/93, *Fiona Shevill*, para. 29.
332 Case C-170/12, *Peter Pinckney*, para. 39 and case C-387/12, *Hi Hotel*, para. 39.
333 Case C-523/10, *Wintersteiger*, para. 29.
334 Case C-324/09, *L'Oréal SA*, paras 64–65.
335 Joined cases C-509/09, *eDate Advertising* and C-161/10, *Olivier Martinez and Robert Martinez*, paras 45–47.
336 Principle 4: Avoiding 'pollution'.
337 *Supra* notes 156–157.

offline context. As to when an infringement is directed to the forum inspiration may be found in *Pammer*[338] (even though the case concerned an online situation under art. 17(1)(c) BR).

As regards the place(s) protecting unregistered trademarks and designs rule it seems likely that the CJEU will require connecting factors offline. Supporting that speaks *Hi Hotel*,[339] which despite concerning copyrights bears a clear resemblance with unregistered trademarks and designs given that they all come into existence without formalities. The CJEU did not specify the connecting factors required but stated that damage could occur in Germany since it was possible to acquire 'a reproduction of the [infringing] work [...] in a bookshop [there]'.[340] Thus, it seems likely that the infringement must have been directed to the forum before an action can be brought under the place(s) protecting unregistered trademarks and designs rule in an offline context. As to when an infringement is directed to the forum inspiration may be found in *Pammer*.[341] **9.62**

The eighth uncertainty is whether the place of establishment of the advertiser rule applies *mutatis mutandis* to offline infringements. The answer to that question is that it does, which is supported by *Hi Hotel*.[342] The place of establishment of the advertiser would in an offline context be the place where the defendant is established.[343] **9.63**

The places to bring an infringement action under art. 7(2) BR considering the nature of the IP right (registered or unregistered) and the nature of the infringement (online or offline) can be illustrated as in Figure 9.2 below:[344] **9.64**

338 Joined cases C-585/08, *Peter Pammer* and C-144/09, *Hotel Alpenhof*, paras 78–89.

339 Case C-387/12, *Hi Hotel*, paras 35–37.

340 It did not make any difference that the defendant had not distributed the photographs in Germany but merely assisted in so doing by handing them over to a third party cf. case C-387/12, ibid., para. 37.

341 *Supra* note 338.

342 Case C-387/12, *Hi Hotel*, para. 27.

343 Eike Scharper, *Durchsetzung der Gemeinschaftsmarke*, Internationale Zuständigkeit, anwendbares Recht und Rechtsfolgen bei Verletzung, Carl Heymanns Verlag, 2006, p. 118 at note 587 with references.

344 Torsten Bjørn Larsen, *The Place Where the Harmful Event Occurred in Exclusive Rights Litigation*, Nordiskt Immateriellt Rättsskydd, 2016, pp. 105 *et seq.*

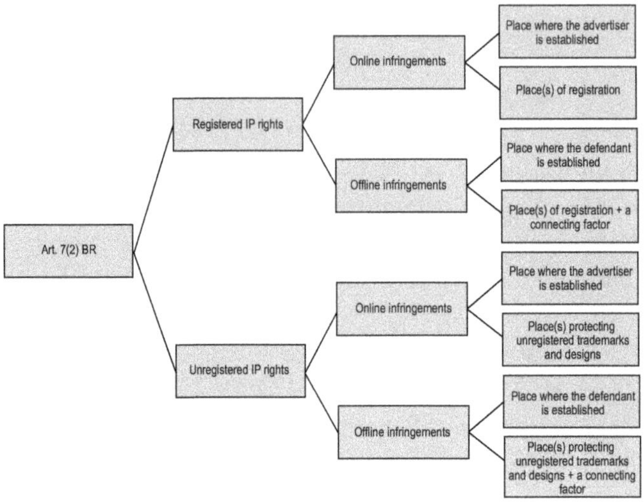

Figure 9.2 Places to bring the action under the forum delicti *rule*

(b) Art. 7(2) BR to non-infringement actions

9.65 National courts have on several occasions addressed whether non-infringement actions fall within the scope of art. 7(2) BR. In some instances the courts have found that they do[345] and in other instances the courts have found that they do not.[346] The CJEU indirectly addressed the issue in

345 *Knorr-Bremse Systems for Commercial Vehicles Ltd. v Haldex Brake Products GmbH* [2008] EWHC 156, (2008); *Equitas Ltd. v Wave City Shipping Co. Ltd.*, Christopher Clarke LJ (2005) EWHC 923, Comm; *Dijkstra Plastics v Saier Verpackungstechnik* [2004] EIPR N151; Oberlandesgericht Düsseldorf on 12 May 2005 (I-2 U 67/03, No 34); Landgericht Düsseldorf, Impstoff II, (4 O 198/97) of 25 March 1999; Landgericht Frankfurt on 25 March 2010 (2-03 O 580/08, 2/03 O 580/08, 2/3 O 580/08, 2-3 O 580/08; Rechtbank Breda on 29 June 2011, *Mivena v Geogreen c.s., LJN*: BR0157; Corte di Cassazione on 17 October 2002 (n. 14769, Riv dir. inter., 2003, p. 238; Tribunale di Milano 6 August 2008 [2009] AIDA 727; Tribunale di Milano 29 March 2005 [2005] AIDA 640; Tribunale di Roma 1 February 2000 [2000] AIDA 870 and Tribunale di Brescia 11 November 1999 [2000] 4107.

346 Landgericht München on 23 October 2008 (7 O 17209/07); Oberlandesgericht Dresden on 28 July 2009 (14 U 1008/08); Oberlandesgericht München, judgment of 25 October 2001 (6 U 5508/00); Högsta Domstolen 14 June 2000, Judgment Ö 2095–99-Flootek; Hof's Gravenhage 22 January 1998 [1999] Nederlandse Jurisprudentie Nr 163; Rechtbank van eerste aanleg Brussel 12 May 2000, Röhm Enzyme [2001], GRUR Int. 170; Rechtbank van eerste aanleg Brussel 19 January 2001, *Novo Nordisk v DSM* [2002] IRDI 304; Court of Appeal of Brussels, 20 February 2001, *Roche v Glaxo Wellcome*, 2001 IER 111; Corte di Cassazione 8 August 1989, No 3657/89 [1989] Riv di rind 224 and Corte di Cassazione 19 December 2003, No 19550 [2004] Riv di rind 429.

Gubisch[347] and *Tatry*[348] where in the context of the *lis pendens* rule[349] the CJEU found that positive and negative claims concern the same subject matter.[350] However, the CJEU directly addressed the issue in *Folien Fischer*.[351] Below a distinction is drawn between the facts and reasoning of *Folien Fischer* (section i), the interpretation of *Folien Fischer* (section ii) and the impact of *Folien Fischer* (section iii).

(i) Folien Fischer (facts and reasoning)

The case concerned a dispute between a Swiss-based manufacturer of paper goods, Folien Fischer AG and an Italian-based manufacturer of similar products, Ritrama SpA.[352] Ritrama SpA had applied for a patent license from Folien Fischer AG, which was denied[353] Folien Fischer AG brought a negative declaration[354] in Germany under art. 7(2) BR claiming, inter alia, that such a denial was not anti-competitive as claimed by Ritrama SpA.[355] Supporting jurisdiction in Germany Folien Fischer AG argued *that* they marketed and sold their products in Germany[356] and *that* their EPO patent designated Germany.[357] Ritrama SpA contested jurisdiction in Germany since they did not operate there[358] despite having a Swiss subsidiary, Ritrama AG with a distinct legal personality (not being part of the case) that did.[359] Based on these facts the question was whether the German courts had jurisdiction to hear the negative declaration under art. 7(2) BR. **9.66**

347 Case 144/86, *Gubisch Maschinenfabrik KG v Giulio Palumbo*.

348 Case C-406/92, *The Owners of the Cargo lately Laden on board the Ship 'Tatry' v the Owners of the Ship 'Maciej Rataj'*.

349 Art. 29 BR.

350 *Conflict of Laws in Intellectual Property, The CLIP Principles and Commentary, supra* note 47, p. 175 (2:602.N01).

351 Case C-133/11, *Folien Fischer*.

352 Opinion of Advocate General Jääskinen in case C-133/11, ibidparas 11–12 and judgment of the CJEU, paras 13–15.

353 Opinion of Advocate General Jääskinen ibid, para. 13 and judgment of the CJEU, para. 16.

354 The term negative declaration and not non-infringement action is used given that the action brought by Folien Fischer AG was not based on non-infringement of an IP right but rather on non-violation of competition law.

355 Opinion of Advocate General Jääskinen in case C-133/11, *Folien Fischer AG*, para. 14 and judgment of the CJEU, para. 17.

356 Opinion of Advocate General Jääskinen ibid, para. 11 and judgment of the CJEU, para. 13.

357 Bundesgerichtshof decision KZR 8/10 of 29 January 2013 between Folien Fischer AG and Ritrama SpA referring to European patents EP0690794 and EP0836953 both designating Germany.

358 Opinion of Advocate General Jääskinen in case C-133/11, *Folien Fischer AG*, para. 24 and judgment of the CJEU, para. 23.

359 Opinion of Advocate General Jääskinen, ibid., para. 24.

9.67 The CJEU stated that art. 7(2) BR is based on predictability[360] and proximity[361] and defined a negative declaration as 'seeking to establish that the pre-conditions for liability, as a result of which the defendant would have a right of redress, are not satisfied'.[362] Given *that* a negative declaration relates to the same law,[363] to the same fact[364] and to the same cause of action[365] as a corresponding positive action; *that* the wording of art. 7(2) BR does not exclude negative declarations[366] and *that* the purpose of art. 7(2) BR is not to protect the weaker party[367] which in turn allows others than the victim to bring an action[368] the CJEU found that negative declarations are covered by art. 7(2) BR.[369] Negative declarations can be brought at the place of action and at the place(s) of effect(s).[370] The extent of jurisdiction at any such places was not addressed.

(ii) Folien Fischer (interpretation)

9.68 *Folien Fischer* was in line with *Wintersteiger* delivered by a small Chamber and not by the Grand Chamber. Again, this seems not surprising given that the latter had already, though indirectly, addressed the issue in *Gubisch* and *Tatry*.[371] *Folien Fischer* carries weight since never before had the CJEU applied art. 7(2) BR to negative declarations.[372]

9.69 In *Folien Fischer* the CJEU basically allowed negative declarations to be brought under art. 7(2) BR, which was contrary to the opinion of the AG[373] but in line with writings of most, but not all,[374] legal scholars.[375] The position is in line with art. 7(1) BR,[376] which in turn creates consistency in contract and

360 Case C-133/11, *Folien Fischer AG*, para. 33 and Chapter 4 section C.1.
361 Ibid., paras 34, 37 and 38 and Chapter 4 section C.2.
362 Ibid., para. 42.
363 Ibid., para. 48.
364 Ibid.
365 Ibid., para. 49 referring to *Tatry supra* note 348.
366 Ibid., para. 36 contrary to the opinion of the AG in the same case, para. 53.
367 Ibid., para. 46 and Principle 9: No protection of the weaker party.
368 Ibid., para. 47.
369 Ibid., para. 54.
370 Ibid., para. 52.
371 *Supra* notes.
372 Opinion of Advocate General Jääskinen, ibid., para. 38.
373 Ibid., para. 73.
374 Ketilbjørn Hertz, *Jurisdiction in Contract and Tort*, Jurist- og Økonomforbundets Forlag, 1998, pp. 278–80. 347–348.
375 *Conflict of Laws in Intellectual Property, The CLIP Principles and Commentary*, *supra* note 47, p. 176 (2:602.N02); Sender, *supra* note 41 at 4.96–4.98; Magnus and Mankowski, *supra* note 8, p. 229; Fawcett and Torremans, *supra* note 41 at 5.37–5.38 and Anna Gardella, 'Torpedos and Actions for Negative Declarations in International IP Law Litigation' in Arnaud Nuyts (ed.), *International Litigation in Intellectual Property and Information Technology*, Kluwer Law International, 2008, p. 206.
376 *Conflict of Laws in Intellectual Property, The CLIP Principles and Commentary*, ibid., p. 176 (2:602.N02).

tort.[377] Despite the fact that *Folien Fischer* concerned a claim for non-violation of competition law a claim for non-infringement of an IP right most likely also falls within art. 7(2) BR,[378] which is supported by the general wording of the CJEU speaking of 'an action [...] seeking to establish the absence of liability in tort [...]';[379] by post-*Folien Fischer* case law at national court level citing *Folien Fischer* in a non-infringement patent case[380] and by scholarly reports.[381] Thus, non-infringement actions of an IP right can be brought where infringement actions of an IP right can be brought i.e. at the place of action[382] defined in *Wintersteiger* as the place of establishment of the advertiser/defendant[383] and at the place(s) of effect(s)[384] defined in *Wintersteiger* as the place(s) of registration[385] or at the place(s) protecting unregistered trademarks and designs.[386] *Folien Fischer* for the infringer, therefore, mirrors *Wintersteiger* for the rightholder and so section B.1(a)(ii) applies *mutatis mutandis*.

(iii) Folien Fischer (impact)

The impact of *Folien Fischer* is that the infringer may choose between potentially several fora under art. 7(2) BR when bringing a non-infringement action. *Folien Fischer* does, therefore, not forestall 'torpedoes'.[387] The position contrasts the EUTMR where non-infringement actions are excluded from the *forum delicti* rule,[388] the CDR where non-infringement actions are also excluded from the *forum delicti* rule,[389] the AUPC where non-infringement actions fall outside the *forum delicti* rule unless an infringement action between the same parties regarding the same patent is pending at any such place in which event the non-infringement action must be brought there[390] but matches the CPVR where non-infringement actions are covered by the *forum delicti* rule.[391] **9.70**

377 Magnus and Mankowski, *supra* note 8, p. 230.
378 Case C-433/16, *Bayerische Motoren Werke AG v Acacia S.r.l.* (pending).
379 Case C-133/11, *Folien Fischer*, paras 56 cf. 42.
380 Corte Suprema di Cassazione, decision of 10 June 2013 in case 14508/13, *General Hospital v Asclepion*.
381 Arts 2:602 cf. 2:202 CLIP Principles and §§ 213 cf. 204 ALI Principles.
382 Case C-133/11, *Folien Fischer*, para. 52.
383 Case C-523/10, *Wintersteiger*, para. 37.
384 Case C-133/11, *Folien Fischer*, para. 52.
385 Case C-523/10, *Wintersteiger*, para. 29.
386 Section B.1(a)(iii).
387 Opinion of Advocate General Jääskinen in case C-133/11, *Folien Fischer*, para. 70. *Folien Fischer* can be criticized accordingly. However, it falls outside the scope of the present study to undertake any such critique given that 'torpedos' are excluded from the present study cf. Chapter 1 section A.5(a) (limit 7).
388 Art. 97(5) EUTMR and section C.1(b).
389 Art. 82(5) CDR and section C.2(b).
390 Art. 33(4) AUPC and section C.4(b).
391 Art. 101(3) AUPC and section C.3(b).

(c) *Art. 7(2) BR to invalidity actions*

9.71 If invalidity is raised during the infringement or non-infringement actions brought under art. 7(2) BR a distinction must be drawn between a registered national IP right and an unregistered national IP right.

9.72 As regards a registered national IP right a sub distinction must be drawn between the place(s) of registration, which leads to joint adjudication since any such place coincides with art. 24(4) BR and *Gat LuK*[392] and the place where the advertiser/defendant is established, which may lead to either joint or split adjudication depending on whether any such place coincides with art. 24(4) BR and *Gat LuK*. Art. 24(4) BR and *Gat LuK* are addressed in Chapter 11 section B.

9.73 As regards an unregistered national IP right no sub distinction needs to be drawn between the place(s) protecting unregistered trademarks and designs and the place where the advertiser/defendant is established. In both situations invalidity leads to joint adjudication since art. 24(4) and *Gat Luk* do not apply.

2. Defendant is domiciled outside the EU/EFTA

9.74 If the defendant is domiciled outside the EU/EFTA the Member States own international forum rules apply.[393] For the reasons in Chapter 1 section A.5(a) (factor 5) any such rules, including the conditions under which they may apply are not examined for the purpose of the present study.

C. THE *FORUM DELICTI* RULE APPLYING TO A EUROPEAN UNITARY IP RIGHT

9.75 Four different *forum delicti* rules apply depending on the corresponding European unitary IP right in question. If an EUTM has been infringed the *forum delicti* rule in the EUTMR applies (section 1); if a CD has been infringed the *forum delicti* rule in the CDR applies (section 2); if a CPV has been infringed the *forum delicti* rule in the CPVR applies (section 3) and if a UP has been infringed the *forum delicti* rule in the AUPC applies (section 4).

392 Case C-4/03, *Gat LuK*.

393 Art. 6 BR.

1. The *forum delicti* rule in the EUTMR

The *forum delicti* rule is found in art. 97(5) EUTMR. The CJEU has interpreted the provision in *Coty Prestige*.[394] Below a distinction is drawn between applying the rule to infringement actions (section a); to non-infringement actions (section b) and to invalidity actions (section c).[395] **9.76**

(a) Art. 97(5) EUTMR to infringement actions

Art. 97(5) EUTMR allows[396] infringement actions[397] to be brought in: '[…] the courts of the Member State in which the act of infringement has been committed or threatened'.[398] **9.77**

The provision, which applies whatever the domicile of the defendant,[399] is modelled on the corresponding provisions in the 1975 Community Patent Convention[400] and in the protocol to the amended 1989 version.[401] The provision is justified in proximity in line with its 'sister' provision in art. 7(2) BR.[402] **9.78**

Compared to its 'sister' provision in art. 7(2) BR the wording is different *since* art. 97(5) EUTMR speaks of 'act(s) of infringement' whereas art. 7(2) BR speaks of 'harmful event(s)'; *since* art. 97(5) EUTMR speaks of 'committed' whereas art. 7(2) BR speaks of 'occurred' and *since* art. 97(5) EUTMR speaks of 'threatened' whereas art. 7(2) BR speaks of 'may occur'. Given the different wordings, which is likely due to the fact that art. 97(5) EUTMR merely covers trademark infringements (IP specific wording) whereas art. 7(2) BR, as also indicated in *Bier*,[403] covers a wide variety of torts (general wording)[404] the **9.79**

---

394 Case C-360/12, *Coty Prestige.*

395 The three kinds of actions are overall defined in Chapter 1 section A.3(b).

396 The reason for using the term 'allows' is that art. 97(5) EUTMR speaks of 'proceedings […] may also be brought […]'. As an alternative to art. 97(5) EUTMR proceedings may be brought under art. 97(1)–(3) EUTMR cf. Chapters 5–7 sections C.1(a) meaning that two alternatives are available to the plaintiff. In addition to that 'fall back' rules apply cf. Chapters 2 and 3 section C.1.

397 Art. 96(a) EUTMR.

398 Art. 97(5) EUTMR.

399 Fawcett and Torremanns, *supra* note 41 at 8.39.

400 Art. 69(2) Convention for the European Patent for the Common Market (Community Patent Convention) (76/76/EEC) of 15 December 1975. The provision differs slightly from art. 97(5) EUTMR given that it speaks of 'was committed' rather than 'has been committed or threatened'.

401 Art. 14(5) Protocol on the Settlement of Litigation Concerning the Infringement and Validity of Community Patents of 30 December 1989 (Protocol of Litigation).

402 Opinion of Advocate General Jääskinen in case C-360/12, *Coty Prestige*, paras. 34–35 cf. Fawcett and Torremanns, *supra* note 41 at 8.23–8.24 and Nuyts, *supra* note 41, p. 106.

403 Case C-21/76, *Handelskwekerij*, para. 18.

404 Nuyts, *supra* note 41, p. 115 and the *CLIP Principles and Commentary, European Max Planck Group on Conflicts of Laws in Intellectual Property*, *supra* note 47, p. 69 (2:202.CO4).

question is whether the distinction under art. 7(2) BR between a place of action and a place(s) of effect(s)[405] similarly operates under art. 97(5) EUTMR or whether art. 97(5) EUTMR must be construed independently. Legal scholars disagree.[406]

9.80 Supporting that the distinction under art. 7(2) BR between a place of action and a place(s) of effect(s) similar operates under art. 97(5) EUTMR it is argued, inter alia, *that* any such distinction has a general nature;[407] *that* the distinction applies in IP[408] and even in trademark[409] cases; *that* even though the distinction does not explicitly appear from art. 97(5) EUTMR does not support that it does not apply given that the same distinction does not appear from art. 7(2) BR; *that* the AG parallels art. 69(2) of the 1975 Community Patent Convention[410] being the inspiration for art. 97(5) EUTMR[411] with art. 7(2) BR in his first opinion in *Shevill* for reasons of territoriality;[412] *that* the reasoning in *Wintersteiger* for a place of action may similarly apply under art. 97(5) EUTMR given that proximity is equally important under the EUTMR[413] and *that* the reasoning in *Wintersteiger* for a place(s) of effect(s) may similarly apply under art. 97(5) EUTMR given that the EUTM is also subject to (regional) territoriality.[414]

9.81 Supporting the opposite result namely that art. 97(5) EUTMR must be construed independently it is argued, inter alia, the drafting history behind the

---

405 Section B.1(a)(ii), Principle 6: Place of action and place(s) of effect(s).

406 Supporting that the distinction under art. 7(2) BR between a place of action and a place(s) of effect(s) similarly operates under art. 97(5) EUTMR see, inter alia, Scharper, *supra* note 343, p. 99 at note 492 with references and Vicente Scordamaglia, 'Jurisdiction and Procedure in Legal Actions relating to Community Trade Marks' in Mario Franzosi (ed.) *European Community Trade Mark, Commentary to the European Community Regulations*, Kluwer Law International, 1997, pp. 386–387. Supporting the opposite result namely that art. 97(5) EUTMR must be construed independently see, inter alia, Tritton, *supra* note 64 at 14–085; Nuyts, *supra* note 41, p. 116 at note 55 cf. p. 130 and (probably) Fawcett and Torremanns, *supra* note 41 at 5.105 cf., however, 8.23–8.24.

407 Case C-21/76, *Handelskwekerij*, para. 25 (environmental case); case C-68/93, *Fiona Shevill*, para. 20 and joined cases C-509/09, *eDate Advertising* and C-161/10, *Olivier Martinez and Robert Martinez*, para. 44 (personality right cases); case C-51/97, *Réunion européenne*, para. 28 (liability of maritime carrier case); case C-18/02, *Danmarks Rederiforening*, para. 40 (labour case); case C-168/02, *Rudolf Kronhofer*, para. 16 (liability of investment consultants case); case C-189/08, *Zuid-Chemie BV*, para. 23 (purchase of unusable products case); case C-133/11, *Folien Fischer*, para. 39 (competition law case) and case C-228/11, *Melzer v MF Global UK Ltd.*, para. 25 (trading in futures case).

408 Case C-170/12, *Peter Pinckney*, para 26; case C-387/12, *Hi Hotel*, para. 27 and case C-441/13, *Pez Hejduk*, paras 18 and 24 (copyright cases).

409 Case C-523/10, *Wintersteiger*, para. 19.

410 *Supra* note 400.

411 *Supra* note 400.

412 Opinion of Advocate General Darmon (first opinion) in case C-68/93, *Fiona Shevill*, paras 87–88.

413 Case C-523/10, *Wintersteiger*, para. 37 cf. Scordamaglia, *supra* note 406, p. 385 and opinion of Advocate General Jääskinen in case C-360/12, *Coty Prestige*, paras 34–35.

414 Case C-523/10, *Wintersteiger*, para. 25 cf. art. 1(2) EUTMR.

EUTMR where it was 'considered necessary, because of the special position with regard to Community trade marks, to modify the rules contained in [art. 7(2) BR]',[415] *that* neither the Explanatory Memoranda[416] nor the sparse comments to art. 69(2) of the 1975 Community Patent Convention or to art. 14(5) of the revised 1989 version being the inspirations to art. 97(5) EUTMR[417] contain any references to art. 7(2) BR; *that* by contrast art. 7(2) BR has been excluded in the EUTMR[418] and a *forum delicti* rule of its own has been introduced;[419] *that* the AG clearly makes a distinction between arts 97(5) EUTMR and 7(2) BR in his second opinion in *Shevill* stating that jurisdiction under the former is 'determined not according to the damage caused but on the basis of the sole causal event: the act of infringement itself';[420] *that* art. 7(2) BR relates to art. 4 BR in a way other than art. 97(5) EUTMR relates to art. 97(1)–(3) EUTMR given that art. 7(2) BR is an exception,[421] which art. 97(5) EUTMR is likely not;[422] *that* even the wordings are different since art. 7(2) BR generally speaks of 'the place where the harmful event occurred' whereas art. 97(5) EUTMR specifically speaks of 'the place where the infringement was committed'; *that* also the scopes are different *since* non-infringement actions are covered by art. 7(2) BR[423] but not by art. 97(5) EUTMR[424] and *since* threatened infringement actions are covered by art. 7(2) BR[425] but only by art. 97(5) EUTMR[426] 'if they are permitted under national

415 Commission Working Paper, Working Group on the Community Trademark, the Need for a European Trademark System, Competence of the European Community to create one, III/D/1294/79-EN, October 1979, p. 31.

416 Memorandum on the Creation of an EEC Trade Mark adopted by the Commission on 6 July 1976, SEC(76)2462 July 1976, p. 36 and Bulletin of the European Communities Supplement 5/80, New Trade Mark System for the Community, proposed Directive and Regulation prepared by the Commission of the European Communities (COM 80 635 final 19 November 1980), p. 76.

417 *Supra* notes 400–401.

418 Art. 94(2)(a) EUTMR; case C-360/12, *Coty Prestige*, para. 28 cf. art. 69(3) Convention for the European Patent for the Common Market (Community Patent Convention) (76/76/EEC) of 15 December 1975 and art. 13(2) Protocol on the Settlement of Litigation Concerning the Infringement and Validity of Community Patents of 30 December 1989 (Protocol of Litigation) where art. 5(3) Brussels Convention was also excluded.

419 Art. 97(5) EUTMR.

420 Opinion of Advocate General Léger (second opinion) in case C-68/93, *Fiona Shevill*, para. 9.

421 Section B.1(a)(ii) Principle 5: Narrow interpretation.

422 If art. 97(5) EUTMR was an exception the plaintiff's EU domicile in art. 97(2) EUTMR would be the main rule if the defendant was domiciled/established outside the EU which, in turn, would require a broad interpretation of any such rule. This seems, and taking into account the hostility against plaintiff's domicile rules cf., inter alia, Section B.1(a)(ii) Principle 6: Place of action and place(s) of effect(s) not a likely interconnection between the 'cascade' rules.

423 Case C-133/11, *Folien Fischer*, para. 56 and section B.1(a).

424 Art. 97(5) EUTMR speaks of 'with the exception of actions for a declaration of non-infringement' and section C.1(b).

425 Art. 7(2) BR speaks of 'may occur'.

426 Art. 97(5) EUTMR speaks of 'threatened'.

law';[427] *that* the nature of the EUTM favours a different interpretation of the *forum delicti* rule since in the EU a place of action will be consumed by a place(s) of effect(s) given that the EUTM is EU-wide[428] whereas for a national trademark right the two places may be segregated[429] and finally *that* the AG in *Coty Prestige* recommends an independent interpretation of art. 97(5) EUTMR[430] which was confirmed by the CJEU.[431]

9.82 It follows, therefore, that art. 97(5) EUTMR must be construed independently. In carrying out the task of how to interpret art. 97(5) EUTMR one may, however, find inspiration *partly* in the principles of, inter alia, predictability and proximity[432] since any such principles express general considerations and common sense[433] and *partly* in art. 7(2) BR given that trademark rights of whatever nature and territorial scope to the largest extent possible should be enforced equally.[434] Determining the impact of art. 97(5) EUTMR a number of options come to mind.

9.83 One option would be to interpret art. 97(5) EUTMR as referring solely to the place of action. Any such interpretation has been favoured by some legal scholars[435] and by the AG in his opinion in *Coty Prestige*.[436] Even though any such interpretation would be congruent with the wording of the provision speaking of 'committed' and meet predictability and proximity[437] and limit forum shopping[438] which is a declared goal under the EUTMR[439] the interpretation is not preferable. The reasons number, inter alia, *that* territoriality[440] would not be applied correctly;[441] *that* a place of action would often, but

427 Art. 96(a) EUTMR.
428 Art. 1(2) EUTMR.
429 Case C-523/10, *Wintersteiger*, paras 29–30.
430 Opinion of Advocate General Jääskinen in case C-360/12, *Coty Prestige*, para. 37.
431 Case C-360/12, *Coty Prestige*, para. 31.
432 Chapter 4 sections C.1–C.2.
433 Opinion of Advocate General Jääskinen in case C-360/12, *Coty Prestige*, para. 35.
434 Tritton, *supra* note 64 at 14–085.
435 Marcus Norrgård, Gemenskapsvarumärket och de Nationella Domstolarnas Internationella Behörighet, Nordiskt Immateriellt Rättsskydd (NIR), 3/1998, p. 460 cf. note 43.
436 Opinion of Advocate General Jääskinen in case C-360/12, *Coty Prestige*, para. 43.
437 Chapter 4 sections C.1–C.2.
438 Chapter 4 section C.3.
439 Bulletin of the European Communities Supplement 5/80, New Trade Mark System for the Community, proposed Directive and Regulation prepared by the Commission of the European Communities (COM 80 635 final 19 November 1980), p. 76; Recital (30) CDR which applies *mutatis mutandis* under the EUTMR; Nuyts, *supra* note 41, p. 116 and opinion of Advocate General Jääskinen in case C-360/12, *Coty Prestige*, para. 42.
440 Chapter 4 section D.
441 Annette Kur, 'Enforcement of Unitary Intellectual Property Rights: International Jurisdiction and Applicable Law' (2015) *Journal of Intellectual Property Law and Practice*, 468–80 at pp. 470 *et seq*.

not always, coincide with art. 97(1) EUTMR[442] and therefore limit the two choices a plaintiff always has under the EUTMR when bringing an infringement action;[443] *that* a place of action could exclude action being brought in Member States where there had in fact been an infringement and finally *that* a place of action would restrict a plaintiff's options more than his/her options under art. 7(2) BR as interpreted in *Wintersteiger* which for reasons of equal enforcement should be avoided.

A second option would be to interpret art. 97(5) EUTMR as referring solely to the place of effect meaning the place of registration.[444] Doing so the courts of Spain would be competent given that Spain is the Member State where the EUTM is registered.[445] Any such interpretation seems, despite meeting predictability[446] and despite limiting forum shopping,[447] also not preferable. The reasons number, inter alia, *that* a place of registration would coincide with art. 97(3) EUTMR and therefore limit the two choices a plaintiff always has under the EUTMR when bringing an infringement action;[448] *that* a place of registration could exclude action being brought in Member States where there had in fact been an infringement and *that* a place of registration would restrict a plaintiff's options more than his/her options under art. 7(2) BR cf. above *mutatis mutandis*. **9.84**

A third option would be to interpret art. 97(5) EUTMR as referring to the place(s) of *de facto* protection. In doing so action could be brought only if the EUTM is enforceable thus excluding jurisdiction, inter alia, *where* the EUTM lacks distinctiveness,[449] *where* the EUTM has not been used for five years[450] or *where* the EUTM has become the common name of the product or service in respect of which it is registered.[451] Any such interpretation seems also not preferable. The reasons number, inter alia, *that* art. 7(2) BR cannot be interpreted to that effect[452] and *that* therefore a place of de facto protection would restrict the plaintiff's options more than his/her options under art. 7(2) BR cf. above *mutatis mutandis*. **9.85**

442 Scharper, *supra* note 343, p. 101 cf. in the interrelationship between arts 4 and 7(2) BR case C-21/76, *Handelskwekerij*, para. 20.
443 Chapter 3 section C.1.
444 Case C-523/10, *Wintersteiger*, para. 29.
445 Art. 87 EUTMR.
446 Chapter 4 section C.1.
447 Chapter 4 section C.3.
448 Chapter 3 section C.1.
449 Arts 52(1)(a) cf. 7(1)(b) EUTMR.
450 Art. 51(1)(a) EUTMR.
451 Art. 51(1)(b) EUTMR.
452 Section B.1(a)(iii) (the first uncertainty).

9.86 A fourth option would be to require connecting factors under art. 97(5) EUTMR in both online and offline situations. In doing so action could only be brought in Member States whereto the defendant had directed the infringement. Any such interpretation seems, despite meeting predictability and proximity,[453] despite being recommended by legal scholars[454] and in scholarly reports[455] and despite limiting forum shopping[456] not preferable either. The reasons number, inter alia, *that* any such general connecting factors approach has been disregarded under art. 7(2) BR[457] and *that* therefore any such approach would restrict the plaintiff's options more than his/her options under art. 7(2) BR cf. above *mutatis mutandis*.

9.87 A fifth option would be to draw a distinction between online and offline infringements under art. 97(5) EUTMR in line with that under art. 7(2) BR. As regards *online infringements* the places of registration rule[458] would have to be adapted to the special circumstances of the EUTM i.e. to a places where the EUTM has taken effect rule. In doing so action could be brought in all of the 28 Member States given that the EUTM has taken effect throughout the EU.[459] Any such interpretation seems preferable despite the risk of forum shopping,[460] which the EUTMR seeks to avoid[461] *since* a places where the EUTM has taken effect rule would create consistency with *Wintersteiger*, which allows for an action to be brought to the same extent under art. 7(2) BR, which similarly seeks to avoid forum shopping;[462] *since* a places where the EUTM has taken effect rule can be justified in the same line of reasoning as *Wintersteiger* given that for EUTMs it can also be argued that territoriality meets predictability and proximity[463] and given that for EUTMs it can also be argued that it is the courts of the Member States where the EUTM has taken effect that are the best to assess whether there has been an infringement;[464] *since* a places where the EUTM has taken effect rule would meet the nature of art. 97(5) EUTMR as an alternative to art. 97(1)–(3) EUTMR and therefore uphold the two choices the plaintiff always has under the EUTMR when

453 Chapter 4 sections C.1–C.2.

454 Scharper, *supra* note 343, p. 120 and the *Conflict of Laws in Intellectual Property, The CLIP Principles and Commentary*, *supra* note 47, p. 72 (2:202.C08–09).

455 Arts 2:605 cf. 2:202 CLIP Principles and §§ 101(5) cf. 204 ALI Principles.

456 Chapter 4 section C.3.

457 Section B.1(a)(iii) (the seventh uncertainty).

458 Case C-523/10, *Wintersteiger*, para. 29.

459 Art. 1(2) EUTMR.

460 Chapter 4 section C.3.

461 *Supra* note 439.

462 Section B.1(a)(ii) Principle 3: Avoiding forum shopping.

463 Case C-523/10, *Wintersteiger*, para. 27.

464 Ibid., para. 28.

bringing an infringement action;[465] *since* a places where the EUTM has taken effect rule would ensure that the EUTM can be enforced in an efficient manner throughout the Community;[466] *since* a places where the EUTM has taken effect rule would give the plaintiff the same options as the ones he/she has under art. 7(2) BR which for reasons of equal enforcement is favourable; *since* there is no reason why the CJEU should interpret art. 7(2) BR extensively for a national trademark right[467] and art. 97(5) EUTMR narrowly for EUTMs and finally since a wide interpretation of art. 97(5) EUTMR is supported by legal scholars.[468] As regards *offline infringements* the places where the EUTM has taken effect rule would have to be supplemented with connecting factors cf. section B.1(a)(iii) *mutatis mutandis*. Any such position would create consistency with art. 7(2) BR.

The CJEU interpreted art. 97(5) EUTMR for the first time in *Coty Prestige*.[469] The case concerned an alleged offline infringement.[470] The CJEU rejected that art. 97(5) EUTMR encompasses both a place of action and a places of effect(s)[471] stating that: 'jurisdiction under [art. 97(5) EUTMR] may be established solely in favour of [EUTM courts] in the Member State in which the defendant committed the alleged unlawful act'.[472] 9.88

Coty Prestige can be interpreted in at least two ways. One way is reading that art. 97(5) EUTMR points at the place of action. Supporting any such interpretation speaks the wording of the decision whereas 'the linking factor provided for by the provision refers to the Member State where the act giving rise to the alleged infringement occurred or may occur [place of action], not the Member State where that infringement produces its effects [places of effect(s)]'.[473] So read, which would be congruent with the AG's opinion,[474] means that art. 97(5) EUTMR grants jurisdiction to the Member State where the central act causing the infringement took place i.e. to one forum only. Any such interpretation is not favourable for the above reasons. Another way to interpret *Coty Prestige*, therefore, is that art. 97(5) EUTMR points at more than one forum. Supporting any such interpretation also speaks the wording of 9.89

465 Chapter 3 section C.1.
466 Recital (29) CDR which applies *mutatis mutandis* under the EUTMR.
467 Case C-523/10, *Wintersteiger*.
468 Nuyts, *supra* note 41, p. 130 stating that 'the "act of infringement" in [art. 97(5) EUTMR] corresponds [...] to the generic notion of "harmful event" in Article [7(2) BR]'.
469 Case C-360/12, *Coty Prestige*.
470 Ibid., paras 18–23.
471 Ibid., para. 32.
472 Ibid., para. 37.
473 Ibid., para. 34.
474 Opinion of Advocate General Jääskinen in case C-360/12, *Coty Prestige*, para. 43.

the decision whereas 'in order to determine whether [art. 97(5) EUTMR] nevertheless leads to [...] a duality of linking factors',[475] which may have been later confirmed[476] given that an unlawful act due to territoriality can be committed in more than one Member State. So read, which is preferable, connecting factors must be applied offline cf. *Blomqvist*[477] where the CJEU held that selling and delivering infringing goods into the EU amounts to trademark use and thus to an unlawful act within the EU.[478] By contrast connecting factors must not be applied online. Any such interpretation ensures consistency vis-à-vis art. 7(2) BR.

9.90 Thus art. 97(5) EUTMR must likely be interpreted as the places where the EUTM has taken effect. Connecting factors are required if the EUTM has been infringed offline.

9.91 The final question is the extent of jurisdiction under art. 97(5) EUTMR. The answer is laid down in art. 98(2) EUTMR under the heading 'extent of jurisdiction' where any such courts: 'shall have jurisdiction only in respect of acts committed or threatened within the territory of the Member State in which that court is situated'.[479]

9.92 The impact of the provision, which in line with the 1975 Community Patent Convention[480] and later in the 1989 version[481] restricts the extent of jurisdiction, has been widely debated. Some legal scholars have argued that art. 98(2) EUTMR restricts jurisdiction more than art. 7(2) BR if the act of infringement must be interpreted as a place of action[482] whereas others have argued that art. 98(2) EUTMR merely limits jurisdiction to acts committed or threatened within the territory of the Member State in which the court is located but not jurisdiction to decide on damages arising out of these acts in other Member States.[483] Given, however, that it seems likely that art. 97(5) EUTMR must be interpreted as the places where the EUTM has taken effect it seems also likely that art. 98(2) EUTMR must be applied literally given the interconnection between the number of available fora and the extent of

475 Case C-360/12, *Coty Prestige*, para. 33.

476 *Infra* note 477.

477 Case C-98/13, *Martin Blomqvist v Rolex SA and Manufacture des Montres Rolex SA*, paras 31–33 cf. joined cases C-585/08, *Peter Pammer* and C-144/09, *Hotel Alpenhof*, paras 80–84 and section B.1(a)(iii).

478 Kur, *supra* note 441, pp. 468–80 at 473–4.

479 Art. 98(2) EUTMR.

480 Art. 69(2) Convention for the European Patent for the Common Market (Community Patent Convention) (76/76/EEC) of 15 December 1975.

481 Art. 17(2) Protocol on the Settlement of Litigation Concerning the Infringement and Validity of Community Patents of 30 December 1989 (Protocol of Litigation).

482 Nuyts, *supra* note 41, p. 130 with references.

483 Metzger, *supra* note 157, p. 260 at note 39 with reference to Scharper, *supra* note 343, pp. 125 *et seq.*

jurisdiction.[484] Accordingly, an art. 97(5) EUTMR court must be subject to limited forum jurisdiction unless the place coincides with art. 97(1) EUTMR in which event the court is subject to unlimited full jurisdiction.[485]

In sum, art. 97(5) EUTMR is likely to be interpreted independently as the places where the EUTM has taken effect. Connecting factors are required offline. The courts are subject to limited forum jurisdiction. The interpretation is consistent with art. 7(2) BR and the place(s) of registration rule in *Wintersteiger*. Thus, the effect of the interpretation is that trademark rights whatever nature and territorial scope can be enforced equally. **9.93**

(b) Art. 97(5) EUTMR to non-infringement actions

Art. 97(5) EUTMR does not allow non-infringement actions[486] to be brought at *forum delicti* given that the rule has been exempted in any such cases: 'with the exception of actions for a declaration of non-infringement of a Community trade mark'.[487] **9.94**

The provision is modelled on the corresponding provision in the 1989 Community Patent Agreement.[488] The reason for the exemption, which is not mentioned in the Explanatory Memorandum,[489] seems to be that art. 97(5) EUTMR is not accepted as a launch pad for a 'torpedo'[490] by contrast to art. 7(2) BR.[491] **9.95**

(c) Art. 97(5) EUTMR to invalidity actions

A distinction must be drawn between invalidity in infringement actions brought under art. 97(5) EUTMR, which leads to joint adjudication given that art. 96(d) EUTMR applies, and invalidity in non-infringement actions brought under art. 97(5) EUTMR, which leads to either split or joint adjudication given that arts 99(2) cf. 56 EUTMR apply. Arts 96(d) and 99(2) cf. 56 EUTMR are addressed in Chapter 11 section C.1. **9.96**

---

484 Case C-523/10, *Wintersteiger*, para. 28; case C-170/12, *Peter Pinckney*, para. 45 and case C-387/12, *Hi Hotel*, para. 38.

485 Art. 98(1) EUTMR.

486 Art. 96(b) EUTMR.

487 Art. 97(5) EUTMR cf. Fawcett and Torremans, *supra* note 41 at 8.23 and Gardella, *supra* note 375, p. 203.

488 Art. 14(5) Protocol on the Settlement of Litigation Concerning the Infringement and Validity of Community Patents of 30 December 1989 (Protocol of Litigation).

489 Bulletin of the European Communities Supplement 5/80, New Trade Mark System for the Community, proposed Directive and Regulation prepared by the Commission of the European Communities (COM 80 635 final 19 November 1980), p. 76.

490 Kur, *supra* note 441, pp. 468–80 at p. 469.

491 Case C-133/11, *Folien Fischer*, para. 56 and section B.1(b).

2. The *forum delicti* rule in the CDR

9.97 The *forum delicti* rule is found in art. 82(5) CDR. The CJEU has yet to interpret the provision[492] and no case is pending.[493] Below a distinction is drawn between applying the rule to infringement actions (section a); to non-infringement actions (section b) and to invalidity actions (section c).[494]

(a) Art. 82(5) CDR to infringement actions

9.98 Art. 82(5) CDR allows[495] infringement actions[496] to be brought in:

> the courts of the Member State in which the act of infringement has been committed or threatened.[497] A Community design court whose jurisdiction is based on Article 82(5) shall have jurisdiction only in respect of acts of infringement committed or threatened within the territory of the Member State in which that court is situated.[498]

9.99 Compared to its 'sister' provision in the EUTMR[499] art. 82(5) is similar[500] *since* it applies whatever the domicile of the defendant;[501] *since* it covers 'act(s) of infringement'; *since* the incidents covered by the provision are located where they have been 'committed'; *since* the option of bringing threatened infringement actions provided that national law so permits[502] is worded as 'threatened'; *since* the courts are subject to limited forum jurisdiction and *since* the justification is similarly proximity.[503]

9.100 Given, however, that the CJEU has yet to interpret the provisions[504] a distinction must be drawn between applying art. 82(5) CDR to the registered CD and to the unregistered CD.

---

492 Curia.eu visited on 1 January 2017.

493 See, however, case C-360/12, *Coty Prestige*, which concerns the 'sister' provision in art. 97(5) EUTMR cf. section C.1(a).

494 The three kinds of actions are overall defined in Chapter 1 section A.3(b).

495 The reason for using the term 'allows' is that art. 82(5) CDR speaks of 'proceedings [...] may also be brought [...]'. As an alternative to art. 82(5) CDR proceedings may be brought under arts 82(1)–(3) CDR cf. Chapters 5–7 section C.2(a) meaning that two alternatives are available to the plaintiff. In addition to that 'fall back' rules apply cf. Chapters 2 and 3 section C.2.

496 Art. 81(a) CDR.

497 Art. 82(5) CDR.

498 Art. 83(2) CDR.

499 Art. 97(5) EUTMR.

500 Memorandum for a European Parliament and Council Regulation on the Community Design presented by the Commission COM (93) 342 final COD 463 Brussels, 3 December 1993, p. 39.

501 Fawcett and Torremanns, *supra* note 41 at 8.116.

502 Art. 81(a) CDR.

503 *Supra* note 402.

504 *Supra* note 492–493.

With respect to the registered CD[505] the above places where the EUTM has taken effect rule subject to limited forum jurisdiction most likely applies *mutatis mutandis* given, inter alia, *that* the wordings of arts 82(5) cf. 83(2) CDR despite slight variations[506] fully equal arts 97(5) cf. 98(2) EUTMR, which is confirmed by the Explanatory Memorandum where the jurisdiction rules in the CD are 'entirely [...] corresponding' to the rules in the EUTMR;[507] *that* the Commission highlights the need for consistency in the Explanatory Memorandum by stating that 'it is extremely important for the users to be presented with rules which are as unitary as possible';[508] *that* the registered CD is EU wide[509] similar to the EUTM;[510] *that* the registered CD is subject to an EUIPO examination prior to registration[511] similar to the EUTM;[512] *that* the fact that the EUIPO examination is purely formal[513] seems irrelevant within the meaning of art. 82(5) CDR given that it is most likely not a requirement that the EUTM is *de facto* protected to bring an action under art. 97(5) EUTMR;[514] *that* legal scholars treat the *forum delicti* rules in the EUTMR and in the CDR equally[515] and *that* interpreting art. 82(5) CDR so that action can be brought where the registered CD has taken effect ensures that the registered CD can be enforced efficiently throughout the Community.[516] In an offline context connecting factors are likely required and section C.1(a) applies *mutatis mutandis*. **9.101**

With respect to the unregistered CD[517] the question is whether *Pinckney* applies *mutatis mutandis* meaning that action can be brought in Member States protecting the unregistered CD[518] or whether the places where the registered CD has taken effect applies *mutatis mutandis*. Any one of these leads to the same result i.e. that action can be brought in 28 Member States. **9.102**

---

505 Art. 35 CDR *et seq.*

506 One variation is that art. 82(5) CDR excludes non-infringement actions from the scope of the provision by referring exclusively to art. 81(a) and (d) CDR whereas art. 97(5) EUTMR explicitly excludes non-infringement actions from the scope of the provision cf. the wording 'with the exception of actions for a declaration of non-infringement'. Another variation is that art. 83(2) CDR speaks of 'acts of infringement committed or threatened' whereas art. 98(2) EUTMR merely speaks of 'acts committed or threatened'.

507 Proposal for a European Parliament and Council Regulation on the Community Design presented by the Commission COM (93) 342 final COD 463 Brussels, 3 December 1993, p. 39.

508 Ibid., p. 37.

509 Art. 1(3) CDR.

510 Art. 1(2) EUTMR.

511 Arts 45 cf. 48 CDR.

512 Arts 36 cf. 45 EUTMR.

513 Art. 45 CDR.

514 Section C.1(a) (third option).

515 Fawcett and Torremanns, *supra* note 41 at 8.116; Nuyts, *supra* note 41, p. 114 and Tritton, *supra* note 64 at 14–087.

516 Recital (29) CDR.

517 Art. 11 CDR.

518 Case C-170/12, *Peter Pinckney*, para. 43 cf. Case C-441/13, *Pez Hejduk*, para. 29.

Supporting that *Pinckney* applies *mutatis mutandis* it is argued, inter alia, that the unregistered CD bears a resemblance with copyrights given that both the former[519] and the latter[520] come into existence without formalities. Supporting that the places where the registered CD has taken effect applies *mutatis mutandis* it is argued, inter alia, *that* the registered and the unregistered CD must be treated equally procedural law wise[521] in particular that the CD courts, despite the differences in acquiring the rights[522] must treat them both as valid in an infringement action[523] and *that* legal scholars do not distinguish between the registered and the unregistered CDs under art. 82(5) CDR.[524] Balancing the interests it seems likely that the latter applies *mutatis mutandis* meaning that action can be brought where the unregistered CD has taken effect, which in turn ensures consistency with the registered CD. In an offline context connecting factors are likely required and section C.1(a) applies *mutatis mutandis*.

9.103 In sum, art. 82(5) CDR is likely to be interpreted as the places where the registered and the unregistered CDs have taken effect. Connecting factors are likely required offline. The courts are subject to limited forum jurisdiction. The interpretation is consistent with art. 7(2) BR and the place(s) of registration of designs in *Wintersteiger* and the places protecting unregistered designs in *Pinckney*.[525] Thus, the effect of the interpretation is that design rights whatever nature and territorial scope can be enforced equally.

(b) Art. 82(5) CDR to non-infringement actions

9.104 Art. 82(5) CDR does not allow non-infringement actions[526] to be brought at *forum delicti* given that the rule has been exempted in any such cases: 'Proceedings in respect of the actions and claims referred to in Article 81(a) [infringement actions] and (d) [counterclaims] may also be brought [...] in the courts of the Member State in which the act of infringement has been committed or threatened.'[527] Similar to art. 97(5) EUTMR[528] the reason for the exception, lacking information in the Explanatory Memorandum,[529]

---

519 Art. 11 CDR.

520 Cornish and Llewelyn, *supra* note 64 at 11.32 and Tritton, *supra* note 64 at 4.001.

521 Proposal for a European Parliament and Council Regulation on the Community Design presented by the Commission COM (93) 342 final COD 463 Brussels, 3 December 1993, pp. 37 *et seq*.

522 Art. 11 CDR (unregistered CD) and arts 35 CDR *et seq*. (registered CD).

523 Art. 85(1) and (2) CDR.

524 Fawcett and Torremanns, *supra* note 41 at 8.116 cf. Tritton, *supra* note 64 at 14–087.

525 Section B.1(a)(iii).

526 Art. 81(b) CDR.

527 At. 82(5) CDR cf. Fawcett and Torremans, *supra* note 41 at 8.116 and Gardella, *supra* note 375, p. 203.

528 Section C.1(b).

529 Proposal for a European Parliament and Council Regulation on the Community Design presented by the Commission COM (93) 342 final COD 463 Brussels, 3 December 1993, pp. 37 *et seq*.

seems to be that art. 82(5) CDR is not accepted as a launch pad for a 'torpedo'[530] by contrast to art. 7(2) BR.[531]

(c) Art. 82(5) CDR to invalidity actions

A distinction must be drawn between invalidity in infringement actions brought under art. 82(5) CDR which leads to joint adjudication given that art. 81(d) CDR applies and invalidity in non-infringement actions brought under art. 82(5) CDR which leads to either split or joint adjudication given that arts 84(4) cf. 52 CDR apply. Arts 81(d) and 84(4) cf. 52 CDR are addressed in Chapter 11 section C.2. **9.105**

3. The *forum delicti* rule in the CPVR

The *forum delicti* rule is found in art. 101(3) CPVR. The CJEU has yet not interpreted the provision[532] and no case is pending.[533] Below a distinction is drawn between applying the rule to infringement actions (section a); to non-infringement actions (section b) and to invalidity actions (section c).[534] **9.106**

(a) Art. 101(3) CPVR to infringement actions

Art. 101(3) CPVR allows[535] actions in respect of claims for infringement[536] to be brought in: 'the courts for the place where the harmful event occurred. In such cases, the court shall have jurisdiction only in respect of infringements alleged to have been committed in the territory of the Member State to which it belongs'.[537] **9.107**

Compared to its 'sister' provisions in the EUTMR and CDR[538] art. 101(3) CPVR is different *since* it speaks of 'harmful event(s)' whereas arts 97(5) EUTMR and 82(5) CDR speak of 'act(s) of infringement'; *since* the incidents covered by art. 101(3) CPVR are located where they have 'occurred' whereas under arts 97(5) EUTMR and 82(5) CDR they are located where they have **9.108**

---

530 *Supra* note 529.

531 Case C-133/11, *Folien Fischer*, para. 56 and section B.1(b).

532 Curia.eu visited on 1 January 2017.

533 See, however, case C-360/12, *Coty Prestige Lancaster Group GmbH v First Note Perfumes NV*, which concerns the 'sister' provision in art. 97(5) EUTMR cf. section C.1(a).

534 The three kinds of actions are overall defined in Chapter 1 section A.3(b).

535 The reason for using the term 'allows' is that art. 101(3) CPVR speaks of 'proceedings [...] may also be brought [...]'. As an alternative to art. 101(3) CPVR proceedings may be brought under art. 101(2)(a)–(c) CPVR cf. Chapters 5–7 section C.3(a) meaning that two alternatives are available to the plaintiff. In addition to that 'fall back' rules apply cf. Chapters 2 and 3 section C.3.

536 Art. 94 CPVR.

537 Art. 101(3) CPVR.

538 Arts 97(5) EUTMR and 82(5) CDR.

been 'committed' and *since* the option of bringing threatened infringement actions is not addressed in art. 101(3) CPVR contrary to arts 97(5) EUTMR and 82(5) CDR which both address and allow for such actions provided that national law so permits.[539]

9.109 It follows that art. 101(3) CPVR does not bear any clear resemblance to arts 97(5) EUTMR and 82(5) CDR except from also applying whatever the domicile of the defendant[540] and from also being justified in proximity.[541] By contrast art. 101(3) CPVR bears a clear resemblance to art. 7(2) BR which also speaks of the place where the 'harmful event occurred'. Thus, the question is whether art. 101(3) CPVR must be construed in line with art. 7(2) BR[542] or in line with arts 97(5) EUTMR and 82(5) CDR.[543] Legal scholars disagree.[544]

9.110 Supporting that art. 101(3) CPVR must be construed in line with art. 7(2) BR it is argued, inter alia, *that* the wording is the same since they both speak of the place where the 'harmful event occurred'; *that* the choice of the wording 'harmful event occurred' seems deliberate taking into account that art. 93(5) of the first CTMR[545] where the wording 'infringement has been committed' was used, was already in force at the time the CPVR was passed[546] and that therefore the latter wording could have been copied into art. 101(3) CPVR, which did not happen; *that* the wording 'may occur' does not appear in neither art. 101(3) CPVR nor in art. 5(3) of the 1988 Lugano Convention, which applied at the time and which is referred to[547] thus supporting corresponding interpretations of the two provisions; *that* art. 5(3) of the 1988 Lugano Convention is not exempted in the CPVR which it most likely would have been if art. 101(3) CPVR was to be given an interpretation different from art. 7(2) BR and finally *that* the AG in *Coty Prestige* seems to indicate that art. 101(3) CPVR must be construed in line with art. 7(2) BR.[548]

---

539 Arts 96(a) EUTMR and 81(a) CDR.

540 Fawcett and Torremanns, *supra* note 41 at 8.162.

541 *Supra* note 402.

542 Section B.1(a).

543 Sections C.1(a) and C.2)(a).

544 Supporting that art. 101(3) CPVR must be construed in line with art. 7(2) BR see Gert Würtenberger, Paul Van Der Kooij, Bart Kiewiet and Martin Ekvad, *European Community Plant Variety Protection*, Oxford University Press, 2006 at 7.66–7.67. Supporting the opposite result namely that art. 101(3) CPVR must be construed in line with arts 97(5) EUTMR and 82(5) CDR see (probably) Fawcett and Torremanns, *supra* note 41 at 8.163.

545 Council Regulation 40/94 of 20 December 1993 on the Community Trademark.

546 Council Regulation 2100/94 of 27 July 1994 on Community Plant Variety Rights.

547 Art. 101(1) CPVR.

548 Opinion of Advocate General Jääskinen in case C-360/12, *Coty Prestige*, para. 29 at note 30.

Supporting the opposite result namely that art. 101(3) CPVR must be construed in line with arts 97(5) EUTMR and 82(5) CDR it is argued, inter alia, *that* both the EUTMR, CDR and the CPVR have unitary characters[549] and that therefore the distinction between a place of action and a place(s) of effect(s) known from art. 7(2) BR does not make sense due to territoriality;[550] *that* arts 97(5) EUTMR, 82(5) CDR and 101(3) CPVR are construed in the same ways as regards the extent of jurisdiction, which is limited to the forum;[551] *that* even though art. 101(3)(first sentence) CPVR ties jurisdiction to the 'harmful event' art. 101(3)(second sentence) CPVR ties the extent of any such jurisdiction to the 'infringements [...] committed' which, as stated by legal scholars,[552] is known from the EUTMR and CDR[553] and finally *that* the strength of the above argument whereas art. 101(3) CPVR must be construed in line with art. 7(2) BR given that the latter has not been explicitly exempted in the CPVR is weak since art. 7(2) BR does not apply as 'fall back' to the CPVR in the EU.[554] **9.111**

Balancing the interests, and despite the literal kinship with art. 7(2) BR, art. 101(3) CPVR is likely to be interpreted as the places where the CPVR has taken effect. Connecting factors are likely required offline cf. section C.1(a) *mutatis mutandis*.[555] Threatened infringement actions cannot be brought under art. 101(3) CPVR based on the motto 'what is generally *excluded* (threatened infringement actions under the CPVR)[556] cannot be specifically *included* (threatened infringement actions under art. 101(3) CPVR)'. The courts are subject to limited forum jurisdiction. The interpretation is consistent with art. 7(2) BR and the place(s) of registration in *Wintersteiger*. Thus, the effect of the interpretation is that plant variety rights whatever nature and territorial scope can be enforced equally. **9.112**

(b) Art. 101(3) CPVR to non-infringement actions

Non-infringement actions are generally covered by the CPVR.[557] Considering the above motto a contrario 'what is generally *included* can be specifically *excluded*' the question is whether non-infringement actions can or cannot be brought under art. 101(3) CPVR. Supporting that non-infringement actions **9.113**

549 Arts 1(2) EUTMR, 1(3) CDR and 2 CPVR.

550 Kur, *supra* note 441, pp. 468–80 at pp. 470–72.

551 Arts 98(2) EUTMR, 83(2) CDR and 101(3) CPVR.

552 Fawcett and Torremans, *supra* note 41 at 8.163.

553 Arts 97(5) EUTMR and 82(5) cf. 83(2) CDR.

554 Chapter 2 sections C.3(a)-C.3(b).

555 A plant variety may also be infringed online given that the exclusive rights cover, inter alia, offering for sale cf. art. 13(2)(c) CPVR.

556 Fawcett and Torremans, *supra* note 41 at 8.146 and 8.179.

557 Chapter 3 section C.3.

can be brought under art. 101(3) CPVRit is argued, inter alia, *that* any such actions have not been excluded and *that* any such actions can be brought under the *forum delicti* rules in scholarly reports.[558] Supporting the opposite result, namely that non-infringement actions cannot be brought under art. 101(3) CPVR, it is argued, inter alia, *that* art. 101(3) CPVR must be interpreted in line with arts 97(5) EUTMR and 82(5) CDR where non-infringement actions are excluded. Balancing the interests, and in particular since any such actions have not been explicitly excluded, non-infringement actions can most likely be brought under art. 101(3) CPVR.

(c) Art. 101(3) CPVR to invalidity actions

9.114 If invalidity of a CPV is raised during the infringement or non-infringement actions brought under art. 101(3) CPVR the CPVO comes into play given their exclusivity to address invalidity,[559] which in turn leads to either split or joint adjudication. Art. 20 CPVR is addressed in Chapter 11 section C.3.

4. The *forum delicti* rule in the AUPC

9.115 The *forum delicti* rule is found in art. 33(1)(a) AUPC.[560] Below a distinction is drawn between applying the rule to infringement actions (section a); to non-infringement actions (section b) and to invalidity actions (section c).[561]

(a) Art. 33(1)(a) AUPC to infringement actions

9.116 Art. 33(1)(a) AUPC allows[562] infringement actions[563] to be brought before: 'the local division hosted by the Contracting Member State where the actual or threatened infringement has occurred or may occur, or the regional division in which that Contracting Member State participates'.[564]

9.117 The provision, which applies whatever the domicile of the defendant,[565] seems to be modelled on its 'sister' provisions in the BR, EUTMR, CDR and

558 Arts 2:605 cf. 2:602 and 2:202 CLIP Principles and §§ 101(5) cf. 213 and 204 ALI Principles.

559 Art. 20 CPVR.

560 Torsten Bjørn Larsen, *Rules of Jurisdiction in the Agreement on a Unified Patent Court*, Nordiskt Immateriellt Rättsskydd, 4/2014, p. 357–374 at pp. 368 *et seq.* and Torsten Bjørn Larsen, *A Bundle of National Patents v a European Patent with Unitary Effect – Jurisdictional Comparison, Intellectual Property and General Legal Principles – Is IP a Lex Specialis?* Edward Elgar Publishing, 2015, pp. 208 *et seq.*

561 The three kinds of actions are overall defined in Chapter 1 section A.3(b).

562 The reason for using the term 'allows', contrary to art. 33(1) AUPC using the term 'shall', is that infringement actions may also be brought under art. 33(1)(b) AUPC cf. Chapters 5 and 6 section C.4(a) meaning that two alternatives are available to the plaintiff cf. Chapter 3 section C.4

563 Art. 32(1)(a) AUPC.

564 Art. 33(1)(a) AUPC.

565 Arts 33(1)(a) and 33(1) (fourth sentence) AUPC.

CPVR. The reason is *that* it speaks of 'infringement', which is an IP specific term known from the EUTMR and CDR;[566] *that* the infringement is located where it has 'occurred' which, by contrast, is a term known from the BR and CPVR;[567] *that* the option of bringing threatened infringement actions is worded as 'threatened [...] may occur' where the former term is known from the EUTMR and CDR[568] and the latter term is known from the BR[569] and *that* the justification for the provision, lacking information in the drafting history,[570] is most likely also proximity.

In carrying out the task how to interpret art. 33(1)(a) AUPC the UPC is as a court outside the judicial and institutional framework of the EU[571] obviously not bound by case law from the CJEU. The UPC may, however, take an interest in interpreting art. 33(1)(a) AUPC consistent with art. 7(2) BR and *Wintersteiger* since the rightholder is free to shop between, inter alia, arts 7(2) BR and 33(1)(a) AUPC for European patents[572] for an extendable period of seven years.[573] Further the UPC may also take an interest in interpreting art. 33(1)(a) AUPC consistent for UPs and European patents *since* the provision combines terms known from European unitary IP right *forum delicti* rules ('infringement' and 'threatened') with terms known from a national IP right *forum delicti* rules ('occurred' and 'may occur') and *since* consistency would create legal certainty for the users.[574] Finally, art. 33(1)(a) AUPC may likely be interpreted in the light of the principles of, inter alia, predictability and proximity,[575] which express general considerations and common sense[576] as well as the principle of territoriality.[577] Determining the impact of art. 33(1)(a) AUPC a number of options, which to a large extent correspond to the ones addressed in section C.1(a), come to mind. **9.118**

One option would be to interpret art. 33(1)(a) AUPC as referring to both a place of action and a place(s) of effect(s). Any such option, which could work **9.119**

566 Arts 97(5) EUTMR and 82(5) CDR.
567 Arts 7(2) BR and 101(3) CPVR.
568 Arts 97(5) EUTMR and 82(5) CDR.
569 Art. 7(2) BR.
570 Chapter 2 notes 248–9.
571 Opinion 1/09 of 8 March 2011 of the CJEU, para. 71.
572 UPC competence for European patents is for the reasons in Chapter 1 section A.5(a) (limit 6) not covered by the present study.
573 Art. 83 AUPC.
574 Recital (5) AUPC.
575 Chapter 4 sections C.1–C.2.
576 Opinion of Advocate General Jääskinen in case C-360/12, *Coty Prestige*, paras 34–35.
577 Chapter 4 section D.

for European patents,[578] seems not preferable since for UPs the former will be consumed by the latter given that the UP is CMS-wide.[579]

9.120 A second option would be to interpret art. 33(1)(a) AUPC as referring solely to the place of action. Even though any such approach could meet predictability and proximity[580] and limit forum shopping[581] the interpretation seems not preferable either. The reasons number, inter alia, *that* the term 'occurred', which in German reads 'erfolgt ist' and in French 's'est produite' all being equally authentic[582] literally does not point at any such place, which in turn is supported by art. 7(2) BR (which similarly uses the term 'occurred' and where more than just a place of action is covered)[583] and by arts 97(5) EUTMR and 82(5) CDR (which despite using the term 'committed' can likely not be interpreted to point at the place of action);[584] *that* a place of action would create inconsistency with art. 7(2) BR and *Wintersteiger* having the effect that the choice of fora would be wider under art. 7(2) BR than under art. 33(1)(a) AUPC, which in turn would make the UPC system less attractive for European patent litigators and thereby contrast the purpose of the AUPC;[585] *that* a place of action would often, but not always, coincide with art. 33(1)(b) AUPC and therefore limit the two choices a plaintiff always has under the AUPC when bringing an infringement action[586] and *that* a place of action would exclude actions to be brought where there had in fact been an infringement which, in turn, would contrast the expected pro patentee approach of the UPC.[587]

9.121 A third option would be to interpret art. 33(1)(a) AUPC as referring solely to the place(s) of effect(s) meaning the place(s) of registration. Any such option, which could work for European patents,[588] also seems not preferable. The reasons number, inter alia, *that* the UP is registered in Germany[589] and *that* therefore a place of registration would exclude actions to be brought where

578 Case C-523/10, *Wintersteiger*, para. 40.
579 Arts 3(2) UPR cf. 2(f) AUPC.
580 Chapter 4 sections C.1–C.2.
581 Chapter 4 section C.3.
582 Art. 88 AUPC.
583 Case C-523/10, *Wintersteiger*, para. 40.
584 Sections C.1(a)–C.1(a).
585 Recital (5) AUPC.
586 Chapter 3 section C.4.
587 Chapter 1 section A.4(b).
588 Case C-523/10, *Wintersteiger*, para. 29.
589 Arts 9(1)(b) cf. 2(d) and (e) UPR.

there had in fact been an infringement, which in turn would not only contrast territoriality[590] but also the expected pro patentee approach of the UPC.[591]

A fourth option would be to interpret art. 33(1)(a) AUPC as referring to the place(s) of *de facto* protection. In doing so action could be brought only if the UP or European patents are enforceable thus excluding jurisdiction where the invention lacks e.g. novelty or inventive step. Any such interpretation seems also not preferable. The reasons number, inter alia, *that* it would create inconsistency with art. 7(2) BR and *Wintersteiger* for European patents, which for the reasons above should be avoided and *that* it could contrast the expected pro patentee approach of the UPC[592] given that it would limit the number of available fora. **9.122**

A fifth option would be to require connecting factors under art. 33(1)(a) AUPC in both online and offline situations. Despite meeting predictability and proximity,[593] despite limiting forum shopping,[594] despite 'striking a fair balance between the interests of right holders and other parties'[595] and despite being recommended by legal scholars[596] and in scholarly reports[597] any such interpretation seems (probably) also unlikely for the two reasons above. **9.123**

A final option would be to draw a distinction between online and offline infringements under art. 33(1)(a) AUPC in line with that under art. 7(2) BR. As regards *online infringements* a places where the UP has taken effect (and a place(s) of registration for European patents) rules would apply. Doing so action could be brought in each of the 25 Contracting Member States given that the UP has taken effect there[598] (and in every Contracting Member State being designated in a European patent). Any such interpretation seems likely *since* it would meet predictability and proximity as applied by the CJEU;[599] *since* it might not lead to more forum shopping given that the exclusive patent **9.124**

590 Chapter 4 section D.
591 Clement Salung Petersen and Jens Schovsbo, 'On Law and Policy in a European and European Union Patent Court (EEUPC), What will it do to Patent Law and What will Patent Law do to it?' in Henning Koch, Karsten Hagel-Sørensen, Ulrich Haltern, Joseph H.H. Weiler (eds), *Europe The New Legal Realism*, DJØF Publishing p. 636 (section IV.4).
592 Ibid.
593 Chapter 4 sections C.1–C.2.
594 Chapter 4 section C.3.
595 Recital (6) cf. art. 42(2) AUPC.
596 *Supra* note 157 *mutatis mutandis.*
597 *Supra* note 156 *mutatis mutandis.*
598 Arts 3(2) UPR cf. 2(f) AUPC.
599 *Supra* note 33.

rights,[600] its limitations,[601] remedies and damages[602] and the ROP are the same; *since* it would meet the nature of art. 33(1)(a) AUPC as an alternative to art. 33(1)(b) AUPC[603] and therefore uphold the two choices the plaintiff always has under the AUPC when bringing an infringement action;[604] *since* it would create consistency with art. 7(2) BR and *Wintersteiger* for European patents; *since* it would create consistency with the expected ways arts 97(5) EUTMR, 82(5) CDR and 101(3) CPVR are interpreted;[605] *since* therefore art. 33(1)(a) AUPC would be interpreted consistently for UPs and European patents which, in turn, would create legal certainty for the users[606] and finally *since* it would be in line with the expected pro patentee approach of the UPC.[607] In order to limit the risk of frivolous lawsuits it must be required that the UPC adopt a similar approach to that of the CJEU in *L'Oréal* whereas there has only been an effect in Contracting Member States whereto the infringement has been targeted.[608] As regards *offline infringements* the places where the UP has taken effect (and the place(s) of registration for European patents) would have to be supplemented with connecting factors cf. section B.1(a)(iii) *mutatis mutandis*. Any such position would create consistency vis-à-vis art. 7(2) BR.

9.125 Thus, it seems likely that art. 33(1)(a) AUPC must be interpreted as the places where the UP has taken effect (and as every place(s) of registration for European patents). Connecting factors are likely required if the UP or the European patents have been infringed offline.

9.126 The final question is the extent of jurisdiction. As stated in Chapter 5 section C.4(a) art. 33(1)(b) AUPC is subject to unlimited full jurisdiction.[609] Below it is addressed whether also art. 33(1)(a) AUPC is subject to unlimited full jurisdiction or whether it is merely subject to limited forum jurisdiction.

9.127 Supporting that art. 33(1)(a) AUPC is also subject to unlimited full jurisdiction it is argued, inter alia, *that* there is nothing in the drafting history

---

600 Arts 24(b) cf. 25–26 AUPC.
601 Arts 24(b) cf. 27 AUPC.
602 Arts 24(b) cf. 56 AUPC *et seq*.
603 Art. 33(1) AUPC speaks of infringement actions to 'be brought before […] *or* […]' (emphasis added).
604 Chapter 3 section C.4.
605 Sections C.1(a)–C.3(a).
606 Recital (5) AUPC.
607 *Supra* note 591.
608 Case C-324/09, *L'Oréal SA*, paras 64–65; case C-98/13, *Martin Blomqvist*, paras 31–33 cf. joined cases C-585/08, *Peter Pammer* and C-144/09, *Hotel Alpenhof*, paras 80–84 and section B.1(a)(iii).
609 Art. 34 AUPC.

indicating a restriction of jurisdiction;[610] *that* unlimited full jurisdiction for patent rights, which are divided (European patents)[611] even more so supports unlimited full jurisdiction for patent rights, which are united (UP) given that the former due to the territorial principle is more extensive than the latter; *that* unlimited full jurisdiction contributes to the required efficiency and cost effectiveness of the functioning of the UPC[612] and thus to an effective enforcement of patent rights[613] and *that* unlimited full jurisdiction removes the risk of diverging decisions being one of the goals behind the AUPC.[614]

Supporting the opposite result namely that art. 33(1)(a) AUPC is merely subject to limited forum jurisdiction it is argued, inter alia, *that* limited forum jurisdiction would contribute to strike a 'fair balance between the interests of right holders and other parties';[615] *that forum delicti* jurisdiction is restricted under the EUTMR, CDR and CPVR[616] having similar unitary characters;[617] *that* unlimited full jurisdiction would create a *forum actoris* which is usually met with hostility and *that* unlimited full jurisdiction could create a risk of forum shopping for non-Contracting Member State rightholders having more than one place of business in the Contracting Member States.[618]

> Changing slightly the example in Chapter 1 section 2 so that Frogs Inc. is based in the US whereas Frox GmbH is based in Germany. Frogs Inc. has places of business in Germany, Denmark, Finland and the UK. Frogs Inc. owns a UP, which has been infringed by Frox GmbH, which markets and sells infringing products in those four Contracting Member States. Frogs Inc. wants to sue Frox GmbH for infringement under art. 33(1)(a) AUPC. No matter in which of those four Contracting Member States Frogs Inc. may sue Frox GmbH, the exclusive patent rights[619] and its limitations,[620] remedies and damages[621] and the ROP are the same. What is not the same are the novelty, inventive step and industrial application requirements, entitlement and the language of the proceedings. The former four follow the laws of the Contracting Member State where Frogs Inc. had its place of business at the time of filing cf. art. 7(1)(b) UPR whereas the latter as a main rule follows the Contracting Member State where the action is brought cf. art. 49 AUPC. Given that Frogs Inc. has

610 Chapter 2 notes 248–9.
611 Art. 34 AUPC.
612 Arts 40(3) and 41(3) AUPC.
613 Recital (5) AUPC and Chapter 4 section B.
614 Recital (2) AUPC.
615 Recital (6) cf. arts 41(3) and 42(2) AUPC.
616 Arts 98(2) EUTMR, 83(2) CDR and 101(3) CPVR.
617 Arts 1(2) EUTMR, 1(3) CDR and 2 CPVR.
618 Art. 7(1)(b) UPR.
619 Arts 24(b) cf. 25–26 AUPC.
620 Arts 24(b) cf. 27 AUPC.
621 Arts 24(b) cf. 56 AUPC *et seq.*

places of business in four Contracting Member States namely in Germany, Denmark, Finland and the UK, it may forum shop between the laws and languages of these four states.

9.128 Balancing the interests and in particular taking into account the drafting history and the position for European patents it seems likely that UP cases brought under art. 33(1)(a) AUPC are also subject to unlimited full jurisdiction, which cannot be restricted. Despite being far-reaching unlimited full jurisdiction allow litigators to return to experienced divisions of the UPC to have the case decided in its entirety, which could strengthen the confidence in the new system.

9.129 In sum art. 33(1)(a) AUPC is likely to be interpreted as the places where the UP has taken effect (and as every place(s) of registration for European patents). Connecting factors are likely required offline. The position is consistent with the expected positions for other European unitary IP rights[622] and the position for a national IP right.[623] The courts are subject to unlimited full jurisdiction, which differs from other European unitary IP rights and a national IP right where the extent of jurisdiction is limited.[624]

(b) Art. 33(1)(a) AUPC to non-infringement actions

9.130 Art. 33(1)(a) AUPC also applies to non-infringement actions.[625] It requires, however, that an infringement action between the same parties relating to the same patent is already pending before an art. 33(1)(a) AUPC court. In that case the non-infringement action, for reasons of procedural economy, may only be brought there.[626] If, however, an infringement action is not already pending art. 33(1)(a) AUPC does not apply. In that case the non-infringement action must be brought at the central division[627] cf. Chapter 10 section C.

(c) Art. 33(1)(a) AUPC to invalidity actions

9.131 If invalidity of a UP is raised during the infringement or non-infringement actions brought under art. 33(1)(a) AUPC the flexible exclusive jurisdiction rule in art. 33(3) AUPC comes into play, which in turn leads to either split or joint adjudication. Art. 33(3) AUPC is addressed in Chapter 11 section C.4.

---

622 Arts 97(5) EUTMR, 82(5) CDR and 101(3) CPVR.
623 Art. 7(2) BR.
624 Arts 7(2) BR, 98(2) EUTMR, 83(2) CDR and 101(3) CPVR.
625 Art. 33(4) AUPC.
626 Art. 33(4) (second sentence) AUPC.
627 Art. 33(4) (first sentence) AUPC.

D. CONCLUSION

A distinction is drawn between the application of the *forum delicti* rule in trademark, design, plant variety and patent cases. **9.132**

In *trademark* cases the applicable *forum delicti* rules are found in arts 7(2) BR, 97(5) EUTMR and in the Member States' own international forum rules, which have not been examined. The justification behind arts 7(2) BR and 97(5) EUTMR are similar whereas the scopes and impacts are both similar and different. **9.133**

They are similar *since* infringement actions can be brought under both; *since* the actions can likely be brought to the same extent; *since* offline infringements are likely subject to connecting factors by contrast to online infringements, which are likely not; *since* both are subject to limited forum jurisdiction and *since* adjudication is joint under both. **9.134**

They are different *since* art. 7(2) BR applies when the defendant is domiciled in the EU/EFTA whereas art. 97(5) EUTMR applies whatever the domicile of the defendant; *since* the harmful event must have occurred in the EU/EFTA under art. 7(2) BR whereas the infringement must have been committed in the EU under art. 97(5) EUTMR; *since* threatened infringement actions can be brought under art. 7(2) BR but only if national law so permits under arts 97(5) EUTMR and *since* non-infringement actions can be brought under art. 7(2) BR but not under art. 97(5) EUTMR. **9.135**

In sum – and generally speaking – art. 7(2) BR is advantageous to the plaintiff acting as the rightholder since threatened infringement actions can always be brought whereas art. 7(2) BR is advantageous to the plaintiff acting as the infringer since non-infringement actions can always be brought. Art. 97(5) EUTMR is advantageous to the plaintiff acting as the rightholder since adjudication is always joint. **9.136**

In *design* cases the applicable *forum delicti* rules are found in arts 7(2) BR, 82(5) CDR and in the Member States' own international forum rules, which have not been examined. The above applies *mutatis mutandis* including to the unregistered CD. **9.137**

In *plant variety* cases the *forum delicti* rules are found in arts 7(2) BR, 101(3) CPVR and in the Member States own international forum rules, which have not been examined. The justification behind arts 7(2) BR and 101(3) CPVR are similar whereas the scopes and impacts are both similar and different. **9.138**

9.139 They are similar *since* infringement actions can be brought under both; *since* the actions can likely be brought to the same extent; *since* offline infringements are likely subject to connecting factors by contrast to online infringements, which are likely not; *since* non-infringement actions are allowed for under both; *since* both are subject to limited forum jurisdiction and *since* adjudication may be joint/split under both.

9.140 They are different *since* art. 7(2) BR applies when the defendant is domiciled in the EU/EFTA whereas art. 101(3) CPVR applies whatever the domicile of the defendant; *since* the harmful event must have occurred in the EU/EFTA under art. 7(2) BR but in the EU under art. 101(3) CPVR and *since* threatened infringement actions are allowed for under art. 7(2) BR but not under art. 101(3) CPVR.

9.141 In sum – and generally speaking – art. 7(2) BR is advantageous to the plaintiff acting as the rightholder since threatened infringement actions can be brought.

9.142 In *patent* cases the *forum delicti* rules are found in arts 7(2) BR, 33(1)(a) AUPC and in the Member States' own international forum rules, which have not been examined. The justification behind arts 7(2) BR and 33(1)(a) AUPC are similar whereas the scopes and impacts are both similar and different.

9.143 They are similar *since* infringement actions can be brought under both; *since* the actions can likely be brought to the same extent; *since* offline infringements are likely subject to connecting factors by contrast to online infringements, which are likely not and *since* threatened infringement actions are allowed for under both.

9.144 They are different *since* art. 7(2) BR applies when the defendant is domiciled in the EU/EFTA whereas art. 33(1)(a) AUPC applies whatever the domicile of the defendant; *since* the harmful event must have occurred in the EU/EFTA under art. 7(2) BR whereas the infringement must have occurred in a CMS under art. 33(1)(a) AUPC; *since* art. 7(2) BR is subject to limited forum jurisdiction whereas art. 33(1)(a) AUPC is subject to unlimited full jurisdiction and *since* non-infringement actions are allowed for under art. 7(2) BR but only under art. 33(1)(a) AUPC if an infringement action between the same parties regarding the same patent is pending at any such place.

9.145 In sum – and generally speaking – art. 7(2) BR is advantageous to the plaintiff acting as the infringer since non-infringement actions can always be brought. Given that the extent of jurisdiction is not flexible under neither art. 7(2) BR (where jurisdiction cannot be extended) nor under art. 33(1)(a) AUPC (where jurisdiction cannot be restricted) none of them are advantageous to the plaintiff whatever their capacity.

Overall, the above similarities and differences as well as the advantages for the plaintiff can be illustrated as shown in Table 9.1 below. As stated in Chapter 3 section D the numbers in brackets refers to the factor identified as an advantage for the plaintiff in Chapter 1 section A.4. **9.146**

Table 9.1 Forum delicti *rule overview*

	GENERAL			JUSTIFICATION	SCOPE				IMPACT					CONCLUSION
											If invalidity is raised			
	Version	*Forum delicti* rule	Wording	Ratio legis	Requirement	Infringement actions	Threatened infringement actions	Non-infringement actions	Places to sue	Connecting factors	In infringement actions	In non-infringement actions	Extent of jurisdiction	Advantages for the plaintiff
Trade Marks	National trademarks	Art. 7(2) BR	'Harmful event occurred or may occur'	Proximity	• Defendant must be domiciled in the EU/EFTA • Harmful event must have occurred in the EU/EFTA	Yes	Yes	Yes	Registered trademarks • Place where advertiser/defendant is established • Place(s) where trademark is registered Unregistered trademarks • Place where advertiser/defendant is established • Place(s) protecting unregistered trademarks	Offline: Yes Online: No	Registered trademarks • Joint/split adjudication where advertiser/defendant is established • Joint adjudication at the place(s) where trademark is registered Unregistered trademarks • Joint adjudication where advertiser/defendant is established and at the place(s) protecting unregistered trademarks		Limited	Art. 7(2) BR is advantageous → To the plaintiff acting as the rightholder since threatened infringement actions can always be brought (8) → To the plaintiff acting as the infringer since non-infringement actions can be brought (9) Art. 97(5) EUTMR is advantageous → To the plaintiff acting as the rightholder since adjudication is always joint (6)
	European Union Trademark (EUTM)	Art. 97(5) EUTMR	'Infringement has been committed or threatened'	Proximity	• Whatever the domicile of the defendant • Infringement must have been committed in the EU	Yes	Yes But require that national law so permits cf. art. 96(a) EUTMR	No	Places where EUTM has taken effect	Offline: Yes Online: No	Joint adjudication Art. 96(a) and (d) EUTMR	N/A	Limited Art. 98(2) EUTMR	

	GENERAL			JUSTIFICATION	SCOPE				IMPACT					CONCLUSION
											If invalidity is raised			
	Version	*Forum delicti* rule	Wording	Ratio legis	Requirement	Infringement actions	Threatened infringement actions	Non-infringement actions	Places to sue	Connecting factors	In infringement actions	In non-infringement actions	Extent of jurisdiction	Advantages for the plaintiff
Designs	National designs	Art. 7(2) BR	What applies to national trademarks applies *mutatis mutandis* to national designs											*Ibid.*
	Community Design (CD)	Art. 82(5) CDR	'Infringement has been committed or threatened'	Proximity	• Whatever the domicile of the defendant • Infringement must have been committed in the EU	Yes	Yes But require that national law so permits cf. art. 81(a) CDR	No	Places where CD has taken effect	Offline: Yes Online: No	Joint adjudication Art. 81(a) and (d) CDR	N/A	Limited Art. 83(2) CDR	
Plant Varieties	National plant varieties	Art. 7(2) BR	What applies to national trademarks applies *mutatis mutandis* to national plant varieties (Except from its unregistered version which does not exist for plant varieties)											Art. 7(2) BR is advantageous → To the plaintiff acting as the rightholder since threatened infringement actions can be brought (8)
	Community Plant Variety (CPV)	Art. 101(3) CPVR	'Harmful event occurred'	Proximity	• Whatever the domicile of the defendant • Harmful event must have occurred in the EU	Yes	No	Yes	Places where CPV has taken effect	Offline: Yes Online: No	Split/joint adjudication Art. 20 CPVR		Limited Art. 101(3) CPVR	
Patents	National patents	Art. 7(2) BR	What applies to national trademarks applies *mutatis mutandis* to national patents (Except from its unregistered version which does not exist for patents)											Art. 7(2) BR is advantageous → To the plaintiff acting as the infringer since non-infringement actions can always be brought (1)
	Unitary Patent (UP)	Art. 33(1)(a) AUPC	'Actual or threatened infringement has occurred or may occur'	Proximity	• Whatever the domicile of the defendant • Infringement must have occurred in a CMS	Yes	Yes	Yes	Places where UP has taken effect	Offline: Yes Online: No	• Joint adjudication Art. 33(3) and (c) AUPC • Split adjudication Art. 33(3)(b) AUPC		Unlimited Art. 34 AUPC	

10

CENTRAL DIVISION RULE

A. INTRODUCTION

10.01 From Chapter 1[1] it follows that the nature of the international jurisdiction rules available to the plaintiff must be identified. The purpose of Chapter 10 is to meet any such objective for the central division rule.[2] Thus, the various versions of the rule, if any, are addressed and compared at the present stage, which leads to identify the advantages for the plaintiff.[3]

10.02 A distinction is drawn between the central division rule, if any, applying to a national IP right (section B) and the central division rule applying to a corresponding European unitary IP right (section C). In the end a conclusion is drawn, inter alia, by Table 10.1 (section D).

B. THE CENTRAL DIVISION RULE APPLYING TO A NATIONAL IP RIGHT

10.03 No central division rule applies to a national IP right. The reasons are that no such rule is found in the BR (applicable to defendants domiciled in EU/EFTA) and that the conditions under which any such rule may apply in the Member States' own international forum rules (applicable to defendants domiciled outside EU/EFTA) for the reasons in Chapter 1 section A.5(a) (limit 5) have not been examined.

1 Section A.3(a).

2 The central division rule is one of the jurisdiction rules covered by the present study cf. Chapter 1 section A.3(c).

3 The factors defining the advantages for the plaintiff are overall identified in Chapter 1 section A.4.

C. THE CENTRAL DIVISION RULE APPLYING TO A EUROPEAN UNITARY IP RIGHT

10.04 No central division rule applies to the EUTM,[4] CD[5] or to the CPV.[6] A central division rule only applies to the UP. The rule comes into play in infringement actions,[7] in non-infringement actions[8] and in invalidity actions.[9]

10.05 As regards infringement actions the central division rule comes into play in three situations. *First*, action shall, if not at *forum delicti*, be brought at the central division if the defendant has his/her residence, principal place of business or, failing either one, place of business outside a Contracting Member State.[10] *Secondly*, action shall be brought at the central division if the Contracting Member State where the infringement action is brought does not host a local or participate in a regional division[11] and *thirdly*, action shall, at the request of the defendant, be brought at the central division in cases of multistate infringement defined as the territories of three or more regional divisions.[12]

10.06 As regards non-infringement actions the central division rule comes into play if an infringement action relating to the same patent is not already pending between the same parties.[13]

10.07 As regards invalidity actions the central division rule comes into play if the local or regional division decides to bifurcate and refer the invalidity claim to any such place[14] or if the parties agree to refer the whole case to any such place.[15]

10.08 If the central division rule applies action must be brought in either Paris (in cases concerning, inter alia, chemical patents), London (in cases concerning, inter alia, physical and electronical patents) or in Munich (in cases concerning, inter alia, mechanical patents).[16] The central division rule is subject to

4 Chapter 3 section C.1.
5 Chapter 3 section C.2.
6 Chapter 3 section C.3.
7 Art. 32(1)(a) AUPC.
8 Art. 32(1)(b) AUPC.
9 Art. 32(1)(e) AUPC.
10 Art. 33(1) (fourth sentence) AUPC.
11 Art. 33(1) (last sentence) AUPC.
12 Art. 33(2) (second sentence) AUPC.
13 Art. 33(4) AUPC.
14 Art. 33(3)(b) AUPC.
15 Art. 33(3)(c) AUPC.
16 Annex II AUPC.

unlimited full jurisdiction,[17] which for the reasons in Chapter 5 section C.4(a) can likely not be restricted.

10.09 The justification for the central division rule is unspoken in the drafting history[18] but may – despite being a forum, which one could argue lacks proximity with France, UK or Germany because neither party may have residence, principal place of business or place of business there or because the patent infringement may have taken place outside France, UK or Germany – be fivefold, namely *that* any such rule is predictable for the parties;[19] *that* requiring non-infringement actions to be brought at the central division limits the risk of 'torpedos';[20] *that* the central divisions 'rank higher' than the local and regional divisions;[21] *that* the central divisions act as 'fall back' to the local and regional divisions;[22] and *that* the central divisions are more specialized than the local and regional divisions.[23]

D. CONCLUSION

10.10 A central division rule comes into play for patents. The rule is found in art. 33 AUPC and possibly in the Member States' own international forum rules, which have not been examined. The similarities and differences between the AUPC and the BR is therefore not addressed. By contrast the effect can be addressed of a central division rule being found in the AUPC and not in the BR, which leads to identify the advantages for the plaintiff.

10.11 If the case is concerned with multistate infringement the regional division shall refer the case to the central division if the defendant so requests whereas under the BR any such change of forum rules does not exist taking into

---

17 Art. 34 AUPC.

18 Chapter 2 notes 248–9.

19 Supporting any such argument speaks that the action shall be brought at the central division in the situations covered by arts 33(1)(last sentence) and 33(4) AUPC.

20 Chapter 1 section A.5(a) (limit 7).

21 Supporting any such argument it is argued that the central divisions are competent in cases concerning multistate infringement cf. art. 33(2) (second sentence) AUPC.

22 Supporting any such argument it is argued that the central divisions come into play if a Contracting Member State does not host a local division or does not participate in a regional division cf. art. 33(1) (last sentence) AUPC.

23 Supporting any such argument it is argued that the central division in Paris (seat) deals with chemical patents, the central division in London (section) deals with physical and electronical patents and the central division in Munich (section) deals with mechanical patents cf. Annex II AUPC whereas the local and regional divisions deal with both chemical, physical, electronical and mechanical patents.

account, inter alia, that a court may not decline jurisdiction of its own discretion (*forum non-conveniens*).[24] The results therefore differ.

If no infringement action regarding the same patent is pending between the same parties the plaintiff must bring the non-infringement action before the central division whereas under the BR any such restriction in available fora does not exist.[25] The results therefore differ. **10.12**

If invalidity is raised the whole case may be referred to the central division, which in turn leads to joint adjudication whereas under the BR invalidity must be addressed by the Member State where the patent is registered following *Gat LuK*,[26] which in turn leads to split adjudication. The results therefore differ. **10.13**

In sum – and generally speaking – the BR is advantageous to the plaintiff acting as the infringer since more fora are available for the purpose of bringing non-infringement actions and since adjudication is split. The AUPC is advantageous to the plaintiff acting as the infringer since he/she may force the rightholder to change forum and is advantageous to the plaintiff acting as the rightholder since adjudication may be joint. **10.14**

Overall, the above similarities and differences as well as the advantages for the plaintiff can be illustrated as in Table 10.1 below. As stated in Chapter 3 section D the numbers in brackets refers to the factor identified as an advantage for the plaintiff in Chapter 1 section A.4. **10.15**

24 Case C-281/02, *Andrew Owusu v N.B. Jackson, trading as 'Villa Holidays Bal-Inn Villas' and Others*, paras 37–43 cf. Annette Kur and Thomas Dreier, European Intellectual Property Law, Text, Cases and Materials, Edward Elgar, 2013, pp. 488 *et seq.*

25 Non-infringement actions may be brought at a number of fora under the BR, inter alia, under art. 7(2) BR cf. case C-133/11, *Folien Fischer AG, Fofitec AG v Ritrama SpA*, para. 56 cf. Chapter 9 section B.1(b).

26 Art. 24(4) BR cf. case C-4/03, *Gesellschaft für Antriebstechnik mbH & Co. KG v Lamellen und Kupplungsbau Beteiligungs KG*, para. 32 and Chapter 11 section B.

Table 10.1 Central division rule overview

	GENERAL			JUSTIFICATION	SCOPE				IMPACT			CONCLUSION
	Version	Central division rule	Wording	Ratio legis	Requirements	Infringement actions	Threatened infringement actions	Non-infringement actions	Places to sue	If invalidity is raised	Extent of jurisdiction	Advantages for the plaintiff
Trade Marks	National trademarks				N/A							
	European Union Trademark (EUTM)											
Designs	National designs				N/A							
	Community Design (CD)											
Plant Varieties	National plant varieties				N/A							
	Community Plant Variety (CPV)											

	GENERAL			JUSTIFICATION	SCOPE				IMPACT			CONCLUSION
	Version	Central division rule	Wording	Ratio legis	Requirements	Infringement actions	Threatened infringement actions	Non-infringement actions	Places to sue	If invalidity is raised	Extent of jurisdiction	Advantages for the plaintiff
Patents	National patents	N/A										The BR is advantageous → To the plaintiff acting as the infringer since more fora are available (2) → To the plaintiff acting as the infringer since adjudication is split (6–7) The UP is advantageous → To the plaintiff acting as the infringer since he/she may force the plaintiff to change forum (5) → To the plaintiff acting as the rightholder since adjudication may be joint (6–7)
	Unitary Patent (UP)	Art. 33(1)(fourth sentence) AUPC	"Actions against defendants having their residence, or principal place of business or, in the absence [of such], their place of business outside [a CMS] shall be brought [inter alia] before the central division"	• Central division rule is predictable	The defendant: • Must not have a residence in a CMS • Must not have a principal place of business in a CMS, and • Must not have a place of business in a CMS	N/A			Paris London Munich (Depending on subject matter)	N/A	Unlimited Art. 34 AUPC	
		Art. 33(1)(last sentence) AUPC	"If a [CMS] does not host a local division and does not participate in a regional division actions shall be brought before the central division"	• Central division rule is predictable • Central division acts as 'fall back'	The CMS: • Must not host a local division, and • Must not participate in a regional division							
		Art. 33(2)(second sentence) AUPC	"[If an infringement or a threatened infringement action] is pending before a regional division and the infringement has occurred in the territories of three or more regional divisions, the regional division concerned shall, at the request of the defendant, refer the case to the central division"	• Central division 'ranks' higher • Central division is more specialized	Infringement or threatened infringement actions must be referred to the central division if: • The case is pending at a regional division, • The infringement has occurred in the territories of three or more regional divisions, and • The defendant requests for a referral							
		Art. 33(3)(b) AUPC	"[The local or regional division may] refer the counterclaim for revocation to the central division […]"	• Central division is more specialized	Invalidity can be referred to the central division if: • The parties are heard							
		Art. 33(3)(c) AUPC	"[The local or regional division may] with the agreement of the parties […] refer the case for decision to the central division"	• Central division is more specialized	Infringement and invalidity can be referred to the central division if: • The parties are heard, and • The parties agree							
		Art. 33(4) AUPC	"[Non-infringement actions] shall be brought before the central division […]"	• Central division rule limits the risk of 'torpedos'	An infringement or a threatened infringement action between the same parties relating to the same patent: • Must not be pending at a local or regional division							

11

EXCLUSIVE JURISDICTION RULE

A. INTRODUCTION

11.01 From Chapter 1[1] it follows that the nature of the international jurisdiction rules available to the plaintiff must be identified. The purpose of Chapter 11 is to meet any such objective for the exclusive jurisdiction rule which is concerned with 'who decides invalidity' if any such is raised in an infringement action or in a non-infringement action.[2] Thus, the various versions of the rule

1 Section A.3(c).

2 The exclusive jurisdiction rules have distinct characters due to the degree of exclusivity. Some – art. 24(4) BR – is exclusive in the sense that it prevents courts other than the ones in the Member State where the IP right is registered to address invalidity of a national registered IP right regardless of whether any such is raised in an infringement action or in a non-infringement action cf. sections B.1 and B.2. Some – arts 96(d) EUTMR and 81(d) CDR – are exclusive on the merits in the sense that they prevent courts other than EUTM and CD courts to address invalidity of a EUTM and a CD if any such is raised in an infringement action pending in the EU cf. sections C.1(a) and C.2(a). Some – arts 99(2) cf. 56 EUTMR and arts 84(4) cf. 52 CDR – are exclusive in the sense that they prevent other than the EUIPO to address invalidity of a EUTM and a registered CD if any such is raised in a non-infringement action pending in the EU cf. sections C.1(b) and C.2(b). Some – art. 20 CPVR – is exclusive in the sense that it prevents other than the CPVO to address invalidity of a CPV if any such is raised in an infringement action or in a non-infringement action pending in the EU cf. section C.3. Some – art. 33(3) AUPC – is exclusive in the sense that it prevents other than the

are addressed and compared at the present stage, which leads to identify the advantages for the plaintiff.[3]

A distinction is drawn between the exclusive jurisdiction rule applying to a national IP right (section B) and the exclusive jurisdiction rule applying to a corresponding European unitary IP right (section C). In the end a conclusion is drawn, inter alia, by way of Table 11.1 (section D). **11.02**

B. THE EXCLUSIVE JURISDICTION RULE APPLYING TO A NATIONAL IP RIGHT

One exclusive jurisdiction rule applies to a national IP right. The rule applies whatever the domicile of the defendant.[4] For the purpose of the present chapter, therefore, no distinction is drawn between defendants domiciled in the EU, in the EFTA and outside the EU/EFTA. Rather a distinction is drawn between whether invalidity is raised in an infringement action (section 1) or in a non-infringement action (section 2).[5] **11.03**

1. Invalidity is raised in an infringement action

Invalidity can be raised in an infringement action. In that case art. 24(4) BR comes into play. Art. 24(4) BR in which *Gat LuK* has been codified[6] states that: **11.04**

court where the UP infringement action is pending or the central division to address invalidity in a Contracting Member State cf. section C.4(a). Finally some – art. 33(4) AUPC – is exclusive in the sense that it prevents other than the central division to address invalidity if any such is raised in a non-infringement action in a Contracting Member State cf. section C.4(b). Despite the distinct characters of the exclusive jurisdiction rules cf. similarly Benedetta Ubertazzi, *Exclusive Jurisdiction in Intellectual Property*, Max Planck Institut für Ausländisches und Internationales Privatrecht, Mohr Siebeck, 2012, the rules are all addressed in the present chapter.

3 Joint adjudication is an advantage for the plaintiff acting as the rightholder whereas split adjudication is an advantage for the plaintiff acting as the infringer cf. Chapter 1 section A.4 (factors 6–7).

4 Art. 24(4) BR speaks of 'regardless of domicile' cf. Report on the Convention on Jurisdiction and the Enforcement of Judgments in Civil and Commercial Matters, signed at Brussels 27 September 1968, by P. Jenard, Director in the Belgium Ministry of Foreign Affairs and External Trade, p. 34 and Report on the Convention on Jurisdiction and the Recognition and Enforcement of Judgments in Civil and Commercial Matters, signed in Lugano on 30 October 2007 by Professor Fausto Pocar, p. 23 (at 91).

5 The reason for the distinction in sections B.1 and B.2 is not that invalidity raised in an infringement action and in a non-infringement action are subject to different rules but rather to follow the structure from section C.

6 Case C-4/03, *Gesellschaft für Antriebstechnik mbH & Co. KG v Lamellen und Kupplungsbau Beteiligungs KG (Gat LuK)*; cf. case C-230/15, *Brite Strike Technologies Inc. v Brite Strike Technologies SA*; and case C-433/16, *Bayerische Motoren Werke AG v Acacia S.r.l.* (pending).

> in proceedings concerned with the registration or validity of patents, trademarks, designs, or other similar rights required to be deposited or registered, irrespective of whether the issue is raised by way of an action or as a defence, the courts of the Member State in which the deposit or registration has been applied for, has taken place or is under the terms of an instrument of the Union or an international convention deemed to have taken place [have exclusive jurisdiction].[7]

11.05 It follows that art. 24(4) BR applies to validity of IP rights registered in a Member State (inter alia trademarks, designs, plant varieties[8] and patents) meaning that validity of IP rights not registered in a Member State (inter alia unregistered trademarks and designs) remain unaffected by the rule.[9] The term 'instrument of the Union'[10] does not refer to the EUTMR, CDR and CPVR given that they have their own exclusive jurisdiction rules,[11] which for the reasons in Chapters 2 and 3 apply. The justification for art. 24(4) BR is that validity of registered IP rights involve an 'exercise of national sovereignty'.[12] The rule must, as an exception to the defendant's domicile rule,[13] be interpreted narrowly.[14] Art. 24(4) BR courts may not address invalidity of IP rights registered in other Member States. The courts are therefore subject to limited forum jurisdiction.

11.06 Art. 24(4) BR was interpreted in *Gat LuK*.[15] Prior to *Gat LuK* the EU was split in two when it came to apply art. 24(4) BR. One view was that the court

7 Art. 24(4) BR.

8 Report by P. Jenard, *supra* note 4, p. 36 and Ulrich Magnus and Peter Mankowski, *Brussels I Regulation*, European Commentaries on Private International Law, 2nd revised edn, 2012, p. 432.

9 *Lucasfilm Ltd. v Ainsworth*, United Kingdom Supreme Court, 2011 UKSC 39; Annette Kur and Thomas Dreier, *European Intellectual Property Law, Text, Cases and Materials*, Edward Elgar Publishing, 2013, p. 505; James J. Fawcett and Paul Torremans, *Intellectual Property and Private International Law*, 2nd edn, Oxford Private International Law Series, 2011 at 7.222 *et seq.* and Magnus and Mankowski, *supra* note 8, p. 433.

10 Art. 24(4) BR.

11 Case C-230/15, *Brite Strike Technologies*, para. 62 and section C.

12 Case C-412/98, *Group Josi Reinsurance Company SA v Universal General Insurance Company (UGIC)*, para. 46; case C-4/03, *Gat LuK*, paras 22–23; *Lucasfilm Ltd.* at 86; Report by P. Jenard, *supra* note 4, p. 36; Annette Kur, 'Are There Any Common Principles of Private International Law with Regard to Intellectual Property' in Stefan Leible and Ansgar Ohly (eds) *Intellectual Property and Private International Law*, Mohr Siebeck, 2009, p. 8; Ubertazzi, *supra* note 2, p. 46; Magnus and Mankowski *supra* note 8, p. 415 and *Conflict of Laws in Intellectual Property, The CLIP Principles and Commentary*, European Max Planck Group on Conflicts of Laws in Intellectual Property, Oxford University Press, 2013, pp. 138–9 (2:401.C04).

13 Art. 4 BR and Chapter 5 section B.1.

14 Case 73/77, *Sanders v Ronald van der Putte*, paras 17–18; case 288/82, *Ferdinand M.J.J. Duijnstee v Lodewijk Goderbauer*, para. 23; case C-8/98, *Dansommer A/S v Andreas Götz*, para. 21; case C-343/04, *Land Oberösterreich v ČEZ as*, para. 26; case C-144/10, *Berliner Verkehrsbetriebe (BVG) v JP Morgan Chase Bank NA, Frankfurt Branch*, para. 30; Report by P. Jenard, *supra* note 4, p. 34; Annette Kur, 'A Farewell to Cross-Border Injunctions?' (2006) *International Review of Intellectual Property and Competition Law* 849–50; Kur and Dreier, *supra* note 9, p. 501; Magnus and Mankowski, *supra* note 8, pp. 417–18; Fawcett and Torremans, *supra* note 9 at 7.30 and *Conflict of Laws in Intellectual Property, The CLIP Principles and Commentary*, *supra* note 12, p. 147 (2:401.N07).

15 Case C-4/03, *Gat LuK*.

should dismiss both infringement and validity once invalidity of a foreign registered IP right was raised[16] (being the approach in the UK,[17] Italy[18] and Belgium[19]) and another view was that the court could address both infringement and invalidity provided that the latter was raised merely as a defence[20] also known as invalidity incidentally raised[21] (being the approach in the Netherlands[22] and in Germany[23]). Presented with *Gat LuK* the CJEU stated that art. 24(4) BR 'concerns all proceedings relating to the registration of validity of a patent, irrespective of whether the issue is raised by way of an action or a plea in objection'.[24]

The effect of *Gat LuK* is that invalidity of patents and other registered IP rights,[25] even if incidentally raised, must be addressed by the courts of the Member State where the IP right is registered.[26] **11.07**

16 Ubertazzi, *supra* note 2, p. 79; Fawcett and Torremans, *supra* note 9 at 7.23–7.25 and Kur and Dreier, *supra* note 9, p. 501.

17 *Coin Controls Ltd. v Suzo International (UK) Ltd. and Others*, 1999 Ch. 33; *Fort Dodge Animal Health Ltd. and Others v Akzo Nobel NV and Another*, 1998, FSR 222 *and Prudential Assurance Co Ltd. v Prudential Insurance Co of America*, 2003, EWCA Civ 327, 2003, 1 WLR 2295.

18 *JA Motte v Tecno SpA*, Rivista di Dritto Internazionale Privato e Processuale 1981, p. 913, D Series I-16.4-B3. Some Italian courts have taken a different view see Ubertazzi, *supra* note 2, p. 78 note 124 with references.

19 Rechtsbank van eerste aanlag te Brussel, GRUR Int. 2001, 170, 171-Röhm Enzyme.

20 Ubertazzi, *supra* note 2, p. 78; Fawcett and Torremans, *supra* note 9 at 7.26 and Kur and Dreier, *supra* note 9, p. 501.

21 Ubertazzi, ibid.

22 *Lincoln v Interlas* (1) BIE 1991, 23; *De Boer Staalinrichtingen v Cewaco*, 28 August 1990, BIE 1992, 78; *Philips v Hermogram*, 30 December 1991, 30 December 1991, BIE 1992, 80; *Pipe Liners v Wavin*, 16 January 1992, BIE 1993, 9; *Vredo v Veenhuis*, 15 April 1992, BIE 1994, 77; *Wiener v Llovera*, 30 November 1993, BIE 1995, 2; *De Groot v Euro Agra*, Aqual Tigra, 12 December 1993; *Applied Research Systems v Organon*, 3 February 1994 (IER 1994, 8); *Chiron v Organon Teknika-UBI*, 22 July 1994 (IER 1994, 24); *Chiron v Organon Teknika-UBI*, 1 December 1994 (IER 1995, 15); *Cordis v Schneider*, 22 December 1994 (IER 1995, 6); *British Telecommunication v Plumetazz*, 31 March 1994 (docket no 94/1044); *Brard v ACS*, 26 January 1995 (docket no 95/87); *Chiron v Murex*, 8 May 1995 (docket no K695/303) and 7 December 1995 (BIE 1998, 879) and 12 December 1996 (BIE 1997, 319); *Hoffmann La Roche v Organon Teknika*, 14 December 1995 (IER 1996, 16); *Raychem Corp. v Thermon*, 22 May 1995 (IER 95, 3) and *Expandable Grafts Partnership v Boston Scientific*, 23 April 1998 in FSR 1999, 352.

23 *Detergent for Plastic Production Machines*, District Court Düsseldorf, 1996, 1, 3, 5 and *Gesellschaft für Antriebstechnik mbH & Co. KG v Lamellen und Kupplungsbau Beteiligungs KG*, District Court Düsseldorf, case 4 0 128/00, 2003 IL Pr 5.

24 Case C-4/03, *Gat LuK*, para. 32.

25 Paul Torremans, 'The Way Forward for Cross-Border Intellectual Property Litigation: Why GAT cannot be the Answer' in Stefan Leible and Ansgar Ohly (eds) *Intellectual Property and Private International Law*, Mohr Siebeck, 2009, p. 206.

26 Case C-230/15, *Brite Strike Technologies Inc.*, para. 61; Fawcett and Torremans, *supra* note 9 at 7.28; *Conflict of Laws in Intellectual Property, The CLIP Principles and Commentary*, *supra* note 12, p. 146 (2:401.N05) and Ubertazzi, *supra* note 2, p. 79.

11.08 *Gat LuK* has been heavily criticized by legal scholars.[27] The points of critique have been, inter alia, *that* the decision goes against the narrow wording of art. 24(4) BR which in the respective German, French, Dutch and Italian versions speak of 'proceedings which have as their object'; *that* the decision goes against the narrow interpretation of art. 24(4) BR;[28] *that* the decision may lead to diverging decisions since invalidity must be addressed on a Member State-by-Member State basis; *that* the decision may lead to more forum shopping since the defendant may raise invalidity where the chances for success are bigger; *that* the decision goes against the principle of *perpetuatio fori* whereas validly established jurisdiction does not shift due to subsequent events[29] and *that* the decision often leads to split adjudication of national registered IP rights by contrast to national unregistered IP rights which remain unaffected by *Gat LuK* and where therefore infringement and invalidity can be adjudicated jointly.[30]

11.09 In the aftermath of *Gat LuK* a relevant question is how an infringement court must react when invalidity is raised during the proceedings. *Gat LuK* itself does not provide any guidance.[31]

11.10 One option is that the infringement court must decline infringement jurisdiction over foreign registered IP rights due to the risk that invalidity is later raised, which renders another court exclusively competent.[32] Any such option, which in line with pre-*Gat LuK* case law has been applied by courts in the

27 Kur, *supra* note 14, pp. 844 *et seq.*; Kur and Dreier, *supra* note 9, p. 503; Torremans, *supra* note 25, p. 191; Paul Torremans, 'The Widening Reach of Exclusive Jurisdiction: Where Can You Litigate After GAT?' in Arnaud Nuyts (ed.) *International Litigation in Intellectual Property and Information Technology*, Kluwer Law International, 2008, p. 61; Paul Torremans, 'Consolidation of Intellectual Property Litigation' in *Europe in Essays in Honour of MP Stathopoulos*, 2010, p. 2985; CLIP, 'Exclusive Jurisdiction and Cross-Border IP (Patent) Infringement – Suggestions for Amendment of the Brussels I Regulation' (2007) EIPR 194; Christian Heinze and Esther Roffael, 'Internationale Zuständigkeit für Entscheidungen über die Gültigkeit Ausländischer Immaterialgüterrechte, GRUR Int., 787, 2006; Klaus Grabinski, 'Cross-Border Injunctions in Patent Litigations Following ECJ Decision in GAT v LUK – Life After Death?' in W Prinz zu Waldeck und Pyrmont, MJ Adelman, R Brauneis, J Drexl and R Nack (eds), *Patents and Technological Progress in a Globalized World: Liber Amicorum*, Joseph Strauss, vol 6, 2009 and *Conflict of Laws in Intellectual Property, The CLIP Principles and Commentary*, *supra* note 12, p. 149 (2:401.N10).

28 *Supra* note 14.

29 *Infra* note 38.

30 *Supra* note 9 and Chapter 3 section B.1.

31 Magnus and Mankowski, *supra* note 8, p. 432.

32 Kur and Dreier, European *supra* note 9, p. 503 and Ubertazzi, *supra* note 2, p. 81.

UK[33] and in Italy,[34] seems unlikely due to the principle of *forum non-conveniens*[35] and since art. 24(4) BR does not deal with infringement.[36]

A second option is that the infringement court is competent until invalidity is raised after which the court looses its competence.[37] Any such option also seems unlikely due to the principle of *perpetuatio fori*.[38] **11.11**

A third option is to allow the infringement court to stay the proceedings until the defendant, within a time limit, has brought the argument before the competent court and that court has decided invalidity. If the defendant fails to bring invalidity the registered IP right is recognized as valid. Any such option, which has been applied by Swiss courts[39] and with a slight variation by Dutch courts,[40] seems the likely one[41] now that the CJEU has not ruled on the issue.[42] **11.12**

---

33 *Sandisk Corp v Koninklijke Philips Electronics NV*, 2007, EWHC 332 (Ch), 2007 IL Pr 22; *Knorr-Bremse Systems for Commercial Vehicles Ltd. v Haldex Brake Products GmbH*, 2008 EWHC 156 (Pat), 2008 IL Pr 26; *Lucasfilm Ltd. v Ainsworth*, Court of Appeal, 2009, EWCA Civ 1328, 2010 FSR 10 and *Berliner Verkehrsbetriebe (BVG) Anstalt Des Offentlichen Rechts v JP Morgan Chase Bank NA*, 2010 EWCA Civ 390 cf. Fawcett and Torremans, *supra* note 9 at 7.102 *et seq.*

34 Tribunale Torino 10.03.2009 in RDIPP, 2010, p. 496 and in GADI, 2009, n. 5407 p. 741; Tribunale Venezia 16.04.2011, unpublished and Tribunale Milano 60696/07, 29.11.2007 cf. Ubertazzi, *supra* note 2, p. 82.

35 *Case C-281/02, Andrew Owusu v N.B. Jackson, trading as 'Villa Holidays Bal-Inn Villas' and Others*, paras. 37–43 cf. Kur and Dreier, *supra* note 9, p. 503 cf. 488.

36 Ubertazzi, ibid., p. 82; Fawcett and Torremans, *supra* note 9 at 7.82–7.89 and Heinze and Roffael, *supra* note 27 at 790.

37 Kur and Thomas, *supra* note 9, p. 503.

38 Ibid; see also Kropholler, Europäisches Zivilprocessrecht, 7th edn, 2002, para. 14 concerning art. 4 BR; Schlosser, EU-Zivilprocessrecht, 2nd edn, 2003, para. 7 concerning art. 7 BR; case C-111/01, *Gantner Electronic v Basch Exploitatie Maatschappij*, para. 26 and case C-39/02, *Maersk Olie & Gas A/S v Firma M de Haan en W. De Boer*, para. 36 (where in both cases the CJEU stated that only the plaintiff's claims and not the defendants counterclaims or defences are relevant when deciding whether the same action is pending before another court within the meaning of the *lis pendens* rule in art. 29 BR) and *Mary Adamson Lorimer Stewart and Others v Trafalgar House Steamship Co. Ltd.*, Outer House, Court of Session, 2013 CSOH 37, paras 16–19 with references.

39 Handelsgericht Zurich, judgment of 23 October 2006, HG 05410, *Eurojobs Personaldienstleistungen SA v Eurojob AG* [sic!] 2006, 854 confirmed by the Swiss Federal Court, judgment of 4 April 2007, I. Zivilabteilung 4C.439/2006 and Handelsgericht Zurich, decision of 16 October 2006 referred in GRUR int. 2007 pp. 258 *et seq.*

40 Dutch Supreme Court, Roche, 2008, IER 37 where the defendant was not given a time limit within which to raise invalidity before the competent court.

41 *Conflict of Laws in Intellectual Property, The CLIP Principles and Commentary*, *supra* note 12, p. 148 (2:401.N09) and Ubertazzi, *supra* note 2, pp. 82 *et seq.* with references.

42 The CJEU was presented with the question how an infringement court must react when invalidity is raised in case C-616/10, *Solvay v Honeywell*. The question remained unanswered given that art. 24(4) BR was found inapplicable in the specific case.

2. Invalidity is raised in a non-infringement action

11.13 Invalidity can be raised in a non-infringement action. In that case art. 24(4) BR also comes into play.[43] Section B.1 applies *mutatis mutandis.*

C. THE EXCLUSIVE JURISDICTION RULE APPLYING TO A EUROPEAN UNITARY IP RIGHT

11.14 Four different exclusive jurisdiction rules apply depending on the corresponding European unitary IP right in question. If invalidity of a EUTM is raised the exclusive jurisdiction rules in the EUTMR apply (section 1); if invalidity of a CD is raised the exclusive jurisdiction rules in the CDR apply (section 2); if invalidity of a CPV is raised the exclusive jurisdiction rule in the CPVR applies (section 3) and if invalidity of a UP is raised the exclusive jurisdiction rules in the AUPC apply (section 4).

1. The exclusive jurisdiction rule in the EUTMR

11.15 Different exclusive jurisdiction rules, neither of which have been interpreted by the CJEU[44] with no cases pending,[45] apply depending on whether invalidity is raised in an infringement action (section a) or in a non-infringement action (section b).[46]

(a) Invalidity is raised in an infringement action

11.16 Invalidity of an EUTM can be raised in an infringement action[47] by way of art. 96(d) EUTMR.[48] The rule, which applies whatever the domicile of the defendant given that it is a provision on the merits, is modelled on the corresponding provision in the 1989 Community Patent Agreement.[49] The effect of the rule is that the EUTM court where the infringement action is

43 *Conflict of Laws in Intellectual Property, The CLIP Principles and Commentary, supra* note 12, p. 176 (2:602.N04) and case C-433/16, *Bayerische Motoren Werke AG v Acacia S.r.l.* (pending).

44 Study on the Overall Functioning of the European Trade Mark System presented by Max Planck Institute for Intellectual Property and Competition Law Munich of 15 February 2011 at 3.126 (p. 156).

45 Curia.eu visited on 1 January 2017.

46 A multitude of CJEU case law, however, exists with respect to art. 56 EUTMR concerning invalidity procedures cf. Study on the Overall Functioning of the European Trade Mark System, *supra* note 44 at 4.194 (p. 195). It is outside the scope of the present study to undertake an analysis of any such case law cf. Chapter 1 section A.5(a) (limit 2).

47 Art. 96(a) EUTMR.

48 Invalidity can also be raised by way of art. 99(3) EUTMR. The differences between the two are outside the scope of the present study cf. Chapter 1 section A.5(a) (limit 4).

49 Art. 15(1)(d) Protocol on the Settlement of Litigation Concerning the Infringement and Validity of Community Patents of 30 December 1989 (Protocol of Litigation).

pending is also competent to address invalidity.[50] The justification for art. 96(d) EUTMR is procedural efficiency[51] even though this may not always correspond to the interests of the infringer.[52] Invalidity raised under art. 96(d) EUTMR is subject to the unitary character principle[53] meaning unlimited full jurisdiction.

Art. 96(d) EUTMR is both similar and different compared to art. 24(4) BR. It is similar *since* invalidity is addressed in one court, namely in the court where the trademark infringement action is pending under art. 96(d) EUTMR and in the court of the Member State where the trademark is registered under art. 24(4) BR. It is different *since* art. 96(d) EUTMR leads to joint adjudication whereas art. 24(4) BR may lead to split adjudication; *since* courts of different Member States are exclusive under art. 96(d) EUTMR[54] by contrast to art. 24(4) BR where courts of one Member State are exclusive and *since* the extent of jurisdiction is unlimited under art. 96(d) EUTMR by contrast to art. 24(4) BR where the extent of jurisdiction is limited. **11.17**

(b) Invalidity is raised in a non-infringement action

Invalidity of an EUTM cannot be raised in a non-infringement action[55] due to art. 99(2) EUTMR.[56] Also this rule is modelled on the corresponding provision in the 1989 Community Patent Agreement.[57] The effect of the rule is that the EUIPO must address invalidity,[58] which in turn leads to either split[59] or joint[60] adjudication. The justification for the rule, which applies whatever the domicile of the defendant, is according to the Explanatory **11.18**

50 Fawcett and Torremans, *supra* note 9 at 8.48.

51 Bulletin of the European Communities Supplement 5/80, New Trade Mark System for the Community, proposed Directive and Regulation prepared by the Commission of the European Communities (COM 80 635 final 19 November 1980), p. 77.

52 Chapter 1 section A.4 (factors 6–7).

53 Art. 1(2) EUTMR cf. Bulletin of the European Communities Supplement 5/80, New Trade Mark System for the Community, proposed Directive and Regulation prepared by the Commission of the European Communities (COM 80 635 final 19 November 1980), p. 77 and Fawcett and Torremans, *supra* note 9 at 8.47.

54 Ubertazzi, *supra* note 2, pp. 74 and 87.

55 Art. 96(b) EUTMR.

56 Fawcett and Torremans, *supra* note 9 at 8.47.

57 Art. 15(4) Protocol on the Settlement of Litigation Concerning the Infringement and Validity of Community Patents of 30 December 1989 (Protocol of Litigation).

58 Art. 56 EUTMR.

59 If the non-infringement action is pending outside Spain contrary to EUIPO's seat infringement and invalidity are adjudicated in different Member States, which in turn leads to split adjudication following the definition in Chapter 1 section A.4 (factor 6).

60 If the non-infringement action is pending in Spain in line with EUIPO's seat infringement and invalidity are adjudicated within the same Member State which in turn leads to joint adjudication following the definition in Chapter 1 section A.4 (factor 6).

Memorandum to 'favor th[e] central action [at the EUIPO]'.[61] Invalidity raised under art. 56 EUTMR is subject to the unitary character principle[62] meaning unlimited full jurisdiction.

2. The exclusive jurisdiction rule in the CDR

11.19 Different exclusive jurisdiction rules, neither of which have been interpreted by the CJEU[63] with no cases pending,[64] apply depending on whether invalidity is raised in an infringement action (section a) or in a non-infringement action (section b).[65]

(a) Invalidity is raised in an infringement action

11.20 Invalidity of a CD can be raised in an infringement action[66] by way of art. 81(d) CDR.[67] The effect of the rule is that the CD court where the infringement action is pending is also competent to address invalidity, which in turn leads to joint adjudication. Section C.1(a) applies *mutatis mutandis* including to the unregistered CD.[68]

(b) Invalidity is raised in a non-infringement action

11.21 Invalidity of a CD cannot be raised in a non-infringement action[69] due to art. 84(4) CDR.[70] The effect is that the EUIPO must address invalidity for the registered CD,[71] which in turn leads to either split[72] or joint[73] adjudication or

61 Proposal for a European Parliament and Council Regulation on the Community Design presented by the Commission COM (93) 342 final COD 463 Brussels, 3 December 1993, p. 39. The reasoning applies *mutatis mutandis* under the EUTMR cf. the wording '[the rules in the CDR] entirely correspond to the parallel provisions relating to the Community Trade Mark', p. 38.

62 Art. 1(2) EUTMR.

63 Curia.eu visited on 1 January 2017.

64 Ibid.

65 A multitude of CJEU case law, however, exists with respect to art. 52 CDR concerning invalidity procedures. It is outside the scope of the present study to undertake an analysis of any such case law cf. Chapter 1 section A.5(a) (limit 2).

66 Art. 81(a) EUTMR.

67 Invalidity can also be raised by way of art. 85 CDR. The differences between the two are outside the scope of the present study cf. Chapter 1 section A.5(a) (limit 4).

68 Fawcett and Torremans, *supra* note 9 at 8.116–8.118 and Ubertazzi, *supra* note 2, pp. 74 and 87.

69 Art. 81(b) CDR.

70 David Stone, *European Union Design Law, A Practitioners Guide*, Oxford University Press, 2012 at 21.26 *et seq.* with references.

71 Art. 52 CDR.

72 If the non-infringement action is pending outside Spain contrary to EUIPO's seat infringement and invalidity are adjudicated in different Member States, which in turn leads to split adjudication following the definition in Chapter 1 section A.4 (factor 6).

73 If the non-infringement action is pending in Spain in line with the EUIPO's seat infringement and invalidity are adjudicated within the same Member State which in turn leads to joint adjudication following the definition in Chapter 1 section A.4 (factor 6).

that the infringer for the unregistered CD cannot raise invalidity but must wait until an infringement action is brought against him/her in which event he/she may do so,[74] which in turn leads to joint adjudication. Section C.1(b) applies *mutatis mutandis*.

3. The exclusive jurisdiction rule in the CPVR

One exclusive jurisdiction rule, which has not been interpreted by the CJEU[75] with no cases pending,[76] applies regardless of whether invalidity is raised in an infringement action (section a) or in a non-infringement action (section b).[77] **11.22**

(a) Invalidity is raised in an infringement action

Invalidity of a CPV cannot be raised in an infringement action[78] given that the CPVR, by contrast to the EUTMR and CDR,[79] does not include any rules on counterclaims[80] but merely an obligation for the 'competent courts' to treat the CPV as valid.[81] Thus, if invalidity is raised action must be brought with the CPVO[82] due to their exclusivity to address invalidity[83] cf. the wording 'the Office shall declare'[84] which in turn leads to either split[85] or joint[86] adjudication. As stated in Chapter 3 section C.3 the decision of the CPVO can be appealed to the Board[87] and further to the CJEU.[88] The justification for art. 20 **11.23**

74 Art. 81(d) CDR and Chapter 2 section C.2.

75 Curia.eu visited on 1 January 2017.

76 Ibid.

77 The reason for the distinction in sections C.3(a) and C.3(b) is not that invalidity raised in an infringement action or in a non-infringement action are subject to different rules but rather to follow the structure from sections C.1 and C.2.

78 Art. 94 CPVR.

79 Arts 96(d) EUTMR and 81(d) CDR.

80 Fawcett and Torremans, *supra* note 9 at 8.179 and Gert Würtenberger, Paul Van Der Kooij, Bart Kiewiet and Martin Ekvad, *European Community Plant Variety Protection*, Oxford University Press, 2006 at 7.09.

81 Art. 105 CPVR.

82 Art. 20 CPVR.

83 Würtenberger et al, *supra* note 80 at 2.01 and 7.09–7.10.

84 In other language versions of art. 20 CPVR the wording 'Office shall declare' is also used i.e. 'Das Amt erklärt' (DE), 'L'Office déclare' (FR), 'Sortsmyndigheden erklærer' (DK) and 'Växtsortmyndigheten skall ogiltigförklara' (SV).

85 If the infringement action is pending outside France contrary to CPVO's seat infringement and invalidity are adjudicated in different Member States, which in turn leads to split adjudication following the definition in Chapter 1 section A.4 (factor 6).

86 If the infringement action is pending in France in line with CPVO's seat infringement and invalidity are adjudicated within the same Member State which in turn leads to joint adjudication following the definition in Chapter 1 section A.4 (factor 6).

87 Art. 67 CPVR.

88 Art. 73 CPVR.

CPVR, which applies whatever the domicile of the defendant, is not mentioned in the Explanatory Memorandum[89] but is likely to favour a central action at the CPVO considering *that* a plant variety has a high technical impact and *that* the courts dealing with a CPV are not specialized as EUTM and CD courts[90] but merely 'competent'.[91] Invalidity raised under art. 20 CPVO is subject to the unitary character principle[92] meaning unlimited full jurisdiction.

(b) Invalidity is raised in a non-infringement action

11.24 Invalidity of a CPV cannot be raised in a non-infringement action[93] but must also be brought with the CPVO.[94] Section C.3(a) applies *mutatis mutandis.*

4. The exclusive jurisdiction rule in the AUPC

11.25 Different exclusive jurisdiction rules apply depending on whether invalidity is raised in an infringement action (section a) or in a non-infringement action (section b).[95]

(a) Invalidity is raised in an infringement action

11.26 Invalidity of a UP can be raised in an infringement action[96] by way of art. 32(1)(e) AUPC. In that case art. 33(3) AUPC, which applies whatever the domicile of the defendant, comes into play. By contrast to art. 24(4) BR,[97] which is exclusive in the sense that only courts of one Member State can address invalidity, art. 33(3) AUPC is flexible[98] in the sense that courts of more Contracting Member States can address invalidity. Thus, if invalidity is raised, after having heard the parties[99] the court hearing the infringement action has three options.[100] *First*, it may decide the case meaning that the

---

89 Memorandum for a Council Regulation on Community Plant Variety Rights presented by the Commission COM(90)347 (90/C 244/01) Brussels 6 September 1990.

90 Arts 95 EUTMR and 80 CDR.

91 Art. 101(4) CPVR.

92 Art. 2 CPVR.

93 Non-infringement actions are not explicitly mentioned in Part Six CPVR. For the reasons in Chapter 3 section C.3 non-infringement actions must, however, be covered by the CPVR.

94 Art. 20 CPVR.

95 Torsten Bjørn Larsen, *Rules of Jurisdiction in the Agreement on a Unified Patent Court*, Nordisk Immateriellt Rättsskydd, 4/2014, pp. 357–74 at 373 *et seq.* and Torsten Bjørn Larsen, *A Bundle of National Patents v a European Patent with Unitary Effect – Jurisdictional Comparison, Intellectual Property and General Legal Principles – Is IP a Lex Specialis?* Edward Elgar Publishing, 2015, pp. 208 *et seq.*

96 Art. 32(1)(a) AUPC.

97 Section B.

98 Fawcett and Torremans, *supra* note 9 at 8.141.

99 Rule 37 ROP.

100 Art. 33(3) AUPC speaks of 'the local or regional division shall [...] have the discretion'.

court will address both infringement and invalidity, which in turn leads to joint adjudication.[101] *Secondly*, it may bifurcate meaning that invalidity will be referred to the central division and that infringement will be either suspended or proceeded with,[102] which in turn leads to either split[103] or joint[104] adjudication.[105] *Thirdly*, it may send the case away to the central division if the parties agree meaning that the central division will decide both infringement and invalidity, which in turn leads to joint adjudication.[106] The court shall give brief reasons for its decision.[107] The justification for the flexible exclusive jurisdiction rule is not mentioned in the drafting history[108] but is likely due to a political compromise.[109] Invalidity raised under art. 33(3) AUPC is subject to the unitary character principle[110] meaning unlimited full jurisdiction.[111]

(b) Invalidity is raised in a non-infringement action

Invalidity of a UP can also be raised in a non-infringement action.[112] In that case a distinction must be drawn between whether an infringement action between the same parties relating to the same patent is pending or not. If any such action is pending the non-infringement action must be brought at the same forum[113] with the effect that the action will be cumulated with the infringement action. If invalidity is then raised the claim becomes a counter-claim in an infringement action meaning that art. 33(3) AUPC applies cf. section C.4(a) *mutatis mutandis*. If by contrast an infringement action is not **11.27**

101 Art. 33(3)(a) AUPC cf. rule 37(3) ROP. This joint way to adjudicate a patent case is common in, inter alia, the UK and the Netherlands cf. Jan Brinkhof and Ansgar Ohly, 'Towards a Unified Patent Court in Europe' in Ansgar Ohly and Justine Pila (eds) *The Europeanization of Intellectual Property Law, Towards a European Legal Methodology*, Oxford University Press, 2013, p. 211.

102 Whether to suspend or proceed with the infringement proceedings is subject to rule 37(4) ROP whereas the court 'shall stay the infringement proceedings where there is a high likelihood that the relevant claims of the patent will be held to be invalid on any ground by the final decision in the revocation proceedings'.

103 If the infringement action is pending outside France, the UK or Germany contrary to the seats of the central divisions infringement and invalidity are adjudicated in different Contracting Member States which in turn leads to split adjudication following the definition in Chapter 1 section A.4 (factor 6).

104 If the infringement action is pending in either France, the UK or Germany in line with the seats of the central divisions infringement and invalidity are adjudicated within the same Contracting Member State which in turn leads to joint adjudication following the definition in Chapter 1 section A.4 (factor 6).

105 Art. 33(3)(b) AUPC cf. rules 38–40 ROP. This bifurcated way to adjudicate a patent case is common in, inter alia, Germany and Austria cf. Brinkhof and Ohly, *supra* note 101, p. 211.

106 Art. 33(3)(c) AUPC cf. rule 41 ROP. The rule, however, requires a complete forum shift, which is not attractive cf. Fawcett and Torremans, *supra* note 9 at 8.141.

107 Art. 37(1) ROP.

108 Chapter 2 notes 248–9.

109 Brinkhof and Ohly, *supra* note 101, p. 211.

110 Art. 3(2) UPR

111 Art. 34 AUPC.

112 Art. 32(1)(b) AUPC.

113 Art. 33(4) (second part) AUPC.

pending the non-infringement action must be brought at the central division[114] and the central division is exclusively competent to address invalidity.[115] Invalidity is in any event subject to the unitary character principle[116] meaning unlimited full jurisdiction.[117] The justification for giving the central division exclusive jurisdiction to address invalidity if any such is raised in a non-infringement action under art. 33(4) AUPC, which applies whatever the domicile of the defendant, seems to be procedural efficiency.[118]

D. CONCLUSION

11.28 A distinction is drawn between the application of the exclusive jurisdiction rule in trademark, design, plant variety and patent cases.

11.29 In *trademark* cases the applicable exclusive jurisdiction rules are found in arts 24(4) BR, 96(d) and 99(2) cf. 56 EUTMR. The rules are both similar and different.

11.30 They are similar *since* art. 24(4) BR often leads to split adjudication if invalidity is raised in a non-infringement action in line with arts 99(2) cf. 56 EUTMR, which may also lead to split adjudication.

11.31 They are different *since* art. 24(4) BR is justified in national sovereignty whereas art. 96(a) EUTMR is justified in procedural efficiency and arts 99(2) cf. 56 EUTMR in favouring a central action at the EUIPO; *since* the extent of jurisdiction is limited under art. 24(4) BR but unlimited under arts 96(d) and 99(2) cf. 56 EUTMR and *since* art. 24(4) BR often leads to split adjudication if invalidity is raised in an infringement action by contrast to art. 96(d) EUTMR, which leads to joint adjudication.

11.32 In sum – and generally speaking – art. 24(4) BR is advantageous to the plaintiff acting as the infringer since adjudication is often split whereas art. 96(d) EUTMR is advantageous to the plaintiff acting as the rightholder since adjudication is joint.

11.33 In *design* cases the applicable exclusive jurisdiction rules are found in arts 24(4) BR, 81(d) and 84(4) cf. 52 CDR. The above applies *mutatis mutandis.*

---

114 Art. 33(4) (first part) AUPC.

115 Art. 33(4) AUPC cf. Fawcett and Torremans, *supra* note 9 at 8.141.

116 Art. 3(2) UPR.

117 Art. 34 AUPC.

118 Another justification for art. 33(4) AUPC is to limit the risk of 'torpedos' cf. Chapter 10 note 20.

In *plant variety* cases the applicable exclusive jurisdiction rules are found in arts 24(4) BR and 20 CPVR. The rules are both similar and different. **11.34**

They are similar *since* art. 24(4) BR often leads to split adjudication in line with art. 20 CPVR, which may also lead to split adjudication. **11.35**

They are different *since* art. 24(4) BR is justified in national sovereignty whereas art. 20 CPVR is justified in favouring a central action at the CPVO; *since* the extent of jurisdiction is limited under art. 24(4) BR but unlimited under art. 20 CPVR and *since* art. 20 CPVO may lead to joint adjudication. **11.36**

In sum – and generally speaking – art. 24(4) BR is advantageous to the plaintiff acting as the infringer since adjudication is often split whereas art. 20 CPVR is advantageous to the plaintiff acting as the rightholder since adjudication may be joint. **11.37**

In *patent* cases the applicable exclusive jurisdiction rules are found in arts 24(4) BR, 33(3) and (4) AUPC. The rules are both similar and different. **11.38**

They are similar *since* art. 24(4) BR often leads to split adjudication in line with art. 33(3) AUPC, which may also lead to split adjudication. **11.39**

They are different *since* art. 24(4) BR is justified in national sovereignty whereas art. 33(3) AUPC is a result of a political compromise; *since* the extent of jurisdiction is limited under art. 24(4) BR but unlimited under art. 33(3) and (4) AUPC and *since* art. 24(4) BR often leads to split adjudication by contrast to art. 33(3) AUPC, which may lead to joint adjudication and art. 33(4) AUPC, which leads to joint adjudication. **11.40**

In sum – and generally speaking – art. 24(4) BR is advantageous to the plaintiff acting as the infringer since adjudication is often split whereas art. 33(3) AUPC is advantageous to the plaintiff acting as the rightholder since adjudication may be joint. **11.41**

Overall, the above similarities and differences as well as the advantages for the plaintiff can be illustrated as in Table 11.1 below. As stated in Chapter 3 section D the numbers in brackets refers to the factor identified as an advantage for the plaintiff in Chapter 1 section A.4. **11.42**

Table 11.1 Exclusive jurisdiction rule overview

	GENERAL			JUSTIFICATION	SCOPE			IMPACT			CONCLUSION
	Version	Exclusive jurisdiction rule	Wording	Ratio legis	Requirement	Invalidity is raised in an infringement action	Invalidity is raised in a non-infringement action	Who decides invalidity	Effect	Extent of jurisdiction	Advantages for the plaintiff
Trade Marks	National trademarks	Art. 24(4) BR	'The courts of the Member State in which the […] registration has been applied for [or] has taken place [have exclusive jurisdiction]'	National sovereignty	Whatever the domicile of the defendant	Yes	Yes	Courts of the Member State where the trademark is registered	Split/joint adjudication	Limited (Art. 24.4 BR)	Art. 24(4) BR is advantageous → To the plaintiff acting as the infringer since adjudication can be split (6–7) Art. 96(d) EUTMR is advantageous → To the plaintiff acting as the rightholder since adjudication is joint (6)
	European Union Trademark (EUTM)	Art. 96(d) EUTMR	'The [EUTM] courts shall have exclusive jurisdiction […] for counterclaims for revocation or for a declaration of invalidity'	Procedural efficiency	Whatever the domicile of the defendant	Yes	No	Court where the EUTM infringement action is pending	Joint adjudication	Unlimited (Art. 1.2 EUTMR)	
		Arts 99(2) cf. 56 EUTMR	'The validity of a [EUTM] may not be put in issue in an action for a declaration of non-infringement' cf. 'An application […] that the trade mark is invalid may be submitted to [EUIPO]'	Favor central action at the EUIPO	Whatever the domicile of the defendant	No	Yes	EUIPO	Split/joint adjudication	Unlimited (Art. 1.2 EUTMR)	
Designs	National designs	Art. 24(4) BR	What applies to trademarks applies *mutatis mutandis* to designs								*Ibid.*
	Community Design (CD)	Art. 81(d) CDR									
		Arts 84(4) cf. 52 CDR									

	GENERAL			JUSTIFICATION	SCOPE			IMPACT			CONCLUSION
	Version	Exclusive jurisdiction rule	Wording	Ratio legis	Requirement	Invalidity is raised in an infringement action	Invalidity is raised in a non-infringement action	Who decides invalidity	Effect	Extent of jurisdiction	Advantages for the plaintiff
Plant Varieties	National plant varieties	Art. 24(4) BR	What applies to national trademarks applies *mutatis mutandis* to national plant varieties								Arts 24(4) BR is advantageous → To the plaintiff acting as the infringer since adjudication can be split (6–7) Art. 20 CPVR is advantageous → To the plaintiff acting as the rightholder since adjudication may be joint (6–7)
	Community Plant Variety (CPV)	Art. 20 CPVR	'The Office shall declare the [CPV] null and void if […]'	Favor central action at the CPVO	Whatever the domicile of the defendant	Yes	Yes	CPVO	Split/joint adjudication	Unlimited (Art. 2 CPVR)	
Patents	National patents	Art. 24(4) BR	What applies to national trademarks applies *mutatis mutandis* to national patents								Art. 24(4) BR is advantageous → To the plaintiff acting as the infringer since adjudication can be split (6–7) Art. 33(3) AUPC is advantageous → To the plaintiff acting as the rightholder since adjudication may be joint (6)
	Unitary Patent (UP)	Art. 33(3) AUPC	'[…] The local or regional division shall […] have the discretion either to [decide the case], [bifurcate] or [send the case away to the central division]'	Political compromise	Whatever the domicile of the defendant	Yes	No	Court where the UP infringement action is pending or the central division	Split/joint adjudication	Unlimited (Arts 3.2 UPR cf. 34 AUPC)	
		Art. 33(4) AUPC	'[Non-infringement actions] and [validity actions] shall be brought before the central division'	Procedural efficiency	Whatever the domicile of the defendant	No	Yes	Central division	Joint adjudication		

Part IV

CONCLUSION

12

CONCLUSION

The purpose of the present study was to identify the jurisdictional advantages for the plaintiff to litigate based on a national IP right compared to litigating based on a corresponding European unitary IP right. To identify the jurisdictional advantages, the number and natures of the international jurisdiction rules available to the plaintiff have been addressed. 12.01

In Chapter 2 the number of the international jurisdiction rules available to the plaintiff were identified. In Chapter 1 section A.4 more jurisdiction rules were generally identified as an advantage for the plaintiff (factor 1). 12.02

From the findings in Part II (Chapters 2–3) it follows *that* a national trademark, design and plant variety right are advantageous to the plaintiff if the defendant is domiciled in the EU since more forum rules are available to him/her (factor 1) whereas an EUTM, CD and CPV are advantageous to the plaintiff if the defendant is domiciled in the EFTA since more forum rules are available to him/her (factor 1), and *that* a national patent is advantageous to the plaintiff if the defendant is domiciled in the EU/EFTA since more forum rules are available to him/her (factor 1). 12.03

In Chapter 3 the natures of the international jurisdiction rules available to the plaintiff were identified. In Chapter 1 section A.4 more available fora within one same forum rule (factor 2) was generally identified as an advantage for the plaintiff unless only the plaintiff acting as the rightholder or as the infringer benefits. A plaintiff's own domicile (factor 3) and discretion between unlimited full jurisdiction and limited forum jurisdiction (factor 4) were generally identified as advantages for the plaintiff. Change of forum principles/rules (factor 5), split adjudication (factors 6–7) and being able to bring non-infringement actions (factor 9) were specifically identified as advantages for the plaintiff acting as the infringer. Joint adjudication (factors 6–7) and being able to bring threatened infringement actions (factor 8) were specifically identified as advantages for the plaintiff acting as the rightholder. 12.04

From the findings in Part III (Chapters 5–11) it follows *that* European unitary IP right establishment rules offer more fora than national IP right establishment rules meaning that the former is advantageous to the plaintiff (factor 2); *that* non-infringement actions can be brought at more fora for a national IP 12.05

right compared to a European unitary IP right meaning that the former is advantageous to the plaintiff acting as the infringer (factor 2); *that* the UP offers a broad and unanimous definition of the defendant's domicile for physical persons by contrast to a national patent right meaning that the former is advantageous to the plaintiff acting as the rightholder (factor 2); *that* a European unitary IP right offers a plaintiff's own domicile by contrast to a national IP right meaning that the former is advantageous to the plaintiff (factor 3); *that* the UP is not subject to discretion when it comes to the extent of jurisdiction by contrast to a national patent right meaning that the latter is advantageous to the plaintiff (factor 4); *that* the UP allows for a forum change by contrast to a national patent right meaning that the former is advantageous to the plaintiff acting as the infringer (factor 5); *that* invalidity of a national registered IP right often leads to split adjudication whereas invalidity of a European unitary IP right often leads to joint adjudication meaning that the former is advantageous to the plaintiff acting as the infringer whereas the latter is advantageous to the plaintiff acting as the rightholder (factors 6–7); *that* threatened infringement actions can always be brought for a national IP right by contrast to a European unitary IP right meaning that the former is advantageous to the plaintiff acting as the rightholder (factor 8) and finally *that* non-infringement actions can always be brought for a national IP right by contrast to a European unitary IP right meaning that the former is advantageous to the plaintiff acting as the infringer (factor 9).

12.06 In sum – and generally speaking – the following conclusion can be drawn from the findings in the present study:

- A national IP right is advantageous to the plaintiff acting as the infringer since more jurisdictional advantages are available to him/her, whereas
- A European unitary IP right is advantageous to the plaintiff acting as the rightholder since more jurisdictional advantages are available to him/her.

12.07 The above findings can be illustrated as in Table 12.1 below. As in Chapters 5–11 the number in brackets refers to the factor identified in Chapter 1 section A.4.

Table 12.1 Conclusions of the study

IP right	Version	Jurisdictional advantageous to the plaintiff whether acting as rightholder/infringer:	Jurisdictional advantageous to the plaintiff acting as rightholder:	Jurisdictional advantageous to the plaintiff acting as infringer:	Conclusion
Trademarks	National trademarks	• *Since* more forum rules are available if the defendant is domiciled in EU (1)	• *Since* threatened actions can always be brought (8)	• *Since* non-infringement actions can always be brought (9) • *Since* non-infringement actions can be brought at more fora, inter alia, at *forum delicti* (2) • *Since* invalidity for registered trademarks often leads to split adjudication (6–7)	• A national trademark is advantageous to the plaintiff acting as the infringer • An EUTM is advantageous to the plaintiff acting as the rightholder
	European Union Trademark (EUTM)	• *Since* more forum rules are available if the defendant is domiciled in EFTA (1) • *Since* more fora are available under the establishment rule (2) • *Since* a plaintiff's own domicile is available if the defendant is domiciled in EFTA or outside EU/EFTA (3)	• *Since* invalidity leads to joint adjudication (6)	N/A	
Designs	National designs	*Ibid.*			• A national design is advantageous to the plaintiff acting as the infringer • A CD is advantageous to the plaintiff acting as the rightholder
	Community Design (CD)				
Plant Varieties	National plant varieties	• *Since* more forum rules are available if the defendant is domiciled in EU (1)	• *Since* threatened actions can be brought (8)	• *Since* invalidity often leads to split adjudication (6–7)	• A CPV is advantageous to the plaintiff whether acting as infringer/rightholder
	Community Plant Variety (CPV)	• *Since* more forum rules are available if the defendant is domiciled in EFTA (1) • *Since* more fora are available under the establishment rule (2) • *Since* a plaintiff's own domicile is available if the defendant is domiciled outside EU/EFTA (3)	• *Since* invalidity may lead to joint adjudication (6–7)	N/A	
Patents	National patents	• *Since* more forum rules are available if the defendant is domiciled in EU/EFTA (1) • *Since* the extent of jurisdiction is subject to discretion except under *forum delicti* (4)	N/A	• *Since* non-infringement actions can be brought at more fora, inter alia, at *forum delicti* (2) • *Since* invalidity often leads to split adjudication (6–7)	• A national patent is advantageous to the plaintiff acting as the infringer • A UP is advantageous to the plaintiff acting as the rightholder
	Unitary Patent (UP)	N/A	• *Since* natural persons are subject to a broad and unanimous definition under the defendant's domicile rule (2) • *Since* more fora are available under the establishment rule (2) • *Since* a plaintiff's own domicile is available (3) • *Since* invalidity may lead to joint adjudication (6)	• *Since* a change of forum rule applies (5)	

BIBLIOGRAPHY

Adolphsen, J. IPRax 15, 2007.

ALI Principles, *Intellectual Property, Principles Governing Jurisdiction, Choice of Law and Judgments in Transnational Disputes*, American Law Institute, 2008.

Andersen, N., A. Carlquist and A. Rubinstein, *Retshåndhævelse af Immaterialrettigheder*, 1st edn, Jurist- og Økonomforbundets Forlag, 2006.

Arnull, A., A. Dashwood, M. Dougan, M. Ross, E. Spaventa and D. Wyatt, *European Union Law*, 5th edn, Sweet & Maxwell, 2006.

Asensio, Pedro A. de Miquel, 'The Unified Patent Court Agreement and the Amendment to the Brussels I Regulation (Recast)', *The EU Patent Protection Lights and Shades of the New System*, a cura di Constanza Honorati G Giappichelli Editore – Torino 2014.

Asensio, Pedro A. de Miquel, 'The Private International Law of Intellectual Property and of Unfair Commercial Practises: Convergence or Divergence?' in S. Leible and A. Ohly (eds), *Intellectual Property and Private International Law*, Mohr Siebeck, 2009.

Asensio, Pedro A. de Miquel, 'Cross-Border Adjudication of Intellectual Property Rights and Competition between Jurisdictions', *Annali italiani del diritto d'autore, della cultura e dello spettacolo (AIDA)*, vol. 16, 2007.

Bariatti, S., La giurisdizione e l'esecuzione delle sentenze in material di brevetti di invenzione nell'ambito della C.E.E, RDIPP, 1982.

Basedow, J., T. Kono and A. Metzger, A, *Intellectual Property in the Global Arena: Jurisdiction, Applicable Law, and Recognition of Judgments in Europe, Japan and the US*, Mohr Siebeck, Tübingen, 2010.

Bengtsson, H., 'Jurisdiktion vid skadegörande handlingar på Internet', *Infotorg Mitt i Juridiken*, 2011.

Bergé, J., 'Le Principe de la Territorialité et la Propriété' in C. Nourissat and E. Treppoz (eds), *Droit International Privé et Propriété Intéllectuelle*, Rueil-Malmaison, 2010.

Bettinger, T. and D. Thum, 'Territorial Trademark Rights in the Global Village – International Jurisdiction Choice of Law and Substantive Law for Trademark Disputes on the Internet', (2000) *International Review of Intellectual Property and Competition Law* 162.

Bogdan, M., 'Website Accessibility as Basis for Jurisdiction Under the Brussels I Regulation in View of New Case Law of the ECJ', in Nordic Yearbook of Law and Informatics 2010–2012: Internationalization of Law in the Digital Information Society, Dan Jerker B. Svantesson and Stanley Greenstein (eds), Ex Tuto Publishing, 2013.

Bogdan, M., 'Website Accessibility as Basis for Jurisdiction under the Brussels I Regulation', (2011) 5(1) *Masaryk University Journal of Law and Technology* 1–10.

Bogdan, M., P. Lindskoug and U. Maunsbach, *Internationellt Privaträttsliga Rätsfall*, 4th edn, Juristförlaget i Lund, 2012.

Bogdan, M. and U. Maunsbach, *EU Private International Law: An ECJ Casebook*, 2nd edn, Europa Law Publishing, 2012.

Biggs, A., 'Jurisdiction over Defences and Connected Claims' (2006) LMCLQ 447.

Brinkhof, J. and A. Ohly, 'Towards a Unified Patent Court in Europe', in A. Ohly and J. Pila (eds), *The Europeanization of Intellectual Property Law*, Oxford University Press, 2013.

Clark, B., 'Off piste? ECJ decides Austrian Supreme Court's "Adwords" Jurisdiction Question in Wintersteiger' (2012) 7(10) *Journal of Intellectual Property Law and Practice* 701.

CLIP, *Conflict of Laws in Intellectual Property, the CLIP Principles and Commentary*, European Max Planck Group on Conflict of Laws in Intellectual Property', Oxford University Press, 2013.

CLIP, 'Exclusive Jurisdiction and Cross Border IP Infringement, Suggestions for Amendment of the Brussels I Regulation', 2006.

Collier, J. G., *Conflict of Laws*, 3rd edn, Cambridge University Press, 2011.

Cornish, W. R. and D. LLewelyn, *Intellectual Property: Patents, Copyrights, Trade Marks and Allied Rights*, 6th edn, Thomson, 2007.

Craig, P. and G. de Búrca, G., *EU Law*, 2nd edn, Oxford University Press, 1998.

Cumming, G., M. Freudenthal and R. Janal, *Enforcement of Intellectual Property Rights in Dutch, English and German Civil Courts*, Wolters Kluwer, 2008.

Cuonzo, G., *Patent Litigation in the Post-Torpedo Era*, Managing Intellectual Property, 2005.

Dickinson, A., *The Rome II Regulation*, Oxford University Press, 2008.

Dinwoodie, G. B., 'Developing a Private International Intellectual Property Law: The Demise of Territoriality?' (2009) 51(2) *William and Mary Law Review* 711.

Drexl, J. and A. Kur, *Intellectual Property and Private International Law*, vol. 24, Hart Publishing, 2005.

Dreyfuss, R. C., J. Ginsburg and F. Dessemontet, *Intellectual Property: Principles Governing Jurisdiction, Choice of Law, and Judgments in Transnational Disputes*, American Law Institute Publishers, 2008.

Echoud, M. v., *Choice of Law in Copyright and Related Rights*, Kluwer, 2003.

Engelen, Th. C. J. A. v., 'Jurisdiction and Applicable Law in Matters of Intellectual Property' (2010) 14(3) *Electronic Journal of Comparative Law.*

Fawcett, J. J. and J. M. Carruthers, *Cheshire, North and Fawcett, Private International Law*, 14th edn, Oxford Univeristy Press, 2008.

Fawcett, J. J. and P. Torremans, *Intellectual Property and Private International Law*, 2nd edn, Oxford University Press, 2011.

Fentiman, R., 'Choice of Law and Intellectual Property' in J. Drexl and A. Kur (eds), *Intellectual Property and Private International Law, Heading for the Future*, Hart Publishing, 2005.

Forsyth, N., C. Mulder, D. Visser and D. Williams, *The Annotated European Patent Convention*, 16th edn, TEL, 2008.

Gardella, A., 'Torpedos and Actions for Negative Declarations in International IP Law Litigation' in A. Nuyts (ed.), *International Litigation in Intellectual Property and Information Technology*, Kluwer Law International, 2008.

Gaudemet-Tallon, H., *Compétence et Exécution des Judgements en Europe*, 4th edn, LGDJ, 2010.

Gervais, D., *The TRIPS Agreement, Drafting History and Analysis*, Sweet & Maxwell, 2012.

Geist, M., 'Is There a There There? Towards Greater Certainty for Internet Jurisdiction', (2001) 16(3) *Berkeley Technology Law Journal* 1345.

Gonzalez Beilfuss, C., 'Is There Any Web for the Spider? Co-Defendants after Roche Nederland, International Litigation' in A Nuyts (ed.) *Intellectual Property and Information Technology*, Kluwer Law International, 2008.

Grabinski, K., 'Cross-Border Injunctions in Patent Litigations Following ECJ Decision in GAT v LUK – Life After Death?' in W Prinz zu Waldeck und Pyrmont, M. J. Adelman, R. Brauneis, J. Drexl and R. Nack (eds), *Patents and Technological Progress in a Globalized World: Liber Amicorum*, Joseph Strauss, vol 6, 2009.

Grabinski, K., 'Zur Bedeutung des Europäischen Gerichtsstands- und Vollstreckungsübereinkommens (Brüsseler Übereinkommens) und des Lugano-Übereinkommens in Rechtsstreitigkeiten über Patentverletzungen', *GRUR International*, no. 3, p. 199, 2001.

Heimdal, L. A., *Rettsvalg ved Erstatning for Krenkende Ytringer*, 1st edn, Universitetet i Bergen, 2012.

Heinze, C. and E. Roffael, 'Internationale Zuständigkeit für Entscheidungen über die Gültigkeit ausländischer Immaterialgüterrechte', *GRUR International*, no. 10, p. 787, 2006.

Heinze, C., *Einstweiliger Rechtsschutz ins europäischen Immaterialguterrecht*, 1st edn, Tübingen, 2007.

Heinze, C., 'Jurisdiction under the CLIP Principles' available at http://www.tomeika.jur.kyushu-u.ac.jp/chizai/symposium/paper/004_08May09_Heinze.pdf

Henningsen, T., *Grenseoverskridende Kjennetegnskonflikter*, Institut for Prviatrett, 2011.

Hertz, K., *Jurisdiction in Contract and Tort under the Brussels Convention*, Jurist- og Økonomforbundets Forlag, 1998.

Hertz, K., *Bruxelles I-forordningen*, 1st edn, Jurist- og Økonomforbundets Forlag, 2007.

Hess, B., *Europäiches Zivilprozessrecht*, Heidelberg, 2010.

Hitsevich, N., 'Article 5 (3) of the Brussels I Regulation and its Applicability in the Case of Intellectual Property Rights Infringement on the Internet' (2013) 7 *World Academy of Science, Engineering and Technology* 2104.

Jacobs, White and Ovey, *The European Convention on Human Rights*, 5th edn, Oxford University Press, 2010.

Karnøe, L., L. Barslev, J. Bundgaard, T. B. Christensen, M. Gudsøe, A. Lotterup, M. Mortensen and P. K. Schmidt, *Immaterialret*, 1st edn, Thomson Reuters, 2008.

Katzenberger, P., 'Anwendungsbereich, Übergangs- und Schlussbestimmungen. Vor §§ 120 ff. Vorbemerkung', in G. Schricker (ed.), *Urheberrecht Kommentar*, C. H. Beck, 2006.

Knaak, R. GRUR Int., 2007, 39.

Koch, H., K. Hagel-Sørensen, U. Halter and J. J. H. Weiler, *Europe The New Legal Realism*, 1st edn, DJØF Publishing, 2010.

Kono, T., *Intellectual Property and Private International Law: Comparative Perspectives*, Hart Publishing, 2012.

Kono, T., 'Intellectual Property Rights, Conflict of Laws and International Jurisdiction: Applicability of ALI Principles in Japan?' (2005) 30(3) *Brooklyn Journal of International Law* 865–83.

Kreuzer, K. and P. Klötgen, *Die Shevill-Entscheidung des EuGH: Abschaffung des Deliksortsgerichtsstands des Art. 5 Nr. 3 EuGVÜ für ehrverletzende Streudelikte*, IPRax, 1997.

Kropholler, J. and J. v. Hein, *Europäsches Zivilprozessrecht*, 9th edn, Frankfurt am Main, 2011.

Kur, A., 'Enforcement of Unitary Intellectual Property Rights: International Jurisdiction and Applicable Law' (2015) *Journal of Intellectual Property Law & Practice* 475.

Kur, A., 'Case C-235/09, DHL Express v. Chronopost, Judgment of the Court of Justice (Grand Chamber) of 12 April 2011, nyr.' (2012) 49(2) *Common Market Law Review* 753.

Kur, A., 'Die Ergebnisse des CLIP-Projekts – Zugleich eine Einführung in die Deutsche Fassung der Principles on Conflict of Laws in Intellectual Property', *GRUR International*, no. 10, p. 857, 2012.

Kur, A., 'Are There any Common European Principles and Private International Law with Regard to Intellectual Property?', in S. Leible and

A. Ohly (eds), *Intellectual Property and Private International Law*, Mohr Siebeck, 2009.

Kur, A., 'A Farewell to Cross-Border Injunctions? The ECJ Decisions GAT v. LuK and Roche Nederland v. Primus and Goldenberg', (2006) 37(7) *International Review of Intellectual Property and Competition Law* 844.

Kur, A., 'Community Trade Marks in National "Community Courts" – a System That's Fit for the Future?', in E. Kooy (ed.), *'Past, Present and the Future' – The Development of Trade Marks, Designs and Related IP Rights in Europe*, Deurne-Antwerpen, ECTA, 2005.

Kur, A., 'Trademark Conflicts on the Internet: Territoriality Redefined?', in J. Basedow, J. Drexl, A. Kur and A. Metzger (eds), *Intellectual Property in the Conflict of Laws*, Mohr Siebeck, 2005.

Kur, A., 'Jurisdiction and Enforcement of Foreign Judgments – the General Structure of the MPI Proposal', in J. Drexl and A. Kur (eds), *Intellectual Property and Private International Law*, Hart Publishing, 2005.

Kur, A., *Jurisdiction and Choice of Law – Perspectives for the Future (Tagungsbericht)*, GRUR International, no. 1, p. 65, 2004.

Kur, A., 'Principles Governing Jurisdiction, Choice of Law and Judgments in Transnational Disputes: A European Perspective' (2003) 3 *Computer Law Review International* 65.

Kur, A., 'International Hague Convention on Jurisdiction and Foreign Judgments: A Way forward for I.P.?' (2002) 24(4) *European Intellectual Property Review* 175.

Kur, A., 'Use of Trademarks on the Internet – The WIPO Recommendations' (2002) 33(1) *International Review of Intellectual Property and Competition Law* 41.

Kur, A., *Territorialität versus Globalität – Kennzeichenprobleme im Internet*, Wettbewerb in Recht und Praxis, 2000.

Kur, A. and B. Ubertazzi, 'The ALI Principles and the CLIP Project – a Comparison', in S. Bariatti (ed.), *Litigating Intellectual Property Rights Disputes Cross-Border*, Milan, 2010.

Kur, A, Knaak, R and Mühlendahl, A, v, 'MPI-Studie zum Funktionieren des Europäischen Markensystems, *GRUR International*, no. 3, p. 197, 2012.

Kur, A. and T. Dreier, *European Intellectual Property Law*, Edward Elgar Publishing, 2013.

Kur, A. and A. Metzger, 'Exclusive Jurisdiction and Cross Border IP (Patent) Infringement Suggestions for Amendment of the Brussels I Regulation', Intellectuelle Eigendom & Reclamerecht, 2007, Volume 23, Nr. 1.

Kurtz, C., *Grenzüberschreitender einstweiliger Rechtsschutz im Immaterialgüterrecht*, 1st edn, V&R Unipress, 2004.

Lando, O., *Kort Indføring i Komparativ Ret*, 3rd edn, Jurist- og Økonomforbundets Forlag, 2009.

Lange, P. GRUR, 2007, 112.
Larsen, B. T., *Trademark Infringements on the Internet in a Jurisdictional Perspective*, Nordiskt Immateriellt Rättsskydd, 2007.
Larsen, B. T., *The Place Where the Harmful Event Occurred in Exclusive Rights Litigation*, Nordiskt Immateriellt Rättsskydd, 2016.
Larsen, B. T., 'Dansk Immaterialret Bind II – Sanktioner og Håndhævelse, Værneting i Immaterialretssager om Krænkelse og Ugyldighed', GAD's Forlag, 2015.
Larsen, B. T., *'A Bundle of National Patents v a European Patent with Unitary Effect – Jurisdictional Comparison', Intellectual Property and General Legal Principles – Is IP a Lex Specialis?* Edward Elgar Publishing, 2015.
Larsen, B. T., *Rules of Jurisdiction in the Agreement on a Unified Patent Court*, Nordiskt Immateriellt Rättsskydd, 2014.
Lassen, B. S. and A. Stenvik, *Kjennetegnsrett*, 3rd edn, Universitetsforlaget, 2011.
Leible, S., Art. 6 Brüssel I-VO in T. Rauscher (ed.), Europäisches Zivilprozess und Kollisionsrecht, 2001.
Leible, S. and A. Ohly, *Intellectual Property and Private International Law*, Mohr Siebeck, 2009.
Leistner, M., 'The Law Applicable to Non-Contractual Obligations Arising From an Infringement of National or Community IP Rights', in S. Leible and A. Ohly (eds), *Intellectual Property and Private International Law*, Mohr Siebeck, 2009.
Lilja, T. M., *Filialbegrebet*, 1st edn, Jurist- og Økonomforbundets Forlag, 2010.
Lindgreen, N. and L. Knudsen, 'Danish High Court Rejects Pan European Injunctions in Patent Cases' (2004) *European Intellectual Property Review* 182.
Lookofsky, J. and K. Hertz, *EU-PIL*, 1st edn, DJØF Publishing, 2009.
Luginbuehl, S., 'The Future of Centralised Patent Litigation in Europe: Between the EPLA and the EU Patent Judiciary', in S. Leible and A. Ohly (eds), *Intellectual Property and Private International Law*, Mohr Siebeck, 2009.
Lundstedt, L., *In the Wake of GAT/LuK and Roche/Primus*, Nordiskt Immateriellt Rättsskydd, 2008.
Lundstedt, L., 'Jurisdiction and the Principle of Territoriality in Intellectual Property Law: Has the Pendulum Swung too far in the other Direction?' (2001) 32(2) *International Review of Intellectual Property and Competition Law* 124.
Lundstedt, L. and U. Maunsbach, *Jurisdiction and Applicable Law: A Swedish Perspective on Cross-Border Enforcement of Intellectual Property Rights*, Nordiskt Immateriellt Rättsskydd, 2003.

Magnus, U. and P. Mankowski, *Brussels I Regulation*, 2nd edn, Sellier European Law Publishers, 2012.

Mankowski, P., 'Das Internet im Internationalen Vertrags- und Deliktsrecht', *Rabels Zeitschrift für ausländisches und internationale Privatrecht*, 1999.

Matulionytė, R., *Law Applicable to Copyright: A Comparison of the ALI and CLIP Proposals*, Edward Elgar Publishing, 2011.

Maunsbach, U., 'Jurisdiction in Relation to Online Cross-Border Infringements: the Code and the Law', in D. J. B. Svantesson and S. Greenstein (eds), *Internationalisation of Law in the Digital Information Society*, Ex Tuto Publishing, 2013.

Maunsbach, U., 'Copyright in a Borderless Online Environment – Comments from a Swedish Horizon', in J. Axamn (ed.), *Copyright in a Borderless Online Environment*, Norstedts Juridik, 2012.

Maunsbach, U. Gränsöverskridande Patenttvister i ny Gemenskapsrättslig Belysning – en Kommentar til EG-Domstolens Avgöranden i Målen C-4/03 (GAT) och C-539/09 (Roche), Nordiskt Immateriellt Rättsskydd, 2007.

Maunsbach, U., *Svensk Domstols Behörighet vid Gränsöverskridande Varumärketvister – Särskilt om Internetrelaterade Intrång*, Lund Universitet, 2005.

Maunsbach, U., 'Some Reflexions Concerning Jurisdiction in Cases on Cross-Border Trademark Infringements Through the Internet' (2004) 47 *Scandinavian Studies in Law* 493.

Maunsbach, U. and U. Wennersten, *Grundläggande Immaterialrätt*, 2nd edn, Gleerups, 2011.

Mentz, T., *Indgåelse af værnetingsaftaler – i Internationale Kommercielle Kontraktforhold*, 1st edn, Jurist- og Økonomforbundets Forlag, 2010.

Metzger, A., 'Jurisdiction in Cases concerning Intellectual Property Infringements on the Internet, Brussels I-Regulation, ALI-Principles and Max Planck Proposals', in S. Leible and A. Ohly (eds), *Intellectual Property and Private International Law*, Mohr Siebeck, 2009.

Muhlendahl, A. v., 'Community Trade Mark Riddles: Territoriality and Unitary Character' (2008) 66(30) *European Intellectual Property Review* 66.

Neergaard, U. and R. Nielsen, *EU Ret*, 6th edn, Thomson Reuters, 2010.

Nielsen, P. A., 'The Recasted Brussels I Regulation' (2014) *Nordic Journal of International Law* 61–71.

Nielsen, P. A., 'The New Brussels I Regulation' (2013) 50(2) *Common Market Law Review* 503.

Nielsen, P. A., *Den nye Domsforordning*, U.2013B.83, Karnov Group, 2013.

Nielsen, P. A., 'The Recast of the Brussels I Regulation', in M. J. Bonell, M. Holle and P. A. Nielsen (eds), *Liber Amicorum Ole Lando*, DJØF Publishing, 2012.

Nielsen, P. A., 'Forslaget til ny Domsforordning', U.2012B.212, Karnov Group, 2012.

Nielsen, P. A., 'The State of Play of the Recast of the Brussels I Regulation' (2012) 81(4) *Nordic Journal of International Law* 585.

Nielsen, P. A., *Den Globale Haager-domskonvention*, U.2010B.289, Thomson Reuters, 2010.

Nielsen, P. A., *Brussels I and Denmark*, IPRax, 2007.

Nielsen, P. A., *International Privat- og Procesret*, Jurist- og Økonomforbundets Forlag, 1997.

Nielsen, R. and C. Tvarnø, *Retskilder & Retsteorier*, 3rd edn, Jurist- og Økonomforbundets Forlag, 2011.

Norrgård, M., 'The European Principles of Intellectual Property Enforcement: Harmonisation Through Communication?', in A. Ohly (ed.), *Common Principles of European Intellectual Property Law*, Mohr Siebeck, 2012.

Norrgård, M., 'A Spider Without a Web? Multiple Defendants in IP Litigation', in S. Leible and A. Ohly (eds), *Intellectual Property and Private International Law*, Mohr Siebeck, 2009.

Norrgård, M., *Immaterialrättens Sanktionssystem och Enforcement-direktivet*, Nordiskt Immateriellt Rättsskydd, 2004.

Norrgård, M, *Gemenskapsvarumärket och de Nationella Domstolarnas Internationella Behörighet*, Nordiskt Immateriellt Rättsskydd, 1998.

Nuyts, A., *International Litigation in Intellectual Property and Information Technology*, Kluwer Law International, 2008.

Nuyts, A., 'Suing at the Place of Infringement: The Application of Article 5(3) of Regulation 44/2001 to IP Matters and Internet Disputes', in A. Nuyts (ed.), *International Litigation in Intellectual Property and Information Technology*, Kluwer Law International, 2008.

Nuyts, A., *International Litigation in Intellectual Property and Information Technology*, Kluwer Law International, 2008.

Nuyts, A., K. Szychowska and N. Hatzimihail, 'Cross-Border Litigation in IP/IT Matters in the European Union: The Transformers of the Jurisdictional Landscape', in A. Nuyts (ed.), *International Litigation in Intellectual Property and Information Technology*, Kluwer Law International, 2008.

Ohly, A., 'Choice of Law in the Digital Environment – Problems and Possible Solutions', in J. Drexl and A. Kur (eds), *Intellectual Property and Private International Law*, Hart Publishing, 2005.

Ohly, A. and J. Pila, *The Europeanization of Intellectual Property Law*, Oxford University Press, 2013.

Pansch, R., 'The Proper Forum for Illicit Acts in Cases of Cross-Border Infringement of Proprietary Commercial Rights' (2000) 5 *European Law Forum* 353.

Petersen, C. S., *Immaterialrettigheder og Foreløbige Forbud*, 1st edn, Jurist- og Økonomforbundets Forlag, 2008.

Petersen, C. S. and J. Schovsbo, 'On Law and Policy in a European and European Union Patent Court (EEUPC), What Will It do to Patent Law and What Will Patent Law do to It?' in H. Koch, H. K. Sørensen, U. Haltern and H. H. J. Weiler (eds), *Europe The New Legal Realism*, DJØF Publishing, 2010.

Peukert, A., 'Territoriality and Extraterritoriality in Intellectual Property Law', in G. Handl and J. Zekoll (eds), *Beyond Territoriality: Transnational Legal Authority in an Age of Globalization*, Queen Mary Studies in International Law, Brill Academic Publishing, Leiden/Boston, 2012.

Picht, P., 'Von eDate zu Wintersteiger – Die Ausformung des Art. 5 Nr. 3 EuGVVO für Internetdelikte durch die Rechtsprechung des EuGH', *GRUR International*, no. 1, p. 19, 2013.

Pii, T. and P. A. Nielsen, *Rom II-forordningen*, U.2008B.283, Thomson Reuters, 2008.

Pontier, J. A. and E. Burg, *EU Principles on Jurisdiction and Recognition and Enforcement of Judgments in Civil and Commercial Matters*, TMC Asser Press, 2004.

Riis, T., 'Merchandising', in *Julebog 1997*, p. 111, Jurist- og Økonomforbundets Forlag, 1997.

Riis, T., *Intellectual Property Law*, 1st edn, DJØF Publishing, 2000.

Roth, H., *Das Konnexitätserfordernis im Mehrparteiengerichtsstand des Artikel 6(1) EuGVO, Die Richtige Ordnung – Festschrift für Jan Kroppholler*, Mohr Siebeck, 2008.

Sachdeva, A. M., 'International Jurisdiction in Cyberspace: A Comparative Perspective' (2007) 13(8) *The Journal of E-commerce, Technology and Communications* 245.

Schack, H., 'The Law Applicable to (Unregistered) IP Rights After Rome II', in S. Leible and A. Ohly (eds), *Intellectual Property and Private International Law*, Mohr Siebeck, 2009.

Schack, H., *International Zivilverfahrensrecht*, 4th edn, C. H. Beck, 2006.

Schaper, E., *Durchsetzung der Gemeinschaftsmarke*, Max Planck Institute for Intellectual Property and Competition Law, Carl Heymanns Verlag, 2006.

Schlosser, F. P., Kommentar Zum EU-Zivilprocessrecht, 2nd edn, München, 2003.

Schlosser, P., B. Hess and T. Pfeiffer, *The Brussels I Regulation 44/2001 – Application and Enforcement in the EU*, Munich, 2008.

Schovsbo, J., M. Rosenmeier and C. S. Petersen, *Immaterialret*, 3rd edn, Jurist- og Økonomforbundets Forlag, 2013.

Schröer, B., 'Einheitspatentgericht – Überlegungen zum Forum-Shopping im Rahmen der Alternativen Zuständigkeit nach Art. 83 Abs. 1 EPGÜ', *GRUR International*, no. 12, p. 1102, 2013.

Schulz, A., 'The Hague Conference Project for a Global Convention on Jurisdiction, Recognition and Enforcement in Civil and Commercial Matters – an Update', in J. Drexl and A. Kur (eds), *Intellectual Property and Private International Law*, Oxford University Press, 2005.

Schønning, P., M. Kyst, M. S. Nielsen, B. Ryberg and K. Wallberg, *Grundlæggende Immaterialret*, 2nd edn, Gjellerup, 2009.

Schønning, P. and J. Blomqvist, *International Ophavsret*, 1st edn, Jurist- og Økonomforbundets Forlag, 2011.

Scordamaglia, V., 'Jurisdiction and Procedure in Legal Actions Relating to Community Trade Marks' in M. Franzosi (ed.), *European Community Trade Mark – Commentary to the European Community Regulation*, Kluwer Law International, 1997.

Scordamaglia, V., 'Die Gerichtsstandsregelung im Gemeinschaftspatentübereinkommen und das Vollstreckungsübereinkommen von Lugano', *GRUR International*, no. 9, 1990.

Sender, M. P., *Cross-Border Enforcement of Patent Rights*, Oxford University Press, 2006.

Sender, M. P., *Cross-Border Enforcement of Patent Rights, An Analysis of the Interface between Intellectual Property and Private International Law*, Oxford University Press, 2002.

Strömholm, S, P. Torremans, G. Davies, U. Maunsbach, J. Rosén, S. v. L. Gervais, G. Karnell, P. Danowsky, M. Levin, M. Norrgård, B. Hogenholtz and J. Axhamn, *Copyright in a Borderless Online Environment*, 1st edn, Norstedts Juridik, 2012.

Smith, H. and J. Gauld, 'The Territorial Effect of Sanctions under the Community Trade Marks Regulation: The ECJ delivers its Judgment in DHL v Chronopost' (2011) 33(9) *European Intellectual Property Review* 588.

Sommer, T., *Can Law Make Life (too) Simple?*, 1st edn, DJØF Publishing, 2013.

Spang-Hanssen, H., *Cyberspace and International Law on Jurisdiction*, 1st edn, DJØF Publishing, 2004.

Stauder, D. and S. Luginbuehl, 'Summary of Argumentation on The ECJ Decisions', in B. Engelbrekt, U. Bernitz, B., Domeij, A. Kur and J. Nordell (eds), *Festskrift till Marianne Levin*, Norstedts Juridik, 2008.

Stone, D., *European Union Design Law, A Practitioners Guide* , Oxford University Press, 2012.

Strömholm, S., *Uphovsrätt och International Privaträtt*, 1st edition, Norstedts Juridik, 2001.

Svantesson, J. B. and S. Greenstein, *Internationalisation of Law in the Digital Information Society*, 1st edn, Ex Tuto Publishing, 2013.

Torremans, P., 'Consolidation of Intellectual Property Litigation in Europe' in *Essays in Honour of MP Stathopoulos*, Ant. N. Sakkoulas Publishers, 2010.

Torremans, P., 'The Way Forward for Cross-Border Intellectual Property Litigation: Why GAT Cannot Be the Answer', in S. Leible and A. Ohly (eds), *Intellectual Property and Private International Law*, vol. 28, Mohr Siebeck, 2009.

Torremans, P., 'The Widening Reach of Exclusive Jurisdiction: Where Can You Litigate After GAT?' in Arnaud Nuyts (ed.), *International Litigation in Intellectual Property and Information Technology*, Kluwer Law International, 2008.

Torremans, P., 'Exclusive Jurisdiction and Cross-Border IP (Patent) Infringement – Suggestions for Amendment of the Brussels I Regulation' (2007) *European Intellectual Property Review* 201.

Tritton, G., *Intellectual Property in Europe*, 3rd edn, Sweet & Maxwell, 2008.

Trzaskowski, J., H. K. Deichmann, S. S. Jakobsen, S. Karstoft, B. Langsted, T. Riis and C. B. Tranberg, *Internetretten*, 2nd edn, Ex Tuto Publishing, 2012.

Ubertazzi, B., *Exclusive Jurisdiction in Intellectual Property*, Max Planck Institut für Ausländisches und Internationales Privatrecht, Mohr Siebeck, 2012.

Ubertazzi, B., 'Intellectual Property Rights and Exclusive Jurisdiction', *GRUR International*, no. 3, p. 199, 2011

Vareilles-Sommiéres, P., *Forum Shopping in the European Judicial Area*, 8th edn, Hart Publishing, 2007.

Virgos Soriano, M. and F. J. Garcimartin Alférez, *Derecho Procesal Civil Internacional: Litigación Internacional*, Thomson-Civitas, 2007.

Warner, S. and S. Middlemiss, 'Patent Litigation in Multiple Jurisdictions: An End to Cross-Border Relief in Europe' (2006) 28(11) *European Intellectual Property Review* 580.

Wichard, C., 'The Joint Recommendation Concerning Protection of Marks, and Other Industrial Property Rights in Signs on the Internet', in Drexl, J., and Kur, A., (eds), *Intellectual Property and Private International Law – Heading for the Future*, Hart Publishing, 2005.

Würtenberger, G., 'The Enforcement of Judgments of Community Trade Mark Courts' (2012) 7(5) *Journal of Intellectual Property Law and Practice* 273–373.

Würtenberger, G., P. v. d Kooij, B. Kiewiet and M. Ekvad, *European Community Plant Variety Protection*, Oxford University Press, 2006.

Zweighert, K. and H. Kötz, *An Introduction to Comparative Law*, 3rd edn, Oxford University Press, 2011.

INDEX

Please note that 'IP' stands for 'intellectual property'.

INTELLECTUAL PROPERTY JURISDICTION STRATEGIES

ELGAR INTELLECTUAL PROPERTY LAW AND PRACTICE

Series Editors: Trevor Cook, *Partner, WilmerHale* and Johanna Gibson, *Herchel Smith Professor of Intellectual Property Law, Queen Mary University of London*

The Elgar Intellectual Property Law and Practice series is a library of works by leading practitioners and scholars covering discrete areas of law in the field of intellectual property. Each title will describe the law in detail, but will also be deeply analytical, highlighting and unpicking the legal issues that are most critical and relevant to practice. Designed to be detailed, focused reference works, the books in this series aim to offer an authoritative statement on the law and practice in key topics within the field, from *Trade Marks* to *Pharmaceuticals*, from *Patent Standards* to *Trade Secrecy* and from *IP Licensing* to *IP Valuation*.

Titles in this series include:

The Law and Regulation of Franchising in the EU
Mark Abell

The Protection of Geographical Indications
Law and Practice
Michael Blakeney

Patent Law in Greater China
Edited by Stefan Luginbuehl and Peter Ganea

Trade Secrecy and International Transactions
Law and Practice
Elizabeth A. Rowe and Sharon K. Sandeen

The Law and Practice of Trademark Transactions
A Global and Local Outlook
Edited by Irene Calboli and Jacques de Werra

Certification and Collective Marks
Law and Practice
Jeffrey Belson

Intellectual Property Jurisdiction Strategies
Where to Litigate Unitary Rights vs National Rights in the EU
Torsten Bjørn Larsen